National Space Law in Poland

Studies in Space Law

VOLUME 21

The titles published in this series are listed at *brill.com/slaw*

National Space Law in Poland

Past, Present and Future

Edited by

Anna Konert and Frans G. von der Dunk

BRILL | NIJHOFF

LEIDEN | BOSTON

The Library of Congress Cataloging-in-Publication Data is available online at https://catalog.loc.gov
LC record available at https://lccn.loc.gov/2022062040.

Typeface for the Latin, Greek, and Cyrillic scripts: "Brill". See and download: brill.com/brill-typeface.

ISSN 1871-7659
ISBN 978-90-04-54285-3 (hardback)
ISBN 978-90-04-54286-0 (e-book)

This book is printed on acid-free paper and produced in a sustainable manner.

Contents

Tables

Foreword

At the turn of the 21st century one can observe a vastly growing tendency towards private space activities. Governments withdraw from their usual function as sponsor of national space programmes and encourage private entrepreneurs like Space X of Elon Musk or Virgin Galactic of Sir Richard Branson to become active and fill gaps in their respective space programmes. As a consequence, there is a growing need for national space legislation. This development has resulted in around 25 countries which by now provide for their national space law granting the possibility to become active in the field of commercial space flight form the own territory.

This book portrays that the space industry and space law in Poland is not in an embryonic stage any more.

It is good that the book editor Anna Konert first introduces different themes presented in this compilation, tracing the evolution of the national space law processes in Poland and highlighting recent activities and legislative developments. Chapter 1 by Jakub Ryzenko and Anna Nałęcz-Kobierzycka provides a brief history of Polish space policy and strategy, accompanied in Chapter 2 by a survey of the Polish involvement in space and space activities, by the same authors. Chapter 3 by Julia Anna Hetlof gives a useful introduction to the complicated – and not yet solved – question of the delimitation of air and outer space. Tomasz Balcerzak and Julia Anna Hetlof then undertake in Chapter 4 to describe such international space treaties to which Poland is a party. This is of course the Outer Space Treaty, the Rescue Agreement, the Liability Convention, the Registration Convention and some of the non-binding United Nations General Assembly Resolutions like the one on Remote Sensing as well as the cooperation agreement of the European Space Agency from 1994. As is well-known, in 2012 Poland became the 20th member state of the European Space Agency, which made Poland also a space power. Tomasz Balcerzak describes in Chapter 5 the Polish space activities in the European Union. There is e.g. an important participation in the Global Navigation Satellite System Galileo. In Chapter 6 Dominika Harasimiuk describes the Polish legal system, whereby it is particularly important to see the context to EU law as well as to public international law because so far ESA is not an entity under European Union law. Ewa Jasiuk then undertakes to analyse in Chapter 7 what has been established as the draft Polish national space act. This is a very important step of the "space development" in Poland in order to make the country an equal competitor in Europe also for private space activities. In addition, Chapter 7 recounts the development of the new Polish Space Agency, its statutory tasks and some perception of Polish space activities based on international agreements. Katarzyna Krupa-Lipińska presents the issue of intellectual property (IP) in the context of space activities in Chapter 8. The final Chapter 9, written by Julia Anna Hetlof and Agnieszka Kunert-Diallo, examines the need and rationale for the implementation of the national (domestic) space legal framework in Poland.

The editor Frans von der Dunk in his concluding remarks presents a compelling case for why the adoption of national space laws would benefit Poland by promoting and supporting private sector participation while protecting the interests of the general public at large.

I personally believe that this book, edited by Anna Konert and Frans G. von der Dunk, is a welcome undertaking. It provides a very solid overview on the present involvement in future cooperation of Poland with regard to space activities. One can only hope that the country's national space law gets ready relatively soon, which will then bring Poland in the first row of the European space fairing nations.

Prof. Dr. Dr. h.c. Stephan Hobe
Director of the Institute for Air Law, Space Law and Cyber Law
University of Cologne

Notes on Contributors

Editors

Frans G. von der Dunk
currently *inter alia* holds the Harvey and Susan Perlman Alumni / Othmer Chair of Space Law at the unique LL.M. Programme on Space, Cyber and Telecommunication Law with the University of Nebraska-Lincoln. He also is Director of Black Holes BV consultancy in space law and policy, based in Leiden, The Netherlands. He has published the first *Handbook of Space Law, the Advanced Introduction to Space Law* and over 200 articles on issues of space law and policy. He is editor of *Studies in Space Law*, has given over 400 presentations and has taught as a guest professor at over 50 universities and other academic institutions worldwide. He has consulted with hundreds of clients all over the world, coming from the governmental, intergovernmental and private sectors. He is the holder of several prestigious awards in the field, and one of the most renowned public speakers world-wide on the subject of space law and policy world-wide, having spoken at TEDX, PINC and TV shows.

Anna Konert
Professor of Aviation Law, attorney-at-law, Dean of the Faculty of Law and Administration, Director of the LL.M in Aviation Law, Director of Aviation Law and Professional Pilot Licence, Director of the Institute of Air and Space Law at Lazarski University in Warsaw, Director of the Lazarski Aviation Academy, Member of the Commitee of European Air Law Association, Former Lawyer for Air France in New York's office.

Authors

Julia Anna Hetlof
attorney-at-law in the State of New York and Colorado, currently US Army liaison at the Multinational Corps North East in Szczecin, Poland. Experienced as a civil litigator and former military prosecutor, with extensive practice in international and operational law, administrative law, military justice, employment and immigration law, and government contracts. As a US Air Force Assistant Staff Judge Advocate, represented the government in numerous courts-martial, discharge boards, employment mediations and negotiations. Received her *Juris Doctor* degree at Fordham Law School in New York, LL.M in Air and Space

Law at McGill University in Montreal, and is currently pursuing a PhD in Space Law at Lazarski University in Warsaw.

Tomasz Balcerzak
PhD Eng.: adjunct at Lazarski University, CEO of Wademekum LTD., Expert European Commission Research Executive Agency (REA), Expert of European Global Navigation Satellite Systems Agency. Extensive experience in the aviation industry in managing projects of the operating companies. Founder and co-founder of several companies. Author and coauthor over 40 publications. Specializes in transportation, logistics, aviation and space.

Dominika Ewa Harasimiuk
PhD and Assistant Professor of EU law at the Faculty of Political Science and International Studies, University of Warsaw. Lecturer of EU law at the Lazarski University, Warsaw. Research interests comprise the fields of EU citizenship, EU constitutional law, Internal market law, in particular free movement of goods and services, as well as regulatory and ethical challenges of algorithmic society.

Ewa Jasiuk
PhD in International Law, attorney-at law, former Deputy Dean for the Quality of Education at Faculty of Law and Administration, Lazarski University in Warsaw.

Katarzyna Krupa-Lipińska
PhD is an adjunct professor of Law at the Nicolaus Copernicus University in Torun (Poland) and lecturer at Lazarski University in Warsaw (Poland). She teaches civil law and intellectual property law. She has published over 40 publications, including books, book chapters and articles on civil law (in particular tort law) and intellectual property law. Katarzyna is also a patent and trademark attorney running practice as a professional representative i.a. before the Polish Patent Office, European Union Intellectual Property Office and World Intellectual Property Organization. At present she holds the position of the Dean of Kuyavian-Pomeranian District of Polish Chamber of Patent Attorneys.

Agnieszka Kunert-Diallo
PhD Aviation lawyer with over 20 years expierience in LOT Polish Airlines. The position of in-house lawyer is being carried out simultaneously with the function of the Compliance Managing Director at Polish Aviation Group. Academic lecturer at Lazarski University. She is a member of the Polish Group of the

International Law Association and the author of a large number of publications on topical issues of aviation law and policy.

Anna Nałęcz-Kobierzycka
Space Research Centre of Polish Academy of Sciences (CBK PAN). Expert in space policy, international relations in space activities and EU-ESA cooperation, currently focused on supporting the use of space applications in public administration via national and international projects. Co-author and editor of Polish Space Strategy from 2017 and Action Programme for the Development of Space Technologies and the Use of Satellite Systems in Poland from 2012. In 2012–2019 Deputy Head of Polish Delegation to ESA and head of Space Policy Unit in the Ministry of Development. In 2017–19 Chair of ESA Programme Board on SSA.

Jakub Ryzenko
Head of Crisis Information Centre, Space Research Centre PAS. He is a space policy and crisis management expert. He is actively involved in several research and development activities and he advises the Polish government and the Polish parliament on space policy matters. In 2004–2008 he was the Head of the Polish Space Office. In 2011–2013 he was involved in the accession of Poland to the European Space Agency. Since then he has regularly acted as a space policy advisor for different governmental institutions and the Polish parliament. Currently he is actively involved in definition of the Polish national space programme. In the safety and security domain, he focuses on effective use of space-related solutions for international security, civil protection and humanitarian operations. Since 2013 he heads the Crisis Information Centre at Space Research Centre PAS, which develops space-related innovative solutions as well as provides operational support for crisis management institutions in Poland. He has coordinated or overseen over 40 operational activations of satellite and UAVs information support for crisis situations.

Introduction

Anna Konert

> Cuius est solum eius est usque ad coelum et ad inferos;[1] this principle inherited from Roman Law, was accepted by international law and adopted to its needs. For centuries States faced no practical questions concerning the control over their airspace nor the height to which their sovereignty extended … Only the first journey of a man-made satellite reopened the issue: what was coelum? Can sovereignty extend ad infinitum?[2]
>
> MANFRED LACHS

The space sector today has an impact on all industries, services and society at large. An ever-increasing number of governmental, institutional, and economic players use more and more space data captured by an exponentially growing number of satellites. This data from space is merged with other data to be transformed into value-added insights allowing companies to perform better in their markets.

"Poland is a country that over the last decades has given the world a number of scientists, engineers and visionaries who not only laid theoretical foundations for cosmonautics, but also took part in the greatest astronautical ventures of mankind. These successes are the basis and foundation of the current efforts to make our country join the group of countries taking an active and active part in the exploration of space – the closer and the more distant."[3]

Poland is a quite new entrant in the space sector and has recently created the Polish Space Strategy (2017) and is currently forming its space legislation.[4] Despite the recent dynamic development of the domestic space sector, Poland is still devoting very little to it – around 0.01 percent of its GDP. Key advantages

1 'Whoever's is the soil, it is theirs all the way to Heaven and all the way to Hell' (Latin).

2 Manfred Lachs, *The Law of Outer Space: An Experience in Contemporary Law-Making* (1979) 42.

3 https://www.gov.pl/web/rozwoj-technologia/polityka-kosmiczna (Access: 4.03.2022).

4 On July 25th 2017 Government Legislation Center published the draft act on space activities and the National Register of Space Objects.

 | DOI:10.1163/9789004542860_002

of the Polish space sector are: building stable cooperation between science and industry, developing innovative technologies and stimulating contacts and foreign cooperation.[5]

In 2012, Poland became a part of the European Space Agency (ESA). This was an opening of the possibilities for intensive technological development thanks to participation in numerous programs and ambitious ESA missions.[6] Poland participates in the following ESA optional programmes: Earth observation, Navigation, Telecommunications and Integrated Applications, Manned Flights and Exploration, Space Situational Information System (SSA), General Technology Support Programme (GSTP) and the ESA Scientific Instrument Building Programme (PRODEX).

In 2014, the Polish Space Agency (POLSA) was established mainly to support the Polish space industry by combining the world of business and science, and to promote the development of satellite technology that can be used in everyday life, including communication, navigation, environmental monitoring and weather forecasting.[7]

On 26 January 2017, the Council of Ministers adopted the Polish Space Strategy by Resolution No. 6, which was published in the Polish Monitor on 17 February 2017, thus becoming formally binding.[8] The Polish Space Strategy presents long-term development directions for the space industry and covers the horizon of 2017 to 2030. It assumes that by 2030, the turnover of Polish companies in this sector should amount to at least 3% of the overall turnover of the entire industry in Europe. Polish public administration will use satellite data for faster and more effective implementation of its tasks, and domestic enterprises will be able to fully meet internal demand for this type of services and export them to other markets; Poland will have access to satellite infrastructure enabling it to meet its needs, especially in the field of security and defense. The Ministry of Entrepreneurship and Technology is responsible for the coordination of activities and supervision over the implementation of the Polish Space Strategy.

5 https://www.esa.int/Space_in_Member_States/Poland/Polska_Strategia_Kosmiczna (Access : 03.03.2022).

6 POLISH PARTICIPATION IN MARS 'TESTS' POLSA, 26 November 2018: https://polsa.gov.pl/images/Inne_publikacje_PAK/Polska_Agencja_Kosmiczna_Polski-udzial_w_badaniach_Marsa.pdf (Access: 20.12.2018).

7 https://polsa.gov.pl/en/about-polsa/about-polsa (Access 20.12.2018).

8 *Resolution No 6 of the Council of Ministers of 26 January 2017 on the adoption of the Polish Space Strategy* (M.P. item 203).

Supporting the space sector is one of the important elements of the Responsible Development Plan (SOR).[9] The basic assumption of this Plan is to create a new model for the development of the Polish economy, based more on knowledge, innovation and technological progress than on low production costs. One of the industries that currently has a niche character in Poland, but which may contribute to achieving this goal, is the space sector.[10]

At the same time, the Polish Space Agency, in close cooperation with scientific and industrial entities as well as the administrative environment of the space sector, prepared the National Space Program for 2019–2021. The current draft of the Polish Space Program for 2021–2026 was completed in mid-2021, but, as of the date of this writing, has not been yet adopted.[11] The most important goal of the National Space Program is to increase the potential and the competitiveness of the Polish space sector by providing a system of optimal tools for financial, advisory and educational support. The activities envisaged in it are aimed at private enterprises, scientific units, government and local government administration, as well as educational activities and raising public awareness of the impact of space technologies on the economic development of the country.

Poland is engaged in multilateral cooperation in the framework of ESA, EU, NASA, EDA. Polish actors more and more often apply to the space programs. POLSA has also started efforts to integrate the national industrial sector in projects implemented by the European Organization for the Exploitation of Meteorological Satellites (EUMETSAT).[12]

Polish enterprises, scientific and research institutions, and universities now have many possibilities to finance their space projects. Polish commercial entities, as well as the researchers, are taking active part in space programs and

9 https://www.gov.pl/web/fundusze-regiony/informacje-o-strategii-na-rzecz-odpowiedzialnego-rozwoju (Access: 03.03.2022).

10 https://www.esa.int/Space_in_Member_States/Poland/Polska_Strategia_Kosmiczna (Access: 04.03.2022).

11 Ministry of the Development and Technology, Krajowy Program Kosmiczny na lata 2021–2026 (Tr. National Space Program for 2021–2026), ver. 0.8, 23 July 2021, https://www.gov.pl/attachment/935b6f52-92ed-41f4-9dc6-fb502c609a84.

12 International cooperation activities provided for in the National Space Policy 2019–2021 included: bilateral and multilateral cooperation, including with the so-called countries Great European Five (Germany, France, Spain, Great Britain, Italy), other ESA Member States with high potential and high spending in the space sector (eg Switzerland, the Netherlands, Norway, Austria, Luxembourg, Belgium), Central and Eastern European countries (in particular, Ukraine, Romania and the Czech Republic), https://www.space24.pl/projekt-krajowego-programu-kosmicznego-zaakceptowany-przez-rade-pak (Access 22.12.2018).

Polish companies are more frequently becoming contractors of elements of devices used in space missions. One of the successes of the Polish industry was participation in the NASA InSight mission where Astronika has built a unique device on a global scale to penetrate the surface of Mars, a drone called – Kret HP3 ("Mole").

Poland has a lot of determination to develop its space industry. One of the major goals now in Poland is to become a significant part of the European space community. Opening up to the world has allowed Poland closer cooperation with many countries and institutions, like ESA, EU, NASA, EDA.

The main goal of the book is to show the perspective of this new entrant in the space sector and to highlight recent activities and actions taken in Poland.

Chapter 1 is focused on the institutional, strategic, and policy perspectives on the development of the Polish space sector. It briefly recalls Polish membership in European organisations involved in operational space activities (the European Union, ESA, EUTELSAT, and EUMETSAT) and related internal governance structures. Next, the definition and evolution of Polish space policy's strategic aims are presented, underlining their step-by-step implementation and possible future directions.

Chapter 2 provides a brief overview of Polish space activities, focusing on scientific and industrial sectors, from historical beginnings to the current state-of-play. Starting in the times of Copernicus, it presents the development of space activities in Poland with particular focus on the road to the accession of Poland to the European Space Agency, the first period of full membership, and the resulting evolution of the Polish space sector.

Chapter 3 provides a brief overview of the evolution of the space industry, from the traditional governmental uses to New Space applications, transforming the sector into the global space economy. One of the outstanding legal issues of the delimitation of outer space is examined from the perspective of having a clearly defined area to which the outer space legal regime applies, as well as, taking into consideration operational and legal implications for air navigation and space traffic management. Different legal approaches, from spatialism, functionalism to hybrid proposals, such as Near Space, are explored, along with the jurisdictional and the State sovereignty implications under both the air law and space law regimes. Finally, State practice on the boundary question, as well as the right of innocent passage for space objects are examined.

Chapter 4 is mostly concerned with the international regime as a set of rules concerning space activities that apply to the relationships between States, forming a branch of international public law. The international space law regime is placed in its historical context, with the contributions of the

Polish thinkers and inventors and the sources of international space law being reviewed in the context of their applicability in the Polish legal system.

Polish space activities in Europe are presented in Chapter 5. Poland has developed its own space sector, which has already gained a lot of experience and has tangible achievements thanks to cooperation with different European organisations and entities, like the Global Navigation Satellite System Galileo, the EGNOS system, the Copernicus system and the ESA programmes. The goal of this part is to show the engagement of Polish entities to develop the European space market.

Chapter 6 provides the general characteristics of the Polish legal system. It discusses the fundamentals of Poland's constitutional legal order by analyzing general rules and principles applied to the State's organisation as well as the scope of freedoms and rights guaranteed by the Constitution. A more detailed analysis concerns the system of sources of the law, indicating the categories of sources that are applied in Poland and their hierarchy. Also, the position of international law in the Polish legal system is examined, with a particular view to the EU legal system. The present chapter also provides an overview of the constitutional political system of government, and general rules of application of the principle of separation of powers are discussed. Finally, the chapter outlines the powers and competences of legislative authorities, executive authorities (indicating the ones responsible for the space policy), and judicial authority.

The aim of Chapter 7 is to present the development of space legislation in Poland – the Act on Space Activity and the National Register of Space Objects (also referred to as Draft Space Act),[13] including the reasons that contributed to its creation. The provisions of the Draft Space Act are analyzed, taking into consideration constructive criticism of the parts therein. The provisions of the applicable international space conventions were also analyzed: the Treaty on Principles Governing the Activities of States in the Exploration and Use of Outer Space, Including the Moon and Other Celestial Bodies (Outer Space Treaty),[14] the Convention on International Liability for Damage Caused by Space Objects (Liability Convention),[15] and the Convention on the Registration of Objects Launched into Outer Space (Registration Conventio),[16] in terms of their implementation in the discussed project.

13 The Act on Space Activity and the National Register of Space Objects, project dated 10 July 2017, available at https://legislacja.rcl.gov.pl/docs//2/12300856/12449052/12449053/dokument300886.pdf.

14 27 January 1967, 610 UNTS 205, Journal of Laws of 1968, no. 14, item 82.

15 29 March 1972, 961 UNTS 187, Journal of Laws of 1973, no. 27 item 154.

16 12 November 1974, 1023 UNTS 15, Journal of Laws of 1979 no. 5 item 22.

Chapter 8 presents the issue of intellectual property (IP) in the context of space activities. There is more and more attention paid to the problems of intellectual property protection since the inevitable shift from State-owned projects concerning space activities to private ones. The goal is to unify patent law relating to outer space activities since there are still differences between national laws. In the Polish legal system, the issues addressing space law and intellectual property law are covered by separate legal acts which were analyzed in this Chapter.

The final Chapter 9 examines the need and rationale for the implementation of the national (domestic) space legal framework in Poland, as reflected by the Act establishing the Polish Space Agency (POLSA),[17] the 2017 Polish Space Strategy,[18] and the developing National Space Program. The ongoing legislative project – 'the Draft Space Act'[19] is reviewed and critically analyzed considering State obligations under international space treaties, while juxtaposing the concepts of jurisdiction and State sovereignty. In addition, general rules contained in the Polish civil and criminal codes, as well as relevant provisions of the domestic telecommunications law, intellectual property law, foreign trade and export control regulations, and the administrative procedures are recalled as applicable to State liability and responsibility in the context of space activities. In conclusion, some proposals *de lege ferenda* are presented for consideration, which might be beneficial for the future Polish Space Act.

Polish space activity supports close cooperation between the science, research and development sectors and industry. The great hopes for a breakthrough in the development of Polish space activities are heralded by a series of announced engineering projects assuming the construction of nano- and microsatellites with the intention of launching them into orbit in the years 2023–2025. One of such ventures is the PIAST project – Polish ImAging SaTellites – a national project, the aim of which is to use the potential of cooperation between scientific units and private entrepreneurs for the development of key solutions for security and defense. Another promising project, financed by the National Center for Research and Development, is to guarantee the first Polish instruments of the national satellite Earth observation

17 Act of 26 September 2014 on the Polish Space Agency, Journal of Laws of 2014 item 1533, as amended by Act of 13 June 2019, Amending The Act On The Polish Space Agency And The Act On Government Administration Departments, Journal of Laws of 2019, item 1248.

18 Council of Ministers Resolution No 6 of 26 January 2017 on the Adoption of the Polish Space Strategy (hereinafter Polish Space Strategy), Official Journal of the Republic of Poland of 2017 (Monitor Polski) item 203, para 1.

19 Ibid (n10).

system for the needs of the Polish Armed Forces. The development of such projects is of key importance for Poland to further increase research centres and enterprises' involvement in space programmes. It will be also necessary to ensure independent European access to outer space, mainly in the field of satellite launches by reusable rockets and its own ground infrastructure and in the field of the EU programme which can support countries in tackling the current and future global crises, to include pandemic, climate or collective defense challenges. Undoubtedly, the development of the space sector has vitally contributed to the growth of innovation in the economy and it will continue to expand the technological possibilities of the industry.

All of the above considerations indicate that now is the time for Poland to create a clear and predictable national legal regime for space activities, which would not only promote its own commercial space sector and national defense capabilities, but also contribute to the continued debate on the extent of space law regulations at the international level. The *corpus iuris spatialis internationalis* – international space law regime, which stems from the Cold War era of governance, is in need of further development to account for the increasingly multi-national and commercialized space sector. Many of the issues that remain ambiguous or unresolved in the current space treaties, provide an opportunity to be developed by the national legal frameworks. Accordingly, the drafters of the Polish Space Act should carefully consider such challenging issues, many of which are discussed in this book – from the extent of the registration and licensing requirements, the scope and extent of State jurisdiction and liability regimes, to the applicability of space law vis-à-vis air law. The importance of setting the legal definitions should not be overlooked, especially in case of: 'space activities' – by inclusion/exclusion of suborbital activities or the status of space mining, and 'outer space' – that is by setting a definitive lower boundary of outer space or incorporating a hybrid Near Space zone for High Altitude Activities such as unmanned high altitude platforms (HAPS) or drones. Finally, many of UN-recommended guidelines and practices should be examined and taken into consideration, such as the Guidelines for the Long-term Sustainability of Outer Space Activities, which should be followed to the largest possible extent and incorporated into the domestic legal framework to foster safety and sustainability of future space operations for Polish and global space operators.

On a final note, we hope this book will serve as a solid overview of the evolution of the Polish space activities and development of the national space sector, against the backdrop of the international space legal regime, and, perhaps will provide some ideas on how to take Poland and other new State entrants to the next level of space activities.

CHAPTER 1

A Brief History of Polish Space Policy and Strategy

Anna Nałęcz-Kobierzycka and Jakub Ryzenko

1 Introduction

The European dimension clearly dominates Polish space policy. Membership in the European Union represents an unprecedented opportunity for growth of the use of space applications in Poland. The European Space Agency and its industrial policy enabled rapid development of the national space sector, particularly commercial companies and space technologies development. Membership in EUMETSAT and EUTELSAT facilitated effective utilization of specific space capabilities.

2 The European Union

At the time of Polish accession to the European Union in 2004, both European space flagship programmes, that is Galileo and GMES (later renamed 'Copernicus'), were in their early development stages. They were just a part of a bigger 'portfolio' of issues dealt with by the already well-established structure of thematic Working Parties and EU Council formations in Brussels. Therefore, they became the responsibility of the respective Polish ministries and remain so until today.

The Galileo Programme was initially regarded as an essential contribution to the European transport infrastructure and as such 'belonged' first to the ministry supervising the infrastructure domain. As a result of numerous internal modifications in the administration's overall structure due to political changes, currently all matters related to Galileo are the Ministry of Digitalisation's responsibility (hereinafter also referred to as MC – Polish abbreviation for Ministry of Digitalisation).

MC experts participate in the GNSS Committee meetings in Brussels, deciding on the next steps in the implementation of satellite navigation systems. The decision-makers took part in the Transport, Telecommunication, and Energy EU Council formation when it was discussing Galileo and EGNOS-related issues. Ministry of Digitalisation representatives also attend the GSA

 | DOI:10.1163/9789004542860_003

Administrative Board meetings, accepting the Agency's action plan and draft budget for another year.

The European Commission is responsible for implementing the Galileo programme, including managing funds and overall supervision, while the Member States play a limited role. The only Galileo functionality independently implemented by the EU Member States[1] is the so-called Public Regulated Service – PRS. This particular service, dedicated only to the public administration, is to provide continuous access to and use of highly accurate location and timing data, secured against the possibility of any unauthorized interference (signal disturbance, jamming, spoofing, and suchlike). Access to the PRS is controlled through operational and technical means, including governmental grade encryption. Users not granted access to the service will be unable to obtain any information from the signal.

In Poland, within the Ministry of Internal Affairs and Administration structure responsible for implementing this service, a special Competent PRS Authority[2] was established. It acts as a necessary intermediary between Polish economic entities interested in obtaining security accreditation issued by the Security Accreditation Board within EUSPA (they cannot apply directly to SAB). In the future it is expected to be responsible for distribution of PRS receivers and encryption keys to duly authorized users. It aims to participate in the process of detailed agreement on the terms of use of the PRS; however, since the service is expected to be fully operational in 2023, the discussions on a European scale are still ongoing.

All issues related to space research as a part of the EU Framework Programmes for Research and Innovation and later on Horizon 2020 are under the Ministry of Science and Education's direct supervision. Its representatives (at an expert and political level, as appropriate) participate in Working Party Research and EU Competitiveness Council in Research and Innovation format. The National Contact Point for Research Programmes of the European Union[3] is very active in promoting Polish scientific and commercial entities'

---

1 In line with point 7 of 'Decision No 1104/2011/EU of the European Parliament and of the Council of 25 October 2011 on the rules for access to the public regulated service provided by the global navigation satellite system established under the Galileo programme' (Official Journal of the European Union L 287, 4.11.2011) "(...) each Member State must be in a position to take its own sovereign decision on which PRS users to authorise and which uses may be made of the PRS, including uses relating to security, in accordance with the common minimum standards."

2 https://archiwum.mswia.gov.pl/pl/bezpieczenstwo/zespol-cpa-polska/15401,Zespol-CPA-Polska-w-ramach-Ministerstwa-Spraw-Wewnetrznych-i-Administracji.html.

3 https://www.kpk.gov.pl.

participation in space-related research programmes and monitoring such involvement.

This ministry is also responsible for the Copernicus Programme – both in the European Union and ESA. It takes part in relevant EU meetings like the Copernicus User Forum to present Polish positions concerning the matters being discussed. It also supports the Polish space sector's broadest possible involvement in developing the programme and using Copernicus data in Poland. To this end, Poland decided to join the so-called Copernicus Collaborative Ground Segment coordinated by ESA. An agreement on this matter was signed in March 2018.[4] As a result, a National Copernicus Operator was selected – the Institute of Meteorology and Water Management – to receive, archive, and share data delivered by Sentinel satellites.

The Treaty of Lisbon through Article 189 of the Treaty on the Functioning of the European Union[5] established space as a 'shared competence' between the European Union and the Member States. The resulting ever-growing role of space policy in the European Union and organisational changes in Brussels, notably the establishment of a new, separate Working Party dedicated to space (WP Space) and later on the Space format of Competitiveness Council,[6] corresponded to a crucial internal change in the Polish Government – the responsibility for overall space policy was moved from the Ministry of Science and Education to the Ministry of Economy (currently named the Ministry of Development). Its representatives (at an expert and political level, as appropriate) participate in Working Party Space and EU Competitiveness Space Council meetings. They also coordinated and presented, during 2-year negotiations in Brussels, Poland's national position on the 'Proposal for a Regulation of the European Parliament and the Council establishing the space programme of the Union and the European Union Agency for the Space Programme,' finally adopted before the end of 2020.

4 https://www.prawo.pl/akty/m-p-2018-1019,18769416.html.

5 Treaty of Lisbon amending the Treaty on European Union and the Treaty establishing the European Community (hereafter Treaty of Lisbon), Lisbon, done 13 December 2007, entered into force 1 December 2009; OJ C 306/1 (2007).

6 The EU Competitiveness Council can meet in four different configurations: (1) internal market, (2) industry, (3) research and innovation and (4) space. In most EU Member States so-called "space ministers" are the ones responsible for either economy/industry/technology domains or science/research/innovation. The exact names of the ministries of course vary in different countries and may change over time, but the political domains related to space remain quite stable.

3 The European Space Agency

The beginning of the negotiations on Poland's accession to ESA in 2011, the Polish EU Council Presidency in the second half of 2011, and preparations of the governmental space strategy 'Action Programme for the Development of Space Technologies and the Use of Satellite Systems in Poland' required efficient coordination among the main stakeholders in the public administration – especially the Ministries of Economy, Science and Higher Education, Defence, Environment, Infrastructure and Transport, and Internal Affairs. At first, it was done at the operational level and later on as a formal inter-ministerial ESA negotiation team. These temporary solutions were transformed into a permanent, high-level political coordination mechanism called the Inter-ministerial Board for Space Policy in Poland, established by Order No 102 of the Prime Minister on 16 November 2012.[7] The Inter-ministerial Board was chaired by the Undersecretary of State in the Ministry of Economy (the Polish 'space minister') and composed of deputy ministers and presidents of central agencies dealing with specific areas of space activities. After the creation of the Polish Space Agency in 2014, its President joined the Board as one of the key members. The Board, meeting regularly every three months, was the primary information and coordination platform for the issues related to space policy. It was focused mainly on coordinating activities related to Poland's membership in the European Space Agency and making relevant budget recommendations regarding Polish participation in ESA's optional programmes[8] (two out of four tasks of the Board).

Poland does not have a dedicated financial line item in the State budget to pay the yearly contribution to ESA – the money comes from the budgets of 5 different ministries: Defence, Economy, Science and Education, Environment, and Foreign Affairs. Therefore, the final decisions on the division of the available amount of funding among different ESA optional programmes were made by the Board before each ESA Ministerial Council, based on results of previous cooperation with the Agency, areas of interest of the ministries, and

7 *Regulation No 102 of the Prime Minister of 16 November 2012, on the Inter-ministerial Board for Space Policy in Poland* (MP item 852, as amended).

8 ESA carries out two kinds of programmes – mandatory and optional. All ESA Member States participate in the mandatory activities, but they are free to decide which optional programmes they intend to join and what financial resources they will allocate for these purposes. ESA Convention, Article XI the Council, point 5 c: "The Council shall (…) as regards the optional programmes referred to in Article V, 1 b: i. accept each programme by a majority of all Member States; ii. determine, as appropriate, in the course of their implementation, the order of priority of programmes".

recommendations of the Polish Space Industry Association and the Polish Academy of Sciences Committee on Space Research. The Board prepared and approved its own detailed Terms of Reference, whereby the resolutions were accepted by a simple majority (in case of an equal number of votes, the vote of the chair would prevail). Apart from key financial decisions regarding ESA optional programmes, the Inter-ministerial Board was also responsible for approving the lists of projects to be carried out under the Polish Industry Incentive Scheme (PLIIS) whenever necessary and accepting the proposals to receive so-called Letters of Support[9] required in specific optional programmes.

The ministries that are Members of the Board (if they so desired) were entitled to nominate their experts to the ESA-Poland Task Force. It was a dedicated body established to implement the provisions of Article 6 of the Accession Agreement:[10] a guarantee that 45% of the Polish mandatory contribution during the transition period would be used only for special projects within PLIIS to support the Polish space sector's adaptation to ESA standards, rules and procedures. The ESA-Poland Task Force was co-chaired by the ESA Director of Industry, Procurement and Legal Services and the Polish Head of Delegation. It was composed of experts from ESA covering all mandatory programmes[11] and the optional programmes that Poland decided to join during the Ministerial Council in 2012 and representatives of the leading institutional stakeholders appointed by the Inter-ministerial Board. The Task Force was mandated to decide on any and all operational issues related to the Polish Industry Incentive Scheme – from the general provisions of each of the calls for proposals to all particular activities' approval. The Task Force officially fulfilled its role by the end of Poland's extended transition period, that is on 31 December 2019.

Polish accession to ESA also required the creation of a dedicated structure – the national Delegation. In line with the ESA Convention and the Council Rules of Procedure, each ESA Member State may have two delegates to the Agency's Committees and Programme Boards, accompanied by experts and advisors if needed. In Poland, following the already established division of roles and

---

9 In specific ESA optional programs, like GSTP or ARTES, obtaining a Letter of Support from the respective National Delegation is a prerequisite for bidding in a tender.

10 *Agreement between the Government of the Republic of Poland and the European Space Agency concerning accession of Poland to the Convention for the establishment of the European Space Agency and related terms and conditions*, signed in Warsaw on 31 July 2012, Journal of Laws item 61, 16 January 2013.

11 ESA Convention, Article V Activities and Programmes: "The activities of the Agency shall include mandatory activities, in which all Member States participate, and optional activities, in which all Member States participate apart from those that formally declare themselves not interested in participating therein."

responsibilities among different ministers dealing with space issues within the European Union and ESA accession negotiation process, it was decided that the Head of Delegation and overall coordination (especially in financial and industrial policy matters) would be placed in the Ministry of Economy. In turn, the Ministry of Science and Education is responsible for scientific and Earth Observation programmes, the Ministry of Digitalization for telecommunication and navigation domains, and the Ministry of Foreign Affairs for International Relations Committee. Later, after creating the Polish Space Agency, its representatives joined the Delegation as advisors.

The Inter-ministerial Board for Space Policy as the main decision-making body at the political level (undersecretaries of state in the ministries and presidents of relevant central agencies like the POLSA and the Industrial Development Agency) existed from November 2012 until January 2019. It was disbanded on 7 January 2019, by Order of the President of the Council of Ministers No 200 of 28 November 2018, on abolishing certain auxiliary bodies of the Council of Ministers and the Prime Minister.

The Minister of Entrepreneurship and Technology, by Order No 15 on 10 May 2019, amended by Order No 9 on 29 June 2020, established the Space Policy Team as an auxiliary body to the Minister responsible for the economy. The team aims to provide support to the Minister in the implementation of tasks in Poland's space policy domain. It is an advisory structure at an expert level and no longer a political one. The institutional members mainly remained the same. Two new tasks were added: proposing solutions aimed at supporting the Polish space sector in acquiring industrial and scientific projects to ensure optimal use of the Polish contribution to ESA and analysis and evaluation of the implementation of the assumptions of Polish space policy and the National Space Programme. The previous tasks like expressing opinions on the projects to be financed from the Polish contributions to ESA optional programmes or recommendations on the distribution of available funds among ESA's optional programmes were also continued, but as suggestions to the 'space minister' and not decisions.

4 EUMETSAT

The European Organisation for the Exploitation of Meteorological Satellites (EUMETSAT) was established in 1986[12] by 16 European countries to ensure the continuity of the operational system of meteorological satellites built by ESA.

12 Convention for the Establishment of a European Organization for the Exploitation of Meteorological Satellites (EUMETSAT), Geneva, done 24 May 1983, entered into force 19

EUMETSAT is responsible for the launch and operation of satellites and for delivering satellite data to end-users, as well as contributing to the operational monitoring of weather and climate and the detection of global climate changes.

Poland started to cooperate with EUMETSAT as soon as the overall political situation made it possible.[13] The formal 'Cooperation Agreement on Use of Images and Information from the EUMETSAT Meteosat Satellites' was signed on 20 January 1993 in Warsaw between EUMETSAT and the Institute of Meteorology and Water Management. Until 1998, the Republic of Poland received data from EUMETSAT free of charge under a license agreement. The situation changed significantly at the end of 1998. The existing license agreement for the free use of meteorological data and satellite information expired because, according to the EUMETSAT Convention,[14] charges for the use of satellite data depend on the country's gross domestic product (GDP). Since the Republic of Poland's GDP exceeded the level of $2,000.00 – in 1997 US dollars (USD) per capita – satellite data may henceforth be shared only for a license fee.[15] A special temporary exception was made between EUMETSAT and Poland for the year 1999. On 15 December 1999, a formal Agreement between the Republic of Poland and EUMETSAT on cooperation was signed in Warsaw.[16]

In accordance with the provisions of the Convention, the Agreement was concluded for a period of 5 years, with the expiry date by the end of 2004. As a result of negotiations, the Republic of Poland extended this contract for another three years, and in December 2007 – for another two years.

In 2008 Poland faced either joining EUMETSAT as a Member State or purchasing a full license to continue using the organisation's meteorological data. Since the data obtained through the purchase of a license were very limited in scope and time of transmission, and without access to the archives, data

June 1986; 1434 UNTS 3.

13 As a sign of political openess and willingness to expand cooperation with the former Soviet bloc countries, in March 1996 EUMETSAT organized in Darmstadt a special forum of users of METEOSAT data for the directors of national water and meteorological state services from Estonia, Latvia, Lithuania, Poland, Czech Republic, Slovakia, Hungary, Romania, Bulgaria, Slovenia and Croatia.

14 Annex III of Resolutions EUM/C/98/Res IV and EUM/C/99/Res VI and amended by Resolution EUM/C/89/18/Res III.

15 Czech Republic, Slovenia and Hungary were faced with the same situation in about the same timeframe and also decided to apply for full membership in EUMETSAT.

16 *Agreement between the Republic of Poland and the European Organisation for the Exploitation of Meteorological Satellites (EUMETSAT) on cooperation*, done and signed in Warsaw on 15 December 1999, Journal of Laws of 2002 No 2020, item 1706.

processing devices, training courses or Polish specialists' participation in EUMETSAT programmes, Poland decided to apply for membership in EUMETSAT, by the formal letter from the Secretary of State, deputy Minister of Environment dated on 3 September 2008.

On 9 January 2009, the Sejm adopted the law on the ratification of the Convention for the establishment of EUMETSAT.[17] It entered into force on 30 June 2009.

Under the Convention and resolutions adopted by EUMETSAT, Poland is entitled and obliged to:

- vote at EUMETSAT Council meetings;[18]
- pay an annual contribution to cover the general budget and mandatory programmes (calculated annually based on GNP over three-year periods, in line with article 10 of EUMETSAT Convention);[19]
- pay a contribution to optional programmes it wishes to join (according to the scale established in these programmes); and
- implement EUMETSAT data sharing rules,[20] including the tasks of the EUMETSAT Licensing Agent.

However, when Poland joined the organisation in 2009, it did not accede to the Protocol on the privileges and immunities of the European Organisation for Exploitation Meteorological Satellites, since the primary motivation for Polish accession to EUMETSAT was to ensure continuous access to meteorological data, as explicitly stated in the "justification of ratification" document. As a result, Polish entrepreneurs were excluded from any tenders for EUMETSAT. Polish citizens could not be employed in the organisation nor participate in foreign courses and internships, and no international EUMETSAT conferences organized in Poland were eligible for funding. However, the rapid development of Polish space sector caused by the increased cooperation with ESA under

17 *Convention for the Establishment of a European Organisation for the Exploitation of Meteorological Satellites* (*EUMETSAT*), done in Geneva on 24 May 1983, Journal of Laws of 2009, No 38, item 297.

18 Ibidem, article 4 and 5.

19 Poland paid a one-off accession fee in the amount of EUR 5,934,000 and its contribution to the mandatory programmes for the period 2009 – 2011 was set for 1,9780% (Annex I and II to EUMETSAT Council Resolution on the accession of the Republic of Poland to the EUMETSAT Convention, EUM/C/66/08/Res. V, adopted at the 66th Meeting of the EUMETSAT Council on 9-10 December 2008, https://www-cdn.eumetsat.int/files/2020-07/pdf_leg_res_full.pdf).

20 EUMETSAT's Principles on Data Policy were laid down in Council Resolution EUM/C/98/Res. IV and amended in Council Resolution EUM/C/57/05/Res. III. These Principles are generic and apply to all present and future EUMETSAT systems. Details available at: https://www.eumetsat.int/legal-framework/data-policy.

the PECS agreement in 2011–12, as well as full accession to ESA and subscription to MetOpSG optional programme in 2012 led to clear interest and willingness of Polish entities with suitable technological competences to participate in EUMETSAT industrial procurements. Therefore, this negative situation was rectified in April 2014, when the President of the Republic of Poland ratified the Protocol on the privileges and immunities of EUMETSAT (which entered into force in May 2014).[21]

At the governmental level, the cooperation with EUMETSAT is under the responsibility of the Ministry of Environment. At the operational level, Poland is represented by the Institute of Meteorology and Water Management (IMGW) – National Research Institute. The Director of the IMGW is the Polish delegate to the EUMETSAT Council, and experts from the Institute participate in the works of the Policy Advisory Committee (PAC), the Scientific and Technical Group (STG), the Administrative and Finance Group (AFG), and the Data Policy Group (DPG). The IMGW is also the Licensing Agent of EUMETSAT for Poland. From October 2016, with the consent of the Minister of the Environment and the IMGW, the EUMETSAT National Contact Point was established within the Polish Space Agency structures. In 2017, a Plan for increasing Polish entities' involvement in ongoing projects by EUMETSAT was prepared (analysis of the competition and ongoing procedures informing entities about tendering processes, assistance in joining consortia, organizing information meetings for industry and science).[22]

As of 2017, on the dedicated tender platform of EUMETSAT, only 13 Polish entities were registered, whereas, in 2019, the number reached 65. In the period 2016–2019, only one Polish company received a contract worth 4,700,000 € (as part of a consortium), while Poland paid total contributions in the amount of 48,900,000 €.

Poland did not participate in any of the optional programmes of EUMETSAT, since in 2009, that is at the time of the Polish accession; the then Ministry of the Environment excluded all optional programmes to reduce costs. However, the rules in EUMETSAT do not limit access by the Member States not participating in the optional programmes to the data generated by these programmes; therefore, the IMGW is allowed to use these data operationally at no cost.

The Polish contribution covered only the so-called general budget and mandatory programmes. Contributions are determined based on the forecast of

21 *The Act of 12 December 2013 on the ratification of the Protocol on Privileges and Immunities of the European Organisation for the Exploitation of Meteorological Satellites* (EUMETSAT), drawn up in Darmstadt on December 1, 1986, Journal of Laws of 2014, item 190.

22 https://polsa.gov.pl/projekty/eumetsat.

the organisation's budget for the following year. The percentage of the individual share for each Member State is updated every three years. Poland's contribution in 2015–2019 was about 2.5% of the general budget, including the mandatory programmes.

Poland participated in five mandatory EUMETSAT programmes:[23]

- Meteosat Transition Programme (MTP) – covering the construction, launching into orbit, and operational exploitation of geostationary satellites Meteosat – 4, 5, 6, and Meteosat – 7.
- Meteosat Second Generation (MSG) – a programme including construction, launching into orbit, and operational exploitation of Meteosat – 8, 9, 10, and 11.
- EUMETSAT Polar System (EPS) – a programme covering the construction, launching into orbit, and operational exploitation of polar satellites Metop – A (start date – 2006), Metop – B (2012), and Metop – C (2018).
- MTG – a programme covering the construction of the third generation of geostationary satellites, including five satellites with exploitation planned for the period 2021–2036.
- EUMETSAT Polar System-Second Generation (EPS-SG) – the programme including constructing the second generation of polar satellites (six satellites in three pairs, launch planned for 2022 and 2023).

In 2005, as part of the terrestrial segment and initiated by Poland, the Satellite Application Centre for Operational Hydrology and Water Management (H-SAF) was established. The IMGW is a member of the H-SAF consortium and co-implementer of the development phase in 2016–2021. Previously, it carried out development phases in the years 2005–2010 and 2010–2016. The consortium consists of 24 institutions from 13 countries and develops, tests, validates, and operationally provides satellite products for hydrology. The IMGW is responsible for the hydrological cluster validation of 74 satellite products.

5 EUTELSAT

EUTELSAT is another 'daughter organisation' of ESA, created with an ambition to build a European industry in the manufacture, launch, and operation of satellites. It was founded in an intergovernmental format in 1977 by 17 European countries, members of the European Conference of Postal and

23 *Development of the space sector – report of the Polish Supreme Audit Office*, KGP.430.017.2019 Reg No 44/2020/P/19/021 / KGP, Warsaw, 20 May 2020.

Telecommunications Administrations, to operate the first generation of communications satellites ordered by the European Space Agency and provide satellite TV programmes in Europe. Its constitutive text, the EUTELSAT Convention,[24] was opened for signature in July 1982 and entered into force on 1 September 1985. Poland decided to join the organisation formally already in December 1991.[25]

Until July 2001, EUTELSAT's primary purpose was the design, development, construction, operation, and maintenance of the space segment of the European telecommunications satellite system or systems. In this context, EUTELSAT's original objective was the provision of the space segment required for international public telecommunications services in Europe. In May 1999, the EUTELSAT Member States decided to restructure the Organisation and agreed to this change's relevant procedures. On 2 July 2001, all the assets, operational activities, and related liabilities and commitments of the intergovernmental organisation EUTELSAT were transferred to Eutelsat SA, a company established in Paris for this purpose.

The original EUTELSAT Convention was amended with the Member States' agreement,[26] and the amendments came into force on a definitive basis in November 2002. Since its restructuring, the structure, role, mission, and activities have evolved to reflect developments in the fields of regulation, technology, and markets for Fixed Satellite Services.

EUTELSAT IGO has a twofold role. It maintains the rights to use radio frequencies and orbital locations assigned collectively to the Member States by the International Telecommunication Union before the 2001 restructuring. EUTELSAT IGO also monitors Eutelsat SA's operations, mainly to ensure that the Basic Principles[27] are observed in accordance with the amended Convention.

---

24 *The Convention Establishing the European Telecommunications Satellite Organization (EUTELSAT)*, Paris, done 15 July 1982, entered into force 1 September 1985; UKTS 1990 No. 15; Cm. 956; Cmnd. 9069; *Space Law – Basic Legal Documents*, C.II.1.

25 *Government Statement of 5 June 1994 on the accession by the Republic of Poland to the Convention Establishing the European Satellite Communications Organisation EUTELSAT*, opened for signature in Paris on 15 July 1982, Journal of Laws of 1995, No 24, item 131.

26 *The Convention Establishing the European Telecommunications Satellite Organization (EUTELSAT), Paris, done 15 July 1982, entered into force 1 September 1985, as amended 20 May 1999, amended version entered into force 28 November 2002; Cm. 4572; Space Law – Basic Legal Documents, C.II.1.*

27 Ibidem, Article III a): "The primary purpose of EUTELSAT is to ensure that the Basic Principles set forth in this Article are observed by the Company Eutelsat S.A. namely: i) public service/universal service obligations: such obligations apply to space segment and to its use to provide services connected to the public switched telephone network;

The organisation's main decision-making body is the Assembly of Parties[28] and is composed of all the Member States, ordinarily meeting every two years. Between the ordinary meetings, the Assembly of Parties is assisted by an Advisory Committee[29] consisting of several Member States. The Advisory Committee, which meets twice per year, provides advice to the Executive Secretary on budget, staffing, and any matters referred to it by the Assembly of Parties. It has no decision-making role.

At the governmental level, Poland is represented in EUTELSAT by the Ministry of Digitalisation (currently under the Prime Minister's direct supervision). Before becoming a separate part of the public administration structure, digitalization used to belong to the Ministry of Internal Affairs and Administration, responsible for Poland's telecommunication matters.

The EUTELSAT IGO Secretariat is headed by the Executive Secretary[30] appointed by the Assembly of Parties for a (renewable) mandate of four years. The Executive Secretary, who is the legal representative of EUTELSAT, acts under the Assembly of Parties' direction and is directly responsible for all the Secretariat functions' performance.

At its 40th meeting in March 2017, the Assembly of Parties appointed Mr Piotr Dmochowski-Lipski from Poland for a mandate of four years from July 2017. From April 2019 until March 2021, Poland was also one of 9 members of the Advisory Committee.

The integration of Poland with the organisational structures of Western Europe, especially with the European Union and the European Space Agency, was undoubtedly the key factor in the development of the national space

audiovisual services and future services will be provided in conformity with the relevant national regulations and international agreements, in particular the provisions of the European Convention on Transfrontier Television, taking account of those applying to the universal service concept and the information society; ii) pan-European coverage by the satellite system: the Company Eutelsat S.A. shall, on an economic basis, seek through the pan-European coverage of its satellite system to serve all areas where there is a need for communications services in Member States; iii) non-discrimination: services shall be provided to users on an equitable basis subject to commercial flexibility and consistent with applicable laws; iv) fair competition: the Company Eutelsat S.A. shall comply with all applicable laws and regulations relating to fair competition."

28 Ibid., Article VII 'Assembly of Parties – Composition and Meetings', Article VII 'Assembly of Parties – Procedure' and Article IX 'Assembly of Parties – Functions.'

29 The *Mandate of the Advisory Committee of the Assembly of Parties of EUTELSAT IGO* was adopted by the Assembly of Parties at its 28th meeting and revised at its 30th, 36th and 39th meetings. Details available at: https://www.eutelsatigo.int/en/wp-content/uploads/sites/2/2016/04/ACMandateEN.2015.pdf.

30 EUTELSAT Amended Convention, Article X 'The Secretariat.'

sector. On the one hand, it offered clear and well-defined milestones to be achieved; on the other, it enabled and stimulated the sector's growth and capabilities. The following part of this chapter presents the process of definition and evolution of Polish space policy and its strategic aims. It started as a bottom-up initiative and concluded with governmental approval of the national space strategy.

6 Committee on Space Research Strategy 2003

The first general analysis of the Polish space sector's current situation, its potential, and perspectives for future development was carried out in 2003 by the Committee on Space Research of the Polish Academy of Sciences and the Polish Space Office. It was prepared on the eve of Poland's accession to the European Union and took into account the developing cooperation between the European Union and ESA, especially the Green Paper on European Space Policy jointly prepared by both organisations.[31]

The process of Poland's integration within the European Union required a new approach to most areas of life and social organisation nation-wide, including academic life covering space research and the application of space technology. From the scientific research perspective, there was a clear need to ensure access to space and international programmes to move knowledge boundaries further. From the practical side, progressive commercialization and privatization of space offered new possibilities also for less-developed countries like Poland. The study of space and the use of space technology were becoming essential elements of implementing the idea of a knowledge-based economy. In Poland, this activity had a long tradition, based on the earlier scientific achievements in astronomy, space research, and technical aviation. This potential in the early 2000s was relatively modest in terms of numbers but certainly not lacking in successful endeavours and international recognition. Therefore, in November 2003, the proposed 'Strategy of actions related to space in Poland in the conditions of membership in the European Union'[32] was officially presented by the Polish Academy of Sciences.

The strategy proposed by the Committee on Space Research aimed to achieve the following goals:

31 *Green Paper on European Space Policy*, Brussels, 21 January 2003, COM (2003) 17 final.

32 http://www.kbkis.pan.pl/images/stories/Strategia_Full_Version.pdf.

- To align Polish space activities with the European Union's space policy;
- To take the proper place among the countries of the European community in the field of exploration and use of outer space;
- To use satellite systems for the benefit of society and public services; and
- To enable Polish companies to operate on the international space technology market.

This document was an attempt to assess Poland's needs and capabilities in space and present a set of activities to achieve the strategic goals with a time horizon of around 2010. The proposed activities were addressed primarily to the State administration at various levels. Still, it was also assumed that economic bodies – including research and development entities – would respond constructively to the conditions and economic incentives created. The year of Poland's accession to the European Union was indicated as 2004, and a rational economic growth / national income scenario was projected as a basis for formulating requests for financial support from the State budget. The value of the desired and possible investments from the private sector was also estimated. The resulting conclusions were as follows:

1. It should be made clear to the Polish decision-makers that as part of the regular contribution paid to the European Union, Poland would finance the European space programme at the level of 350 million PLN per year.
2. To actively participate in the European space programme and at least partially recover this money in a way beneficial for the Polish economy and science, it is necessary for Poland to join the European Space Agency and to take advantage of the PECS[33] mechanism enabling gradual integration with ESA activities.
3. The Polish national space programme's financing in 2010 should be at the level of 125 million PLN, of which approximately 75 million PLN is to come from the State budget, with a gradual increase starting from the next financial year.
4. Poland needs to participate in the international space exploration effort by deepening the space research scientific programme, both within ESA and in cooperation with other space agencies.

33 'The Plan for the European Co-operating States (PECS)' was a special mechanism elaborated by ESA in 2001 to stimulate cooperation with the former Soviet bloc countries. For details please refer to: *Towards an Enlarged Partnership – ESA's Relations with the Czech Republic, Hungary, Poland and Romania*, C. Baudin, Legal Affairs Department, ESA, Paris; K. Bergquist, International Relations Department, ESA, Paris, ESA Bulletin 107 – August 2001.

5. It is necessary to establish an efficient organisational structure, considering the solutions existing in other countries. The mechanism of a 'government programme' may be an appropriate form of financial management.
6. It is necessary to extend educational and promotional activities at the postgraduate, university, and popular levels.

7 Committee on Space Research Strategy Revision 2009

The specific actions of the 2003 proposed strategy were never implemented. However, significant progress in cooperation between Poland and ESA led to Poland's accession to the Plan for European Cooperating State (PECS) Agreement in April 2007.[34] These developments, as well as crucial changes at the European level – a further evolution of European Space Policy, cooperation between the European Union and ESA (the EU-ESA Framework Agreement,[35] Resolution on the European Space Policy from May 2007,[36] Article 189 of the Treaty on the Functioning of the European Union following the Treaty of Lisbon)[37] – resulted in the revision of the proposed strategy in October 2009.[38]

Whereas the four strategic aims defined in 2003 remained valid, the Committee suggested revised and more detailed lines of activity to be pursued to achieve them. These updated objectives were as follows:

1. Elaboration of the Polish space policy and the national space programme, establishing a dedicated body coordinating Polish space activities and full membership in ESA.
2. Launching several large industrial and research projects financed under the national programme, which would allow for the development of skills and expansion of technological potential and native know-how.

---

34 *European Cooperating State Agreement between the European Space Agency and the Government of the Republic of Poland*, Journal of Laws No 154, 26 August 2008.

35 *The Framework Agreement Between the European Community and the European Space Agency*, Brussels, done 25 November 2003, entered into force 28 May 2004; OJ L 261/64 (2004); 53 *Zeitschrift für Luft- und Weltraumrecht* (2004), 89.

36 9052/07 RECH 115 COMPET 115 ENV 218 COSDP 348 TRANS 132 + ADD1 ADD2 ADD 3 – COM (2007) 212 final, Brussels, 25 May 2007.

37 *Treaty establishing the European Community as amended by the Treaty of Lisbon amending the Treaty on European Union and the Treaty establishing the European Community* (hereafter TFEU), Lisbon, done 13 December 2007, entered into force 1 December 2009; OJ C 326/47 (2012).

38 http://www.kbkis.pan.pl/index.php?option=com_content&view=article&id=71&Itemid=49.

3. More active involvement of Poland in the implementation of the European Space Policy, in particular full use of the opportunities created by the development of the GMES and Galileo Programmes.
4. A guaranteed budget for implementing technological projects based on the cooperation between the public sector and industry, which could lead to the development of advanced products and services at home and abroad, supporting the transfer of knowledge and experience between units of both sectors.
5. The development of space technology applications based on (i) publicly funded and elaborated programmes aimed at specific needs of the public administration (with specified beneficiaries, defined project implementation, and approval criteria), and (ii) market mechanisms.
6. Attracting foreign investments in the space industry sector.
7. Construction and modernization of the research and laboratory infrastructure and providing education and continuous replenishment of scientific and technical staff for the needs of the R&D sector of the Polish space programme.
8. An ambitious and comprehensive public information strategy on the benefits and availability of specific products and services based on space technologies and their applications.

8 Action Programme for the Development of Space Technologies and the Use of Satellite Systems in Poland 2012

The overwhelming interest of the Polish space sector in cooperation with ESA under the PECS Agreement leading to the formal request of Poland to begin accession negotiations, the EC Communication from April 2011 'Towards a space strategy for the European Union that benefits its citizens'[39] and the initial discussions about space programmes for the next EU Multiannual Financial Framework as well as the Polish EU Council Presidency in the second half of 2011, resulted in the elaboration and approval by the Government of the first official Polish space strategy. The 'Action Programme for the Development of Space Technologies and the Use of Satellite Systems in Poland' was approved

39 Communication from the Commission to the Council, the European Parliament, the European Economic and Social Committee and the Committee of the Regions *Towards a space strategy for the European Union that benefits its citizens*, Brussels, 4.4.2011, COM (2011) 152 final.

by Resolution No 121 of the Council of Ministers on 26 June 2012,[40] and the Minister of Economy was appointed to implement the provisions of the document.

The strategic goals of the 'Action Programme' were as follows:

1. Growth of innovativeness and competitiveness of enterprises through development of advanced technologies (satellite and space technologies) and support of cooperation between the R&D sector and enterprises,
2. Improved efficiency and effectiveness of the public administration functioning through the development and implementation of solutions based on satellite technologies to use the existing resources and infrastructure more effectively, and
3. Satisfy national security and defense needs through available instruments and development of autonomous potential in selected areas.

These key aims were to be implemented through the following operational objectives:

1. Development of cooperation between Poland and the European Space Agency, including in particular full ESA membership of Poland,
2. Participation of Poland in EU programmes, including the projects of the European Defense Agency,
3. Setting up an organisational structure for coordination of Poland's space activities, and
4. Development and implementation of a national space sector programme.

In contrast to the previous strategic documents prepared by the Committee on Space Research and therefore naturally focused on the scientific community's perspective, the 'Action Programme' as a governmental strategy elaborated by the Ministry of Economy presented an overall picture of the space sector in Poland, its scientific and technological potential, possible industrial development and institutional and organisational aspects (both in terms of relations between Poland, the European Union, and ESA and internal Polish structures related to space activities). The SWOT analysis concluded that the main barriers for Poland's space industry's growth were organisational and financial in nature, and State intervention was required to overcome these obstacles.

Therefore, the 'Action Programme' proposed a vision of a robust pro-space State policy, which would ensure the maximization of benefits from Poland's accession to ESA and guarantee the optimal use of expenditures and the maintenance of national competences in the field of research, implementation, and industrial activities, enabling the implementation of the strategic interests of

40 Resolution No 121 of the Council of Ministers of 26 June 2012.

the State. Thanks to participation in the optional ESA programmes, Poland would quickly develop its competencies in selected technological areas considered essential for the State's national interest. The domestic space sector would have sufficient funds for sustainable development (ensuring a minimum balance between investments in the upstream and downstream segment, enabling constant access to the latest technologies in the long term, without the risk of remaining only a user of satellite applications produced by other countries), as well as benefit from all large projects with a special financing path. Thanks to implementing this vision, Poland would not only be a customer of solutions developed abroad, but would also actively participate in creating and using new technologies in both the European Union and ESA.

On the eve of Poland's accession to ESA, the 'Action Programme' emphasized the political, technological, and economic benefits of joining the Agency, specification of related financial conditions, possible coordination and organisation structure, and thematic areas of interest of Poland in space activities. These priorities were set based on the following three factors: (1) the needs of the users, primarily the public and local authorities, followed by representatives of research and scientific circles and entrepreneurs; (2) the analysis of long-term benefits of the application of space technologies for Poland; and (3) technological potential of the national space sector and its competitiveness compared to the European and global stakeholders. They covered satellite observations, navigation and positioning, satellite communications generic space technologies, defense and national security, crisis management and promotion and education as a horizontal component. These priority areas were duly reflected by the Polish contribution to ESA's optional programmes during the Ministerial Council in Naples in 2012.

As far as the organisational structure was concerned, it was decided to set up a coordination model with the Ministry of Economy playing the key role as the Polish 'space ministry,' in close cooperation with the other governmental stakeholders gathered in the Inter-ministerial Board for Space Policy. At the same time, the competent organisational unit in the Polish Agency for Enterprise Development (PARP) would implement tasks related to State policy, especially in supporting entrepreneurship and developing the space sector. The establishment of a separate government agency, supported by research and development centres, focused on the management of major projects and coordination of the Polish industry activities, could be considered in the longer run, depending on the evolution of the Polish space sector and available financial resources.

The 'Action Programme' also underlined the need to increase Polish involvement in the European space flagship initiatives Galileo and Copernicus, as well as the planned Space Situational Awareness domain. The importance of participation in relevant projects within the European Defense Agency and European Framework Cooperation (EFC) pilot programme (an initiative of the EDA, the European Commission, and ESA aimed at coordinating the works in research and technology for security and defense) was indicated.

Finally, last but not least, it was recommended to initiate preparations to develop and implement a national space programme. This national programme would be complementary to Polish space activities undertaken within the European Union and ESA. It was intended to build national capacity in the field of research, implementation, and industrial operations, allowing the realization of the State's strategic interests. On the one hand, the national programme would support the domestic space sector's development to acquire experience and scientific and technological expertise, making it easier to apply for contracts with ESA, under the EU Framework Programmes, or on the commercial market. At the same time, on the other hand, it would provide the opportunity to implement the acquired *know-how* at a national scale, as well as to promote the use of satellite technologies by the administrative authorities and the members of society.

9 National Space Strategy 2017

In the following years, full membership in ESA resulted in the Polish space sector's vigorous growth. Unfortunately, however, the opening of international opportunities was not complemented by a national space programme, which had not been initiated.

In 2016 a new, comprehensive strategy of economic development for Poland was presented – the so-called Responsible Development Plan (SOR).[41] This strategy's basic assumption was to create a new model for the Polish economy's development, based more on knowledge, innovation, and technological progress than on low production costs. The SOR defined the country's primary conditions, goals, and directions in the social, economic, regional, and spatial dimensions in the 2020 and 2030 timeframe.

One of the industries that had a niche character in Poland but could contribute to achieving this goal was the space sector, with its already-proven key advantages: building stable cooperation between science and

41 https://www.gov.pl/web/fundusze-regiony/informacje-o-strategii-na-rzecz-odpowiedzialnego-rozwoju.

industry, developing innovative technologies, stimulating contacts and foreign collaboration.

In October 2016 the European Commission published the Communication 'Space Strategy for Europe.'[42] It provided several measures to increase the competitiveness of this sector of the European economy on the global market and increase the use of satellite data for the implementation of many sectoral EU policies. At the same time, the European Space Agency also developed a new vision of space activity called 'Space 4.0'[43] taking into account the dynamically changing conditions of space activities (increasingly faster technological development including digitization and miniaturization, an increased number of countries conducting space activities, and a growing role of the private sector).

Therefore, the Polish Space Strategy was an attempt at a national response to these challenges, and at the same time, taking advantage of the opportunities created by the new conditions for the Polish economy. According to the overall vision, by 2030 the space sector would become an important element of the Polish economy based on knowledge and innovation. Its linkage with other areas of the economy would be conducive to increasing competitiveness.

On 26 January 2017, the Council of Ministers adopted the Polish Space Strategy by Resolution No. 6. Both documents were published in the Polish Monitor on 17 February 2017, thus becoming formally binding.[44]

The document defined the following strategic objectives to be achieved by 2030:

- To enable the Polish space sector to compete on the European market successfully and to raise its share of turnover up to at least 3% of the total turnover of the market (in proportion to the Polish economic potential);
- The Polish public administration will use satellite data for faster and more efficient implementation of its tasks while Polish enterprises will be able to meet the domestic demand for such services fully and to export them to other markets; and

42 *Communication from the Commission to the European Parliament, the Council, the European Economic and Social Committee and the Committee of the Regions 'Space Strategy for Europe,'* Brussels, 26 October 2016, COM (2016) 705 final.

43 https://www.europarl.europa.eu/cmsdata/111744/ITRE2016%20-%20ESA%20-%20point%2013.pdf.

44 *Resolution No 6 of the Council of Ministers of 26 January 2017 on the adoption of the Polish Space Strategy* (M.P. item 203).

- The Polish economy and the public authorities will gain autonomous access to satellite infrastructure within a scope that allows their needs to be fully met.

These strategic, long-term aims would be gradually achieved by implementing five specific objectives, each of them with corresponding defined areas of intervention and dedicated tools. They are as follows:

- Increasing competitiveness of the Polish space sector and its share in the turnover of the European space sector,
- Development of satellite applications – contributing to the process of building the digital economy,
- Strengthening capacities in the area of security and defence by using space technologies and satellite applications,
- Creating an environment conducive to the development of the space sector in Poland, and
- Building human capacities for the Polish space sector.

The first three specific objectives focus on 'hard', tangible activities and require more significant financial resources and administrative efforts, whereas the last two rely on rather 'soft' implementation mechanisms.

In order to increase competitiveness of the Polish space sector and its share in the European market it is necessary to increase participation in ESA optional programmes (targeted at 150%–200% of mandatory contributions, which is a normal ratio for most ESA Member States) and at the same time develop and implement the National Space Programme. These two key measures should be accompanied by several other supporting actions to be pursued simultaneously: increasing participation in EU space programmes (Horizon2020, Copernicus, Galileo, SST, GovSatCom) as well as in other international initiatives (EUMETSAT, ESO), developing bilateral cooperation with other countries (in Europe and outside, notably with the United States) and initiating Polish participation in the so-called *New Space* sector. A necessary pre-requisite for all that is the identification of the most promising technology areas for the Polish space industry (existing competence, technology niches, and development potential). By implementing the above-mentioned activities, Poland should strive to elevate its national space sector from the level of a supplier of components to that of a supplier of satellite subsystems.

The second operational objective of the Strategy is focused on the development of satellite applications and supporting their market uptake and use in the public administration at all levels. Here the condition sine qua non is providing continuous, fast, and reliable access to satellite data, mostly by joining the Copernicus Collaborative Ground Segment coordinated by ESA (Poland signed the agreement with ESA in March 2018,[45] established a National Copernicus Operator and created a dedicated system within Sat4Envi project). This should enable and encourage the widespread use of satellite data at various levels of the public administration and facilitate the provision of commercial services. Intensified participation in international programmes (European Union, ESA, EUMETSAT, the European Investment Bank, World Bank) is also foreseen here.

The third specific objective is strengthening capacities in the area of security and defence by using space technologies and satellite applications. It also requires additional investments and well-coordinated efforts of governmental administration focused on development of dual-use space technologies and capabilities: the construction of a national satellite Earth Observation system, construction of a space situational awareness system, ensuring availability of satellite communication and navigation systems and development of launcher technologies. It is worth to mention that in December 2018 Poland formally joined the EU SST Consortium.[46]

The areas of intervention defined under specific objective number four aim at creating an environment conducive to the development of the space sector in Poland. These are mostly informational and promotional activities and fostering science and business, particularly for SMEs. It is planned to establish an ESA Business Incubator Centre in Poland (in conjunction with the IAP Ambassadors Platform), following the example of most ESA Member States, as well as conduct other support activities to increase the level of private investments in the Polish space sector. And – last but not least – enacting the Law on the National Register of Space Objects to meet Poland's obligations under international treaties is also planned.[47]

The last specific objective is focused on building human capacities for the Polish space sector. It is foreseen to continue and increase already ongoing support mechanisms for high-schools and universities competitions and students' projects and foster programmes, internships, and apprenticeships in the space sector (Polish companies, universities, international organisations – at all education levels, from undergraduate to post-doc). If needed, new university departments may be established. Finally, the efforts should be made to increase participation of the Polish staff in international organisations (the European Union, ESA and others).

45 https://www.prawo.pl/akty/m-p-2018-1019,18769416.html.

46 https://polsa.gov.pl/en/events/events/15-latest/943-poland-has-joined-the-space-surveillance-and-tracking-sst-consortium-established-to-track-space-debris.

47 For details please refer to.7

As of the beginning of 2021, the Polish Space Strategy remains in force and guides the development of space activities. It is an instrument for programming, management, and coordination of the government's public policies concerning the space sector in partnership with public and private entities and society. The strategy is the basis for updating the existing programming documents relating to this sector, as well as for reassessment of the current instruments. There should also be a consistency between the Polish Space Strategy as approved by the Council of Ministers and the secondary documents on the Polish space sector, in particular the executive documents, such as the National Space Programme to be prepared by the Polish Space Agency, Industrial Development Agency and other action plans of public bodies involved in Polish space programmes.

The goals and indicators are the basis for continuous monitoring of the development and the impact of the Strategy. Representatives of business, academia, and NGOs will be involved in a partnership to achieve the Strategy's objectives. They had already been involved in the strategy programming phase, among others, through participation in the strategy drafting and during public consultations.

The strategic goals and specific objectives laid down in the Polish Space Strategy should be achieved by 2030. The Ministry of Development is responsible for its comprehensive implementation in cooperation with the relevant institutions, particularly with other ministries and the Polish Space Agency, which should define and implement the National Space Programme.

All activities described in the Strategy will be conducted simultaneously; however, to help monitor its implementation and take corrective actions, indicators have been defined for each specific objective chosen to be implemented in 2020, which represents the first 'checkpoint.'[48] At this early stage, the majority of the proposed indicators are binary (fail/pass) but once attained, they will continue to be monitored for quality (for instance, development and implementation of the National Space Programme are followed by evaluation of the effectiveness of its implementation, building receiver stations for the Copernicus satellite data and then monitoring the number of users of these

48 In June 2021 Polish Space Professionals Association published a report *"Evaluation of implementation of Polish Space Strategy and its KPIs"*. According to this document out of 13 KPIs indicated in Polish Space Strategy to be fulfilled by the end of 2020 only 4 were fully met, 1 was partially achieved and 8 were not realized. Source: https://kosmonauta.net/2021/06/pspa-ocena-realizacji-polskiej-strategii-kosmicznej/. There has been no official report on the implementation of the Polish Space Strategy presented by any of the governmental institutions (until September 2021), nor any comments to PSPA document.

data and running an NCBiR programme for building a national satellite system of Earth observation and evaluation of the process of its implementation). Another 'checkpoint' is planned for 2025 when detailed indicators will be defined after the verification exercise of the proposed measures and tools' effectiveness.

10 Concluding Remarks

The first Polish space policy strategic document was elaborated (2003) and revised (2009) by the Polish Academy of Sciences' Space Research Committee. Due to this fact, it was not a binding document; it could only be regarded as a set of evidence-based recommendations, but without any dedicated implementation mechanisms nor State funding. Nevertheless, it provided a comprehensive vision and suggested lines of activities to be pursued by interested stakeholders. Owing to continuous efforts of the space scientific community and later on also the developing space industry, it was possible to achieve significant progress within most of the indicated domains (especially an increase in the cooperation level with the European Union and ESA) and convince the Polish public administration of the ever-growing importance of the space sector for the development of innovation and a knowledge-based economy.

As a result, the following strategic document was approved by the Council of Ministers in 2012 and had the status of an official governmental policy; in contrast to 2003 and 2009 including dedicated implementation mechanisms. As such, it was accompanied by a defined organisational structure responsible for its implementation (the Inter-ministerial Board for Space Policy, Ministry of the Economy as 'space ministry,' with a clear division of roles among the other governmental stakeholders). It also had some dedicated funding available to develop the scientific and industrial space sector, mainly through the Polish Industry Incentive Scheme and Polish contributions to ESA optional programmes. The coordinated information and promotion activities were implemented – and paid for – by the relevant ministries and the Polish Agency for Enterprise Development (PARP). Due to the systematic cooperation of different governmental institutions in the implementation of objectives set out in the 'Action Programme' and the positive reaction of industrial entities and the scientific community to the opportunities offered by Polish accession to ESA and the EU Horizon 2020 programme by 2016 three out of four operational goals were mostly met: full Poland's membership in ESA, increased participation in EU space activities and the establishment of the Polish Space Agency in 2015. Only the national space programme remained at the stage of analytical and conceptual work. Consequently, the Polish space sector's development was mainly based on international mechanisms and lacking specific funding aimed at national priorities.

The fulfilling of most of the operational objectives of the 'Action Programme' from 2012, as well as the evolution of European space policy and dynamic development of the national space industry, led to the formulation of a new, long-term (until 2030) governmental Polish Space Strategy, approved in January 2017. From the very beginning, its implementation was planned as a gradual, step-by-step process, taking maximum possible advantage of already-existing financial support mechanisms (EU space and R&D programmes, structural funds, contribution to ESA, national structures like NCN and NCBR) and whenever necessary complementing them with new ones, notably the national space programme to be elaborated by the Polish Space Agency. Efficient coordination of efforts made by all involved stakeholders to further support the Polish space sector's development was deemed crucial to the strategy's overall successful implementation.

The report of the Supreme Audit Office in 2019[49] indicated that in some areas, the progress was faster (like support for the operational use of EO data by the public administration in the Sat4Envi project, Poland's accession to the EU SST Consortium, a system of internships in the companies and research institutes from the space sector, and support for students and education initiatives) and in some others slower (for example, an elaboration of the national space programme). The COVID-19 pandemic and related economic crisis also had a negative impact on the implementation of the Polish Space Strategy objectives. Still, it is expected that the sector will once again prove its resilience and innovation potential.

10.1 *Bottom-Up vs. Top-Down Approach – Advantages and Disadvantages*

To explain the gradual evolution of the definition and implementation of Poland's national space policy, it must be stressed that – contrary to the practice common among most space-faring nations – this process was based on a bottom-up and not a top-down approach. Unlike the space superpowers (the United States, the Soviet Union/Russia, China, or even France), it was never driven by geopolitical, military, and strategic objectives defined by the central government and then "given" to the respective national space sectors for

49 *Development of the space sector – report of the Polish Supreme Audit Office,* KGP.430.017.2019 Reg No 44/2020/P/19/021/KGP, Warsaw, 20 May 2020.

implementation. Neither has it ever been treated as one of the critical priorities of innovation and economic development, like in Germany or Luxembourg.

Space policy in Poland developed as a kind of 'organic growth' inspired by tangible successes of the national space sector and then progressing to the governmental level. This bottom-up approach has certain advantages – mostly diversity and strength of its foundations. It leads to a more resilient situation, less prone to fall victim to potential political disturbances and changes in government-funded space programmes. Furthermore, the strategic aims defined in this way reflect the space sector's real needs and capabilities and remain stable and gradually achieved.

However, the downside of this approach is the comparatively slower progress than in the case of top-down formulation of objectives that are given the appropriate funding and implementation mechanisms from the start. Some efforts may be more fragmented and yield less short-term results than a well-coordinated, centrally-driven programme. Also, what is particularly important is that such an approach misses an opportunity to gather support and resources to achieve all-important successes[50] – delivering results of significant political importance and high visibility.

Taking the above into account, the fact that the Polish space sector managed to prove its importance to the high-level political authorities and inspire the elaboration of two government-approved space policy strategy documents (in 2012 and 2017) is the best evidence of its current and future potential. At the same time, other countries' experience seems to prove that effective use of space to address national economic, social and strategic goals requires rather a top-down approach. The question of when it is an optimal time to introduce it in Poland remains open.

50 Like the first human spaceflight or landing on the Moon.

CHAPTER 2

A Survey of Polish Involvement in Space and Space Activities

Jakub Ryzenko and Anna Nałęcz-Kobierzycka

1 The Foundations

Polish interest in space reaches back to the early days of the 16th century. The most prominent scientific figure of that time was Polish astronomer Mikołaj Kopernik (1473–1543), whose work "On the Revolutions of the Heavenly Spheres" laid the foundations for the most significant scientific revolution at that time – the Copernican Revolution. A century later, the astronomer, mathematician, and constructor of astronomic instruments, Jan Heweliusz (1611–1687), lived and worked in Gdańsk. His regular observations of the sky resulted in a series of landmark astronomical studies. The same period saw Kazimierz Siemienowicz (1600–1651), an engineer and artillery theoretician, develop the basis for multistage rocket construction.

After the end of World War II, Poland was actively involved in shaping the international organizational environment for space activities. Poland was one of the founding member states of the UN Committee of COPUOS in 1958.[1] The internationally recognized Polish lawyer Manfred Lachs provided significant contributions to the formulation of international space law. In 1963, the COSPAR General Assembly was held in Warsaw and the International Astronautical Congress in 1964. A dedicated structure facilitating space-related research was established in 1965 as part of the Polish Academy of Sciences, currently named the Committee on Space Research.[2]

The first flight of the Polish meteorological rocket *Meteor* took place in 1963. More than 200 flights of different models were conducted until 1974 when the programme was ended. A number of those flights reached an altitude of 90 km, and in one flight, the rocket crossed the 100 km threshold of space.[3]

1 https://www.unoosa.org/oosa/en/ourwork/copuos/members/evolution.html.

2 Interview with Prof. Zbigniew Kłos, former Director of the Space Research Centre, PAN.

3 *Rola Instytutu Lotnictwa w badaniach kosmicznych,* Witold Wiśniowski, Piotr Wolański, Prace Instytutu Lotnictwa, No. 1 (234), 2014 10–11.

 | DOI:10.1163/9789004542860_004

The beginning of Polish participation in space flights was realized as part of the international programme *Interkosmos*,[4] based on collaboration with the Soviet Union. The first Polish research instrument was flown in space in 1970 on the *Vertical-1* rocket. The first orbital instrument was sent on board the satellite *Kopernik-500* (*Interkosmos-9*) in 1973.[5] Three years later the Space Research Centre of the Polish Academy of Sciences was established as a research entity focused entirely on exploring space and developing space technologies. Until today, it has developed more than 80 instruments deployed in space. In 1978, the first and to date only Polish astronaut, Mirosław Hermaszewski†, flew in space onboard the USSR spaceship *Soyuz-30*. This 8-day mission aimed to carry out experiments in the Soviet space station *Salut-6*.

In parallel with research activities, the foundations for the practical utilization of space were laid out. In 1967, the first receiving satellite station was established in the National Hydrological-Meteorological Institute, which regularly collected data from meteorological satellites. The station was gradually expanded, and today it represents the core of the Polish Copernicus Collaborative Ground Segment.[6]

In 1972, the Polish State telecommunication company's satellite communication centre was established, initially as part of *the Intersputnik*[7] system. The following years it expanded and offered services within INMARSAT, INTELSAT and EUTELSAT's[8] framework. The Centre terminated its services in 2010 as a result of competition from terrestrial services.[9]

In 1976, the 'Opolis' Teledetection Centre was created as part of the Institute of Geodesy and Cartography to develop Earth Observation (EO) applications. Throughout the years, a wide variety of EO analyses were created, and the Institute remains one of the leading institutions in the field of EO applications.[10]

---

4 Agreement for Cooperation in the Exploration and Use of Outer Space for Peaceful Purposes (INTERKOSMOS), Moscow, done on 13 July 1976, entered into force 25 March 1977; 16 ILM 1 (1977).

5 *Polish Space Instruments, Period 1970–2016*, 2016.

6 https://www.imgw.pl/en/institute/history.

7 Agreement on the Establishment of the "INTERSPUTNIK" International System and Organization of Space Communications, Moscow, done on 15 November 1971, entered into force 12 July 1972; 862 UNTS 3; TIAS 859 (1973) No. 12343; *Space Law – Basic Legal Documents*, C.VIII.1.

8 Poland joined INMARSAT already in 1979, INTELSAT in 1993 and EUTELSAT in 1994.

9 Urania, *Postępy Astronomii*, No 1/2011, 34–35.

10 http://www.igik.edu.pl/pl/a/Seminarium-Jubileuszu-75-lecia-Teledetekcja-OPOLIS-w-Instytucie-Geodezji-i-Kartografii.

After 1989, geopolitical changes enabled Poland and other former Eastern Bloc countries to initiate cooperation with the Western world's foremost international organizations, particularly the European Economic Community, the North Atlantic Treaty Organization (NATO), and the Organisation for Economic Co-operation and Development (OECD). For the space communities of these countries, the European Space Agency was a natural target. Their previous experience and achievements in space research, including under the *Intersputnik* programme and the overall geopolitical environment, represented a solid ground for establishing direct contacts.

In Poland, entering into cooperation with ESA represented a game-changer for the space sector. In the following years, opportunities offered by cooperation with ESA and later by full membership represented the major source of funding for space projects, becoming by far the mainstream of Polish space activities.

2 Beginning of Cooperation with ESA – 1994 and 2002 Agreements

The first formal cooperation agreement between ESA and new Eastern partners was signed with the Republic of Hungary in April 1991 and the second with the Government of Romania in December 1992. Poland was the third country from the Central-Eastern European region to sign such an agreement. It was done on 28 January 1994, at the ESA Headquarters in Paris by Jerzy Łukaszewski, Polish Ambassador to Paris, and Jean-Marie Luton, the ESA Director-General.

This agreement, covering cooperation on the exploration and use of outer space for peaceful purposes, was an expression of ESA's political will to cooperate with the countries of Central and Eastern Europe recently reaffirmed in a resolution on international cooperation adopted by the ESA Council meeting at the ministerial level in Granada. It mentioned several activities, such as regular exchanges of information, visits, the award of fellowships, joint symposia, mutual access to databases and laboratories, and studies on joint projects in fields of mutual interest.

To reinforce existing relations between Poland and ESA, both parties decided to renew the agreement. On 24 January 2002, the agreement was signed in Warsaw by Antonio Rodotà, the ESA Director-General, and the Polish science Minister Professor Kleiber. As at that time Poland was finalizing its preparation to join the European Union, Mr. Rodotà also met with Poland's principal negotiator with the EC, Mr. Truszynski, to introduce the ESA/EC space strategy and stress the need to work in close relation with the candidate countries.

Owing to both cooperation agreements with ESA, Polish institutions had a chance to participate as co-investigators in almost all the ESA Science projects: Ulysses; ISO (archive data); SOHO; XMM (observing time; archive); Cluster; Double Star; Huygens; Mars Express; Herschel (hardware for the HIFI instrument); Planck; XEUS; Integral; Rosetta and BepiColombo. Polish researchers also undertook some activities related to the ExoMars rover instruments. The Polish scientific community was also very active with the utilization of Envisat data. Training opportunities and several fellowships at ESA and Member States' establishments were granted to Polish students. Several of them were also involved in ESA educational project known as the Student Space Exploration and Technology Initiative (SSETI).

3 PECS Agreement and Beginnings of the Space Industry in Poland

After the ESA Council's decision of 21–22 March 2001, the European countries' accession procedure was detailed in 'The Plan for the European Co-operating States (PECS).'[11] It was primarily addressed to the former Eastern Bloc countries, which were at that time finalizing their accession negotiations to the European Community and had already signed cooperation agreements with ESA. This initiative was aimed at gradual integration of the potential future member states into ESA programmes, rules and procedures and building up their space sectors to be able to participate in ESA projects.

The analysis of the Polish space sector conducted at the request of the European Space Agency in 2004 showed that in many Polish enterprises that had not been involved in space activities so far, there was an immense potential of knowledge, experience, and organizational culture that would enable them to join such activities relatively quickly. This primarily included aerospace and defense companies, which are the cradle of the space industry in all other countries as well. It was also necessary to add companies from the information technology, telecommunications, and electronics sector, which, due to their technical competences, could be placed somewhere in the production and satellite service chain, from the production of components and elements of rockets and satellite platforms, through the ground segment (data reception stations, satellite signal receivers, et cetera), up to the downstream segment of services using satellite technologies.

11 Towards an Enlarged Partnership – ESA's Relations with the Czech Republic, Hungary, Poland and Romania, C. Baudin, Legal Affairs Department, ESA, Paris K. Bergquist, International Relations Department, ESA, Paris, ESA Bulletin 107 – August 2001.

This analysis, as well as positive experiences from both cooperation agreements and interest in developing the space sector in Poland, resulted in the signature of the European Cooperating State Agreement[12] in Warsaw on 27 April 2007, by Paweł Poncyljusz, Secretary of State in the Polish Ministry of Economy, and René Oosterlinck, ESA Director of Legal Affairs and External Relations.

Poland became the fourth European Cooperating State (ECS), following Hungary (April 2003), Czech Republic (November 2003), and Romania (February 2006).

The PECS Agreement represented a real breakthrough in relations between Poland and ESA both from a legal and industrial perspective. Compared to the previous agreements, the PECS Agreement bound Poland to ESA as a technological and industrial partner, and not only in the field of scientific cooperation, while maintaining the powers granted to the Agency in previous accords. In particular, pursuant to Article 7 of the Agreement of 24 January 2002, and the PECS Agreement:[13]

- ESA had legal personality in the Republic of Poland;
- ESA had immunity from jurisdiction and execution (with some precisely indicated exceptions);
- The Agency had the right to the free circulation of publications and information materials;
- ESA employees and their family members were exempt from income taxes;
- The Agency, its property, and income were exempted from all taxes on the Republic of Poland's territory. ESA's assets enjoyed immunity from all legal proceedings, except where the Agency expressly waived this right in an individual case;
- The Government of the Republic of Poland and ESA were to determine together the procedure that would apply to the export and import of goods used for cooperation purposes; and
- The Agency had the right to receive and possess any funds in the Republic of Poland and might freely dispose of them for any purpose provided for in the Convention on the European Space Agency or in this agreement and might open bank accounts in any currency.

12 *European Cooperating State Agreement between the European Space Agency and the Government of the Republic of Poland*, Journal of Laws No 154, 26 August 2008.

13 Ibidem.

From the perspective of the nascent Polish space industry, due to the PECS Agreement for the first time it was allowed to apply directly for ESA projects.[14] Poland was obliged to pay a minimal financial contribution of 1 million euro per year (in 2001 economic conditions), and the Agency, after deducing a fixed rate of 7%, used the remaining funds to implement projects submitted by Polish entities in open calls for proposals organized in line with ESA technical rules and procedures. Poland was exempted from participation in the Basic Research Technology Programme but was allowed to take part in activities related to:

- space science, in particular space astronomy and astrophysics, solar system exploitation and solar-terrestrial physics;
- Earth observation research and applications, in particular environmental monitoring, meteorology, aeronomy, and geodesy;
- telecommunications, in particular service demonstrations and satellite navigation;
- microgravity research, in particular space biology and medicine, and materials processing; and
- ground segment engineering and utilization.

The categories of activities covered by the PECS were the following: technology and equipment relating to those ESA optional programmes which were not on the critical path for the execution of the Agency's programmes; scientific projects and/or experiments; data exploitation; and support to Small and Medium Enterprises. The specific areas and projects for cooperation were to be defined jointly by Poland and ESA and subscribed to within one year in the form of the so-called PECS Charter. It was signed in Warsaw by Rafał Baniak, Secretary of State in the Polish Ministry of Economy, and Chris de Cooker, Head of the International Relations Department of ESA, on 28 April 2008.

Since the PECS Agreement was related to the payment of financial contribution from the State budget, according to the Polish Constitution it had to be ratified by the Parliament. The ratification law draft was submitted on 20 February 2008, unanimously approved on 28 March (with a vote of 433 to 0) and signed by the President on 11 April 2008.

The interest of the Polish space sector in developing cooperation with ESA was overwhelming. The sum of the budgets of projects submitted by Polish entities and positively assessed by ESA in two PECS competitions more than twice exceeded the minimum obligatory contribution for the PECS for five

14 *Plan for European Cooperating States (PECS): Objectives, Rules and Procedures*, Journal of Laws No 154, 26 August 2008.

years (that is, it amounted to approximately 11 million euros). As a result, by a special amendment to the State budget, it was decided to add another 5 million euros to the overall PECS budget.[15] This allowed to perform 3 PECS calls, in which more than 135 proposals were submitted. The first two calls were for a total of 29 projects and 8,143,000 €. The third call,[16] using a new approach based on standard ESA procurement processes, recommended the implementation of 16 further projects for a total of 2,347,000 €. The total funding for the three PECS calls amounted to 10,490,000 €.

The considerable interest of entrepreneurs and research units and the high quality of project applications (high overall success rate) confirmed the Polish space sector's great potential. It should also be emphasized that, in contrast to other PECS countries, where scientific and educational projects dominated, in the case of Poland, the practical and applicative nature of the interests of Polish entities and their significant technological potential were observed – the projects chosen for implementation concerned, among others, Earth observation, navigation and development of new technologies for space missions.

4 Accession to ESA in 2012

The fast development of the space sector in Poland, proven not only by the results of the PECS programme but also by ever-growing interest and participation in the EU space activities, combined with strategic and political considerations described in the first chapter, led to another crucial decision – the beginning of negotiations on Poland's becoming a full ESA Member State.

One of the critical elements accompanying the accession process was the review of Polish scientific and industrial potential in the space sector, carried out jointly with ESA. The evaluation took place in two stages. The Ministry of Economy sent out special questionnaires to enterprises and research and development units.[17] After analyzing the collected responses, entities with the most significant potential were invited to meetings with ESA and Polish experts. This review's results had an impact on the scope and subjects of the participation of Polish entities in the Agency's programmes in the coming years. Information was received on over 115 entities, including about 50 companies. This review

15 http://orka2.sejm.gov.pl/iz6.nsf/main/5f1c822e, Odpowiedź podsekretarza stanu w Ministerstwie Gospodarki – z upoważnienia ministra -na zapytanie nr 9394 w sprawie działań zmierzających do przystąpienia Polski do Europejskiej Agencji Kosmicznej.

16 https://kosmonauta.net/2011/12/3-pecs/.

17 https://kosmonauta.net/2011/12/ocena-esa/.

took place throughout 2012. A preliminary report was produced, which was favorably assessed by the ESA Industrial Policy Committee. Agency representatives highly appreciated the Polish intellectual and technical potential in the space sector. At the same time, they drew attention to the fact that many PECS projects coordinated by scientific and research units had a robust industrial component in the form of cooperation with commercial companies. This element was especially valuable in the context of cooperation between science and industry, which is necessary for space activities. Also, companies participating in the evaluation considered space activities to enable the development of new technologies and products that could then be used in their primary market activity. This pragmatic approach to space activities was regarded as potentially promising a high return on investment.

Under the Polish Constitution, the international agreement resulting in Poland becoming an ESA Member State required ratification. Therefore it was necessary to prepare a dedicated draft law authorizing the President of the Republic of Poland to ratify two documents at the same time: the Agreement between the Government of the Republic of Poland and the European Space Agency concerning the accession of Poland to the Convention for the establishment of a European Space Agency and related terms and conditions, which was done in Warsaw on 31 July 2012,[18] and the Convention for the Establishment of a European Space Agency, done in Paris on 30 May 1975.[19]

It is worth underlining that Poland's accession to ESA was the fastest-ever ratification process in the Polish Parliament. The governmental project was formally submitted on 16 October 2012, discussed during relevant parliamentary commissions, approved by unanimity on 24 October (434 votes to 0), approved by unanimity by the Senate on 9 November (82 votes to 0), and signed by the President on 12 November 2012 (effective immediately upon publication). The ratification document was officially deposited with the French Ministry of Foreign Affairs on 19 November 2012, and from this date, Poland became the 20th ESA Member State.

After Polish accession to ESA, the legal status of the Agency within Poland mainly remained the same, since the PECS Agreement already in force in terms

---

18 *Agreement between the Government of the Republic of Poland and the European Space Agency concerning the accession of Poland to the Convention for the establishment of the European Space Agency and related terms and conditions*, signed in Warsaw on 31 July 2012, Journal of Laws No 61, 16 January 2013.

19 Convention for the Establishment of a European Space Agency (hereafter ESA Convention), Paris, done on 30 May 1975, entered into force 30 October 1980; 1297 UNTS 161; UKTS 1981 No. 30; Cmnd. 8200; 14 ILM 864 (1975); *Space Law – Basic Legal Documents*, C.I.1.

of immunities and privileges for the Agency was based on the relevant articles of the Convention and Annex I. The situation of Poland, however, changed entirely because it gained all the rights of a Member State, including:

- *de facto* full right of access (through participation in consortia formed for the implementation of projects by the industries of the ESA members, including classified tenders) to the EU funds transferred to ESA for the implementation of joint projects (Galileo, GMES/Copernicus);
- the right to participate and vote in the ESA Council and all bodies (in all matters of the Agency, including the location of new ESA investments in the common infrastructure; previously, Poland, apart from the PECS Committee, had the right to participate as an observer in the work of the Council and other ESA bodies only when matters related to the Plan for European Cooperating Countries were being considered);
- full access to all ESA programmes (per Article 2 of the PECS Agreement, only to jointly selected programmes and activities further specified in Annex 1, excluding the Agency's core technology research programme); and
- full access for Polish entities to the Electronic System of Invitations to Tender – EMITS (before Polish entities could use this essential administrative and technical tool of ESA only for PECS purposes and only for the information concerning the Agency's programmes, and not to submit their contract offers or soliciting to participate in joint consortia).

As already mentioned, Poland's accession to ESA was associated with the necessity to incur expenses from the State budget, which included:

- a one-time 'entrance fee' for acquiring the right of joint ownership of ESA infrastructure – 11,100,000 € in 2011 economic conditions, payable in 4 annual installments starting from 2012;
- annual contribution to ESA mandatory programmes[20] – the amount is calculated in relation to the value of the net national income (NNI) of a given country in three-year periods (at the time of the accession 2007 – 2009) according to the statistics published by OECD or EUROSTAT. The obligatory contribution for Poland for 2012 was set at 19,200,000 €, which represented 2.57% of ESA's annual budget (the amount paid was calculated proportionally to the number of days from the date of joining ESA to the end of the calendar year); and

20 ESA Convention, Article V Activities and Programmes: "The activities of the Agency shall include mandatory activities, in which all Member States participate, and optional activities, in which all Member States participate apart from those that formally declare themselves not interested in participating therein."

- contribution to ESA optional programmes – the amount and scope of participation in these programmes depend on each interested country's individual decision.[21]

In line with the financial limits defined in the 'Action Programme for the Development of Space Technologies and the Use of Satellite Systems in Poland' approved by the Government in June 2012, the Polish contribution to ESA's optional programmes was set at 50% of the mandatory one. Taking into account the results of PECS calls, the survey of the Polish space sector, and the recommendations from the ministries involved in the negotiations with ESA during the Ministerial Council in Naples in November 2012, Poland decided to subscribe to the following optional programmes:

- Earth Observation programmes: EO Envelope Programme (EOEP4) – 16,000,000 €, MetOp Second Generation Programme (MetOpSG) – 5,000,000 €, GMES Space Component-3 (GSC-3) – 750,000 €;
- General Support Technology Programme (GSTP) – 11,000,000 €;
- European GNSS Evolution Programme (EGEP) – 3,750,000 €;
- ARTES 20 – Integrated Applications Promotion (IAP) – 3,000,000 €, ARTES 1 – 480,000 €;
- Space Situational Awareness (SSA) – 2,200,000 €;
- Mars Robotic Exploration Programme 2 (Mrep2) – 750,000 €; and
- PRODEX – 1,000,000 €.

The indicated amounts reflect the total declared contributions, but the programmes' implementation periods opened for subscription in November 2012 were multiannual and varied (3–5 years, some even longer).

5 The European Space Agency's Organizational and Financial Mechanisms

Taking into account the fact that the accession of Poland to ESA was the major breakthrough in the history of Polish space sector, both from political and industrial perspectives, it is worth to describe in more detail how the Agency is organized and what the mechanisms of cooperation with its Member States are.

21 ESA Convention, Article XI the Council, point 5 c: "The Council shall (…) as regards the optional programmes referred to in Article V, 1 b: i. accept each programme by a majority of all Member States; ii. determine, as appropriate, in the course of their implementation, the order of priority of programmes".

The Convention for the establishment of a European Space Agency was signed on 30 May 1975 in Paris by 10 States: Germany, Belgium, Denmark, Spain, France, Italy, the Netherlands, United Kingdom, Sweden and Switzerland and in December 1975 by Ireland. The Convention entered into force on 30 October 1980.

Gradually more and more States decided to join ESA, bringing up the number of full members to 22: Austria and Norway in 1986, Finland in 1995, Portugal in 2000, Greece and Luxembourg in 2005, Czech Republic in 2008, Romania in 2011, Poland in 2012, Estonia and Hungary in 2015, with a special arrangement for Canada under a Cooperation Agreement (since 1978). Slovenia, Latvia and Lithuania are Associate Members. As of 2021, five other EU states have Cooperation Agreements with ESA: Bulgaria, Croatia, Cyprus, Malta and Slovakia.

According to the Convention, the main decision-making body is the ESA Council, composed of the representatives of all Member States, either at delegate or ministerial level. The Council at delegate level meets 4 times per year – every March, June, October and December,[22] in order to take all measures necessary for the fulfilment of the goals of the Agency, like reviewing the course of the implementation of duly adopted programmes, prioritising them if necessary, approving the budgets, the financial and staff regulations.

The Council elects a chair and 2 vice-chairs from amongst its members for a period of 2 years, with one-year extension. The term starts on the first of July. Each Member State has one vote. The decisions are usually taken by a simple majority of Member States present and voting, with a quorum formed by the majority of all Member States. The exceptions to that rule are explicitly defined in the Convention. There are different options possible, depending on the "gravity" of the issue put to vote. For instance, the level of resources for 5 years or the accession of a new Member State have to be approved by the unanimity of all Member States. The appointment of a Director General for a defined period, the annual general budget, Financial Regulations and all other financial arrangements of the Agency, establishment and terms of reference of subordinate bodies, Staff Regulations require a two-thirds majority of all Member States (although not legally necessary, unanimity is usually expected – and achieved – especially for the appointments of the Director General).

22 Additional meetings may be convened by the Chair, either on its own initiative or on a join request from at least 3 Member States. According to the Council Rules of Procedure, the Council has to meet at least twice a year, but a long-term practice is 4 meetings per year.

Mandatory programmes and the list of optional programmes are approved by a majority of all Member States. A Member State has no right to vote in matters related to an optional programme in which it does not take part (it can vote on the decision whether or not to establish such a programme; once accepted by the Council an optional programme is governed by the participating Member States). A Member State may lose its right to vote in the Council "if the amount of its arrears of contributions to the Agency in respect of all activities and programmes covered by Article V in which it participates exceeds the assessed amount of its contributions for the current financial year".[23] In such a case this Member State is not taken into account when determining the unanimity or different majorities specified in the Convention. The other Member States may, by a two-thirds majority of all Member States, decide that the non-payment of contributions is caused by the circumstances beyond the control of the Member State in financial difficulties and allow it to vote in the Council.

The key political and financial decisions concerning ESA activities are taken by the Ministerial Council. There is no fixed calendar for such meetings, but recently they have been synchronized with the 3-year period for determining the level of resources (the most recent ones being the ESA Ministerial Council in Lucerne in 2016 and in Sevilla in 2019, with the next one planned for 2022). It is important to distinguish the chairmanship of a normal ESA Council and the Ministerial one (sometimes called "ESA Presidency") – these are separate roles performed by different Member States. ESA members gathered for the Ministerial meeting elect a new Chair (or two co-Chairs),[24] who immediately takes over both the chairmanship of the current meeting and ESA Presidency for the period leading up to the next Ministerial session.

The ministers of all ESA Member States decide by unanimity on the level of resources to be made available to the Agency for the coming five-year period and "towards the end of the third year of each five-year period and after a review of the situation, the level of resources (…) for the new five-year period starting at the end of this third year".[25] The level of resources covers the costs of the normal functioning of the Agency and the realization of its mandatory programmes. The agreed amount is "divided" among all Member States

23 ESA Convention, Article XI – The Council, point 5 a ii and iii.

24 The Ministerial Council in Naples in November 2012, when Poland officially became ESA Member State number 20, was prepared by Italian Presidency. During this meeting Switzerland and Luxembourg were elected as co-Chairs for the next period. In Lucerne in December 2016 Spain was chosen to organize the next Ministerial Council, which took place in Sevilla in November 2019. Then France and Portugal were elected as co-Chairs.

25 ESA Convention, Article XI – The Council, point 6 b.

according to a scale of contributions adopted by the Council,[26] on the basis of the average national income of each Member State for the three latest years for which statistics are available.[27] There is a maximum limit of contributions that may be required from a single Member State – no more than 25% of the total approved level-of-resources budget, regardless of the scale and its NNI level.

ESA mandatory programmes, however, represent only about 20–25% of the Agency's activities[28] – the rest is focused on the optional programmes. ESA Ministerial Council approves the optional programme proposals prepared by the ESA executive in cooperation with the Member States – the Programme Declarations, Implementing Rules and the overall budget envelopes. It is also an opportunity for the Member States to declare their willingness to participate[29] – or not – in a given optional programme and specify their financial contributions. In contrast with the mandatory activities there is no fixed scale of contributions to be paid; the Member States are in principle[30] free to decide on the amount of money they want to spend for these purposes, according to their national priorities and budgetary resources available.

ESA Ministerial Council meetings also serve to give general political messages and guidelines to address strategic issues faced by the Agency. Some examples of such policy declarations are the "Political Declaration Towards the European Space Agency That Best Serves Europe" and the "Resolution on the Role of ESA in Sustaining Competitiveness and Growth in Europe", adopted in Naples in November 2012. Strategic programme decisions about the development of the Ariane 6 launcher and continuation of the ExoMars mission were taken by the ESA Ministerial Council in Luxembourg in December 2014 and the 10% increase in the ESA Science budget and adoption of Space Safety as a new basic pillar of ESA's activities by the Ministerial Council Meeting in Sevilla in November 2019.

26 Council at delegate level, by a two-thirds majority of all Member States.

27 ESA Convention, Article XIII – Financial Contributions, point 1. The scale of contributions is reassessed when a new Member State joins the Agency.

28 Excluding activities funded by the European Union.

29 A Member State may also join an optional programme during the course of its implementation (between Mininisterial Council meetings), but it needs an approval of the participating states, which may specify some additional conditions to be met.

30 "In principle", because there is a minimum limit of expected financial contribution to an optional programme defined in Article XIII point 2 of the ESA Convention – 25% of the mandatory scale of contributions. This minimum limit is applied unless all the participating states decide otherwise. To give a precise example: Poland's share in mandatory activities at the time of its accession to ESA in November 2012 was 2,57%, and 25% of that is 0,64%. Therefore, if Poland wanted to join an optional programme with a budget of 100 M€, it should declare its minimum financial contribution of 640 K€.

ESA Member States are also represented in the Council's subordinate bodies – Committees, dealing with "horizontal" issues concerning the Agency as a whole and therefore composed of delegations of all Member States, and Programme Boards, responsible for the respective domains of optional activities, composed of representatives of Member States formally participating in these programmes.

The only subordinate body established directly by the Convention (pursuant to Article XI(8)(a)) is the Science Policy Committee, supervising the mandatory scientific programme. All the others were created by the Council, which has to approve their terms of reference by a two-thirds majority of all the Member States. Apart from the Science Policy Committee, there are 4 other Committees in ESA: the Industrial Policy Committee (IPC – responsible for implementation and monitoring of ESA industrial policy,[31] approving procurement and contracts proposals in mandatory and optional programmes, supporting competitiveness of European space industry, authorizing technology transfers outside ESA Member States if required by a given project), the Administrative and Finance Committee (AFC – dealing with all budgetary, financial and legal issues, staff regulations), the International Relations Committee (IRC – dealing with all relations and contacts of ESA with other international organizations and individual states), and the Security Committee (SEC – taking care of protection of classified information, including industrial security policy, and physical security of ESA establishments).

Six ESA Programme Boards supervise the implementation of duly approved optional programmes:

- The Programme Board on Satellite Navigation (PB NAV) – satellite navigation programmes (EGNOS and Galileo),
- the Joint Board on Communication Satellite Programmes (JCB) – telecommunication activities (ARTES programmes),
- the Earth Observation Programme Board (PB EO) – EO programmes including Copernicus (in cooperation with the EU), Earth Observation Envelope Programme (EOEP), MetOp programmes (in cooperation with EUMETSAT),
- the Programme Board for Human Spaceflight, Microgravity and Exploration (PB HME) – human spaceflight development and exploitation, life and physical sciences and application in space, exploration programmes, European contribution to the International Space Station,

31 Including, but not limited to, the geographical return rules and their practical implementation.

– the Launchers Programme Board (PB LAU) – initially established to deal with the Ariane Programme, later on new areas of responsibility were added: CSG, Vega, Soyuz and other launcher-related technology development, and
– the Programme Board for Space Situational Awareness (PB SSA) – Space Situational Awareness programme, after the Ministerial Council Meeting of 2019 transformed into Space Safety.

Given their broad and diverse areas of responsibility (including international cooperation elements), two Programme Boards – the PB EO and the PB HME – are supported by permanent sub-groups: the Data, Operations, Science and Technical Advisory Group (DOSTAG) and the Exploration and Utilisation Board (HME–EUB). There is also a Technology Harmonization Advisory Group (THAG) affiliated to the IPC.

All Committees and Programme Boards have their own terms of reference, specifying the detailed competences and internal rules and procedures, based on the ESA Convention, its Annex III, Council Rules of Procedure and – in case of the PBs – respective Programme Declarations and Implementing Rules. All Member States are represented in each ESA subordinate body by no more than two delegates,[32] who have the formal right to vote. During the meetings delegates may be accompanied by experts and advisors as needed; they can participate in the discussions but without the right to vote on behalf of their Member State. The decisions to start a new phase of an optional programme or discontinue it have to be taken by a two-thirds majority of all participating states, representing at least two-thirds of contributions.

In principle, all deliberations and decisions of the ESA Council and its subordinate bodies are confidential and carried out only in the presence of duly authorised delegations from Member States and the ESA Executive. However, representatives of other international organizations (like the European Union and EUMETSAT), non-ESA Member States or individual experts may be invited as observers for the meetings (whole meetings or just some points on the agenda), if all Member States (or participating states for the PBs) agree so in advance. The observers may participate in the relevant discussions, but obviously without the right to vote. In the period of time after the signature of the Accession Agreement (31 July 2012) and the formal accession[33] (19 November 2012) Poland was invited to take part in all ESA meetings with such a status.

32 The same person may be – and quite often is – appointed as a delegate or advisor to more than one Committee or PB.

33 A state becomes a full member of ESA on the day when the required instruments of accession are deposited with the Government of France.

6 The Polish Industry Incentive Scheme with ESA – Evolution, Results, and Impact on the Space Sector

In line with Article 6 of the Accession Agreement[34] "an amount representing 45 % of Poland's overall contribution to the Agency's mandatory activities until the end of the transition period, shall be used by the Agency, in accordance with the Agency's rules and procedures, to finance activities aimed at adapting Poland's industry, operators, the scientific community and other actors to the Agency's requirements, in particular within the mandatory activities."

This was the legal basis for establishing the Polish Industry Incentive Scheme – the key instrument dedicated to developing Poland's space sector. In practice, these funds were at the disposal of a specially created joint Task Force composed of representatives of Poland and ESA, which supervised the organization of tenders available only to Polish entities (a mechanism similar to PECS), especially in the areas of activity of the Agency of special interest to Poland. They undertook other activities aimed at the maximum integration of the Polish industry with ESA activities (for instance, workshops, training, et cetera). Polish enterprises were allowed to apply for the remaining part of the Polish mandatory contribution and the optional part allocated to contracts for the industry per the general ESA tender rules and procedures. According to Article 6.2 of the Accession Agreement, "the final objective of the Agency is to reach at the end of the transition period, an industrial return at the same level as the one applicable to all Member States."

As agreed during the accession negotiations, the Poland-ESA Task Force started to work as soon as possible. It pursued its main line of activity, that is the organization, evaluation, and implementation of calls for proposals dedicated only for the Polish space sector. However, especially during the first two years, much emphasis was placed on information days about the ESA programmes to which Poland subscribed, training courses (like 'How to write a successful proposal'), workshops, study visits in and from the major ESA Member States, dedicated meeting with the so-called Large System Integrators (LSIs),[35] et cetera.

---

34 *Agreement between the Government of the Republic of Poland and the European Space Agency concerning the accession of Poland to the Convention for the establishment of the European Space Agency and related terms and conditions*, signed in Warsaw on 31 July 2012, Journal of Laws No 61, 16 January 2013.

35 Large System Integrators (LSIs) in the space industry specialise in bringing together component subsystems into a whole and ensure that those subsystems function together. These enterprises have at least one ongoing prime contract worth over €200 million that involves space-related infrastructures, launchers or satellites; and in this area either an annual turnover of over €200 million or an annual balance sheet total of more than €200

These efforts, combined with the Polish space sector's technological potential and enthusiasm, did pay off.

In reply to the open calls[36] for proposals that were concluded before July 2016 under the PLIIS (Polish Industry Incentive Scheme) launched in 2013, 236 proposals were received, of which 99 were approved for implementation with a total value of approximately 19,500,000 €. About 80% of the accepted projects had been submitted by industry and 20% by academia. The programmes' stable and relatively high success rate was worth emphasizing, proving a good quality of applications as one out of three indeed received funding.

Also, the results achieved in the ten selected optional programmes subscribed to by Poland in November 2012 were positive. The best proof of the commitment of Polish industry and science and high quality of their proposals were the results achieved under the GSTP technology development programme (including the participation of the Polish organizations in the Proba-3 mission) or in the integrated applications programme (IAP – Integrated Application Promotion), both of which encompassed projects on the use of satellite data in agriculture, in monitoring the condition of forests, and in marine navigation in harbors. Also, the Polish space sector delivered excellent results in the Mrep-2 robotic exploration programme, the Space Situational Awareness programme, the Copernicus space component construction programme, and the Prodex programme for the construction of scientific instruments, exhausting the pool of available funds a full year before the end of the programme. In programmes with a longer time horizon, especially those related to Earth Observation, the fund allocation level was proportional to the planned duration.

Halfway through the intended duration of the agreed transition period (initially planned for the end of 2017) and a year before the ESA Ministerial Council in Lucerne planned for December 2016, the Poland-ESA Task Force conducted an in-depth analysis (detailed questionnaires followed by dedicated meetings with key players) of the Polish space sector status and perspectives. The results of the 'Joint ESA/Poland Mid Term Review Report' were presented during a high-level political event in June 2015 (with the participation of Polish Deputy Prime Minister/Minister of Economy Mr. Janusz Piechociński, Director General

million. On this basis, the list of space-related LSIs would be: Airbus Defence and Space, ArianeGroup, Arianespace Avio SpA, OHB System, Thales Alenia Space.

Source: https://www.esa.int/About_Us/Business_with_ESA/Large_System_Integrators.

36 'Open call' means a call where any eligible entity whose project idea is in line with the call's general requirements may apply; there are no pre-defined topics, and everyone may submit their own idea.

of ESA Jean-Jacques Dordain, Daniel Calleja y Crespo, the Director-General at the European Commission's Directorate-General for Internal Market, Industry, Entrepreneurship, and SMEs as well as Professor Johann-Dietrich Wörner, Chairman of the Executive Board of the German Aerospace Centre (DLR) and as of 1 July 2015, the next Director-General of ESA.

The main conclusions of the 'Joint ESA/Poland Mid Term Review Report' were positive, pointing out the increasing competitiveness of the Polish industry (especially in the downstream added value industry), as well as its involvement in the development of innovative space technologies. There were reasonable expectations that the geographical return would be achieved at the end of the respective optional programme subscription periods and the mandatory programme.

ESA observed that Polish economic operators were actively involved in the ESA tender system EMITS. Remarkable results were achieved by, among other things, three different economic operators winning contracts in open competition for Sentinel 5 and Exomars missions and Proba-3 mission.

Nevertheless, it was underlined that the pacing of ESA programmes (where typically, on average, there is one opportunity for the selection of EOEP satellite subcontractors every three years and a selection of subcontractors for large science missions every five) did not work easily in terms of timing with the accession of Poland to the ESA Convention. This timing did not provide Polish economic operators sufficient opportunities to bid on large ESA projects. A period of seven years for the Industry Incentive Scheme would compensate for the effect of the sub-contractor selection timing in ESA programmes.

Therefore, the Mid-Term Review's key recommendation, wholeheartedly supported by the Polish space sector, was to extend the transition period and its associated Polish Industry Incentive Scheme by two years, that is until the end of 2019. It was also suggested to put more effort into dedicated thematic calls for proposals while keeping the open call as the basic support mechanism. It was recommended that PLIIS should, in its following period:

- re-enforce the support in the creation of industrial partnerships and the participation of Polish industry in international consortia;
- re-enforce the emphasis on flight hardware activities, especially those using previously developed platform-related technologies in Poland;
- support R&D in advanced technologies for future spacecraft and increase of TRL,[37] and activities to prepare small missions; and

37 Technology Readiness Levels (TRL) are different points on a scale used to measure the progress or maturity level of a technology. The scale ranges from 1 to 9, where TRL 1 is the lowest and TRL 9 is the highest. When a technology is at TRL 1, scientific research is

– re-enforce the emphasis on preparatory activities that support the qualification of staff, facilities and processes, development of supplier networks, et cetera.

Several other important observations were also made in the Mid-Term Review about Poland's space sector's status and actions to stimulate its dynamic growth further. They are described in the section below since they mostly remain valid until today.

It was noted that there is an excellent academic knowledge base to grow future competitive space firms. However, there is not yet sufficient space industrial heritage and still little motivation for private capital investment. The academic institutions have experience in developing scientific instruments or parts of them (in particular, optical), but availability of spacecraft platforms and microwave technologies are not demonstrated yet in the ESA programmes. Efforts should be made to focus the interest of Polish economic operators having the needed capacities. Cooperation between industry and academia, building on the academic network's strengths and respecting their natural roles, should be encouraged and reinforced, maintaining an adequate balance between academic institutions and industry. It is also recommended to increase students' awareness and interest in scientific and engineering disciplines related to space.

It is essential to encourage the involvement in space activities of national firms from other sectors than space to consolidate Polish industrial capacity and foster national and foreign investment in Polish space companies.

The detailed knowledge about ESA space missions, the upstream infrastructure space market, and procurement practices in these missions often remains, in industry, at the theoretical level. It looks like the full practical implications have not yet been understood. More dedicated information activities, tailored to the needs of Polish industry (like specific courses on procurement, process and policy on ESA missions, access to information on the space market by sectors to allow Polish industry to have clearer views of the market, their competitors, and potential partners, courses on Quality and Product Assurance and Cost audits for Polish industry and academia) would be beneficial.[38]

One very significant administrative change was introduced into PLIIS in response to the opinions of the sector and as a way to speed up the contracting

beginning and those results are being translated into future research and development, while at TRL 9 the technology has already been proven to work during a flight mission in space. Source: https://www.esa.int/Enabling_Support/Space_Engineering_Technology/Shaping_the_Future/Technology_Readiness_Levels_TRL.

38 *Joint ESA/Poland Mid Term Review Report*, Warsaw June 2015.

process and offer more flexibility – the open call for proposals was transformed from an annual event into a permanent announcement of opportunity, with fixed submission and evaluation deadlines four times per year. The permanently open call covered four categories of projects:[39]

- Flight Hardware activities, with a preference for those related to satellite platform technologies and sensors or generic technologies with the potential for re-use (at the start a TRL of at least 3 and with a target TRL of at least 5);
- Research and Development activities (including technology demonstrations, industrial processes, and their qualification/certification) leading to products (hardware or software) or generic technologies with the potential for re-use (at the start a TRL of at least 2 and with a target TRL 4 or below);
- Preparatory activities (for instance, feasibility studies, technology assessments, user requirements, or market surveys) and ESA mission-related services to support national competitiveness in ESA programmes (optional and mandatory) to which Poland subscribes; and
- Space applications, products, and services using space infrastructure that is already existing or scheduled for operation in the near term (with at the start a TRL of at least 4), education and awareness activities are excluded.

The Polish space sector very warmly received this change since it "transformed the race from a sprint into a marathon."[40] The space industry was able to plan their activities better, ensuring a steady and sustainable workload for the personnel – if one project failed, they did not have to wait for a year for another chance for submission. Also, ESA experts were not overwhelmed once a year with hundreds of proposals to be evaluated but instead received smaller amounts regularly. This new approach worked perfectly well for both ESA and the national space sector – so well in fact that it was later adopted as a general rule for all future new ESA Member States in their Industry Incentive Programmes.

Formally, the agreement to extend the Polish Industry Incentive Scheme duration until the end of 2019 was signed by ESA Director General J. Woerner and Polish Deputy Prime Minister M. Morawiecki on 12 January 2017. On the same day, a new Polish Space Strategy was presented to the general public.[41]

---

39 http://emits.sso.esa.int/emits/owa/emits.main, AO 8433.

40 Interview with Pedro Baptista, https://kosmonauta.net/2015/09/niebawem-ruszy-trzeci-konkurs-polski-w-esa/.

41 For details please refer to the previous chapter.

These two critical milestones in the development of the space sector in Poland were additionally strengthened by an increased (by 25%) contribution to ESA optional programmes during the Ministerial Council in Lucerne in December 2016. Poland decided to continue its involvement in most of the programmes (thematic lines) subscribed four years before, with some modifications in the declared levels of funding (including additional payments made after the Council Meeting):

- Earth Observation Envelope Programme EOEP 5 – 9,700,000 €
- General Support Technology Programme GSTP – 9,850,000 €
- Space Situational Awareness Programme SSA – 6,500,000 €
- Integrated Application Promotion IAP – 5,000,000 €
- Scientific Experiment Development Programme PRODEX – 8,000,000 €
- Future Launchers Preparatory Programme FLPP – 4,000,000 €
- European Exploration Envelope Programme E3P (Exploration) – 3,800,000 €
- Next Generation Platform (Neosat) – 2,000,000 €
- Navigation Innovation and Support Programme NAVISP – 2,100,000 €
- Advanced Research in Telecommunications Systems Programme ARTES (Future Preparation) – 250,000 €

In 2017, the ESA-Poland Task Force initiated a Working Group to suggest changes to PLIIS for the last two years of operation. The Working Group used questionnaires to Polish industry and ESA technical officers of Polish activities as the basis of recommendations together with face-to-face meetings, Polish optional programmes and their georeturn.[42] It was decided from 2018 to implement several top-down activities (initiated by ESA through specific ITTs,[43] with defined Statements of Work) under several technology roadmaps,[44] in order to focus the support on higher TRL activities enabling future

42 'Georeturn' is an informal, but very widely used term referring to the basic rule of ESA industrial policy established by article VII point 1c of ESA Convention and elaborated in detail in Annex V. The Agency is obliged to place contracts in the entities located in the Member States in proportion to their financial contribution to mandatory and optional programmes. In line with Article IV of Annex V to the ESA Convention "The geographical distribution of all the Agency's contracts shall be governed by the following general rules: 1. A Member State's overall return coefficient shall be the ratio between its percentage share of the total value of all contracts awarded among all Member States and its total percentage contributions (…) 3. Ideally the distribution of contracts placed by the Agency should result in all countries having an overall return coefficient of 1."

43 ITT is an abbreviation for Invitation to Tender – a term meaning procurement used in ESA.

44 http://space.biz.pl/wp-content/uploads/2018/05/ESA-Stephane-Combes.pdf.

participation in mandatory programmes. The majority of the remaining PLIIS budget was directed towards these roadmap activities, with some limit set aside for the last open call.

The Polish Industry Incentive Scheme officially ended on 31 December 2019 – after that date, no new financial commitments may be undertaken under the programme. However, the projects accepted previously are expected to run for 2–3 years more, depending on their particular schedules.

According to the data from the report of the Supreme Audit Office published in 2020 (but carried out in 2019), taking into account the ESA settlement mechanism, in 2015–2019, ESA allocated 46,700,000 € under the PLIIS mechanism, that is 42% of the sum of mandatory contributions shown on ESA invoices. This amount was reduced by ESA's internal costs, which effectively put at the disposal of Polish entities contract options with a total value of 37,400,000 €. The amount for contracts concluded between ESA and Polish entities from 1 January 2015, to 30 September 2019, amounted to 28,900,000 €, which means a 'return' of 77.3%.

Under the ESA mandatory programmes, apart from PLIIS, Polish entities concluded 42 contracts worth 15,700,000 €.

By 2016, under 11 optional programmes, 81 contracts were concluded with a total contract value of 21,900,000 €. In 2017–2019, 64 contracts were concluded under six optional programmes with a total value of 20,700,000 €.[45]

In July 2021, the Ministry of Development, Technology and Labour published a draft project of the National Space Programme for public pre-consultations. This document contains updated statistics regarding Polish participation in ESA activities[46] (in comparison with the Supreme Audit Office Report quoted above). 145 Polish entities submitted 487 project proposals for 102 600 000 € under PLIIS support mechanism, out of which 210 projects worth 58 000 000 € were financed, covering 20 out of 25 ESA technology tree domains. The overall success rate was 43%, which is quite high. According to ESA 65% of the activities carried out under PLIIS have a very good chance for continuation in the other ESA programmes (optional ones on the condition that there is sufficient funding from Poland available) and only 10% turned out to be one-off

45 *Development of the space sector – report of the Polish Supreme Audit Office*, KGP.430.017.2019 Reg No 44/2020 / P / 19/021 / KGP, Warsaw, 20 May 2020.

46 *National Space Programme 2021–2026*, draft version 0.8, 23 July 2021, p. 55–58, https://www.gov.pl/web/rozwoj-technologia/prekonsultacje-krajowego-programu-kosmicznego-na-lata-2021--2026-kpk.

initiatives.[47] Between 2015 and the first quarter of 2020 156 Polish entities[48] participated in different ESA projects as contractors and subcontractors. The overall value of projects signed between 2012 and end 2019 (PLIIS included) was 143,000,000 €.[49]

According to the report "Polish space sector 2020. Analysis of current situation, trends and technologies from national and international perspective" published by the Polish Space Agency in 2021, the overall number of Polish entities registered in ESA STAR (System for Tendering And Registration) system was 331 in August 2020. 79% are commercial entities and 21% R&D institutions and universities. 60% of companies are Small and Medium Enterprises.

In conclusion, Poland's decision to join ESA in November 2012 can be rightly perceived as the beginning of creation of a 'real' space industry in the country. Some space-related commercial activities were initiated in the early 1990s, mainly in the area of satellite observation, navigation, and geoinformation. During the first decade of the 21st century, several advanced products and services were offered on the national market.[50] Even the commercial EO satellite *Ikonos* receiving station was operated by one of the Polish companies.

Nevertheless, it was the second decade when ESA activities became the major incentive for the Polish space industry's development. Accession to ESA did not only provide the sector with a stable, multiannual possible source of funding under georeturn rules of the Agency but also PLIIS calls for proposals, numerous dedicated information activities and training courses enabled the companies to learn ESA procurement rules and procedures and establish contacts and cooperation with foreign partners, including LSIs, which was beneficial for them in EU space activities and on the commercial market.

To illustrate that process, it is enough to look at the Polish Space Industry Association. It was founded on 31 October 2012, on the eve of Polish accession to ESA, by only 19 companies and R&D institutes. By 2020, it has 72 active

47 *Polish space sector 2020. Analysis of current situation, trends and technologies from national and international perspective*, Polish Space Agency, May 2021, Warsaw, p 48.

48 15 entities signed about 70% of all ESA contracts with Poland. About 30% of all the projects were carried out by small and medium enterprises.

49 To compare these numbers with the Polish participation in EU Horizon 2020 space calls: in 2014–2019 35 Polish entities participated in 39 projects worth about 13 000 000 €. Source: *Polish space sector 2020. Analysis of current situation, trends and technologies from national and international perspective*, Polish Space Agency, May 2021, Warsaw, p.52.

50 It is worth to underline that 74% of the current Polish space sector entities started their activities after 2001, when Poland was preparing to join ESA PECS programme – it is not a coincidence.

members and is a part of the pan-European network SME4Space and the national Lewiatan Federation.

7 Non-ESA Space Activities in Poland

While ESA activities represented the primary funding source for space projects, some national opportunities are also available. Contrary to the Polish Space Strategy's objectives, up until today, there is no separate, coordinated National Space Programme formally in force. However, there are two national funding mechanisms supporting space activities outside of ESA and the European Union's scope. One mechanism is aimed at basic research and one at more market-oriented projects.

The National Science Centre (NCN) is a government agency supporting basic research in Poland. The NCN funds research projects carried out by individual researchers and research teams, both at the domestic and international level, and doctoral fellowships and post-doctoral internships.

The formula of competitions for funding basic research projects, periodically announced by the National Science Centre, allows the applicants to define themselves those matters they want to focus on. Detailed issues are only subject to general classification into domain and order panels to ease the substantive review of submitted applications and select the best proposals within each panel to be financed. Depending on the project's exact topic, the activities related to space fall into either life sciences or physical sciences and the engineering domain.

From 1 January 2016, to the end of December 2019, the NCN granted scientific and research units financial support for implementing 250 research projects related to space or the use of satellite data for the total amount of PLN 101,330,000 (about 23,000,000 €). Individual projects were co-financed with amounts from PLN 1,600 up to PLN 3,300,000.[51]

The National Centre for Research and Development (NCBiR) is a government entity supporting and developing innovative technological and social solutions. It organizes and implements different undertakings contributing to the civilizational growth of the country.

Competitions for project co-financing announced periodically by NCBiR are dedicated to a specific topic and concern R&D projects, usually ending in prototypes of devices or implementations of new processes or services.

51 Ibid, p. 20.

NCBR, in the period from 1 January 2016, to 31 December 2019, concluded 24 contracts for co-financing research or development projects related to space activities or the use of satellite data run by academic units or entrepreneurs. By 31 December 2019, a total of PLN 55,950,000 (about 13,000,000 €) was paid out. Value of co-financing of individual projects ranged from PLN 390,000 to PLN 14,990,000.[52]

In 2019, a special competition dedicated only to space activities was conducted – the so-called 'Space Technologies' fast track. It lasted from 2 September to 29 November. On 3 December, NCBR announced that it had received a total of 33 applications for funding for this competition. The total amount of requested funding reached PLN 311,000,000, exceeding slightly the amount allocated by the NCBR for funding under this competition.

On 21 February 2020, NCBR announced the final list of projects selected for funding. In total, NCBR approved 15 projects – seven from the Mazowieckie Voivodeship and eight from other regions of Poland. The total value of co-financing of selected projects amounted to slightly over PLN 143,800,000. The chosen projects included satellite systems, satellite technologies, missile technologies, rocket propulsion, the use and processing of satellite data, and sub-orbital technologies. The smallest approved project had a total value of PLN 2,000,000 (co-financing amount – PLN 1,560,000) – while the largest project has a total value of PLN 53,100,000 (co-financing amount – PLN 33,400,000).

It is interesting to note that NCBR decided to allocate a value slightly lower than 48% of the total available funds for this competition; for an amount of 144,000,000 PLN, corresponding to about 33,500,000 €.[53]

As part of national space activities, six satellites have been funded and developed in Poland in 2012–2019. These were two scientific satellites, *'Lem'* and *'Heweliusz'* conducting astronomical observations as part of international constellation BRITE, commercial technology demonstrator *'Światowid'* and three educational nanosatellites: *'PW-Sat,' 'PW-Sat 2'* and *'KRAKsat.'*[54]

52 Ibid.

53 https://archiwum.ncbr.gov.pl/o-centrum/aktualnosci/szczegoly-aktualnosci/news/zakonczenie-oceny-wnioskow-zlozonych-w-ramach-konkursu-51112019-technologie-kosmiczne-61345/.

54 Up until today (end of 2021) Poland has no law on a National Registry of Space Objects, despite some preparatory works being carried out since 2013. For details please refer to chapter 7. As far as the satellites are concerned, both 2 BRITEs and PW-Sats were duly notified to the UN by the Polish Ministry of Foreign Affairs, since they were treated as "public" satellites (built by public institutions and financed by public money). This is not the case for Swiatowid and Kraksat – for details please refer to the Supreme Audit Office Report on Polska Agencja Kosmiczna, page 20–21, https://www.nik.gov.pl/kontrole/P/19/021/KGP/.

Participation in the EU Horizon 2020 programme represents the last major funding source of space activities in Poland. In the period 2016–2019, Polish entities received contracts for 13,600,000 €, of which commercial companies realized 30%.[55]

8 Perspectives for the Polish Space Sector

The Polish space sector has been and for several years will remain highly dependent on public funding. This situation is not untypical for the space industry worldwide. However, due to the relatively young age of the companies, it is more significant. Only a minor part of sector's income is based on commercial activities; the maturity of technologies is not sufficient for substantial spin-off activities; independent investments are also minimal. As a consequence, future development of the sector is very sensitive to directions defined by public policies.

The main policy goal driving public activities from pre-accession to ESA until today was an increase in industrial competitiveness. In 2017, the Polish Space Strategy defined as its first objective 'Increasing competitiveness of the Polish space sector and its share in the turnover of the European space sector.' The abovementioned objective was to be implemented by, among others, the following actions:

- Increasing participation in ESA optional programmes (targeted 150% – 200% of obligatory contribution);
- Development and implementation of the National Space Programme; and
- Identifying the most promising technology areas for the Polish space industry (existing competence, technology niches, development potential).[56]

Unfortunately, the practical implementation of this policy in recent years is not pursued at a sufficient level.[57] The Supreme Audit Office, in its 2020 report on space activities, stated:

---

55 *Development of the space sector* – report of the Polish Supreme Audit Office, p. 21.

56 *Polish Space Strategy*, 2017, Resolution No 6 of the Council of Ministers of 26 January 2017, on the adoption of the Polish Space Strategy (MP item 203).

57 See also *"Evaluation of implementation of Polish Space Strategy and its KPI s"*, https://www.pspa.pl/index.php/pl/projekty/polska-strategia-kosmiczna-psk/ocena-realizacji-wskaznikow-polskiej-strategii-kosmicznej.

- Poland's participation in ESA optional programmes has not been increased; in 2019, this share amounted to 78.2%, and in 2020 the proportion of the optional contribution to the obligatory contribution will be 59.6%;
- the 2018 National Space Programmes draft has not been approved or implemented, and as of December 2019, it is undergoing a major overhaul; and
- The responsible minister also did not indicate – in an official form – a list of the most promising technological specialties in the space sector and did not comprehensively monitor such specializations.[58]

Since 2008, participation in ESA activities enabled the creation of strong foundations for self-definition and growth of the Polish space sector. ESA programmes represented the main funding opportunity for the Polish space sector, which was utilized quite efficiently. This was particularly visible in the effectiveness in obtaining contracts in ESA optional programmes. According to the Supreme Audit Office: "The minister responsible for the economy was active and effective in obtaining contracts with ESA for Polish entrepreneurs, as a result of which the so-called rate of return on contributions paid to this Agency by Poland was significantly higher than that achieved by other countries at a comparable stage of development of the space sector. [...] The geographical return ranged from 0.86 to 1.04 and was significantly greater than that of other countries ending the so-called transition periods. It is a noticeable achievement of the Minister of Development and space sector entrepreneurs."[59]

Unfortunately, not only did the planned increase of contribution to ESA optional programmes not materialize, but the contribution was decreased. Furthermore, the space sector perspectives for future development are also determined by a relatively high level of mandatory contribution – about 25,000,000 € per year (however, now without a dedicated support mechanism of the Polish Industry Incentive Scheme). For the period 2020–2022, in line with the subscriptions from Ministerial Council in Sevilla in November 2019, the overall Polish optional contribution amounts to 39,000,000 € in total:[60]

- Space Safety Programme (S2P) – 9,900,000 €
- Earth Observation (EO) [Period 2020–2028] – 8,500,000 €
- Programme for Advanced Research in Telecommunication Systems (ARTES 4.0) [The period 2020–2025] – 7,300,000 €
- European Exploration Envelope Programme (E3P) – 6,000,000 €

58 *Development of the space sector* – report of the Polish Supreme Audit Office, p. 26.
59 Ibid, p. 34.
60 https://www.gov.pl/web/rozwoj-praca-technologia/wsparcie-dla-polskich-firm.

– Scientific Experiment Development Programme (PRODEX) – 4,000,000 €
– General Support Technology Programme (GSTP) – 3,000,000 €
– Navigation Innovation and Support Programme (NAVISP) – 300,000 €

For most European countries, implementing a significant part of their space activities through ESA is a natural choice. ESA ensures the achievement of synergies at the European level, allowing for more effective use of resources of countries pursuing similar goals. However, when deciding to implement their space policy, most European countries recognize that ESA activities need to be supplemented by national space programmes. It is natural, as ESA, being an international organization, needs to mainly focus on areas that are of interest to a significant number of Member States. Activities undertaken under national programmes allow the space industry to develop its potential and strengthen its competitive position outside of ESA programmes, including highly competitive areas considered as strategic by national authorities.

The Polish space community's level of competence already achieved enables the establishment of a more focused industrial policy aimed at specific technology and utilization priorities. This will intensify the growth of the space industry's desired capabilities and facilitate the realization of national strategic goals in space utilization.

In the opinion of the Polish space community, the establishment and proper funding of the National Space Programme remains the key factor for the future development of the sector: "A stable development plan for the sector for several years together with a proposal for its financing would allow enterprises for better and more effective planning of their activities in a long-term perspective. Such a programme should be, apart from the ESA funds, the main driver of the industry development. The programme should also finance projects that are strategic from the country's perspective and that are not of interest to ESA."[61]

The role of such a programme may not be substituted by the existing mechanisms of funding national research activities. They usually require a significant own financial contribution, and they expect achieving results at a high technology readiness level within 3 to 4 years. Such criteria are both business- and technology-wise unrealistic for the space sector.

At the beginning of 2020, the summary assessment of perspectives for the sector was the least optimistic for over a decade: "Space projects are long-term undertakings that require consistent investments. Meanwhile, the decreasing contribution to optional ESA programmes and the lack of the National Space Programme may cause stagnation in the industry, and even its

61 *Development of the space sector* – report of the Polish Supreme Audit Office, p 77.

slowdown and gradual regression. With the current level of financing, it will be challenging for several dozen entities in the space industry to stay on the market that requires the highest qualifications, even if they conduct diversified activities."[62]

The Polish space sector's future development will be a direct result of the level of participation in ESA optional programmes, the establishment of a sustainably funded and efficiently managed National Space Programme, and the ability to focus both mechanisms on a limited number of well-defined priority areas.

62 Ibid.

CHAPTER 3

Defining Outer Space – the Continued Debate on the Scope and Applicability of Space Law

Julia Anna Hetlof

1 Introduction[1]

On 4 October 1957, the first artificial satellite *Sputnik-1* was launched into Earth's orbit, marking the onset of the Space Age. Now, well over 60 years later, the international legal regime for outer space activities is being tested by new participants and the emerging space activities and capabilities. Outer space – "a domain that no nation owns but on which all rely, is becoming increasingly congested, contested, and competitive"[2] – congested, as the number of satellites and accumulated space debris have increased; and contested and competitive with the emergence of new space-faring nations and the active participation of private entities. This increasingly multi-national and commercial nature of the space sector calls for revisiting the basis and scope of the legal framework for space activities. One of the fundamental, but still unresolved legal issues, concerns the scope of and applicability of space law, or, in other words, *when or where exactly should space law apply*? While it is generally accepted that space law applies to satellites actively orbiting the Earth, should it not also apply to the rocket or launch vehicle that propels and carries that satellite into orbit? If so, should space law apply to that launch vehicle while it is passing through another State's airspace or only once it transfers into outer space? What about if that space-bound vehicle takes off and lands horizontally, like conventional aircraft, but is carrying space tourists on their way to enjoy a few minutes of microgravity and views of the Earth from space – should air law or space law, or in some instances both, apply to such flights? If space law applies only to the objects that are already in outer space, where does outer

1 The opinions, conclusions, and recommendations expressed or implied in this article are those of the author and do not necessarily reflect those of the United States Air Force, United States Army, the Department of Defense, nor any other agency of the United States Government.

2 Robert M.Gates, Secretary of Defense and James R. Clapper, Director of National Intelligence, *National Security Space Strategy* (January 2011) i.

 DOI:10.1163/9789004542860_005

space actually begin? These are but a few questions that remain unresolved by the current international legal regime.

While there are no ready answers, this article frames the issue of applicability of space law in the context of the emerging uses of outer space and takes a fresh look at the underlying causes of the *status quo,* such as the still undefined lower boundary of outer space and State sovereignty implications.

2 Introduction to Space Applications

The launch of *Sputnik-1* marked the onset of a new era in human history – a scientific revolution that, in a way, was comparable to that in Copernicus' day.[3] The ability to launch objects into outer space, or space transportation, has enabled the development of all modern satellite-based activities in the fields of communication, navigation, remote sensing and science.[4] Satellite-derived data has improved our science and knowledge of our planet (through Earth Observation from space), impacting many fields and branches of the economy, including weather forecasting, geodesy and cartography, energy, forestry and water management and disaster response; it has revolutionized the food and fiber industries with precise farming and other applications improving agriculture (satellites for agriculture).[5]

The impact of satellites and their applications cannot be overstated, both from the civil society and global economy perspectives. The improvements in navigation, mass telephone, television and radio communications were surpassed by the 21st century's advances in small satellite platforms, miniaturization of instruments and the availability of low-cost launches, significantly lowering the costs of entry into the space sector. Consequently, the outer space sector is a rapidly developing market expanding beyond the traditional, government-controlled, and publicly-funded projects into new entrepreneurial activities – dubbed the NewSpace.[6] The next generation of satellites already harness innovations in computing, electronics, big data, imaging, sensors and

3 Paul G. Dembling, 'Some Thoughts about Sovereign Rights Arising From Space Activities' in Proceedings of the ASIL Annual Meeting, vol 88 (Cambridge UP, 1994) 260.

4 Peter van Fenema, 'Legal aspects of launch services and space transportation,' in Frans G. von der Dunk with Fabio Tronchetti, eds, *Handbook of Space Law* (Edward Elgar Pubs, 2015) 382.

5 Dembling (n5) 261.

6 Julia Hetlof, 'Delimitation of Airspace and Outer Space: Challenges and Opportunities for the Creation of a Unified Legal Regime for Suborbital Flights' in Anna Konert, ed, *Rola prawa lotniczego w procesie budowy bezpieczenstwa transportu lotniczego* (Uczelnia Lazarskiego, Warszawa, 2021) 65–66.

artificial intelligence; while ongoing developments in space transport, space tourism, asteroid mining, lunar operations, and missions to Mars promise setting new frontiers in the not so distant future. The development of low-cost reusable launch vehicles has been a vital element in the NewSpace markets, especially involving suborbital flights. Suborbital reusable launch vehicles are instrumental in a long anticipated space transport and space tourism industry, and could be destined to become point-to-point transportation vehicles for high speed transnational flights, much like the Concorde once was.

Another key aspect of space activities relates to the military uses for security and defense of nation States. In addition to opening up a new sphere for a wide range of human endeavors, the launch of *Sputnik -1* clearly demonstrated that the (former) Soviet Union had the missile technology to deliver payloads at global ranges.[7] The duality of applications for both civilian and military uses was apparent from the beginning of the Space Age in the 1960s. In fact, the underlying security concerns of both the United States and the Soviet Union contributed to the successes of the United Nation's Committee on the Peaceful Uses of Outer Space (COPUOS) in negotiating and drafting a series of multilateral space law treaties, starting with the Outer Space Treaty in 1967.[8] Both superpowers, entrenched in a Cold War, apparently perceived the resulting legal constraints in the new realm of outer space as more restraining on the opponent than on themselves.[9]

Outer space continues to be an important domain for national military capabilities, as confirmed by the launch of the United States Space Force (USSF) as a separate branch of the US Armed Forces in December 2019.[10]

---

7 Jane Gibson and Jeremy Powell, 'Current Space Law and Policy' in AU-18 Space Primer (Air Command and Staff College and Space Research Electives Seminars AUP, 2009) 46, www.jstor.com/stable/resrep13939.10.

8 Treaty on Principles Governing the Activities of States in the Exploration and Use of Outer Space, Including the Moon and Other Celestial Bodies, 27 January 1967, 610 UNTS 205 (Outer Space Treaty or 'OST').

9 Frans G. von der Dunk, 'International Space Law' in *Handbook of Space Law* (n 6) 35.

10 Of note, in November 2019, NATO Member States recognized space as a new operational domain, alongside air, land, sea and cyber. This announcement followed the introduction of NATO's first space policy which underscored the risks of space being used for aggressive, non-peaceful purposes such as the hacking, jamming or weaponization of satellites. Thomas Jones et alia, 'Space Alert: Review of the legal, regulatory and political developments for the space sector in 2019' (2019) www.twobirds.com/en/news/articles/2019/global/space-alert-review-of-the-key-legal-developments-for-the-space-sector-in-2019 'accessed 1 February 2021.'

3 Applicability of Space Law: Framing the Question

Space law is broadly described as 'all the law that may govern or apply to outer space in and relating to the outer space'[11] or, more precisely, as 'the cumulative body of *national and international legislation*, regulations, treaties, agreements, and conventions created to enable, manage, and regulate world-wide, regional, and national commercial civil governmental, and national or regional defense activities *in or related to outer space*.'[12] This definition indicates that the laws governing outer space are a complex mix of laws, drawn from a variety of sources, including international and domestic (national), which may be appliable directly (*lex specialis* – international space treaties) or indirectly (*lex generalis*).[13] Moreover, the space law regime encompasses both public international law, as a set of legal rules that govern relations between *States* (and *international organizations*), as well as private international law, regulating interactions between *private entities in an international context.*

The importance of applicability of space law is predicated on the distinct character of outer space and, hence, different legal status of the activities that are conducted therein. Outer space has become the fourth geographical realm of human activity (following land, sea and airspace) which is generally viewed as 'without frontiers' (except for its still undefined lower boundary with airspace).[14] The status of this new realm has been accepted as 'province of all mankind' – with global commons character, where territorial sovereignty does not exist, and freedom of activity is a default rule (at least for the States).[15]

Defining the scope of the international space law regime involves fundamental, if rather theoretical, debate between 'spatialists,' who advocate for a clearly defined upper limit to national airspace, with a precise baseline marking the beginning of outer space, and 'functionalists,' who disagree, believing the regulation of space activities should be determined solely by the nature of the activity or of the vehicle.[16] Finally, some thinkers and space-faring States (including the United States) continue to believe there is no need to decide

11 Francis Lyall and Paul B. Larsen, *Space Law: A Treatise* (Ashgate, 2009) 2.

12 Stephen E. Doyle, 'A Concise History of Space Law' in Mark J. Sundahl & V. Gopalakrishnan eds, *New Perspectives On Space Law: The Proceedings Of The 53rd Iisl Colloquium On The Law Of Outer Space: Young Scholar's Session 1* (Int'l Inst. Space L. 2011) 1 https://iislweb.org/docs/NewPerspectivesonSpaceLaw.pdf 'accessed on 1 February 2021.'

13 Gibson and Powell (n9).

14 Frans G. von der Dunk, *Advanced Introduction to Space Law* (Edward Elgar, 2020) 2–3.

15 Ibid.

16 Bin Cheng, 'International Responsibility and Liability for Launch Activities' 20 Air & Space L 6 (1995) 298.

the issue, claiming that so far no legal or practical problems have arisen in the absence of such a definition and no issue of State sovereignty would be solved by defining (and delimiting) outer space.[17] Similar sentiment has been expressed by the Polish jurists, including Professor Zdzisław Galicki, who stated: 'there is not much hope on any imminent agreement between States on a common position on whether or not to delimit outer space (…) the international community does not feel too severely the lack of appropriate international regulations.'[18]

Under a strict spatialist analysis, the determination of the applicable legal regime depends on the location of the vehicle – if it is below the demarcation line, it is in airspace and air law applies; when it is above the line, it is in outer space and space law applies. Conversely, functionalists focus on the nature of the activity (whether it is aviation or space mission) and/or of the technical aspects of the vehicle in question (aircraft or spacecraft). Accordingly, the determination of whether the space law regime applies involves several options: i) location of the activities (outer space) – spatialist approach; ii) character or function of those activities (space activities) – functional approach; iii) character of the object subject to the regulations (spacecraft or, more broadly, space object)- functional approach; or a combination thereof.[19]

To recapitulate, the application of international air law, with the corresponding principle of the sovereign jurisdiction of individual States over their national airspaces and their nationally registered aircraft, hinges on the concepts of *airspace* and *aircraft*.[20] Correspondingly, the applicability of space law depends on the definitions of *outer space* and *space object*.[21] While the

17 Jose Monserat Filho, 'Definition and Delimitation of Outer Space – a Deadlock Discussion?' 2nd ICAO/UNOOSA Symposium, Abu Dahbi, UAE (15–17 March 2016) https://www.icao.int/Meetings/SPACE2016/Presentations/2%20-%20J.%20Filho%20-%20Chair%20of%20COPUOUS%20LSC%20WG%20on%20DefDel%20of%20Outer%20Space.pdf.

18 Andrzej Misztal, Lukasz Kulaga, 'Znaczenie Prawa Kosmicznego w Polskiej Polityce Zagranicznej' (Tr. 'The Significance of the Space Law on the Polish Foreign Policy') in Katarzyna Myszona-Kostrzewa, ed., *Kosmos w Prawie i Polityce, Prawo i Polityka w Kosmosie* (Tr. *Cosmos in law and politics, law and politics in space*) (Warsaw 2017) 21.

19 Frans G. von der Dunk, 'The Delimitation of Outer Space Revisited: The Role of National Space laws in the Delimitation Issue' (1998) Space, Cyber, and Telecommunications Law Program Faculty Publications 51, 255, https://digitalcommons.unl.edu/spacelaw/51; Paul Stephen Dempsey and Maria Manoli, 'Suborbital Flights and the Delimitation of Air Space vis-à-vis Outer Space: Functionalism, Spatialism and State Sovereignty' 42 Annals Air & Space L. 209 (2017), 213; Hetlof (n8).

20 Frans G. von der Dunk, 'Legal aspects of private manned spaceflight' in *Handbook of Space Law* (n6) 676.

21 Ibid.

determination as to which legal regime to apply is not a simple function of definitions, their lack thereof makes the process even more daunting. The resulting legal uncertainty reflects a mix of legal, political, and State sovereignty concerns, which, to a large extent, are further compounded by the actual, geophysical attributes of Earth's atmosphere, to wit: it gradually decreases in density with height, thus making the precise physical boundary between airspace and outer space difficult to ascertain.[22]

4 The Relationship between Airspace, Outer Space and State Sovereignty

Historically, the attempts to define the legal status of airspace can be traced at least to ancient Rome and legal distinction between the words *aer* (air) as the atmosphere we breathe, and *coelum*, as the area (translated as sky or airspace) in which air circulates.[23] Air, just like the flowing water, the sea and the seashore, was, as a general principle, considered by the Roman jurists as *res communis* – common to all by natural law.[24] In contrast, none of the Roman texts ever refer to the *coelum* (airspace) as being 'common to all,' but rather it was considered *res soli*, subject to appropriation by the owner of the land.[25] Adopting the legal maxim of *Cujus est solum ejus est usque ad coelum* (who owns the land, owns even to the skies), the common law *ad coelum* doctrine developed in the English and American property law, protecting the right of property owners to the airspace superjacent to their land.[26] It is worth noting that even under Roman law such rights were never absolute or unlimited, but rather were subject to State control of public places, right of eminent domain or other restrictions on the land and real estate owners, including servitudes (urban – relating to buildings, such as height or access to sunlight, or

22 Ruwantissa Abeyratne, 'Commercial Space Travel Security' J. Transp Secur (2013) 262; Erik Seedhouse, *Suborbital: Industry at the Edge of Space* (Springer, 2014) 5.

23 John Cobb Cooper, 'Roman Law and the Maxim *Cujus Est Solum* in International Air Law' McGill LJ 1 (1952–1955) 37–38.

24 Ibid 36–37; Charles Henry Monro, *The Digest of Justinian* (Cambridge, Cambridge UP, 1904–09) vol 2, 39–40.

25 Cooper (n25) 38; Henry Goudy, 'Two Ancient Brocards' in Paul Vinogradoff, ed, *Essays in Legal Hisotry read before the International Congress of Historical Studies held in London in 1913* (London/NY, Oxford Univ. Press, 1913) 231.

26 Christy Collis, 'The Geostationary Orbit: A Critical Legal Geography of Space's Most Valuable Realt Estate' in Lisa Parks and James Schwoch, eds, *Down to Earth: Satellite Technologies, Industries, and Cultures* (Rutgers UP, 2012) 61–81.

rustic – relating to cultivated lands).[27] Von Jhering, upon re-examination of the original sources, concluded that the owner of the soil was also the owner of the airspace above, but only to the extent required to satisfy his practical needs, and that Roman jurists would not have accepted such an 'abuse of logic' as property in space without limit.[28]

Moreover, the *Cujus est solum* maxim cannot be traced *verbatim* to the original texts of the Roman law as such *Corpus Juris Civilis* or even to the original glosses to the Digest.[29] According to Copper, the closest reference likely stems from a 13th Century gloss of Franciscus Accursius to Digest VIII.2.1.[30] The original text of the Digest reads that the airspace over the public highway should be free (*'quia coelum, quod supra id solum intercedit, liberum esse debet'*),[31] while the gloss, as attributed to Accursius, notes: '*Nota. Cujus est solum, ejus debet esse usque ad coelum, ut hic & infra "qoud vi aut clam" i fi. § pen,*' which may be translated: 'Whose is the soil, his it *ought to be* up to the heaven; as here and later in Digest XLIII.24.22.4' [emphasis added].[32] The cross refence is to the passage in the Digest stating that the airspace (*coelum*) over a tomb is part of the tomb.[33] According to Cooper, this gloss expressed Accursius' belief that airspace over private lands should be (*debet esse*) free and unobstructed without limit, expanding the rule in the Digest applicable to space over public lands (such as the highway or tomb).

The creation or the extent of the property rights of the landowners in airspace above their land are not important, *per se*, in the context of international law except as proof of the underlying principle of State sovereignty. As was well stated by one of pioneers in the development of air law: "The State cannot give landowner a right of property or of use over the airspace above his land, if that airspace is not submitted to its sovereignty. Consequently, by giving such a

27 *See* Copper (n25) 27, 33–34, 49–50. According to de Montmorency, under Roman law, the State enjoyed a right of eminent domain in space Roman soil and that control of the airspace was retained by the Roman State insofar as the airspace was not essential to the enjoyment of the land beneath. James E.G. de Montmorency, 'The Control of the Air Spaces' in Grotius Society, *Problems of the War* (London, Sweet & Maxwell, 1917) vol 3, 67.

28 Cooper (n25), 27–28; Rudolf von Jhering,'Zur Lehre von den Beschrdnkungen des Grundeigenthiimers in Interesse der Nachbarn,"Jiering Jahrbiicher filr die Dogmatik des Biirgerlichen Rechts" Vol. 6, 1863, Translated by O. Meulenaere "Des restrictions imposes aux proprietaires fonciers dans l'interet des voisins,"' in Rudolf von Jhering, *Oeuvres choisies* (Paris, A. Marescq, 1893) Vol. 2, 101–144.

29 *See* Copper (n25) 40–9.

30 Ibid 41.

31 Ibid 29, Monro (n26) 68.

32 Cooper (n25), 41–42.

33 Ibid.

right to the landowner, the State says that it considers itself sovereign over the airspace."[34] As such, the rights of ownership (*'dominium'*) are closely related and, in effect, derive from State sovereignty ('right of imperium').

According to the writings of the Roman jurists and later interpretations of the original texts, the authority of the Roman State as to airspace over Roman lands was exercised without limit and to such height as was found necessary to protect public or private rights to occupy and use such space.[35] The concept of usable space will be undertaken again in later parts of this Chapter in relation to the State's ability to exercise effective control over such airspace.

Internationally, State interest in controlling and regulating the airspace became more urgent with development of modern air travel in early 20th century. Each State's 'complete and exclusive sovereignty over the airspace above its territory' was recognized and legally formalized, for the first time, at the Paris Peace Conference of 1919.[36] The principle of State sovereignty over airspace was firmly established in customary international law and codified in the Convention on International Civil Aviation (also known as the Chicago Convention).[37] At the same time, the upper limit of airspace and, henceforth, the legal extent of State sovereignty has not been clearly defined either by treaty or by customary recognition.[38] The only court reference, by the Permanent Court of International Justice, in the 1933 *Eastern Greenland's Case,* unhelpfully stated that the natural meaning of the term 'airspace' was its geographical meaning, which, in effect, means that it is space where air is present.[39]

The early 20th century legal scholars and scientists had already began to recognize not only the physical differences between the realms of airspace (in the layer of 'breathable air') and what laid beyond, the layers of 'unbreatheable gas' and 'ether,' but also to postulate that the latter should be governed by a separate legal regime – free of and unconstrained by considerations of sovereignty over airspace, to be termed 'space law.'[40] In the 1940s, Arthur C. Clarke explained that there must be an upper limit to national sovereignty because

34 Johanna F. Lycklama a Nijeholt, *Air Sovereignty* (The Hague, M. Nijhoff, 1910) 34.

35 Copper (n25) 40.

36 Convention Relating to the Regulation of Aerial Navigation Signed at Paris, October 13, 1919 (Paris Convention) 1 J. Air L. & Com. 94 (1930) Article 1.

37 Convention on International Civil Aviation (Chicago Convention) (1994) 15 U.N.T.S. 295, Article 1; Georgetown Space Law Group, The Geostationary Orbit: Legal, Technical and Political Issues Surrounding Its Use in World Telecommunications, 16 Case W Res J Int'L 223 (1984) 232.

38 Abeyratne, (n24) 262; Seedhouse (n24) 5.

39 PCIJ Series A/B, No. 53.

40 Doyle (n14).

otherwise 'in the course of a day, [on a rotating globe] every country will lay claim to a large portion of the Universe!'[41]

The modern day debate on the issue of where airspace ends and outer space begins has continued in the international arena since the late 1950s, so far without a consensus on the legal boundary issue.[42] Consequently, neither 'airspace' nor 'outer space' is defined in the relevant international air law, space law, or any other treaties and no uniform or legally binding delimitation, interpretation, definition of these terms has been agreed upon on the international scale, to this date.[43] Increasingly, individual States, through the national legislation process, have undertaken to the define the area of space activities as applicable to their respective regulation – by adopting a functional approach or unilaterally setting the altitude, as addressed at Section 7 of this Chapter.

5 In Search of the Boundary: Operational Considerations for Spatial Approach

According to the spatialists, space law applies to all activities, which are conducted in the area of outer space. This, however, necessitates defining such area, at least the lower boundary of outer space as the demarcation point with the airspace. But what are the boundaries of outer space?

It is generally accepted and uncontroverted that the artificial satellites that are operating (orbiting) are doing so in 'outer space.'[44] However, where, along that aerospace continuum, should the boundary be placed, continues to be debated. There are several spatially-based operational characteristics that exist

41 Arthur C. Clarke, 'The Challenge of the Spaceship' VI J of the British Interplanetary Soc (1946–47) 66–67. Clarke was at the time the President of the British Interplanetary Society and was not yet recognized for any of his eventual world-famous science fiction. See Doyle (n14) 12, ft 13.

42 The first mention of the issue of delimitation took place at the *ad hoc* COPUOS in 1959. Although the Committee noted that there was no consensus on the matter and that 'it might eventually prove essential to determine these limits,' States 'generally believed that the determination of precise limits for air space and outer space did not present a legal problem calling for priority consideration at this moment.' Report of the Ad Hoc Committee on the Peaceful Uses of Outer Space, UN Doc A/4141 (14 July 1959) 25; see also Stephen Hobe and Kuan-Wei Chen, 'Legal Status of Outer Space and Celestial Bodies' in Ram Jakhu and Paul Stephen Dempsey, eds, *Routledge Handbook of Space Law* (Routledge, 2017) 27.

43 Von der Dunk, *Delimitation* (n21) 254, Hetlof (n8).

44 Cheng (n18) 298; see Thomas Gangale, *How High the Sky? The Definition and Delimitation of Outer Space and Territorial Airspace in International Law* (Brill | Nijhoff, 2018) 391.

TABLE 1 Operational boundaries for aviation and space operations[a]

Altitude	Operational significance
18 km	upper limit of civil aviation traffic (managed airspace)
50 km	upper limit of atmospheric buoyance (balloons)
80 km	operational lower boundary of space as recognized by the USA (USAF/NASA/FAA) for the purpose of awarding astronaut status to anyone flying above that altitude
100 km	operational lower boundary of space as recognized by FAI (World Air Sports Federation) for the purpose of record setting flights – misnamed as the 'Kármán Line'
120 km	re-entry threshold for space systems – the height at which significant heating occurs to a re-entering spacecraft. Natural space objects (meteoroids) also start to ablate or burn up at around this altitude, creating the visible meteors we see in the night sky.[b]
160 km	lower limit of practically sustainable orbital flights

a Andrea Harrington, 'The Definition and Delimitation of Outer Space and the Safety of Aerospace Operations' Presentation in collaboration with the Research Team at the McGill University Institute of Air and Space Law, available at www.unoosa.org/documents/pdf/copuos/lsc/2016/tech-03.pdf.

b Australian Space Academy, Space Law Guide at https://spaceacademy.net.au/spacelaw/splawguide.htm.

for the purposes of aviation and space operations, which have been used in the delimitation discussions, as detailed in Table 1 below.[45]

The FAI and many other groups and institutions recognize 100 kilometers (62.5 miles), as the boundary between aeronautics and astronautics, where, in theory, the atmosphere becomes too thin to provide enough lift for conventional aircraft to maintain flight.[46] While this demarcation point has been increasingly accepted at the 'edge of space,' and popularly referred to as the von Kármán Line, it has not been uniformly adopted as a legal boundary. In fact, not only the altitude of 100 km appears arbitrary and disputable even by astrophysical standards, it might have been incorrectly attributed to the work

45 Dempsey & Manoli (n21) 249.

46 Abeyratne (n24) 26.

of Theodore Von Kármán, the aeronautical engineer after whom the 'line' was named.[47] Von Kármán arguably never set the limit at 100 km and his engineering work was misinterpreted by lawyers seeking an altitude of physical significance as the basis for delimitation.[48] Several authors, including Polish jurist Andrzej Górbiel referred to the effective Kármán line as closer to 83/84km, others noted many of the 'science' arguments as inconsistent, or inaccurate representation of laws of physics, based on 1950s aerospace technology and, in part, complicated by the various types of miles-to-kilometers calculations used.[49] Accordingly, as succinctly put by Gangale, any references to the 100-kilometer von Kármán line should be treated as a misnomer and urban legend, not based on facts and science.[50]

Furthermore, it should be noted that any such Non-Kármán line, whether set at 100 or 84 km, is concerned with the maximum altitude of feasible aviation.[51] Another marker for the same boundary is based on the outer space operational perspective, measuring the minimum altitude of feasible orbits, so called 'lowest perigee rule,' referring to the point closest to Earth in (usually) elliptical Earth orbits.[52] Accordingly, taking the spatial approach to the generally accepted view that international space law applies to any object in orbit around Earth, it is uncontroverted that outer space extends at least "no lower than from where satellites have been observed to continue in orbit for at least one revolution."[53] Using the lowest perigee theory is the most objective solution, however it is likewise not static, depending on whether the rule would adopt the lowest *sustainable* altitude – currently accepted around 100 km, or encompass lowest recorded or even the lowest theoretical altitudes – which might lower the boundary to 81 or even 78 km.[54]

---

47 Thomas Gangale, 'The Non Karman Line: An Urban Legend of the Space Age' 41 J of SP 2017, vol 2, 151; Jonathan C. McDowell, 'The edge of space: Revisiting the Kármán Line' 151 Acta Astronautica (2018) 676.

48 Andrew G. Haley was the main proponent of the 'von Karman line' as the line of 'primary jurisdiction.' Ibid.

49 Andrzej Górbiel, *Międzynarodowe prawo kosmicznev* (Tr. *International Space Law*) (Warsaw 1985) 160; Gangale, ibid 164; Von der Dunk, *International Space Law* (n11) 66.

50 Gangale, ibid 162.

51 Von der Dunk (n11) 66.

52 Ibid 68.

53 Gangale, *How High the Sky* (n46).

54 Von der Dunk, *International Space Law* (n11) 68, Gangale, *How High the Sky* (n46) 392.

6 Applying Spatial, Functional or Yet Another Approach?

Assuming the boundary line is drawn and legally accepted (for example, using the widely accepted lowest perigee theory or the popular Non-Karman line at 100 km), applying the strict spatial approach would subject the same flight to two different regulatory regimes. For example, given that all space-bound missions start at the surface of the Earth and must pass through airspace on the way up to outer space, a rocket (or launch vehicle) during its ascent phase would be subject to the air law regime with all of its applicable regulations (including, but not limited to, aviation navigation, safety, security, and environmental standards, as well as over-flight and other sovereignty implications) up to the altitude of 100 km. Once the vehicle has crossed that boundary line and moved to outer space, it then would have to follow all the obligations required under the space law treaties and the applicable domestic space regulations.[55] Applying a pure spatial approach would not only lead to theoretically inconsistent requirements. In practice, some of the existing space law rules already apply below any boundary, that is regardless of where the activity at issue takes places. For example, the Liability Convention applies as long as the damage is caused by a 'space object', irrespective of whether that object is in outer space or not.[56] The launching State is liable for all damage caused by its space object, wherever such damage occurs – on the surface of the Earth, in the air or outer space, the only difference being in the extent of such damages – absolute (if damage occurs on the surface of the Earth or 'to aircraft in flight'),[57] or fault-based for damages caused in space ('elsewhere than on the surface of the Earth').[58] Consequently, many national space laws also handle third-party liability to that extent.

Applying the functional approach renders it unnecessary to solve the theoretical dispute concerning the existence and location of the boundary between airspace and outer space as space law would be applicable to all space objects and space-based activities, notwithstanding their location. The qualifying determination, under this approach, would be the intended purpose of the

55 Michael Chatzipanagiotis, 'Regulating the Safety of Suborbital Flights in Europe: Navigation Through the Labyrynth of Competences of the EU, its Member States and EASA' Proceedings of the 64th International Astronautical Congress (Beijing 2013) 2; https://papers.ssrn.com/sol3/papers.cfm?abstract_id=2424764.

56 Von der Dunk, *The Delimitation* (n21) 256, Convention on International Liability for Damage Caused by Space Objects (Liability Convention), 29 March 1972, 961 UNTS 187 Journal of Laws of 1973, No 27, item 154.

57 Ibid Article II.

58 Ibid Article III.

flight or activity- if the vehicle's primary purpose is to go to outer space (for example space tourism – to experience weightlessness, to deploy a satellite, or conduct scientific experiments), it is a space object subject to space law throughout the entire duration of the flight. If, taking the example of a sub-orbital flight, the purpose would be to provide transportation between two points on the surface of the Earth (an Earth-to-Earth mission), then the vehicle, arguably, is not a space object but rather should be considered as an aircraft subject to the aviation rules only.[59]

Another, related method of determining whether the vehicle in question is an 'aircraft' or a 'space object' is to consider its technological properties, functional characteristics, or design and aerodynamics.[60] According to the International Civil Aviation Organization (ICAO), an 'aircraft' is '[a]ny machine that can derive support in the atmosphere from the reactions of the air other than the reactions of the air against the earth's surface.'[61] While there is no internationally accepted definition of 'space object', the existing treaty provisions and the national space laws indicate that a space object is any artificial device launched or intended to be launched into outer space, designed to move and operate therein, as well as any component parts and launch vehicle therein.[62] Under the current ICAO definition of aircraft, an aerospace vehicle launched by a rocket might not be considered an aircraft on the ascent phase of the flight, but might be on the descent phase, when it would be using its wings to glide to its destination.[63] Depending on specifications of each sub-orbital vehicle type, it might require licensing solely as a space object or both certification as an aircraft and licensing as a space object.[64]

Apart from the definitional ambiguities, practical and operational issues are bound to arise due to different registration and liability standards under the legal regimes of air and space law, in addition to safety standards and traffic management problems.[65] This situation would likewise lead to legal uncertainty, distort competition, and hinder innovation.[66] Moreover, Górbiel

59 Dempsey & Manoli (n21) 219.
60 Ibid.
61 Chicago Convention (n41) Annex 1,2, and 6 *definitions*; see also Dempsey & Manoli (n21) 221.
62 Dempsey & Manoli (n21) 224, Michael Chatzipanagiotis, *The legal status of space tourists in the framework of commercial suborbital flights* (Cologne 2011) 20–25.
63 Dempsey & Manoli (n21) 222.
64 Ibid 224.
65 Thomas Cheney and Lauren Napier, 'Policy Analysis: Air versus Space. Where do Suborbital Flights Fit In for International Regulation?' 7 JSPG 1 (August 2015) 8–11.
66 Ibid 10.

submitted that applying the functional approach would render meaningless the treaty principles that had already been established for outer space.[67] As an example, under functionalism, a suborbital vehicle that briefly passes through outer space in the course of earth-to-earth transportation presumably would remain subject to air law during the entire journey.[68] Specifically, there are certain activities which are expressly prohibited by international space law, for example placing the weapons of mass destruction (WMD) on the space object (as per Article IV of the Outer Space Treaty),[69] but which would not necessarily be considered illegal in case of the aircraft.[70] By extension, applying the functional theory, such suborbital vehicle would not be prohibited from carrying WMD on board even when in outer space (provided no other air law or general international law was violated by such act). Such an interpretation would obviously violate the express provisions of the Outer Space Treaty.

At the same time, certain space treaty provisions are clearly functionally based, such as the already mentioned liability regime which applies to 'space objects' regardless of where they are present the moment damage is caused by them. The above considerations show that neither spatialism nor functionalism can provide a definitive and universal guidance that would result in a uniform application of the law. In addition, despite a perhaps more natural tendency for a vertical limitation (at least for this author), setting the legal lower boundary of outer space at the proposed Non-Karman line of 100 km or, alternatively, at the lowest perigee point (approximately between 80 to 100 km), could still severely restrict the free access to outer space absent a right of innocent passage through the national airspaces below that boundary line.[71] Consequently, various hybrid ideas have emerged, including the 1983 former Soviet Union's proposal combining the spatial and functional approaches – with a defined boundary not exceeding 110 km, and the right of 'innocent flight' below that line for the purpose of reaching orbit or returning to Earth.[72]

Other proposals have also ensued in efforts to provide less restrictive access to space, especially for the emerging space activities (such as suborbital vehicles, stratospheric balloons, pseudo-satellites or high-altitude drones, with

67 Górbiel (n53) 174–75.

68 Dempsey and Manoli (n21) 19.

69 Outer Space Treaty (n10) Article IV.

70 See, e.g., International Court of Justice, Advisory Opinion, *Legality of the Threat or Use of Nuclear Weapons*, 1996 ICJ 226 (July 8), reprinted in 35 ILM 809 (1996)(possession of nuclear weapons not per se unlawful; use of nuclear weapons must conform to the U.N. Charter and the law of war).

71 Gangale, *How High the Sky* (n46) 393.

72 Ibid 416.

many commercial applications.)[73] Since many of such NewSpace applications primarily use lower altitudes, starting from approximately 18km to 160 km, different authors have advocated for a separate legal regime in that region (or, alternatively, between 50 to 120 km) called 'Near Space,''Proto Zone' or 'mesospace.'[74] This proposed intermediate zone between airspace and outer space, which would be legally distinct from either of the two spheres, could be compared to the region between 'territorial seas' and 'high seas' under United Nations Convention on the Law of the Sea (UNCLOS).[75] At various periods of history different States have claimed limited rights in areas of high seas adjacent to their territorial seas in order to enforce customs, fiscal, immigration or sanitary regulations (contiguous zones) or to claim sovereign rights over all the economic resources of the sea or the seabed (exclusive economic zones).[76] Loosely modelling on the UNCLOS, innocent passage (for commercial activities) would be allowed in Near Space, but the safety risk for the overflown population should be compliant with the international norms (to be defined).[77] The economic exploitation of such a zone (for instance the use of pseudo-satellites) would be the exclusive prerogative of the country underneath. In addition, overflights for military purposes (for instance ICBM tests) could be undertaken in Near Space only if authorized by the overflown country, thus

73 Dempsey & Manoli (n21) 248, Gangale (n46) 403.

74 Ibid; Joseph Pelton, 'Urgent Security Concerns in the "Proto-Zone"' Presentation at the 4th International Manfrech Lachs Conference on Conflicts in Space and the Rule of Law, McGill University, Institute of Air and Space Law (Montreal, 2016). http://www.mcgill.ca/iasl/files/iasl/mlc4_presentation_jpelton.pptx, slide 3.

75 United Nations Convention on the Law of the Sea (UNCLOS), Dec. 10, 1982, 1833 U.N.T.S. 397.

76 Peter Malanczuk, *Akehurst's Modern Introduction to International Law*, 7th ed (Routledge, 1997) 182–83 *Contiguous Zone* is an area extending seaward from the baseline up to 24 nautical miles in which the coastal nation may exercise the control necessary to prevent or punish infringements of its customs, fiscal, immigration, and sanitary laws and regulations that occur within its territory or territorial sea, UNCLOS, Article 33. At the same time, ships and aircraft enjoy high seas freedoms, including overflight, in and above the contiguous zone. Malanczuk, id; Air Force Operations and the Law (2020) 54. Cf. *Exclusive Economic Zones* (EEZ) are resource-related zones adjacent to a State's coast and extending beyond its territorial sea. They may extend up to 200 nautical miles from the baselines used to measure the territorial sea. UNCLOS, Article 55. In the EEZ, States enjoy the right to exercise the traditional high sea freedoms of navigation and overflight, and, additionally, of the laying of submarine cable and pipelines, and of all other traditional high sea uses by ships and aircraft that are not resource related. UNCLOS, Article 58(1); Malanczuk, ibid, DoD Law of War Manual, para 14.2.1.2.

77 Ibid.

extending the territorial sovereignty beyond the proposals associated with the Non-Kármán line.[78]

While theoretically possible and perhaps justifiable, creating legal fiction of yet another, separate legal zone between airspace and outer space would not be politically expedient and hence, is not a realistic solution. Especially since neither the concept of innocent passage nor of a contiguous zone exists in air law, the arguments for this approach would need to be very persuasive.[79] Moreover, it is highly unlikely the any State would be prepared to accept any proposal which would be a de facto limitation of their air sovereignty to 18 km (or even 50 km) above sea-level.[80]

As already indicated, establishing the lower boundary of outer space would clearly mark the point beyond which State sovereignty does not extend. From the private sector's perspective, the boundary line should be set as low as possible to enable free access to outer space and hence, foster the sector's development; on the other hand, from the State security perspective, the vertical limit of sovereign airspace should extend as far as the State is able to defend against (military) threats to its security. Interestingly, the expansion of military capabilities and more reliance on space-based capabilities should not factor in that determination. As pointed out by Gangale, the altitude capability of anti-missile or anti-satellite weapons is irrelevant in this context, since the threat posed by such targets comes from outer space, which has no upper limit.[81] Given this, it would be impractical (not to mention in violation of the already established *lex specialis* and customary international law) to extend national sovereignty as high as the highest spaceborne threat.[82] Accordingly, the spatial determination of sovereignty should reflect a prevailing State practice with regard to aviation, namely, the capabilities combat aircraft, air-to-air defensive system, and surface-to-air defensive systems.[83] According to Gangale, modern air defense systems are typically capable of operating at up to 30 km (98,000 ft) while a few older systems were capable at up to 40 km (131,000 ft) which has been pretty stable since the 1960s.[84]

Assuming that competing State interests of defending airspace and of accessing outer space converge at about 30 km, it might be argued that this

78 Ibid.
79 Gangale (n 51) 402.
80 Ibid 405.
81 Ibid 394.
82 Ibid.
83 Ibid 395.
84 Ibid.

altitude should serve as a line delimiting *sovereign* airspace.[85] In retrospect, John Cobb Cooper, one of the founders of space law, already wrote in the 1950s on the effective control theory, which would have established a ceiling on State sovereignty, as well as postulated for the necessity of an intermediate zone, emphasizing, in 1964, that the principle of free access to outer space precluded setting the boundary of State sovereignty too high.[86]

Circling back to the modern-day proposals related to mesospace, this author considers any proposals bringing mesospace (especially if defined as the area starting at 18 km) under *corpus juris spatialis* or under a separate legal regime akin to 'contiguous zone' with right of innocent passage, as not feasible and without legal precedent in air law. However, another more moderate option is worth examining, as it also would secure less restrictive access to outer space, specifically, to designate mesospace as international airspace, while taking into account the effective control of the States.[87] This would have subtly different yet important considerations, specifically, the freedom of passage would apply to mesospace as it does in international airspace over international waters at lower altitudes. Moreover, precedent in air law would permit States to establish zones analogous to air defense identification zones (ADIZs), where aircraft are identified, monitored, and controlled in the interest of national security.[88] Finally, treating mesospace as international airspace would facilitate the integration of mesospace traffic with traffic in national air space.

However, this proposal would require States to agree on yet another delimitation – between their sovereign airspace and a super-adjacent international atmospheric space. Setting the sovereignty limit at the highest altitude of *effective control* by the most technologically advanced State would enable international airspace to extend from approximately 30 km all the way up to outer space. Of course, the reach of effective control is not fixed either, but rather dependent on the advancements in aerospace technologies and physical properties of the atmosphere; yet, it had remained stable at the approximate altitude of 30 km for the last six decades.[89] At the same time, international consensus on defining the effective control limit is just as unlikely as setting

85 Ibid 409.

86 Ibid 422; John Cobb Cooper, 'Contiguous Zones in Aerospace: Preventive and Protective Jurisdiction' 7 Air Force L. Rev. 15 (1965); John Cobb Copper, 'High Altitude Flight and National Sovereignty' 4 Int'l L.Q. 41, 411 (1951); John Cobb Cooper, 'The Problem of a Definition of "Air Space"'1 Proc. On the L. of Outer Space 38,42 (1958).

87 Gangale (n 51) 405.

88 Ibid.

89 ibid 403.

the upper limit of airspace – politically motivated reasoning might prevail based on the apparent, even if not actual State sovereignty concerns.

7 Air Law versus Space Law: The Territorial Limit of State Sovereignty

It is a basic principle of international air law that every State has complete and exclusive sovereignty over the airspace above its territory.[90] It is undisputed that any object within the national airspace would be subject to that State's sovereignty, including a prohibition of unauthorized flights and an obligation to conform to territorial laws and regulations by foreign aircraft.[91] In addition, air law imposes liability on the airline or aircraft operator and requires States, *inter alia*, to certify and register aircraft, and to regulate safety, navigation, security, as well as noise and emissions and other detailed standards and recommended practices (SARPs) of the international civil aviation in the Chicago Convention and its 19 Annexes.

In contrast to the air law regime, the international law of outer space establishes the freedom of outer space and outlaws any claims of sovereignty. The 1967 Outer Space Treaty affirms that outer space is 'free for exploration and use by all States' and 'is not subject to national appropriation by claim of sovereignty, by means of use or occupation, or by any other means'[92] while imposing liability and oversight responsibility upon the space-faring State.[93] The international registration regime is set up for space objects;[94] however, there are yet no legally binding, universal safety, navigation, or security standards, which continue to be governed by alternative mechanisms in the form of voluntary norms, standards, and recommendations – so called 'soft law'

---

90 Chicago Convention (n41) Article 1, Paris Convention of 1919 (n40) Article 1. National airspace consists of the airspace above its land and territorial waters. See Abeyratne (n24) 261. Terms synonymous with national airspace include 'territorial airspace' or 'sovereign airspace,' Air Force Operations and the Law, 4th ed (2020).

91 Abeyratne (n24); Article 3 of Chicago Convention provides that '[n]o state aircraft of a contracting State shall fly over the territory of another State or land thereon without authorization by special agreement or otherwise, and in accordance with terms thereof.' (n41) Also see Article 6 and Article 12, respectively.

92 Ibid OST (n10) Article I and Article II, respectively.

93 Ibid Article VI.

94 Ibid Article VIII; Convention on Registration of Objects Launched into Outer Space, 6 June 1975, 1023 UNTS 15 (Registration Convention) Article II.

TABLE 2 Major differences between the air law and space law regimes[a]

Air law	Space law
Applies to 'airspace' and 'aircraft'	Applies to 'outer space' and 'space object'
States enjoy 'complete and exclusive sovereignty' over their territorial airspace	State sovereignty claims over outer space are prohibited; outer space is 'free for exploration and use' by all States
Imposes liability on the airline, or the aircraft operator	Imposes liability on the 'launching State,' and oversight responsibility upon the 'appropriate State'
Requires States to certify and register aircraft	Creates an international registration regime
Requires States to regulate safety, navigation, and security	No universal safety, navigation, or security standards
Requires States to regulate noise and emissions	Environmental standards are 'soft law'

a Ibid.

instruments, in addition to national space regulations.[95] A brief overview of the major differences between the air law and space law regimes is provided in Table 2 below.[96]

This simplified comparison chart highlights major legal principles between the two distinct regimes of air law and space law, thus illustrating that the decision which regime is applied has many important legal, regulatory, and political (including national security) implications.

In addition to issues of State sovereignty, as discussed above, the question of international responsibility for 'national activities' is of crucial importance. Under the space law regime, States are internationally responsible for their 'national activities' conducted in outer space and, consequently, are obliged to undertake proper 'authorization and continuing supervision' of such

95 Julia Hetlof, 'Space Security: Space Debris Removal Under the International Legal Regime' in A. Hrycaj, A. Lazarska, P. Szustakiewicz, eds, *Prawo a Nowoczesność: Wyzwania-problemy-nadzieje* (Warszawa, 2019) 236.

96 Dempsey & Manoli (n21) 218.

activities – at least if they are held to be the 'appropriate State' to do so.[97] Under the general public international law principle of 'state responsibility,' States also remain internationally responsible *below* the geographical threshold of outer space, in particular with respect to the national activities taking place within their respective *national airspace*.[98] As explained by Professor Von der Dunk, the main difference, which is of key importance in the context of private manned spaceflight in particular, is that under general State responsibility rules, States are only directly and fully responsible for their *own* activities, whereas under the space law regime they are equally responsible for non-governmental (that is, private or commercial) activities.[99]

Finally, the definition of 'space object' is relevant to the application of the space law regimes of liability and registration-*cum*-jurisdiction.[100] The liability-related issues have been raised in the context of sub-orbital vehicles and on the separate issue of space debris remediation.[101] The Registration Convention mandates each 'space object' to be registered by the relevant 'launching State.'[102] Formally, the registration obligation is limited to space objects 'launched into Earth orbit or beyond,' which would ipso facto exclude sub-orbital spacecraft.[103] However, Von der Dunk submits that this formal limitation was mainly intended to exclude one-off sounding rocket launches and deep space probes, (semi-) failed launches and launches of intercontinental ballistic missiles, and should not be interpreted as making it principally impossible to register sub-orbital vehicles under the Registration Convention's terms.[104] This grey area, however, might lend support to the creation of other registration regimes for sub-orbital activities, under the umbrella of aviation law, as proposed by the ICAO or the European Space Agency (ESA).

---

97 Outer Space Treaty (n10) Article VI, Von der Dunk, *Legal Aspects* (n21) 680.

98 Ibid 680; see Draft Articles on the Responsibility of States for Internationally Wrongful Acts (Draft Articles) UN Doc. A/RES/56/83 (2001); Report of the ILC on the Work of its Fifty-third Session, UN Doc A/56/10 (2001), 26; cf. Chicago Convention (n41) Article 28.

99 Von der Dunk, *Legal aspects* (n22) 680.

100 Ibid 681.

101 For discussion on state liability in connection with space debris remediation, see Hetlof, Space Security (n99).

102 Registration Convention (n98) Article II.

103 Von der Dunk, *Legal aspects* (n22) 681.

104 Ibid.

8 Customary Law: State Practice Considerations

While there is no agreement on the definition and delimitation question within COPUOS or in the international community at large, several States have taken steps to clarify their domestic regulatory frameworks on this issue. The existence of the national regulations in the area of outer space activities is of twofold importance. First, it is crucial for the domestic legal framework of such States, as it can, consequently, impact (positively or negatively) the development of the space sector and its domestic economy in general. The evidence of State practice is important from the international space law perspective not only as illustrative of possible solutions (for comparative law purposes), but also because it can contribute to forming the rules of customary law. Customary law arises from the practice of States coupled with the acceptance of the practice as law (*opinio juris sive necessitates*), which, once established, is binding on all nations.[105] The point at which a consistent State practice becomes customary international law binding on all States is open to interpretation. The evidence of custom may be found in international agreements, declarations of international organization, judicial decisions of international tribunals, and other acts of States.[106]

In 2005, COPUOS invited States to submit and update information on national legislation or any national practices that might exist or were being developed, relating directly or indirectly to the definition and/or delimitation of outer space.[107] While most States indicated no relevant national legislation defining the outer space boundary, from the nations that opined on the issue, a trend can be seen towards the adoption of the spatial approach. Australia's Space Activities Act 1998 was amended in 2002 to replace the words 'outer space' with a description of an area beyond the distance of 100 km above mean sea level.[108] Similarly, Kazakhstan's national legislation, the 2012 Outer Space Activities Act, provides that 'outer space is defined as space extending beyond airspace at a height exceeding 100 kilometers above sea level.'[109] In addition, the Act provides for innocent passage by a space object 'in the process of its launch into outer space or return to Earth on condition of prior agreement with the Ministry of Defence of Kazakhstan and the competent bodies dealing with natural and man-made emergencies and environmental protection.'[110]

105 Von der Dunk, *Delimitation* (n21) 255, Air Force Operations and the Law (n54) 11.

106 Ibid 12.

107 COPUOS, Report of the Working Group (A/AC.105/850, annex I, para 5 (e)).

108 COPUOS, Report [Australia, 2012] A/AC.105/865/Add.11.

109 COPUOS, Report [Kazakhstan, 2013] Article 1, para 6, A/AC.105/865/Add.12.

110 Ibid Article 7, para 5.

Some States embraced the spatial approach without indicating the exact altitude of the demarcation point, *to wit*, South Africa, by defining outer space as 'the space above the surface of the Earth from a height at which it is in practice possible to operate an object in an orbit around the Earth,'[111] or Austria, which adopted maximum altitude for feasible aviation by defining 'Upper State Boundary – USB: the altitude at which aircraft can no longer move by aerodynamic lift but only according to Kepler's force.'[112]

Other States, however, have adopted the functional approach in their national laws. The Netherlands defined 'space activities' as 'the launch, flight operation or guidance of space objects in outer space' and 'space objects' as 'any object launched or destined to be launched into outer space' without defining the outer space.[113] Similarly, Belgium defined 'space objects' as 'any object launched or intended for launching on an orbit around the Earth or to a destination beyond Earth orbit' as well as its launching devices and component parts.[114]

The amendments clarified that the operation of small satellites (small sats) that are not maneuverable (such as cube sats) is covered by the Belgium space law, however, sub-orbital fights are excluded from its scope because of the definition of the space object.[115]

The functionalist States do not advocate any legal delimitation between airspace and outer space, believing that such definition is not relevant and has no impact on the development of the outer space activities.[116] This view has been shared by the United States, which continues to oppose any proposals to define or delimit outer space claiming that it is not necessary, does not hamper the space sector's development and it would not help in safeguarding any sovereignty issues.[117]

Russia (formerly the Soviet Union), on the other hand, which had initially favored the functional approach, has been advocating spatialism since 1979, when it proposed at the COPUOS Legal subcommittee (and reiterated in 1983) that the region above 100/110 km above sea level is outer space and should be established as such by a treaty, and that the States should 'retain'

111 COPUOS, Report, Space Affairs Act of 1993, as amended in 1995 [South Africa, 2017].

112 COPUOS, Report, Austrian Federal Law Gazette II No. 297/2014 (2017).

113 COPUOS, Report [Netherlands, 2010] A/AC.105/865/Add.8.

114 COPUOS, Report [Belgium, 2012] V.13-80419 3 A/AC.105/865/Add.1.

115 Irmgard Marboe, 'National Space Law' in *Handbook of Space Law* (n6) 162.

116 COPUOS Report (n116), Netherlands and Belgium response.

117 UN COPUOS (2010); also see Bhavya Lal and Emily Nightingale, 'Where is Space? And Why Does That Matter' (2014), Space Traffic Management Conference, 16, https://commons.erau.edu/stm/2014/wednesday/16.

the right to fly over the territory of other States at the altitudes below that line 'for the purpose of reaching orbit or returning to Earth in the territory of the launching State.'[118]

The existence of the right of innocent passage by spacecraft through the airspace of foreign States is another grey area under the international law. The concept derives from the maritime law, where 'innocent passage' is defined as 'navigation through the territorial sea for the purpose of:

a. traversing that sea without entering internal waters or calling at a roadstead or port facility outside internal waters; or
b. proceeding to or from internal water or a call at such roadstead or port facility.'[119]

The right of innocent passage does not exist in the air law regime, as confirmed by the Chicago Convention, but the concept was resurrected by outer space lawyers with respect to the passage through the national airspace above conventional air traffic.[120]

Sputnik-1, as the first successful satellite that achieved Earth's orbit in 1957, overflew various States, including the United States, yet no State ever protested that its legal airspace had been violated by the satellite.[121] The question remains whether the evidence of actual State practice has been sufficient to date and, whether it has been confirmed by the general *opinio juris* of States. According to the ICAO Council, as presented by the ICAO Observer to the COPUOS Legal Subcommittee at its 1986 session:

> 'The right of innocent passage of spacecraft through the sovereign airspace is proposal *de lege ferenda* (i.e. a legislative proposal not reflecting the existing law); such right does not exist under the present international law of the air; an unconditional right of passage through the sovereign airspace does not exist even with respect to the civil aircraft and is specifically subject to a special authorization with respect to State aircraft and pilotless aircraft;(...) and the operation of spacecraft in the airspace may require operational co-ordination with air navigation services to ensure the safety of air navigation.'[122]

118 COPUOS [USSR proposal, 1979] A/AC.105/L.112.
119 UNCLOS (n 79), Article 19.
120 Gangale (n 46) 323.
121 Collis (n28).
122 ICAO Doc. C-WP/8158 (1985).

It appears there is no consensus between different jurists regarding the existence of an international customary law relating to the right of innocent passage for the spacecraft. As noted by Gangale, no State has declared it has a right of overflight, but those that did simply acted as though such right existed.[123]

9 Conclusion

A clear and unambiguous determination of the applicability of space law is needed for the effective regulation of both current and, particularly, emerging space and aero-space operations. The current legal regimes of air and space law are not well defined as to their spatial or functional applicability. As discussed in this Chapter, the issues of State sovereignty, to a large degree, explain a continuing lack of will on the part of some major space powers (including the United States) on the legal delimitation of the lower boundary of outer space. Etablishing such a boundary would clearly mark the point beyond which the air law regime, with its principle of State sovereignty, does not extend. While, from the private sector's perspective, such boundary line should be set as low as possible to enable free access to outer space and hence, foster the sector's development; from the State security perspective, setting a vertical limit on sovereign airspace must take into account vital State interest in defending against threats to its security.

Notwithstanding whether one is a proponent of spatialism, functionalism or a hybrid approach, the decision on space law applicability should reflect the interests and principles, which are already firmly established by the applicable regimes of air and space, including, but not limited to, State sovereignty in national airspace, on the one hand, and common interest and freedoms of outer space, on the other. Getting to the 'right' compromise would seem to involve the wisdom of King Solomon combined with a Herculean effort. However, as the US Supreme Court Justice Frankfurter once noted (in an unrelated matter),

> In law as in life lines have to be drawn. But the fact that a line has to be drawn somewhere does not justify its being drawn anywhere. The line must follow some direction of policy, whether rooted in logic or experience. Lines should not be drawn simply for the sake of drawing lines.'[124]

---

123 Gangale (n 46) 365.

124 *Pearce v. Commissioner,* 315 U.S. 543, 558 (1942) (Frankfurter, J. dissenting); see Howard J. Taubenfeld, 'Outer Space: The "Territorial" Limits of Nations' 38 Fordham Law Rev 1, 6 (1969).

Given the ever-developing technological capabilities, a determination on the scope and extent of the Polish space law ultimately might be based on the mutual political accommodations. It should, nonetheless, focus on advancing safety of the inherently risky space operations while, to the greatest possible extent, allowing the industry to develop in a uniform and fair legal regime.

CHAPTER 4

The International Legal Regime for Space Activities Applicable to Poland

Tomasz Balcerzak and Julia Anna Hetlof

1 Legal and Historical Introduction

Since outer space has developed as a fourth realm for human activity (following land, sea and airspace), 'space law' ultimately reflects a conglomerate of different legal regimes, international as well as national, which were developed in different contexts and from various angles and which may be applicable to space activities directly (*lex specialis* of space law) or indirectly (*lex generalis*).[1] Polish jurist, Professor Jerzy Górbiel, in 1985, defined international space law, in a narrow sense, as 'the entirety of the treaty and the customary law norms, based on the reciprocal rights and obligations of States (and intergovernmental organization to some extent) concerning the activities carried on by them in the exploration and use of outer space, ' and 'in the broader sense contains also provisions of the domestic laws delivered by particular States in order to regulate space activities.'[2] The contemporary scholar and space law expert, Professor Frans G. von der Dunk succinctly described 'space law' as 'all law that actually, one way or another, follows humans into outer space.'[3]

Since Space Law is a function of both international and national legal regimes, it is formulated at the international level following the established international law-making process, while national (domestic) space law is formulated at the national level pursuant to national law-making procedures in each State.[4] This Chapter is mostly concerned with the former – the international regime with a set of rules concerning space activities that apply to the

1 Frans G. von der Dunk, *Advanced Introduction to Space Law* (Edward Elgar, 2020) 9; Jane Gibson and Jeremy Powell, 'Current Space Law and Policy' in AU-18 Space Primer (Air Command and Staff College and Space Research Electives Seminars AUP, 2009) 46, www.jstor.com/stable/resrep13939.10.

2 Andrzej Górbiel, *Międzynarodowe prawo kosmicznev* (Tr. *International Space Law*) (Warsaw, 1985), 10–11.

3 Von der Dunk (n1) 1.

4 COPUOS, 'Space Law', www.unoosa.gov/oosa/en/ourwork/spacelaw/index.html; *See further* von der Dunk, *Advanced Introduction* (n1).

 | DOI:10.1163/9789004542860_006

relationships between States, forming a branch of international public law ('the law of nations' or *ius gentium*).[5]

First, we will place the international space law regime in its historical context, with the contributions of the Polish thinkers and inventors. Next, the sources of international space law will be reviewed in the context of their applicability in the Polish legal system. The substantial analysis of this Chapter will be limited to the 'core' of international space law regime, *the corpus iuris spatialis internationalis,* which primarily includes five international treaties applicable to basically all space activities as well as the non-binding UN Resolutions.[6] Other international agreements, intergovernmental organizations, and multinational or bilateral agreements affecting space activities, to which Poland is a party, will be noted and expanded in some cases in the final section.

1.1 *Polish Contributions to Early Explorations*

While human interest in space research and observation predates the modern era, space law is a recent body of law that started with visionary concepts and theories of early 20th century legal scholars, philosophers, inventors, thinkers, and intellectual enthusiasts who propagated the idea that outer space (or area 'beyond airspace') was a different region with distinct physical characteristics and advocated for its separate governance, free of and unrestrained by the considerations of sovereignty over the airspace.[7] In addition to early discoveries and revolutionary works of such scientists as Nicolaus Copernicus and

5 It should be noted that the Roman notion of *ius gentium* (common to all mankind) was different than its modern meaning as it regulated relationships between private persons – Roman citizens and foreigners (*peregrines*). The founder of international law, famous Dutch scholar Hugo Grotius (1583–1645) had understood *ius gentium* as law regulating affairs among independent states, but he did not introduce the term international law. English professor Richard Zouche (1550–1660) used the term *ius inter gentes* (law between peoples) to differentiate it from *ius gentium*, while English jurist and philosopher Jeremy Bentham (1748–1832), the contemporary of the French revolution, was the first scholar to introduce the term 'international law.' Genc Trnavci, 'The Meaning and Scope of the Law of Nations in the Context of the Alien Tort Claims Act and International Law,' Penn Law: Legal Scholarshipo Repository (2014) 199–206. Also See Remigius Bierzanek and Janusz Symonides, *Prawo Miedzynarodowe Publiczne* (Tr. International Public Law) (Wolters Kluwer, Warsaw 2004) 19.

6 Von der Dunk (n1) 8.

7 Stephen Doyle, 'A Concise History of Space Law' in New Perspectives On Space Law: The Proceedings Of the 53rd Iisl Colloquium On the Law of Outer Space: Young Scholar's Session 1, Sundahl M J and Gopalakrishnan V eds, (Int'l. Inst. Space L. 2011) 1, https://iislweb.org/docs/NewPerspectivesonSpaceLaw.pdf; Also See Francis Lyall and Paul B. Larsen, *Space Law: A Treatise*(Ashgate, 2009) 7. Notable early dissenter should be noted, the Russian E. Korovin, (1933) argued in favor of state sovereignty over airspace, to extend indefinitely on the grounds of safety and military security. Ibid. 6.

Jan Heweliusz in the 16th and 17th centuries, Polish scientists and scholarly contributions to the area of space law and technologies should also be noted.[8] Polish scholars, including Jerzy Sztucki[9] and Andrzej Górbiel[10] also considered the legal aspects of extra-atmospheric flights, the branch of international law's theory systems, and the existence and functioning of outer space.

The onset of the Space Age was closely tied to the intense rivalry between the United States and the former Soviet Union, two superpowers that had already been entrenched in the Cold War, entering in a space race. As the international timeline of early explorations and developments portrays (Table 3), it was marked by such milestones as the first launch of the artificial satellite, *Sputnik-1* (the Soviet Union in 1957), and the first humans on the moon (the United States in 1969).[11]

Polish interest in space exploration dates to 1954 when the Polish Astronautical Society was admitted to the International Astronautical Federation. At the beginning of the Space Era, Poland organized two important world events: the COSPAR General Assembly was held in Warsaw in 1963, and the International Astronautical Congress in 1964. Starting in 1966, Poland became involved in international cooperation in the field of research and use of outer space with the former Soviet Union, resulting in designing and launching more than 200 sounding rockets – *Meteor,* from which one reached the so-called Kármán line.[12] On 19 April 1973, the first Polish scientific instrument (radiospectrograph) was launched into space onboard the *Kopernik-500* satellite (also known as *Interkosmos-9*). On 29 September 1976, the Space Research Center of the Polish Academy of Sciences was established as a research unit focusing on space research and the development of space technologies. On 27 June 27 1978, the first (and so far the only) Polish cosmonaut, Mirosław Hermaszewski, conducted medical and material science experiments and

8 M. Kopernik, J. Heweliusz, K. Siemianowicz, I. Łukasiewicz, K. S. Olszewski, Z. Wróblewski, whose works contributed to the development of the space sector to a large extent, and their research was used for the construction of, among others, the Russian Sputnik I rocket carried out into orbit around the Earth.

9 He published the work, *Legal problems of the cosmos*, published in 1965.

10 He published the *International Space Law*, published by PWN in 1985.

11 Peter Jankowitsch, 'The background and history of space law' Frans G. von der Dunk with Fabio Tronchetti, eds, *Handbook of Space Law* (Edward Elgar Pub, 2015) 1 et seq.

12 The so called 'Kármán line' or 'von Karman line' is commonly but inaccurately referred to as boundary between airspace outer space at 100 km (62 miles), as recognized by FAI (World Air Sports Federation) for record setting purposes. For discussion on how this alleged boundary line was misconstrued, see Chapter 3 of this book; Also See Thomas Gangale, 'The Non Karman Line: An Urban Legend of the Space Age' 41 J of SP 2017, vol 2, 151.

TABLE 3 Timeline of early exploration and developments (1957–1969)[a]

1957	The first artificial satellite, *Sputnik-1*, launched into Earth's orbit (USSR). First animal (the dog Laika) orbits the Earth (USSR). UNGA Res 1348 – first resolution related to outer space 'Question of the Peaceful Use of Outer Space.'[b]
1958	The 18-member ad hoc UN COPUOS was established to discuss the scientific and legal aspects of the exploration and use of outer space.
1959	First spacecraft to reach escape velocity and orbit the Sun – *Luna-1* (USSR). First pictures of the never-before-seen far side of the moon by the space probe *Luna-3* (USSR). UNGA Res 1472 – established a 24-member permanent UN COPUOS.[c]
1960	First successful weather/earth observation satellite launched – TIROS-1 (USA).
1961	First manned spaceflight – cosmonaut Yuri Gagarin orbits the Earth in *Vostok 1* (USSR). A few weeks later, astronauts Alan B. Shepherd and Virgil Grissom (USA) made short ballistic journeys. UNGA Res 1721 – increased COPUOS to 28 members.[d] UNGA Res 1721B – established first UN register of space objects.[e]
1962	UNGA Res 1802 International Cooperation in Outer Space.[f]
1963	First woman to orbit the Earth – cosmonaut Valentina Tereshkova (USSR). UNGA Res 1962 (XVIII) Declaration of Legal Principles – first legal principles governing outer space adopted.[g]
1964	First geostationary satellite launched – *Syncome-3* (USA).
1965	First space walk by cosmonaut Alexei Leonov (USSR) in March, followed by Edward E. White III (USA) in June.
1966	First probe to land on the moon – *Luna-9* (USSR). First probe to reach Venus – *Venera-3* (USSR).
1967	First international treaty on outer space (the Outer Space Treaty) signed (entered into force on October 10, 1967).[h] First human fatalities – Virgin Grissom, Edward White & Roger Chaffee (USA) while undergoing tests for *Apollo* flights; Vladimir Komarov in *Soyuz 1* parachute-failure after completing the mission (USSR).

TABLE 3 Timeline of early exploration and developments (1957–1969) (*cont.*)

1968	Rescue and Return Agreement signed (entered into force December 3, 1968).[i]
	First UNISPACE conference on outer space.
	First humans to witness Earthrise – the crew of *Apollo 8* (USA).
1969	First spacecraft docking – *Soyuz 4* and *Soyuz 5* (USSR).
	First humans on the Moon, astronauts Neil Armstrong & Edwin Aldrin of Apollo 11 (USA).

a A Timeline of the Exploration and Peaceful Use of Outer Space, www.unoosa.org.
b UNGA Res 1348, Question of the Peaceful Use of Outer Space, 13 December 1958, UN Doc. RES 1348(XIII)
c UNGA Res 1472, International Co-operation in the Peaceful Uses of Outer Space, 12 December 1959, UN Doc RES 1472(XIV).
d UNGA Res 1721, International Co-operation in the Peaceful Uses of Outer Space, 20 December 1959, UN Doc RES 1721(XVI).
e Ibid.
f UNGA Res 1802, International Co-operation in the Peaceful Uses of Outer Space, 14 December 1962, UN Doc RES 1802(XVII).
g UNGA Res 1962, Declaration of Legal Principles Governing the Activities of States in the Exploration and Use of Outer Space, 13 December 1963, UN Doc. RES 1963 (XVIII).
h Treaty on Principles Governing the Activities of States in the Exploration and Use of Outer Space, Including the Moon and Other Celestial Bodies (Outer Space Treaty or OST) 27 January 1967, 610 UNTS 205, Journal of Laws of 1968, No 14, item 82.
i Agreement on the Rescue of Astronauts, the Return of Astronauts and the Return of Objects Launched Into Outer Space (Rescue Agreement), 22 April 1968, 672 UNTS 119 Journal of Laws of 1969, No 15, item 110.

Earth observation during his flight onboard the *Salut-6* space station, making Poland the fourth nation after the Soviet Union, the United States, and Czechoslovakia, to send its citizen to space.

1.2 *Post-Cold War Developments*

After 1989, with the demise of communism and Poland's successful political and economic transition to democracy, it was finally possible to develop cooperation with countries outside the (former) Eastern Bloc. In 1994, Poland signed an agreement with the European Space Agency (ESA) on cooperation in the peaceful use of outer space, extended in 2002.[13] On its basis, Polish

13 Agreement between the European Space Agency and the Government of the Republic of Poland concerning space cooperation for peaceful purposes, signed Paris, 28 January 1994.

entities could participate in ESA's scientific programs, resulting in Polish devices appearing on most of the flagship research missions (Cassini– Huygens, Integral, Mars Express, Rosetta, Venus Express, and Herschel). The beginning of the 21st century brought an intensification of cooperation with ESA. In 2007, the Agreement on a European Cooperating State (PECS)-3 was signed with ESA.[14] Thanks to creating this mechanism, 45 projects were financed by Polish companies, research institutions, and universities in cooperation with ESA. Simultaneously, the number, quality, and advancement of products and services using the satellite techniques offered by the Polish companies, have significantly increased.

Two Polish satellites of the BRITE Constellation, *LEM* (launched in 2012) and *Heweliusz* (launched in 2013), together with similar satellites built by Austria and Canada, were launched to study the dynamics of bright stars. In 2018, CubeSat PW-Sat2, the second satellite created by Polish students (at the Faculty of Power and Aeronautical Engineering of the Warsaw University of Technology) was sent into orbit to study its own innovative deorbiting system consisting of a sail with the surface area of 4 m^2.[15] In 2019, Światowid – the first Polish commercial satellite, constructed by SatRevolution, a Wrocław company, was launched successfully.[16] The Institute of Aviation in Poland is

14 The European Cooperating State Agreement between the European Space Agency and the Government of the Republic of Poland, done in Warsaw on 27 April 2007, and ratified by Poland on 28 March 2008, entered into force on 26 April 2008, Journal of Laws of 2008 No 154, item 959.

15 The satellite was carried to earth's orbit aboard the Falcon 9 rocket on December 3, 2018. The PW-Sat 2 was registered by Poland with the UN Office for Outer Space Affairs on 16 January 2019; see ST/SG/SER.E/874; other registrations by Poland in the UN register can be found at https://www.unoosa.org/oosa/en/spaceobjectregister/submissions/poland.html. During the primary part of the mission, all satellite subsystems were tested successfully: the power supply system, the communication system, the onboard computer, the cameras, as well as the sun and space radiation sensor. Over that period, PW-Sat2 also took the first Polish photograph from a satellite. After 813 days, PW-Sat2 deorbited on February 23, 2021. The satellite burnt up completely in the earth's atmosphere. Currently, over 20 students specializing in various engineering fields are working to get ready PW-Sat3 for launch in 2023. See Jakub Olesz, 'Stay tuned, PW-Sat3 is coming!' (5 October 2021) https://pw-sat.pl/en/whats-next-pw-sat3/.

16 The Światowid satellite was launched on April 17, 2019, on board the Cygnus NG-11 unmanned spacecraft providing supplies for the International Space Station. Together with it, another Polish KRAKsat satellite was launched into orbit, built in cooperation with SatRevolution and the AGH University of Science and Technology. The ship with the Światowid satellite on board reached the International Space Station on April 19 and moored to the Unity module. Światowid was released into space from the Japanese module of the Kibō International Space Station on July 3, 2019. After its release, the satellite began broadcasting signals that were picked up by amateur radio ground stations on the

also leading in developing a new green propellant and rocket engines for small satellites and small rocket launchers.

1.3 *Polish Contributions to the Legal Framework for Activities in Space*

Manfred Lachs, a distinguished Polish legal scholar, Judge of the International Court of Justice (1967–1993), and one of the instrumental contributors to the United Nation's space treaties, remarked that: '[f]rom the very day his instruments entered outer space, man was faced with a range of important problems, which have intensified and proliferated with the speedy development of science and technology. The response of law became an urgent necessity.'[17]

In addition to humankind's first exploits in outer space, the decade of the 1960s witnessed the initiation and substantial successes of the United Nation's Committee on the Peaceful Uses of Outer Space (COPUOS) as the primary forum for negotiating and drafting applicable legally binding commitments in the form of multilateral treaties regulating outer space activities. COPUOS was first established in 1958 as an *ad hoc* Committee of the General Assembly with 18 Member States and made permanent with 24 States as members a year later.[18] Secretarial and administrative assistance to COPUOS is provided by the Office of Outer Space Affairs (OOSA) since 1993 relocated to the UN Office in Vienna. The Committee has two subsidiary bodies: the Scientific and Technical Subcommittee, and the Legal Subcommittee, both established in 1961. It is a unique body of the United Nations in which there is no voting, and all decisions are taken by consensus, that is in the absence of objections.[19] The Committee was tasked with reviewing international cooperation in peaceful uses of outer space, studying space-related activities that could be undertaken by the United Nations, encouraging space research programs, and studying legal problems arising from the exploration of outer space. The Committee was instrumental in creating five space treaties and many recommendations and guidelines, as discussed in the following Section. Over the years, its membership has increased to its present 102 (as of 2022) to equitably represent the developed and developing countries' interests and provide suitable geographic

same day. From the beginning of the mission, the satellite has been taking and transmitting images of the earth's surface.

17 Manfred Lachs, *The Law of Outer Space: An Experience in Contemporary Law-Making* (1979) xvii.

18 UNGA Res 1348 (n13).

19 Doyle (n 7) 8.

world coverage.[20] At the same time, as the size of COPUOS increased, obtaining consensus became substantially more difficult.

Poland has always supported the creation of a legal framework for the activities of States in space. Since the inception of COPUOS in 1959, Professor Manfred Lachs – then the director of the Legal and Treaty Department of the Ministry of Foreign Affairs in Poland – strove to create a special UN body for space law.[21] As Poland's representative, Manfred Lachs became the first chairman of the Legal Subcommittee of COPUOS in 1962 (until 1966). Under his chairmanship, the Declaration of Legal Principles was adopted in 1963,[22] which was the immediate precursor to the Outer Space Treaty.[23] As Manfred Lachs remarked concerning the Declaration, 'the principles it mentions do not constitute a closed chapter. After adopting this declaration, some of the proposals and suggestions already made and some others that may be made in the future will require further consideration and negotiations.'[24] The 1963 Declaration, developed by the Sub-committee headed by the Polish diplomats, also inspired other basic space treaties, particularly the 1968 Rescue Agreement and the 1972 Liability Convention.[25]

After Ambassador Lachs ceased his function in connection with an appointment as a judge of the International Court of Justice, the next Chairman of the Legal Subcommittee of COPUOS (for 16 years) was also a Pole – Ambassador

20 UNGA Res 76/76, International Co-operation in the Peaceful Uses of Outer Space, 9 December 2021, UN Doc A/RES/76/76.

21 Andrzej Misztal and Łukasz Kułaga, 'Znaczenie prawa kosmicznego w polskiej polityce zagranicznej' (Tr. 'The importance of space law in Polish foreign policy') in Katarzyna Myszona-Kostrzewa, ed, *Kosmos w prawie i polityce, Prawo i polityka w Kosmosie* (Tr. *Kosmos in law and politics, law and politics in space*) (Warsaw 2017); Marcin Nowacki, 'Działalność dyplomatyczna profesora Manfreda Lachsa' (Tr. 'Diplomatic activity of Professor Manfred Lachs') in Zdzislaw Galicki et alia, eds, *Manfred Lachs – wybitny pranik swiata* (Tr. *Manfred Lachs – an outstanding world lawyer*) (Warsaw, 2011) 59.

22 UNGA Res 1962 (n18).

23 Renata Szafarz, 'Manfred Lachs – światowej sławy uczony, sędzia i patron' (Tr. 'Manfred Lachs – world-famous scientist, judge and patron') in Galicki, *Manfred Lachs* (n30) 2.

24 Minutes of the COPUOS meeting of 22 November 1963, see: Jerzy Sztucki, *Problemy Prawne Kosmosu* (Tr. *Legal Problems of the Cosmos*) (Polish Institute of International Affairs, 1965) 109.

25 Rescue Agreement (Table 3), Convention on International Liability for Damage Caused by Space Objects, 29 March 1972, 961 UNTS 187 (Liability Convention); Łukasz Kułaga, 'Współczesne tendencje regulacyjne międzynarodowego prawa kosmicznego' (Tr.'Contemporary regulatory tendencies of international space law') Kwartalnik Prawa Publicznych, No 4 (2007) 49–57; Łukasz Kułaga, 'Odpowiedzialność międzynarodowa za szkody wyrządzone przez obiekty kosmiczne' (Tr. 'Liability for damages caused by space objects') in Galicki, *Manfred Lachs* (n30), 447–466.

Eugeniusz Wyzner.[26] Poland's continued involvement at the COPUOS forum also meant that relatively quickly – still in the 1970s – Poland became a signatory and legally bound by all but one of the core space treaties (the Moon Agreement being the exception).[27]

1.4 *The Development of Space Law: Four Stages*

According to Stephen Doyle, the development of space law during the 20th century evolved in four interrelated phases: the first phase established early concepts of space law before Sputnik's first launch (1910–1957); the second phase clarified and adopted basic law applicable to exploration and uses of outer space (1957–1966); the third phase involved the expanding uses of space and national and international laws and regulations to manage such uses (a continuing process since 1957).[28] Finally, the fourth phase pertains to the regulation of extra-terrestrial human settlements and activities, which has only started to be addressed in recent years.[29]

Frans von der Dunk likewise described the development of the International Space Law legal regime as four distinct yet overlapping phases, by emphasizing the role of COPUOS as the main venue for creating the international space legal regime and focusing on the legal character of the resulting regulations.[30]

The first phase encompassed the early UN Declarations and Resolutions, such as Resolution 1721 (XVI) of 1961[31] positing the principles of international cooperation in the peaceful uses of outer space, and of registration with the United Nations of any space object launched into outer space, and Resolution 1962 (XVIII) of 1963,[32] hailed as the Principles Declaration as it achieved a blueprint for an all-encompassing legal regime for outer space. While the early resolutions were considered to have considerable political and moral force, they were legally non-binding – although the principles established therein arguably formed the rules of customary international law, thus binding on all nations.[33]

26 Eugeniusz Wyzner, 'Manfred Lachs – Profesor, Szef, Mentor i Przyjaciel' (Tr.Manfred Lachs – Professor, Boss, Mentor and Friend), in Galicki *Manfred Lachs* (n30) 1.

27 The Agreement Governing the Activities of States on the Moon and Other Celestial Bodies, 5 December 1979, 1363 UNTS 3 (Moon Agreement).

28 Doyle (n7) 1.

29 Ibid.

30 Frans von der Dunk, 'International Space Law' Von der Dunk, *Handbook* (n11) 38.

31 UNGA Res 1721 (n15).

32 UNGA Res 1962 (n18).

33 Von der Dunk, International Space (n39).

The second phase was termed the golden age of UN space law treaty-making, which commenced with the Outer Space Treaty of 1967, and followed with four more conventions – the 1968 Rescue Agreement, 1972 Liability Convention, 1974 Registration Convention, and 1979 Moon Agreement.[34] These five treaties created the foundational framework of a legal regime that governs space activities, the *corpus juris spatialis internationalis*, which is characterized by, *inter alia*, the freedom of exploration and use, the non-appropriation of outer space by any one country, partial arms control, liability for damage caused by space objects, the safety and rescue of spacecraft and astronauts, the prevention of harmful interference with space activities and the environment, the notification and registration of space activities, and the settlement of disputes. Each of the treaties underlines the notion that space exploration and international cooperation should be peaceful and conducted for the common interest and benefit of all States and all humanity.

In addition to the binding nature of treaty obligations on their signatories,[35] some of the obligations included in the space treaties are considered to have transformed into customary law with *erga omnes* effects – obligations towards the international community as a whole, designed to protect the international community's interest and common values and which would authorize invoking State responsibility without proving injury in case of their breach.[36]

In this context, only the first four of the space treaties provide the real inner core of the governing space law as they have been widely ratified and, in most cases and respects, considered to constitute customary international law.[37] In contrast, the Moon Agreement, the fifth UN space treaty to enter into force,

34 Ibid, Rescue Agreement (n20), Liability Convention (n34), Convention on Registration of Objects Launched into Outer Space, 12 November 1974, 1023 UNTS 15 (Registration Convention), and Moon Agreement (n32) respectively.

35 States explicitly consent to their terms by signing these contracts, Vienna Convention on the Law of Treaties (VCLT), 23 May 1969, 1155 UNTS 331, Article 11. For the treaty to come into legal force, in addition to the signing, the signatory State must also ratify and enact into its national law (depending on the terms of the Treaty), VCLT arts 2(1)(b), 14; See: Ram S. Jakhu and Joseph N. Pelton, eds, *Global Space Governance: An International Study* (Springer, 2017) 21.

36 Ibid 29, Lachs, (n 26), Cassandra Steel, 'Sources and law-making processes relating to space activities' in Ram S. Jakhu and Paul S. Dempsey, eds, *Routledge Handbook of Space Law* (Routledge, 2017) 7, International Law Commission (ILC), Draft Articles on Responsibility of States for Internationally Wrongful Acts (Draft Articles), Supplement No 10 (A/56/10), chp. IV.E.1 (2001), Article 42(a). For discussion on the limited scope of the erga omnes, see: Ioannis Prezas, 'A bilateral treaty developing legal effects erga omnes? Reflections on the Prespa Agreement between Greece and North Macedonia settling the name dispute' 65 QIL Zoom-in (2020) 33.

37 Von der Dunk, *Advanced Introduction* (n1).

is ratified marginally (and by that token of limited legal impact). The Moon Agreement's lack of success is mostly related to the controversial designation of the moon (and other celestial bodies within solar system except for the Earth) as the 'common heritage of mankind' and the uncertain consequences thereof for prospective mineral exploitation.[38]

With no political will at the international level to conclude any more space law treaties since 1979, the efforts to further develop international space law have continued at the COPUOS level by means of essentially non-binding UN Declarations and Resolutions (the third phase).[39] The use of formally non-binding principles, guidelines, and industry practices, has also been described as a process of 'soft law.'[40]

Von der Dunk described the final, fourth phase of space law development as overlapping with the other phases but forming a different layer of space activities outside of the COPUOS' purview and associated with the entrance of private actors into the space arena.[41] During the early phases of exploration, States were the main spacefaring actors – space activities were directed by the governments, financed with public funds, and conducted primarily by the military. Starting as early as the 1970s, several operational, inter-governmental organizations (IGOs) have emerged at international or regional levels, at first mainly in the area of telecommunications, such as INTELSAT, INMARSAT, EUTELSAT, INTERSPUTNIK, or ARABSAT, which gradually commercialized and privatized, and finally, transformed into private operators.[42] In addition to the operational IGOs, the space activities and space law *lato sensu* have been affected by many international and regional international organizations, multilateral and bilateral agreements (to include public-private partnerships, private aspects via contract, or MOUs), and many other international and regional

38 Von der Dunk, International Space Law (n39) 103.

39 Ibid.

40 The issue of the presence of "soft" law in the Polish system of legal sources means the closed catalog of sources of universally binding law does not exclude the existence of soft law norms, not only those derived from international or community law. A special example of such norms in Poland may be the codes of professional ethics which, although they do not constitute legally binding norms, undoubtedly affect the legal position of persons, not only representing a given profession (which would be a proof of their nature similar to domestic law), but also indirectly for other entities. They constitute normative acts created on the basis of the performance of functions assigned to the state administration and from this point of view they may be subject to review by the Polish Constitutional Tribunal.

41 Von Der Dunk, International Space (n39) 107.

42 Ibid 107–112, 282–300; Also See Jakhu & Pelton (n44) 88–89.

initiatives (such as COSPAS-SARSAT).[43] A more detailed overview of such entities and the related agreements to which Poland is a party to is presented in Section 4.

Finally, the 21st century's advances in small satellite platforms, miniaturization of instruments, and the availability of low-cost launches for small satellites, significantly lowered the costs of entry into the space sector and changed the nature of the activities, broadly termed as NewSpace. This newest phenomenon transformed the space sector from a few State actors to a global space economy with a rapidly growing number of spacefaring States, organizations, and especially private entities. In this new era of space activities, national governance of space activities has become necessary to ensure compliance with international treaty obligations and foster the development of the private space sector.[44]

2 Space Law as Part of Public International Law and Its Implementation in the Polish Legal System

International space law is part of ordinary public international law and shares in its sources.[45] Although the international legal order lacks any central mechanisms, the UN Charter and the Statute of the International Court of Justice (ICJ)[46] are both considered constitutive documents, with the ICJ being the primary judicial organ.[47] Article 38(1) of the Statute of the ICJ lists sources applicable to disputes under international law:

> Article 38 (1). The Court, whose function is to decide in accordance with international law such disputes as are submitted to it, shall apply: (a.) international conventions, whether general or particular, establishing rules expressly recognized by the contesting States; (b.) international custom, as evidence of a general practice accepted as law; (c.) the general principles of law recognized by civilized nations; (d.) subject to the provisions of Article 59, judicial decisions, and the teachings of the most

43 Ibid.

44 Jakhu and Pelton (n44) 88–89.

45 Lyall and Larsen (n 7) 39.

46 United Nations, Charter of the United Nations, 24 October 1945, 1 UNTS XVI (UN Charter); United Nations, Statute of the International Court of Justice, 18 April 1946.

47 Steel (n45) 5.

> highly qualified publicists of the various nations as subsidiary means for the determination of rules of law.

While Article 38(1) provides the foundation and a reference point, there is a growing acceptance of the view that it is not an exhaustive list and that the sources of international law may include elements not enumerated therein.[48] Space law is an area in which this may be particularly true, as evidenced by the continuing question of the legal weight or significance of the various UN Resolutions on Principles on space law matters.[49] Space law has a rich literature on the policy of application in many countries, which is of constant interest to UN bodies and other international organizations dealing with space issues.[50] Although the ICJ is recognized *de facto* as authoritatively clarifying and even creating international law, to date, there have been no ICJ decisions that would directly involve the contentious application of the space treaties.[51] Indirectly, however, judicial decisions in other areas of international law, such as environmental law, the law on the use of force, the law of armed conflict, and others that might apply to space activities are likewise of importance to the space law regime.[52]

International space law is essentially conventional in nature as treaties or conventions are considered the primary, or the strongest, source of law listed in Article 38 of the Statute of the ICJ.[53] While international law is created independently of any domestic legal system, its legal effect, or how it applies

48 Ibid 40. See also Israr Khan, 'Article 38 of the International Court of Justice Statute: A Complete Reference Point for the Sources of International Law?' The New Jurist (5 April 2019). https://newjurist.com/article-38-of-the-statute-of-the-international-court-of-justice.html#:~:text=Article%2038(1)of%20the,principles%20recognized%20by%20civilized%20nations.

49 Lyall and Larsen (n 7) 41.

50 Marek Żylicz, 'O początkach międzynarodowego prawa kosmicznego' (Tr. On the beginnings of international space law) in Zdzislaw Galicki, *et alia*, eds, *Wykorzystanie Przestrzeni Kosmicznej Świat-Europa-Polska* (Tr. *The Use Of Outer Space-World-Europe-Poland*) (Warsaw, 2010) 15.

51 Steel (n45) 11. The closest potential case was following a nuclear-powered USSR satellite; the Cosmos 954 satellite failed and disintegrated over Canadian territory in 1977, resulting in an expansive nuclear cleanup operation that ultimately was settled out of court.

52 Ibid.

53 Ibid 5. Ram S. Jakhu and Steven Freeman, *The Sources of International Space Law* (Beijing, 2013) 463. Conventions are Treaties negotiated by States, including Agreements, Arrangements, Memoranda of Understanding (MOUs), Exchange of Letters, Contracts, etc. See VCLT (n44) Article 1.

within a State, depends on that State's approach to international obligations.[54] Traditionally, two theories or doctrines have been used to describe the interaction between international law and domestic (internal) laws: monism – which sees international law and domestic law as part of one and the same legal system, with either international law at the top of a hierarchy (monism with primacy of international law- also called Kelsenian monism),[55] or conversely, monism with primacy of domestic law; and dualism – which sees international law and domestic law as separate legal systems where it is for each State to determine how international rules are applied at the national level.[56] According to monism, international law is automatically and directly incorporated into national law, whereas dualism requires implementation of international law into an internal norm. In reality, States adopt approaches that may include a mix of the two, so it depends on a case-by-case basis how States apply international law domestically.

While opining on the relationship between domestic and the European Union Law, the Polish Constitutional Tribunal remarked that 'the very conception and the model of European Law, have created a new situation, where there are two autonomous legal systems simultaneously in effect. Their mutual interrelation cannot be described comprehensively by the traditional theories of monism and dualist, in the alignment: domestic-international law.'[57]

Some scholars question the continued validity or usefulness of these 19th century-derived theories when applied to the contemporary legal systems, which have evolved with the gradual elaboration of international law, the processes of globalization and, above all, the inclusion of positive constitutional

54 Patrick Butchard, 'Principles of International Law' House of Commons Library, Briefing Paper 9010 (21 September 2020) 3, https://researchbriefings.files.parliament.uk/documents/CBP-9010/CBP-9010.pdf; 26–27.

55 After Hans Kelsen, one of its most preeminent proponents. See Bierzanek and Symonides (n5) 26.

56 Ibid, 27. It should be noted that the conception of monism with domestic law primacy was taken to its extreme by the National Socialist doctrine of Nazi Germany in following the theories of Georg Wilhelm Friedrich Hegel who denied the existence of the international community as a reality of its own and therefore its capacity to have a law of its own; consequently, Hegel declared international law to be nothing else than domestic law *ad extra* (as compared to ordinary domestic law that takes effects *ad intra*) and, such, it was totally dependent on the will of the State. See Heribert Franz Koeck, 'Alfred Verdross – A Visionary of Contemporary Doctrine and Practice of International Law' Lecture delivered at the Faculty of Law and Administration of the Nicolaus Copernicus University of Toruń on 13 December 2010, Studia Iuridica Toruniensia VIII, 18–20.

57 Judgment of 11.5.2005, K18/04, para 6.3.

provisions on the role of international law within domestic systems.[58] Such constitutional norms are also present in Poland, and they include: the principle of respecting international law (article 9 of the Constitution), the principle of the democratic State ruled by law (Article 2) and Article 91(1), stating that:

> After promulgation thereof in the Official Journal of Laws of the Republic of Poland (*Dziennik Ustaw*), a ratified international agreement shall constitute part of the domestic legal order and shall be applied directly, unless its application depends on the enactment of a statute.[59]

The Constitutional Tribunal, in the judgment regarding the European arrest warrant (EAW judgment) emphasized the validity of the interpretation of Article 9 of the Constitution as 'reflecting the international legal principle of *pacta sunt servanda*.'[60] The requirement of implementation of international agreements in the Polish legal system was reiterated by the Supreme Administrative Court in the judgment of 29 December 1999, providing that 'the binding force of the treaty on the grounds of the international law is insufficient for its application by the domestic court.'[61]

Moreover, the implementation requirement is, at times, defined directly in some international agreements.[62] Such is the case which the five core space law treaties, which will be discussed in the following Section 3.[63] Poland is a signatory to all core space law treaties, except for the Moon Agreement. In addition, there are other treaties and agreements relevant to space activities, particularly those in the area of disarmament and telecommunication law, as well numerous inter-governmental organizations (IGOs) and other initiatives (to include public-private partnerships and increasingly private entities), established internationally or regionally, or space-related activities regulated

58 Armin von Bogdandy, 'Pluralism, direct effect, and the ultimate say: On the relationship between international and domestic constitutional law,' Int'l J of Con Law 3 no 3 and 4 (Oxford University Press, 2008) 399–400.

59 Constitution of the Republic of Poland of 2 April 1997, Dz.U. 1997 nr 78 poz. 483.

60 Judgment of 27.4.2005, P1/05, para 5.3, para 5.4. See Łukasz Kułaga, 'The Implementation of International Agreements in the Polish Legal System. The Selected Aspets of Practice in Recent Two Decades,' 9 Polish Rev of Int'l and Eur Law 1 (2020) 130.

61 Judgement of 29.12.1999, ISA/Po 3057/98, ONSA 2001, no 1, item 34, 331. 129.

62 Kulaga (n69) 128.

63 Outer Space Treaty (n19) article XIV (2) provides: 'This Treaty shall be subject to ratification by signatory Sates. Instruments of ratification and instruments of accession shall be deposited with the Governments (...) which are hereby designated the Depositary Governments.' The provisions to the same effect are included in the Registration Convention, Liability Convention, Rescue Agreement and Moon Agreement.

through multilateral and bilateral agreements (private aspects via contract, or MOUS), which will presented in Section 4 infra.

3 The Framework of Public International Space Law (*corpus juris spatialis internationalis*)

The core of the *corpus iuris spatialis internationalis* is generally viewed as consisting of five treaties drafted under the auspices the United Nations, notably its Committee on the Peaceful Uses of Outer Space (COPUOS), and eight key UN General Assembly Resolutions.[64]

3.1 *Space Treaties*

3.1.1 The 1967 Outer Space Treaty

The Treaty on Principles Governing the Activities of States in the Exploration and Use of Outer Space, including the Moon and Other Celestial Bodies,[65] was considered by the COPUOS Legal Subcommittee in 1966, adopted by the General Assembly on 19 December 1966, in its Resolution 2222 (XXI), opened for signature on 27 January 1967, and entered into force on 10 October 1967. On the same day, Poland signed (27 January 1967), and it entered into force on 22 December 1967.

The Outer Space Treaty has been recognized as one of the most successful multilateral international treaties ever promulgated.[66] As of 1 January 2022, it was accepted by 135 States (with 112 ratifications, 23 signature-only), which constitute a large majority of the world's nation-States, including all of the world spacefaring and space-capable States. The Treaty was based mainly on the non-binding UN General Assembly Resolution 1962, the Principles

64 Von der Dunk, *Advanced Intro* (n1) 14.

65 Outer Space Treaty (n19).

66 Joanne I. Gabrynowicz, 'The Outer Space Treaty and Enhancing Space Security' United Nations Institute for Disarmament Research, Building the Architecture for Sustainable Space Security, Conference Report 30–31 March 2006, UNIDIR/2006/17. It is interesting to note that owing to the preliminary discussions during the negotiations of the 1963 Declaration and the conclusion thereof, it became easier to reach agreement on fundamental principles in the draft Treaty, whereas some more specific questions relating to the second category of topics led to controversial and sometimes lengthy discussions. A number of such issues were reconciled only during the final stages of the negotiations by informal consultations between the representatives of the two major space powers with the participation of United Nations Secretary-General U Thant, the COPUOS Chairman, Kurt Waldheim of Austria, and the Chairman of the COPUOS Legal Subcommittee, Manfred Lachs of Poland.

Declaration.[67] The Outer Space Treaty contains the following fundamental legal principles governing space activities:

- '[t]he exploration and use of outer space [...] shall be carried out for the benefit and in the interests of all countries [...] and shall be the province of all mankind.'[68]
- '[o]uter space [...] shall be free for exploration and use by all States;'[69]
- '[o]uter space [...] is not subject to national appropriation by claim of sovereignty, by means of use or occupation, or by any other means;'[70]

67 UNGA Res 1962 (n 18).

68 Outer Space Treaty (n19) Article I provides 'common interest' and 'province of mankind' principles. This notion reiterates that in conducting space activities, one must take those interests into consideration. Cf. 'Common heritage of mankind' principle under the Moon Agreement.

69 Ibid, para 2 provides for the 'freedom principle': to explore and use outer space, and of scientific investigation. Freedom to use – includes different types of human activities, which may or may not be aimed at gaining economic profit. Questionable whether that freedom covers only activities that are taking place in outer-space or whether it is also extended to space-related activities such as the construction of satellites or even when the object is transiting through air space on its way to outer space. See: Bin Cheng, 'Revisited: International Responsibility, National Activities, and the Appropriate State' 27 J of SL (1998) at 19; Frans von der Dunk, *Private Enterprise and Public Interest in the European 'Spacescape'* (Leiden 1998) 13; H.A. Wassenbergh, 'An International Institutional Framework for Private Space Activities' XXIII Annals of A&SL 529 (1997) 533. The term 'freedom' in general international law indicates that all entities entitled to partake in those freedoms may do so without asking for permission from other States or international entities. *France v. Turkey,* PCIJ, A/10, 18. This is not an absolute freedom. In Lachs' opinion, 'there can be no doubt that States' freedom of action in outer space or on celestial bodies is neither unlimited, absolute, or unqualified, but is determined by the right and interest of other States. Therefore, it can be exercised only to the extent to which as indicated it does not conflict with those rights and interests.' (n26) 117.

70 Outer Space Treaty (n19) Article II espouses the 'non-appropriation principle,' which prohibits States from declaring sovereign or territorial claims over outer space and celestial bodies, thus limiting the principle of freedom. Concerning celestial bodies, the non-appropriation principle is reaffirmed in the Moon Agreement under Article 11. The exact meaning is not clear. It is still subject to further interpretation of whether only the celestial bodies' surface or that what lies underneath (such as resources) is protected by this provision. See Stephan Hobe and Kuan-Wei Chen, 'Legal Status of outer space' in *Routledge Handbook* (n45) 29; Cf Lachs (n 26) 58 (who claims that non-appropriation must be understood as 'including not only sovereign rights but also property rights' thus barring States from establishing proprietary links regarding the new dimension.) This principle was challenged by the 1976 Bogota Declaration, whereby several equatorial States declared their sovereignty over those portions of the geostationary orbit that are above their national territories. These claims have generally been dismissed as contrary to the established principles of international law. See: Ram Jakhu, 'The legal status of the Geostationary Orbit' VII Annals of Air and Space Law (1982) 333 et seq. Generally, the non-appropriation principle prohibits claims to ownership in outer space unless an international regime for

– States 'shall carry on activities [under the Treaty] in accordance with international law, including the Charter of the United Nations, in the interest of maintaining international peace and security and promoting international cooperation and understanding;'[71]
– States shall not 'place in orbit around the Earth any objects carrying nuclear weapons or any other kinds of weapons of mass destruction;'[72]
– '[t]he Moon and other celestial bodies shall be used […] exclusively for peaceful purposes;'[73]
– Astronauts shall be regarded as the envoys of mankind and States 'shall render to them all possible assistance in the event of accident, distress, or emergency landing;'[74]
– States shall 'bear international responsibility for national activities in outer space […] whether such activities are carried out by governmental agencies or non-governmental entities;'[75]

exploitation of the resources is established. (Hobe & Chen, 30). In telecom law, closely related to space law, the allocation of orbital slots in GEO by the ITU represents such a regime for governing the exploitation (use) of scarce resources.

71 Outer Space Treaty (n19) Article III further limits the freedom of action by subjecting space activities to international law and the UN Charter. The principle of cooperation is another fundamental principle in space law, articulated in arts III, IX, and X. No specific definition of the exact scope and meaning of the cooperation principle.

72 Ibid. Article IV limits certain military uses of outer space by specifically prohibiting, among other things, the placement of nuclear weapons or weapons of mass destruction in orbit around the earth and the establishment of military bases and testing of weapons on celestial bodies. The moon and celestial bodies designated 'exclusively for peaceful purposes.' Cf. outer space need only be explored and used for 'peaceful purposes' (Preamble, Article IX). The 'peaceful purposes' is not defined, but the predominant opinion is that peaceful means non-aggressive, signifying that certain military activities are acceptable if exercised lawfully (US position). See: Jakhu, Steer, and Chen, 'Conflicts in Space and the Rule of Law' Space Policy (Spring 2016) available at SSRN https://papers.ssrn.com/sol3/papers.cfm?abstract_id=2722245.

73 Ibid.

74 Outer Space Treaty (n19) Article V was further developed in the Rescue Agreement and the concept of 'rescue and return' of the astronauts in distress.

75 Ibid. Article VI is seen as further limitation to the freedoms set out under Article I by providing for State responsibility in space activities. Only State parties can bear international responsibility for any national outer space activities, both by governmental agencies and non-government or private entities. Private activities in space are allowed, but States must provide authorization and continuing supervision not to revoke their international responsibility. In terms of OST and its foundational provision Article I, any human activity taking place in or intended for space is a space activity, is subject to Article VI requirements. From the launching to the operation and re-entry of a space object, all activities may entail international responsibility. Hobe & Chen, (n 79) 37 .

- 'The activities of non-governmental entities in outer space [...] shall require authorization and continuing supervision by the appropriate State [...];'[76]
- A State 'that launches or procures the launching of an object into outer space,[...] and each State [...] from whose territory or facility an object is launched, is internationally liable for damage [...] by such object or its component parts on the Earth, in air space or in outer space [...];'[77]
- A State 'on whose registry an object launched into outer space is carried shall retain jurisdiction and control over such object, and over any personnel thereof, while in outer space or on a celestial body. Ownership of [such] objects is not affected by their presence in outer space or on a celestial body or by their return to the Earth;'[78]
- States 'shall be guided by the principle of cooperation and mutual assistance and shall conduct all their activities in outer space [...] with due regard to the corresponding interests of all other States;'[79] and
- States 'shall conduct exploration of [outer space, the Moon and other celestial bodies] to avoid their harmful contamination and adverse changes in Earth's environment.'[80]

---

76 Ibid.

77 Outer Space Treaty (n16) Article VII imposes liability for damages caused by a space object on the launching State and does not require any unlawfulness of the activity itself. Private entities are not a subject of international law and are not directly bound by international treaties – Article VII must be read in conjunction with Article VI. Space activities are high-risk activities, and therefore, the international community was aware of the necessity of a strict and clear liability regime. The liability regime was more fully developed with 1972 Lability Convention.

78 Ibid Article VIII further expanded by the Registration Convention.

79 Ibid Article IX embodies the 'cooperation principle' and is the basis for environmental protection of outer space based on the principle of non-interference and due regard to the corresponding interests of other States when conducting space activities. Note: under general international law, the Corfu Channel case is instructive on State responsibility. *Corfu Channel* (*the UK v Albania*) (1949) ICJ Reports 4, 22. The 'due regard' principle also applies to the law of the sea (UNCLOS, Article 87). Another attempt to clarify the meaning and significance of the cooperation principle was undertaken in the 1996 Space Benefits Declaration, which empowers the States to freely determine 'all aspects of their participation in international cooperation in exploring and using outer space on an equitable and mutually acceptable basis,' para 2.

80 Ibid.

3.1.2 The 1968 Rescue Agreement

The Agreement on the Rescue of Astronauts, the Return of Astronauts and the Return of Objects Launched into Outer Space,[81] was considered and negotiated by the COPUOS Legal Subcommittee from 1962 to its adoption by the General Assembly in its Resolution 2345 (XXII) in 1967, opened for signature on 22 April 1968, and entered into force on 3 December 1968. As of 1 January 2022, it was accepted by 122 States (99 ratifications, 23 signature-only). On the same day, Poland signed the treaty on 22 April 1968, and it entered into force on 28 December 1968.[82]

The Agreement, elaborating on Articles V and VIII of the Outer Space Treaty, symbolizes the spirit of cooperation that has existed between spacefaring and non-spacefaring nations even during and since the Cold War; as such, it is one of the more successful instruments in protecting the global public interest.[83] According to the Agreement, States must take all possible steps to rescue and render all necessary assistance to 'the personnel of a spacecraft in the evidence of an accident, distress, emergency, or unintended landing and safely and promptly return them to the launching State.'[84] The Agreement also establishes obligations to share information, to help recover objects collaboratively, and, upon request, aid launching States in recovering space objects and to return such objects to, or hold them for the disposal of, the launching State.[85] While the signatories' intent for the astronauts' safety was clearly expressed, especially in conjunction with Article V of the Outer Space Treaty and its designation of astronauts as 'envoys of mankind,' it is unclear whether the 'rescue and return' obligation would extend to 'space tourists' or other spaceflight participants in the commercial spaceflight context.[86]

3.1.3 The 1972 Liability Convention

The Convention on International Liability for Damage Caused by Space Objects[87] was considered and negotiated by the Legal subcommittee from 1963 to 1972. The Agreement was reached in 1971, and the General Assembly adopted it in its Resolution 2777 (XXVI), opened for signature on 29 March 1972, and entered into force on 1 September 1972. Poland acceded to the

81 Rescue Agreement (Table 3).
82 Journal of Laws of 1969, No 15, item 110.
83 Jakhu and Pelton (n 44) 24.
84 Rescue Agreement (Table 3) Article 428.
85 Ibid Article 6.
86 *See* Lyall and Larsen (n 7) 131.
87 Liability Convention (n 34).

Convention, which became effective on 25 January 1973.[88] As of 1 January 2020, it was accepted by 117 States (98 ratifications, 19 signature-only).

The concept of liability for damage was first included in the Outer Space Treaty, specifically in its Article VII, establishing that a launching State is internationally liable to compensate for damages caused by its space object on Earth, in the air, or outer space.[89] Expanding on this principle, the Liability Convention specified that the launching State's liability to pay compensation for damage caused by its space object is 'absolute,' that is, there is no need to prove any fault, if such damage occurs on the surface of the Earth or in airspace ('to aircraft in flight').[90] For damages caused in space ('elsewhere than on the surface of the Earth'), liability is fault-based ('if fault can be attributed to the launching State or to persons for whom it is responsible'),[91] that is, it must be shown that the accused State acted with negligence or could avert damage and failed to do so.[92] Consequently, under international space law, a State cannot be held liable for accidents in orbit where there was no fault, such as the 2009 Iridium-Cosmos collision (between a defunct and-presumably uncontrollable Russian satellite with a fully operational US commercial telecom satellite).[93] However, invoking the Liability Convention would not necessarily lead to an easy or unequivocal assignment of fault as there are no clear, legally binding standards to measure 'fault' in the novel context of space operations. Moreover, given that the Liability Convention (just like all current space treaties) is an instrument of public international law, it does not properly account for the increasingly commercial nature of space activities. As a result of confining the liability for damage to the 'launching State' (or States) defined as 'a State that launches or procures the launching of a space object' or 'from whose territory or facility a space object is launched,'[94] even proper identification of responsible parties might be a daunting process.

88 Journal of Laws of 1973, No 27, item 154.

89 OST (n19) Article VII. Also See Ram S. Jakhu and Tanveer Ahmad, 'The Outer Space Treaty and States' obligation to remove space debris: A US perspective' The Space Review, 13 November 2017, 6.

90 Liability Convention (n 34) Article II; Jakhu and Pelton (n 44) 25.

91 Ibid Article III.

92 Jakhu and Pelton (n44) 25.

93 Frans G. von der Dunk, 'Too-Close Encounters of the Third Party Kind: Will the Liability Convention Stand the Test of the Cosmos 2251-Iridium 33 Collission?' (2010) Space, Cyber and Telecom. L Program Faculty Publications 28, https://digitalcommons.unl.edu/spacelaw/28.

94 LC (n 34) Article I(c); note RC (n 43) Article Ia contains the same definition.

The above liability clauses should be considered in conjunction with other obligations stemming from the Outer Space Treaty, including Articles I and III, reiterating that States must conduct their activities 'following international law,' therefore making the general rules on State responsibility and liability also applicable.[95] Moreover, Article VI of the Outer Space Treaty is of paramount importance in the context of the space sector's increasing privatization since it explicitly designates States as responsible for all 'national activities' in space, including those conducted by non-governmental (ie private) entities. Accordingly, under the existing space law regime, if the launch is conducted or procured by a private company, it is legally considered an action of the State of that company's nationality, with the possible liability for damages to be incurred by that State in connection therewith.[96]

3.1.4 The 1974 Registration Convention

The Convention on Registration of Objects Launched into Outer Space[97] was considered and negotiated by the Legal Subcommittee from 1962 to its adoption by the General Assembly in 1974 (General Assembly Resolution No. 3235 (XXIX), opened for signature on 14 January 1975, and entered into force on 15 September 1976). Poland acceded to the Convention on 5 October 1978.[98] As of 1 January 2020, it was accepted by 72 States (69 ratifications, three signature-only).

Building upon the desire, expressed by States in the Outer Space Treaty, the Rescue Agreement, and the Liability Convention, to facilitate identification of space objects, the Registration Convention expanded the scope of the UN Register of Objects Launched into Outer Space that had been established by Resolution 1721 (XVI) of December 1961 relating to the States' responsibilities concerning their space objects.[99] Once again, the Secretary-General was requested to maintain the Register and ensure full and open access to the information provided by States and international intergovernmental organizations. The Convention has been criticized for allowing a very fragmented national registry system and limited information on orbital data, which makes the identification of space debris more difficult.[100] As space objects become more complex and the orbits increasingly congested, it would be beneficial to

95 Lyall and Larsen (n 7) 104, Jakhu and Pelton (n 44) 25.
96 Jakhu & Ahmad (n 98).
97 Registration Convention (n43).
98 Journal of Laws of 1979, No 5, item 22.
99 UNGA Res 1721B, (n15).
100 Lyall and Larsen (n 7) 931, Jakhu & Pelton (n 44) 27.

have more detailed registration requirements, to enable identification of more parts or clearer identifiers of the more significant parts.[101]

The Registration Convention designated the launching State as responsible for registering its space object upon launch and making appropriate notifications to the UN Secretary-General.[102] In case of a joint launch, the States should agree which of the launching States will be the State of registration 'bearing in mind the provisions of Article VIII [of the Outer Space Treaty] and without prejudice to appropriate agreements concluded or to be concluded among the launching States on jurisdiction and control over the space object and over any personnel thereof.'[103] Read together, while there might be multiple launching States, the treaties allow for only one State of registration.

Increased commercialization and privatization of space activities exposed some inconsistent rights and obligations under the space treaties, for example between the State of registration and the launching State, which particularly affect the transfer of ownership or other aspects of private contracts. Article VIII of the Outer Space Treaty provides that the State 'on whose registry an object launched into outer space is carried shall retain jurisdiction and control over such object, and over any personnel thereof, while in outer space or on a celestial body. Ownership of objects launched into outer space [...] is not affected by their presence in outer space.'[104]

Accordingly, the State of the registration has the right, as well as the obligation, to exercise jurisdiction and control over its space object and personnel. Moreover, in the context of commercial space activities, an 'appropriate State' is required to authorize and continuously supervise space activities conducted by its non-governmental entities (ie, private companies and organizations).[105] It is difficult to imagine a situation where the jurisdiction and control referred to in this provision can be retained where a third country (or third country's entity) has become the space object's owner. In such cases, it seems necessary to lay down rules on the exercise of jurisdiction and control based on a bilateral agreement between the State that still has the object in its registry and the State that owns it.[106]

101 Ibid.
102 RC (n 43) Article II.
103 Ibid Article II.2.
104 OST (n 19) Article VIII.
105 Ibid Article VI.
106 Stephan Hobe, *et alia*, eds, *Cologne Commentary on Space Law*, Vol. 2 (Köln 2013) 256 et seq.

Since there is no definition of the 'appropriate State' provided in the Outer Space Treaty, this gap can be filled by general international law norms relating to the exercise of jurisdiction, including territoriality, nationality, the protective principle, universality, et cetera.[107] In particular, factors such as the State of incorporation, the headquarters' location, or the controlling shareholders of a private entity may become relevant in identifying the 'appropriate State.'[108]

The determination and the extent of State obligations under the space treaties circles back to the notion of international responsibility for 'national activities' under Article VI of the Outer Space Treaty. According to Article VI, States remain ultimately responsible for their 'national activities' in outer space, whether carried out by the State or private actors and for assuring that such activities comply with treaty obligations.[109] The determination of nationality, connecting responsibility with a State or its nationals again might need to be determined in accordance with the norms of international law, such as the test of 'effective control' used in the *Nicaragua* case,[110] or the 'overall control' test in the *Prosecutor v Tadic* case.[111]

However, in order to fulfill such responsibility, a State must be in a position to exercise jurisdiction over the concerned person or entity. The ownership of the satellite or other space objects may be transferred after launch (for example, by sale to a different operator). On the face of it, there is no objection to a transfer of registration in the Registration Convention or other treaties. The international responsibility for 'national activity' under Article VI of the Outer Space Treaty might transfer with such a change of ownership as it appears to be linked to the operator's nationality, however the ability of the new owner to register (or change the registration) is more problematic under the current regime.[112] While the Registration Convention does not implicitly prohibit it, it does not account for the possibility of transferring the registration to the third state, which was not one of the launching States. This is confirmed by the

---

107 For jurisdiction in space, see PJ Blount, 'Jurisdiction In Outer Space: Challenges Of Private Individuals In Space' 33 J. Space L. 299 (2007).

108 Nottebohm Case, *Liechtenstein v Guatemala*, ICJ Reports 1955, 23; the Barcelona Traction Case, *Belgium v Spain*, ICJ Reports 1970, 85, 88.

109 OST (n 19) Article VI.

110 Military and Paramilitary Activities in and against Nicaragua, *Nicaragua v USA*, ICJ Reports 1986, para 115.

111 *Prosecutor v Tadic*, IT-94-1-T, 10/8/1995, para 120, 131, 137, *Prosecutor v Tadic*, IT-94-1A, 15/7/1999, para 137–138, 146.

112 Frans G. von der Dunk, 'Transfer of Ownership in Orbit: From Fiction to Problem' in Mahulena Hofmann and Andreas Loukakis, eds, *Ownership of Satellites: 4th Luxembourg Workshop on Space and Satellite Communication Law* (2017) 36.

definition of the term 'State of registry' to mean 'a launching State on whose registry a space object is carried in accordance with article II.'[113] Accordingly, the State of the new owner can register it and have jurisdiction and control over the space object *only if* it is also one of the launching (issuing) States.[114]

This launching State criterion is related to the concept of liability under the Liability Convention, which is solely dependent on the State's status as a launching State – regardless of whether that space object is owned, controlled, or operated by a private operator.[115] Since the launching State status is fixed at the time of the launch, it is not affected by any subsequent transfer of ownership. Hence 'once a launching State, always liable' – the original launching State always remains liable for damages of the transferred object under both Article VII of the Outer Space Treaty and the Liability Convention, irrespective of whether the transfer of registration might be effective or not, and irrespective of whether it can exercise control over the object.[116] At the same time, the State of the 'national activity' is required, under Article VI of the Outer Space Treaty, to authorize and supervise this activity, even if it cannot register it or have jurisdiction and control over it.

Critics rightly point out that this is one of the signs that the Cold War period of space governance is breaking down in the face of 21st century economics and politics.[117] Similarly, the definition of a launching State that is present in the space treaties refers to either the entrepreneurial State, which launches or procures the launch, or the territorial State, from which a launch takes place or whose facility has been used to launch.[118] This definition and, in fact, the entire State of registration versus the launching State distinction does not account for the complexity of the multinational and transnational relationships with many private and commercial entities involved in the procurement, subcontracting, and financing of launches (as well as other space-related activities). The resulting determination of any potential liability or the risk thereof might be often a very complex, unrealistic, and ultimately, although perhaps unintentionally, unjust, both from the perspective of the developing industry and the potential victims seeking damages.

113 Registration Convention (n43) Article I (c).

114 Ibid Article II.

115 Von der Dunk, *Transfer of Ownership* (n 121) 35; OST (n 19) Article VII, Liability Convention (n 34).

116 Von der Dunk, Transfer of Ownership (n121) 36.

117 Jakhu and Pelton (n 44).

118 OST (n 19) Article VII, LC (n 34), Article I, RC (n 43) Article I.

Since it is mostly the launching State that bears international responsibility and liability, it is in the interest of States to ensure that the activity planned by their non-governmental entities can be properly supervised. While there is no hard obligation under the treaties requiring States to enact any national space legislation, it will be increasingly difficult for any State engaged in space activities to discharge its existing treaty obligations (including to authorize and supervise activities of their national private entities) without setting out clear national rules on licensing and other requirements.

3.1.5 The 1979 Moon Agreement

The Agreement Governing the Activities of States on the Moon and Other Celestial Bodies[119] was considered and elaborated by the Legal Subcommittee from 1972 to 1979. The Agreement was adopted by the General Assembly in 1979 in Resolution 34/68. However, it was not until June 1984 that the fifth country, Austria, ratified the Agreement, allowing it to enter into force in July 1984. Poland is not a party to this most controversial and least successful of the five UN treaties on space; as of 1 January 2020, it was accepted by only 22 States, with 18 ratifications and four signatories-only.

The Agreement reaffirms and elaborates on many of the provisions of the Outer Space Treaty as applied to the Moon and other celestial bodies, providing that those bodies should be used exclusively for peaceful purposes, that their environments should not be disrupted, and that the United Nations should be informed of the location and purpose of any station established on those bodies. Also, the Agreement provides that the Moon and its natural resources are the 'Common Heritage of Mankind' and that an international regime should be established to govern the exploitation of such resources when such exploitation is about to become feasible.[120]

It is worth noting that Poland initially supported the development of a space treaty regarding the Moon in the early 1970s, which was reflected in the sponsorship of General Assembly resolutions indicating legitimacy of this type of work.[121] Ultimately, however, after the negotiation of the Agreement, Poland, like other countries of the Eastern bloc and most countries actively involved in the use of outer space, did not decide to be bound by this treaty.[122] Such a

119 Moon Agreement (n36).

120 Ibid Article 11, s 1–3.

121 Relevant motions for resolutions are available on the website: http: // www. unoosa.org/pdf/gadocs/c1/A_C1_L572E.pdf; http://www.unoosa.org/pdf/gadocs/ c1 / A_C1_L712E.pdf, (accessed 26 January 2021).

122 For a critical issue of the significance of the 1979 Moon Agreement, see: Kazimierz Lankosz, 'Eksploracja i eksploatacja Kosmosu. Czy helium 3 zmieni status prawny

position seems to result from the fact that the Moon Agreement embraced a different philosophy compared to the provisions of the 1967 Outer Space Treaty, one of the fundamental controversies being the determination that the natural resources of all celestial bodies constitute a common human heritage[123] In this context, the position presented in June 2016, by the Minister of Development should be noted, the leading body in the field of space law in the Polish government administration. In response to the interpellation, he indicated *inter alia*:

The Ministry of Development appreciates the growing role of space mining in the world and constantly monitors global trends related to the potential possibilities of exploiting natural resources outside our planet (...). The Ministry of Development remains in contact with Polish entities with the potential in the field of space mining. It supports their efforts to join the Luxembourg government's initiative to amend international law in such a way that it allows acquiring ownership of natural resources" asteroids (...). Polish companies and research units in the space industry have competences in the field of space mining. The currently available technologies do not yet enable the development of a complete resource extraction and transport process but only focus on mapping and sampling. Over time, however, these competencies should be strengthened, *inter alia*, by Poland's participation in optional ESA programmes that enable the improvement of the existing ones and the development of new technologies, e.g., in the field of robotics or autonomous systems. It is planned that these themes constitute one of the elements of the developed strategy for the space sector.[124]

przestrzeni kosmicznej?'(Tr. 'Exploration and exploitation of space. Will Helium 3 change the legal status of outer space') in Elzbieta. Mikos-Skuza et alia, eds, *Prawo międzynarodowe – teraźniejszość, perspektywy, dylematy. Księga Jubileuszowa Profesora Zdzisława Galickiego* (Tr. *International Law – present, perspective, dilemmas. The anniversary edition of Prof. Zdzislaw Galicki*) (Warszawa 2013) 374–375.

123 See, eg position paper presented at the 786th meeting of the COPUOS Legal Subcommittee on 24 March 2009, COPUOS / LEGAL / T.786. For more, see Łukasz Kułaga, 'Przestrzeń kosmiczna – jako wspólne dziedzictwo ludzkości. Kontrowersje wokół Porozumienia regulującego działalność państw na Księżycu i innych ciałach niebieskich' (Tr. 'Outer space – as a common heritage of humanity. Controversies around the Agreement regulating the activities of States on the Moon and other celestial bodies') in Galicki, *Wykorzystanie Przestrzeni Kosmicznej* (n59) 25–41.

124 Reply to interpellation No 3297 on the 'adoption by Poland of a new space law. Responsible: Undersecretary of State in the Ministry of Development Adam Hamryszczak (Warsaw, 16 June 2016) available at: www. sejm.gov.pl; See also M. Polkowska, *The space law in the new era of space activity*, (Oficyna Allerhanda, 2016) 67–68.

3.2 *UN Recommended Principles and Other Soft Law Instruments*

The development of a binding international space governance regime (often referred to as 'hard law') more or less stopped after adopting the 1979 Moon Agreement.[125] Since then, the alternative mechanisms in the form of non-legally binding, voluntary measures and norms of behavior, so-called 'soft law' instruments, along with national laws, regulations, and policies, have taken precedence.[126] Because soft-law instruments are not binding, they are not enforceable. Nevertheless, they provide incentives in other ways for international actors to modify their behavior since they represent political agreements and reflect requirements of good faith. This might be more effective in reaching particular goals or regulating behavior than the slow and politically charged process of negotiating a new treaty. Consensus-based COPUOS has been politically deadlocked for years on the question of restraining the arms race in space, or even proposals for a non-binding International Code of Conduct have been put on hold.[127]

General Assembly (GA) resolutions can be considered to be soft law since they are statements adopted by vote to express international government opinion on specific matters, with aspirational calls to action.[128] According to the UN Charter, the GA may only make 'recommendations' while the Security Council makes binding resolutions.[129] But GA resolutions may still have normative value, especially when they are adopted by consensus. In some cases, GA resolutions may be indicative of emerging customary law as they may express evidence of *opinion juris.*[130] While GA resolutions can provide evidence of

125 Jakhu and Pelton (n 44) 8–9; Julia Hetlof, 'Security: Space Debris Removal Under the International Legal Regime' Anna Hrycaj, et alia, eds, Prawo a Nowoczesność: Wyzwania-problemy-nadzieje (tr. Law and Modernity: Challenges-issues-expectations) (Warsaw 2019) 235.

126 Soft law instruments include technical guidelines for how to safely conduct space operations as well as transparency and confidence-building measures (TCBMs). One must distinguish between binding, but 'weak' treaty obligations (such as the OST Article IX obligation to conduct space activities with 'due regard to the corresponding interests of other States' – unclear what is considered as due regard. So, it is a weak obligation, nonetheless, it is binding). See Steel (n 45) 19.

127 Steven Freeland, 'The Role of "Soft Law" in Public International Law' in Irmgard Marboe, ed, *Soft Law in Outer Space: The Function of Non-binding Norms in International Space Law* (2012) 22; Steel (n45) 20.

128 Ibid.

129 Articles 10 and 11 of the UN Charter mandate the General Assembly to make recommendations on matters within the scope of the Charter; Article 25 determines that decisions of the Security Council bind States. See Steel (n45).

130 *The legality of the Threat or Use of Nuclear Weapons*, Advisory Opinion (1996) ICJ Rep 226, 254–55. See Steel, ibid 21.

States' opinion (especially if they are adopted unanimously), customary law also requires a consistent State practice to develop.

The General Assembly has adopted a series of resolutions of direct importance to space law:

- 1963, The Declaration of Legal Principles Governing the Activities of States in the Exploration and Uses of Outer Space ('Declaration of Legal Principles');[131]
- 1982, The Principles Governing the Use by States of Artificial Earth Satellites for International Direct Television Broadcasting ('Broadcasting Principles');[132]
- 1986, The Principles Relating to Remote Sensing of the Earth from Outer Space ('Remote Sensing Principles');[133]
- 1992, The Principles Relevant to the Use of Nuclear Power Sources in Outer Space (The 'Nuclear Power Sources Principles');[134]
- 1996, The Declaration on International Cooperation in the Exploration and Use of Outer Space for the Benefit and the Interest of All States, Taking into Particular Account the Needs of Developing Countries ('Benefits Declaration');[135]
- 2004, Launching State Resolution, Application of the concept of the 'launching State' ('Launching State Resolution');[136]
- 2007, Recommendations on enhancing the practice of States and international intergovernmental organizations in registering space objects ('Registration Practice Resolution');[137]
- 2013, Recommendations on national legislation relevant to the peaceful exploration and use of outer space ('National Space Legislation Resolution).[138]

Another form of soft-law creation are recommended guidelines or recommended practices, such as the 2007 Space Debris Mitigation Guidelines, first started by the Inter-Agency Space Debris Coordination Committee (IADC), then further developed and ultimately adopted by the COPUOS and endorsed by the General Assembly, and which consequently formed a basis of the ISO

131 UNGA Res 1962 (n 18).
132 UNGA Res 37/92, of 10 December 1982; UN Doc. A/RES/37/92.
133 UNGA Res 41/65, of 3 December 1986; UN Doc. A/RES/41/65.
134 UNGA 47/68, of 14 December 1992; UN Doc. A/RES/47/68.
135 UNGA Res 51/122, of 13 December 1996; UN Doc A/RES/51/122.
136 UNGA Res. 59/115, of 10 December 2004; UN Doc. A/RES/59/115.
137 UNGA Res. 62/101, of 17 December 2007, UN Doc. A/RES/62/101.
138 UNGA Res. 68/74, of 16 December 2013, UN Doc. A/RES/68/74.

Standard 24113 'space systems – space debris mitigation.'[139] GA Resolution 62/217 of 22 December 2007, endorsing the Space Debris Mitigation Guidelines, agreed that those voluntary guidelines reflected the existing practices developed by several national and international organisations and invited the Member States to implement them through relevant national mechanisms.[140] Since then, the space debris guidelines have been incorporated into specific technical, operational, and management measures, or space industry standards, and even enacted in the national legislation of several spacefaring nations.[141]

The most recent example of promoting best practices via soft-law mechanisms is the voluntary Guidelines for the Long-Term Sustainability (LTS) of Outer Space Activities, formally adopted by COPUOS in June 2019.[142] The LTS Guidelines include a set of 21 internationally recognized measures for ensuring the long-term sustainability of outer space activities and enhancing the safety of space operations. They address the policy, regulatory, operational, safety, scientific, technical, international cooperation, and capacity-building aspects of space activities. The guidelines are intended to support the development of national and international practices and safety frameworks for conducting outer space activities while allowing for flexibility in adapting such practices and frameworks to specific national circumstances.

4 Broader International Legal Regime for Space Activities Applicable to Poland

The following are additional treaties, organizations, and agreements to which Poland is a party that are applicable in the Polish domestic space framework.

139 Compendium, Space Debris Mitigation Standards Adopted by States and International Organisations, 5 September 2018, http://www.unoosa.org/documents/pdf/spacelaw/sd/Space_Debris_Compendium_COPUOS_5_sep_2018.pdf.

140 UNGA Res 62/217, 'International cooperation in the peaceful uses of outer space' of 22 December 2007, UN Doc. A/RES/62/217.

141 Team Project, 'Space Debris: Team Project Report' International Space University 2012, 11 http://www.isunet.edu The guidelines include several recommended mitigation rules, such as collision avoidance maneuvers (to prevent on-orbit collisions), passivation of space objects at the end of their operational life (depletion of all latent energy sources, like fuel, batteries to prevent accidental post-mission explosions) or 25-year rule of post-mission disposal (to limit the long-term orbital presence). See Hetlof (n 134).

142 Report of the Committee on the Peaceful Uses of Outer Space, COPUOS 62nd session, A/74/20, 20 August 2019.

a) The Treaty Banning Nuclear Weapon Tests in the Atmosphere, in Outer Space, and Under Water,[143] which forbids nuclear weapons tests or any other nuclear explosion underwater, in the air, and outer space.

b) The International Telecommunication Union Constitution and Convention (ITU),[144] with ITU Radio Regulations, as amended, which regulates the use of radiofrequency spectrum and access to orbital slots at the geostationary orbit, since they are considered limited natural resources to which all States are authorized to equitable access.[145]

c) The European Space Agency (ESA), which was established under the Convention on the Establishment of the European Space Agency (Convention) done in Paris on May 30, 1975.[146] In 2007, Poland concluded the European Cooperating State Agreement with ESA, and on July 31 2012, an agreement on accession to the Convention.[147] ESA aims to ensure and promote, solely for peaceful purposes, cooperation between European countries in space research and technology and their applications in space to be used for scientific purposes and operational systems utility.

d) The Agreement on the Establishment of the Intersputnik International System and Organization of Space Communications (as amended by the Protocol on Amendments of 30 November 1996)[148] established the Intersputnik International Organization of Space Communications (INTERSPUTNIK), an international intergovernmental organization (IGO), founded in 1971 in Moscow by the former Soviet Union along with a group of eight formerly socialist States (Cuba, Czechoslovakia, East Germany, Hungary, Mongolia, Poland, and Romania). Poland's membership continues to this day, and the organization increased to 26 Member States (as of 2020). Intersputnik is engaged in the design, construction,

143 The Treaty Banning Nuclear Weapon Tests in the Atmosphere, in Outer Space and Under Water, 5 August 1963, 14 U.S.T. 1313, 480 UNTS 43 (Limited Test Ban Treaty), entered into force 10 October 1963, Journal of Laws of 1963, No 52, item 288.

144 Constitution and Convention of the International Telecommunication Union (ITU), 22 December 1992, 1825 UNTS 143, UN Reg No I-31251.

145 Ibid Article VII.

146 Convention for the establishment of a European Space Agency, opened for signature on 30 May 1975 and entered into force on 30 October 1980.

147 The European Cooperating State Agreement (n23) and the Agreement between the Government of the Republic of Poland and the European Space Agency Concerning the Accession of Poland to the Convention for the Establishment of a European Space Agency and Related Terms and Conditions, done in Warsaw on 31 July 2012, ratified on 24 October 2012, and entered into force on 19 November 2012, published 16 January 2013, Journal of Laws of 2013, item 61.

148 861 UNTS 3, in effect in Poland as of 12 July 1972, Journal of Laws of 1974, No 40, item 234.

operation, and development of a satellite communication system for the benefit of Member States and commercial entities. Its area of operation is mainly in the Northern Hemisphere.

e) The International Mobile Satellite Organization (IMSO) as intergovernmental organization is a successor to the former International Maritime Satellite Organization (INMARSAT). The IGO INMARSAT was first established in 1976 to supply maritime and other mobile communications services via satellite.[149] In Poland, both the INMARSAT Convention and Operating Agreement entered into force on 16 July 1979, following the Government Statement of 28 January 1980, on the Convention and the Operating Agreement's ratification.[150] Adapting to the changing economic reality, INMARSAT went through a complex privatization process that ultimately transformed it into a much smaller IGO under the new acronym – IMSO. It had the sole task of overseeing the newly-created operating company Inmarsat, which took charge of all the satellite operations, service provisions, and attendant market operations.[151] The entry into force of these changes resulted in the expiration of the INMARSAT Operating Agreement. IMSO acts as the supervisory board to Inmarsat within the scope of the Core Principles, that is, providing global emergency services, providing services without national discrimination, providing services to remote regions in developing countries, and providing services following the principles of fair competition and compliance with the law. Poland is a party to IMSO, while INMARSAT shareholders

149 By way of the Convention on the International Maritime Satellite Communications Organization (the INMARSAT Convention) on 3 September 1976, entered into force on 16 July 1979, 1143 UNTS 105; and the Operating Agreement on the International Maritime Satellite Organization (INMARSAT Operating Agreement) on 3 September 1976, entered into force 16 July 1979, 1143 UNTS 2013, Journal of Laws of 1980, No.7, items 19 and 20, and the Government Declarations to the Amendments to the Agreements as mentioned above, Journal of Laws of 2003, No 140, items 1342 and 1344.

150 Ibid. Poland also ratified the subsequent amendments to the said Convention and Agreement. Ratification took place on 22 October 1987, 7 December 1996, and 13 March 2000 (Poland is not bound by the Amendments adopted by the Organization's Assembly in 1994).

151 The Convention on the International Mobile Satellite Organization (IMSO Convention), London, 3 September 1976, entered into force 16 July 1979, as amended in 1998. The amended version entered into force 31 July 2001; ATS 2001 No 11. In Poland, the amendments were ratified on 13 March 2000, and entered into force on 31 July 2001, Government declaration of 20 September 2002, Journal of Laws of 2003, No 140, item 1347. The new IMSO has 104-Member States (as of 2018). Also See Frans von der Dunk, 'International organizations in space law' *Handbook of Space Law* (n 11) 290–294.

are telecommunications operators, including Polish communications operators.[152]

f) The International Telecommunications Satellite Organization (ITSO) is an intergovernmental organization with 149-Member States (as of 2020). Initially established in 1973, as the International Telecommunications Satellite Organization (INTELSAT),[153] it was restructured in 2001. As a result, INTELSAT was transformed into the International Telecommunication Satellite Organization (ITSO)[154] and the operating company Intelsat, Ltd. In this case, the Operating Agreement also expired. The relationship between ITSO and Intelsat, Ltd is governed by the Fundamental Principles contained in the contract. Poland is a member of ITSO,[155] with only States as parties. ITSO acts as a supervisory board, monitoring the performance of Intelsat's public service obligations and

152 In Poland, there is a satellite communication station in Psary near Kielce. Unfortunately, the potentially large opportunities for intensive participation in the Inmarsat system, and thus for earning considerable money, are almost completely missed. The Psary station operates only on one of the few Inmarsat subsystems, historically the oldest first-generation system, Inmarsat A. It offers only a very narrow range of services, almost completely useless in modern mobile satellite communications. It is practically impossible to make settlements for users outside the constant, for years the same and ever-decreasing group. This situation is caused by the lack of automatic billing devices in telephone exchanges and currently the only possibility, and rather theoretical, to use the services of the station in Psary is to order a telephone call. It is even difficult to determine how many users Psary has per month. The tariff policy is not conducive to the development of services, as the connection via Psary today costs over USD 10 per minute. Providing a wider range of services is effectively limited by the poor development of our telecommunications network. In this situation, it is not surprising that there is an almost complete lack of marketing. Finally, the development of satellite communication services is completely blocked by the legal status in Poland, which makes it practically impossible to register a mobile satellite communication station, and the use of such terminals requires overcoming numerous bureaucratic barriers.

153 By way of the Agreement Relating to the International Telecommunications Satellite Organization (the INTELSAT Agreement), Washington, done 20 August 1971, entered into force 12 February 1973, 1220 UNTS 21 (1971), and the Operating Agreement Relating to the International Telecommunications Satellite Organization (INTELSAT Operating Agreement), Washington DC, done 20 August 1971, entered into force 12 February 1997, 1220 UNTS 149 (1971); Poland acceded to the Agreement on 30 April 1993, and it entered into force on 15 December 1993. Journal of Laws of 1994, No 110, item 530.

154 Agreement Relating to the International Telecommunications Satellite Organization (ITSO), (the ITSO Agreement), Washington DC, done 20 August 1971, entered into force 12 February 1973, as amended 13 November 2000, amended version entered into force 30 November 2004, 23 UST 3813 and 4091, TIAS 7532.

155 In Poland, in Psary-Kąty near Kielce, there are Intelsat ground stations (cooperation with satellites of the Atlantic O.O. since 1982 and Indian O.O. since 1989).

safeguarding the Parties' Common Heritage that had been outlined in Resolution 1721 (XVI),[156] establishing that communication employing satellites should be available to all nations worldwide as soon as practicable on a global and non-discriminatory basis.

g) The Convention Establishing the European Satellite Communications Organization (EUTELSAT), entered into force 1 September 1985, amended in May 1999 in connection with a decision to restructure.[157] As of 2 July 2001, EUTELSAT evolved into the intergovernmental organization EUTELSAT IGO and the operating company Eutelsat SA. The Maintenance Agreement has expired. The relationship between EUTELSAT IGO and Eutelsat SA is defined by the Basic Principles that oblige the operating company to ensure public and universal access to services, TV broadcast coverage throughout Europe, and to ensure non-discriminatory and fair competition. Currently, Eutelsat SA is a public company listed on the Paris Stock Exchange since 2005. Poland is a member of EUTELSAT IGO.[158] Poland joined EUTELSAT in 1992 and, since 1993, it has been operating the ground stations of the system in Psary-Kąty and Poręby Leśne near Warsaw and several hundred terminals with a small antenna (VSAT) located throughout Poland.

h) The European Organization for the Exploitation of Meteorological Satellites (EUMETSAT) was established in 1986 to ensure the continued operation of the meteorological satellite system built by ESA.[159] The organization's main task is to implement its own satellite program to provide Member States with, among others, weather and earth monitoring along with climate forecasting and monitoring. Poland established relations with EUMETSAT in 2000 as a cooperating member and obtained full membership in 2009 when it acceded to the EUMETSAT Convention.[160] However, at the time of its signing, the 'Protocol on the privileges and

156 Ibid (n 15).

157 UK Misc. No 4, Cmnd. 9154 (1984), Journal of Laws of 1995, No 24, item 130.

158 Ibid.

159 By way of the Convention for the Establishment of a European Organization for the Exploitation of Meteorological Satellites (EUMETSAT), (the EUMETSAT Convention), done in Geneva on 24 May 1983, entered into force on 19 June 1986. Germany, *Bundersgesetzenblatt, Jahrgang* 1987, part II (1987) 256 (this Convention has been published in the national bulletins of the ratifying States).

160 The Act on the Ratification of the Convention on the Establishment of the European Organization for the Exploitation of Meteorological Satellites (EUMETSAT) drawn up in Geneva on May 24, 1983, Journal of Laws of 2009, No 38, item 297 (adopted by the Parliament of the Republic of Poland 9 January 2009 entered into force on 27 March 2009).

immunities of the European Organization for the Exploitation of Meteorological Satellites,' done in Darmstadt on 1 December 1986, was not taken into account, thus depriving Poland of the possibility of financing EUMETSAT international conferences organized in Poland and excluding Polish specialists from courses and internships abroad. Moreover, Polish entrepreneurs were also excluded from any tenders for EUMETSAT. Poland joined the Protocol only in 2014.[161] In Poland, the Institute of Meteorology and Water Management ('IMWM') – National Research Institute, which participates in the work of EUMETSAT bodies, is responsible for relations with the organization. IMWM's representatives participate in the meetings of EUMETSAT program councils and committees. As a result of its membership in the organization, Poland has full access to satellite data from its satellites. Imaging provided by EUMETSAT is used by the State hydrological and meteorological services to prepare forecasts, for hydrometeorological protection of the society and economy, and monitoring of climate change, as well as by the Polish Armed Forces, universities, and research institutes. Images from the meteorological satellites can also be utilized in: agriculture, forestry, land management, spatial management, investment planning, monitoring of water areas (including the Baltic Sea) and the atmosphere, including measuring trace gases and aerosols.

i) The International COSPAS-SARSAT Programme Agreement (COSPAS-SARSAT Agreement)[162] was established as an inter-governmental organization by four parties to the Agreement: Canada, France, the USA, and the former USSR. Currently, 44 Member States belong to the COSPAS-SARSAT Programme. Poland has been a full member of the COSPAS-SARSAT Programme since 16 September 2005.[163] The Civil Aviation Office is responsible for the following tasks resulting from Poland's membership in the COSPAS-SARSAT Programme: keeping records of on-board and personal distress signal transmitters ELT, EPIRB and PLB 406 MHz

161 Journal of Laws 2019, No 190 and 1042 (effective 16 February 2014).

162 The International COSPAS-SARSAT Programme Agreement (COSPAS-SARSAT Agreement), Paris, done 1 July 1988, entered into force on 30 August 1988.

163 On 31 May 2005, in Warsaw, the President of the Civil Aviation Authority, authorized by the Resolution of the Council of Ministers No. 107/2005 of 25 April 2005, signed the Note on the accession of the Republic of Poland to the COSPAS-SARSAT International Programme as a User State (Monitor Polski of 2006, No 13, item 171), of which it is the contractor. Following the Government Statement of 30 December 2005, on binding the Republic of Poland to the Note on Joining the International Programme COSPAS-SARSAT as a User State, signed in Warsaw on 31 May 2005 (Monitor Polski of 2006 No 13, item 172).

and forwarding the information contained therein to the Center for Coordination of Search and Aviation Rescue (ARCC Warsaw); preparation of annual reports assessing the elements of the COSPAS-SARSAT system; cooperation with the COSPAS-SARSAT Programme Secretariat; supervision over the Polish Air Navigation Services Agency (SPOC Polska) in the field of cooperation with the System Mission Control Center (CMC Moscow); implementation and supervision over the protocols for coding transmitters of the danger signal adopted by the COSPAS-SARSAT Programme Council in Poland; coordination of the distress signal transmitters' testing in accordance with the procedure recommended and approved by the COSPAS-SARSAT Programme Council, published in document C / S S. 007 "Handbook of Beacon Regulations" and on the website of the Civil Aviation Authority; monitoring of the proper use of danger signal transmitters registered in Poland; cooperation with the Polish Air Navigation Services Agency, ARCC Warsaw and the Maritime Search and Rescue Service in matters related to the Programme.

The COSPAS-SARSAT Programme's mission is to provide a search and rescue service with accurate, up-to-date, and reliable information about detected danger signals through satellites and ground components of the system emitted by the ELT (Emergency Locator Transmitter),[164] EPIRB (Emergency Position-Indicating Radio Beacon),[165] and PLB (Personal Locator Beacon)[166] distress

164 ELT (Emergency Locator Transmitter) for aviation use. The 121.5 MHz band service emergency beacons are required on many aircraft, referred to as ELT 121.5, with a smaller number carried on maritime vessels. The 121.5 MHz frequency band is used by an older type of beacons which do not transmit any encoded information. It is also the frequency used for low-power homing transmitters included in most beacons. The more recent ELT devices on aircraft are provided with dual frequency alert systems, 121.5 and 406.025 MHz.

165 EPIRB (Emergency Position Indicating Radio Beacon) for use in maritime applications. A small battery-powered transmitting device which is carried on vessels (several nations require EPIRB devices on all vessels). It can be activated in times of trouble to send out help signals. EPIRB devices operate on a frequency of 121.5/243 MHz (the 243 MHz frequency is used only in some older beacons), they may also include the 406.025 MHz alert signal for global detection.

166 PLB (Personal Locator Beacon) used for land-based applications (basically an ELT when carried by a person, but not used in aviation or maritime applications). These are handheld or pocket size dual frequency (121.5 and 406 MHz) or single frequency (either 121.5 or 406.025 MHz) devices which transmit distress signals to search and rescue authorities via the COSPAS-SARSAT satellite system. On July 1, 2003, FCC (Federal Communication Commission) of the USA authorized the use of PLBs (406 MHz digitally encoded) on a nationwide basis.

signal transmitter operating at 406 MHz.[167] By the decision of the Council of the International COSPAS-SARSAT Programme, from 1 February 2009, the satellites of the system no longer monitor the distress signals emitted by the distress signal transmitters on the 121.5 MHz frequency. Nevertheless, the frequency of 121.5 MHz, following the international standards and recommended practices contained in the Chicago Convention[168] Annex 10 is still the emergency frequency. The frequency of 121.5 MHz is also used by search and rescue aircraft, carrying out searches using the instrumental method during a search and rescue operation.[169]

Since December 2016, the COSPAS-SARSAT Programme has been supported by the MEOSAR satellite system, consisting of three satellite constellations: American GPS, European Galileo, and Russian Glonass. Once the MEOSAR system is fully operational, it will ensure continuous and complete coverage of the globe and enable faster and more precise localization of the danger signal transmitter. The MEOSAR system also has a Return Link Service function, which will be available with the second generation distress signal transmitters. The Return Link Service function relies on the feedback system's terrestrial component to send the distress signal that generated the distress signal to the transmitter as confirmation of receipt of the distress signal by COSPAS-SARSAT satellites. Thirty years after the inception of COSPAS-SARSAT,

167 The development of the new generation of beacons transmitting at 406 MHz commenced at the beginning of the COSPAS-SARSAT project in the mid-1970s. Although the COSPAS-SARSAT system was primarily designed to function on the much improved 406 MHz frequency, it still had to make a provision for the thousands of 121.5 MHz beacons already in use. For this reason, the satellites were designed to receive 121.5 MHz as well. The 406 MHz units were designed specifically for satellite detection and Doppler location by having: high peak power output and a low duty cycle – Improved radio frequency stability; a unique identification code in each beacon; digital transmissions that could be stored in a satellite's memory; a spectrum dedicated by the ITU (International Telecommunication Union) solely for distress beacons. The 406 MHz beacons transmit a 5 W, half-second burst approximately every 50 seconds. The carrier frequency is phase-modulated with a digital message. The low duty cycle provides a multiple-access capability of more than 90 beacons operating simultaneously in view of a polar orbiting LEO satellite, versus only about 10 for 121.5 MHz beacons.

168 Convention on International Civil Aviation (the 'Chicago Convention') (1994) 15 UNTS 295.

169 On February 1, 2009 an era of emergency beacon support ended: the 121.5 and 243 MHz emergency beacons were phased out for satellite distress alerting (in accordance with the 2000 Council decision). The decision to stop satellite processing of 121.5 / 243 MHz signals is due to problems in this frequency band which inundate search and rescue authorities with poor accuracy and numerous false alerts, adversely impacting the effectiveness of lifesaving services. See http://www.sarsat.noaa.gov/, http://www.sarsat.noaa.gov/Phaseout_Brochure.pdf.

a new chapter is opening for this international program: analog beacons have been phased out, digital 406 Mhz beacons are fully operational, new generation SARSAT-3 instruments are launched on the US NOAA and the European MetOp satellites. Furthermore, the COSPAS-SARSAT organization is preparing for the future, with the integration of a MEOSAR component that will use the GNSS (Global Navigation Satellite Systems) constellations.[170]

5 Conclusion

The exploration and use of outer space for peaceful purposes, made possible under the international space law regime set up by the five UN space law treaties and several UNGA resolutions, has brought unprecedented economic and social benefits to the entire humanity.

Currently there are over 3300 active satellites orbiting the Earth that belong to over 50 countries and provide services of various kinds to all the nations of the world.[171] In the years between 2008 and 2019, the global satellite industry almost doubled to reach 271 billion U.S. dollars. However, by the 2040s, this is expected to grow between 1 to 2.7 trillion U.S. dollars. The space sector has become a significant industry on its own, but it is also a very important catalyst for a host of other industries.

Despite increasingly commercial nature of the space sector, the international space legal regime, which originates in the 20th century Cold War period, continues to primarily govern the relationships between the State actors only. The United Nations has continued to play a central role in advancing the peaceful uses of outer space. Although, since 1979, the international community has been paralyzed by political impasse and unable to conclude any new space treaties (or update any of the existing ones), COPUOS remains an essential forum for space-related legal discussion, cooperation and formation of soft-law norms, recommended guidelines and best industry practices. Poland's continuing contributions to this forum and its representatives indicate their strong commitment to further developing international space law and its compliance. Polish entities have also been involved in the European Union's scientific and research programs related to space. Poland is a member of EUMETSAT (European Organization for the Exploitation of Meteorological

170 EO Portal Directory, 'COSPAS-SARSAT', https://directory.eoportal.org/web/eoportal/satellite-missions/c-missions/cospas-sarsat#foot14%29.

171 3,372 active (operational) satellites as of 1 January 2021, https://www.geospatialworld.net/blogs/how-many-satellites-are-orbiting-the-earth-in-2021/.

Satellites) and ESO (European Southern Observatory). Since joining the European Space Agency in 2012, Poland has 'opened the door' for its domestic space sector to develop through participation in ESA tenders. Increasingly, the fact that the company has documented experience in space activities, for example, in ESA projects, is a kind of 'quality certificate' confirming the credibility of the potential partner and its technological competence worldwide.

Poland has scientific and industrial potential and constantly growing experience that enables it to be involved in this innovative sector. The equipment developed for space missions needs to be reliable, light, and energy-saving due to the satellite's limited energy. The space sector stimulates new materials and technologies and introduces new forms of work organization and quality control. Besides, innovations implemented in the space sector are used in other areas to increase their competitiveness. All this makes the space sector, one of the most modern and technologically advanced industries, of growing importance for the European and world economies.

The increased involvement in space activities, especially starting with the first launches of the Polish satellites in 2012, prompted a need to conform Poland's obligations under the core space treaties. The Polish Space Strategy, adopted in 2017, takes into account the obligations resulting from Poland's membership in ESA, NATO, and the European Union. The development of the National Space Program and the draft Act on Space Activity and the National Register of Space Objects (as discussed elsewhere in the book), once implemented into the national space legal framework, will certainly have an impact on Polish space industry and the opportunities of international cooperation in the space sector.

CHAPTER 5

Polish Space Activities in Europe

Tomasz Balcerzak

1 Introduction

Over the past 20–30 years, Poland has developed its own space sector, which has already gained a lot of experience and has tangible achievements. It was done based on cooperation with European, European Union, global organisations, entities, and international space agreements. The sector consists of several research centers, a dozen research groups in universities, and several dozen small and medium-sized enterprises. They, in turn, undertake projects related to satellite techniques or space technologies.

Many Polish enterprises also have a great potential of knowledge and experience that would enable them to join this activity quickly. These are primarily companies from the aviation and defense sectors, which are the cradle of the space industry and other countries. Enterprises from the ICT sector[1] also have great potential, which due to their technical competencies, can successfully engage in activities in the field of production and satellite services.

The beginning of the 21st century brought an intensification of cooperation with the European Space Agency (ESA).[23] In 2007, the Agreement on

---

1 The new Information and Communication Technology – ICT sector comprises the manufacturing and services sectors whose main activity is linked to development, production, commercialization, and intensive use of new technology.

2 The European Space Agency. It was established under the Convention on the Establishment of the European Space Agency (Convention) drawn up in Paris on 30 May 30 1975. Poland's cooperation with ESA dates back to 1994 when Poland signed the Agency's first cooperation agreement. In 2007, Poland concluded an agreement on the European Cooperating State with ESA, and on 31 July 2012 – an agreement on accession to the Convention. The text of the Agreement and the text of the Convention were published in January 2013. The purpose of ESA is to ensure and promote, for peaceful purposes only, cooperation between European countries in space research and technology and their applications in space, with a view to being used for scientific purposes and for operational user systems.

3 ESA is an intergovernmental organisation, whereas the European Union is supranational. The two institutions have different competencies, different Member States, and are governed by different rules and procedures. However, the European Union and ESA share a common aim: to strengthen Europe and benefit its citizens. While ESA and the European Union are separate organisations, they are increasingly working together towards common objectives. Because it implemented the European Union's flagship programmes, Galileo and Copernicus,

© KONINKLIJKE BRILL NV, LEIDEN, 2023 | DOI:10.1163/9789004542860_007

European Cooperating States (PECS) was signed. Thanks to the creation of this mechanism, 45 projects were financed for a total amount of EUR 11,500,000, implemented by Polish companies, scientific and research institutions, and universities in cooperation with ESA. Simultaneously, the number, quality, and advancement of products and services using satellite techniques, which are offered on the market by Polish companies, have significantly increased.

In November 2012, Poland became the twentieth Member State of the European Space Agency, paying a premium of approximately EUR 30,000,000 annually. For Polish companies and research centres, this opened the way to a faster development of space technologies and satellite techniques through the possibility of full participation in most of the Agency's programmes.[4]

Currently, Poland participates in the following ESA optional programmes:

- Earth observation
- Navigation
- Telecommunications and Integrated Applications
- Manned Flights and Exploration
- Space Situational Information System (SSA)
- General Technology Support Programme (GSTP)
- The ESA Scientific Instrument Building Programme (PRODEX).

---

and its support of the European Union's research and development programme, Horizon 2020, some 20% of the ESA funds managed recently have originated from the EU budget. The legal basis for EU/ESA cooperation is provided by a Framework Agreement entered into force in May 2004. In recent years, the two institutions have worked towards reinforcing their cooperation in light of the global developments challenging the European Space Sector. In 2016, ESA and the European Commission made an effort to coordinate their vision of a future European space sector that maintains Europe's world-class space industry and ensures that future space programmes' scientific discoveries shall be fully integrated into European societies and economies. In December 2016, ESA and the European Commission signed a Joint EU/ESA Statement on the shared vision and goals for Europe in space. In this joint statement, ESA and the European Union list several common goals and emphasized their intention to reinforce their cooperation in the future.

4 The space sector is divided into two basic segments. The first of them, the so-called upstream, includes manufacturers of space equipment and the launch of instruments and satellites into space. Generally, this segment comprises satellite system integrators and suppliers of the necessary subsystems, components, and instruments. The second segment, called downstream, concerns the use of all kinds of satellite data by end-users and includes suppliers of products and services produced or provided with the help of this data (applications for individual or institutional customers – environmental data, meteorological data, telecommunications services, crisis management, traffic supervision, etc.).

2 Key Actors of Polish Space Policy

From a general perspective, the key actors in the space sector which therefore also represent the key stakeholders in the context of Polish space policy, can be subsumed under four headings: (governmental) teams and committees; the Ministries more formally part of the Polish government; non-governmental entities; and a residual category of other supporting entities.

As for the teams and committees, they especially comprise the following four:

- The Interministerial Team for Space Policy in Poland, which is responsible for shaping the national space policy, is the coordinator of the government administration's activities in this area and takes key decisions, also of a financial nature.
- Task Force PL – ESA (TASK FORCE PL – ESA), which was established to protect the interests of domestic entities operating in the space sector undertaking cooperation with ESA. Its tasks include the organization of the Polish Industry Incentive Scheme. The Ministry of Entrepreneurship and Technology in Poland is responsible for coordinating the work of the team.
- The Polish Task Force (TASK FORCE PL), whose tasks include among others monitoring the spending of funds by ESA on contracts with Polish entrepreneurs and taking actions aimed at supporting the Polish space sector in acquiring industrial and scientific projects in order to ensure optimal spending of the Polish contribution to ESA.
- The Space and Satellite Research Committee of the Polish Academy of Sciences (KBKIS PAN), which brings together many award-winning scientists working in the field of space in Poland for integrating and stimulating domestic research, cooperation with foreign and international scientific organizations in this field and representing Poland in them, as well as giving opinions on legal acts and projects of scientific and research programs.

Next, the main Ministries involved concern:

- The Ministry of Entrepreneurship and Technology (MPiT), which is the leading ministry in the field of implementation of Polish space policy, and which represents Poland in the European Space Agency and in forums devoted to space policy in the European Union.
- The Ministry of Science and Higher Education (Ministry of Science and Higher Education), which is responsible for scientific research under the national programs of the National Center for Research and Development (NCBiR) and the National Science Center (NCN), as well as international ones, including Horizon 2020, Copernicus program, and ESO (European South Observatory) programs.

- The Ministry of National Defense (MON), which is a body responsible for military aspects and the use of space technologies and satellite techniques for the purposes of state defense. The following programs are of interest to the Ministry of National Defense: SST / SSA, FLPP and GOVSATCOM. The ministry also cooperates with NATO and the European Defense Agency (EDA).
- The Ministry of Digitization (MC), which is the ministry dealing with the EU satellite navigation program – Galileo (except for the PRS part, which falls under the competences of the Ministry of Interior and Administration) and issues related to satellite telecommunications.

Among the non-governmental organizations, the following are key:
- The Space Sector Employers' Union (ZPSK), an institution established in 2012 associating enterprises and research institutes involved in space activities. The union works to increase the economic potential of the space industry in Poland. Currently, it associates over 60 entities.
- The Aviation Valley Employers Group Association "Aviation Valley", an association founded in 2003 in Rzeszów representing an innovative sector of the aviation industry, located in south-eastern Poland. Currently, it associates over 150 entities.
- The Polish Association of Space Professionals (PSPA), an association registered in 2016, which is actively involved in building a network of contacts between Polish professionals working in the domestic and foreign space sector, as well as disseminating knowledge related to the space sector.
- The Polish Rocket Society (PTR), a nationwide organization of rocket modellers and enthusiasts of experimental rockets and space technologies, which was established in 2010. One of the goals of the association is the construction of rocket engines, rockets and their use.
- The Polish Astronautical Society (PTA), an association founded in 1954 bringing together both professionals, professionally dealing with space issues, and enthusiasts of all fields of astronautics.
- The Polish Astronomical Society (PTA), a scientific association of professional astronomers, operating since 1923. The main goal of the association is to popularize astronomy in society, including by organizing conventions, conferences and workshops.
- The European Space Foundation, which is an institution established in 2014 dealing with educational and promotional activities in the field of space exploration, as well as supporting the development of space policy in Poland (it organized, among others, 3 editions of the European Mars Robot Competition – European Rover Challenge in the years: 2014, 2015 and 2016).

- The Mars Society Polska (MSP), which forms the Polish branch of the Mars Society, focusing on the promotion of research on the Red Planet and the vision of its colonization. The organization develops IT projects and supports Mars rovers projects.
- The Association "Astronomia Nova", established in 2009 in Częstochowa. The statutory goals of the Association are, *inter alia*, increasing the knowledge of society in the field of natural sciences, with particular emphasis on astronomy and its related sciences.

Finally, an array of other supporting entities should be mentioned here:

- The Industrial Development Agency S.A. (ARP), a state-owned company that runs dedicated support programs for the space technology sector, for instance business incubations or internships and training for young engineers.
- The Polish Space Agency (POLSA), a government executive agency established in 2014. Its tasks include supporting representatives of science and industry operating in the field of space technologies and satellite techniques. This support is implemented, *inter alia*, through cooperation with the European Space Agency (ESA), the European Union (EU) or the European Organization for the Exploitation of Meteorological Satellites (EUMETSAT), which aims to include Polish entities in European space projects. POLSA organizes industry events and conferences and participates in national and international space-related fairs, promoting Polish entities. All these activities make it possible to establish contacts between domestic and foreign entities in the space sector, as well as to learn about the current trends of the international space market. The priority tasks of the Agency also include the development of Poland's defense capabilities, including the security of its citizens, through the use of space and satellite systems and ensuring their effective use by state institutions. POLSA is responsible for the preparation and implementation of the National Space Program (NFP). The agency also conducts educational activities aimed at popularizing knowledge in the field of space research among students of primary and secondary schools, and initiates and supports the creation of new fields of study related to space technologies and satellite techniques at Polish universities.

3 Participation in ESA Space Missions

The signing of a cooperation agreement by Poland with ESA in 1994 opened the way for Polish entities to participate in the Agency's missions. At the Space

Research Centre of the Polish Academy of Sciences, several scientific instruments have been built in cooperation with a dozen Polish companies. Devices made in Poland took part in missions aimed at remote sensing and direct study of the properties of the solar system's planets and space bodies' atmospheres and surfaces.

3.1 *The Most Exciting Missions with the Participation of Polish Research Instruments*[5,6]

The Polish space sector began to form in the 1970s, when the institutes of the Polish Academy of Sciences headed by the Space Research Center and state research institutes started their scientific, research and development and implementation activities in the field of space technologies and satellite techniques. The instruments designed and built by them participated in over 70 international space missions, such as Cassini-Huygens, Mars Express, Rosetta, Herschel, PROBA-3, and InSight.

The catalyst for the development of the Polish space sector has become the cooperation with the European Space Agency (ESA), and its important point was the signing by Poland in 2007 of the Agreement on European Cooperating States (PECS). In this way, representatives of Polish industry and science gained the opportunity to participate in the first international space projects. In 2012, Polish entities regularly participate in the competitions of this organization, both in the program dedicated exclusively to Polish entities (the Polish Industry Incentive Scheme – PLIIS), as well as in optional and compulsory programs. Along with participation in subsequent space projects, the experience of Polish entities in the production of advanced technological solutions verified in space (space heritage) is constantly growing. Since joining ESA, the number of Polish entities registered on the ESA EMITS tendering portal has increased more than eightfold (420 entities at the beginning of 2018, compared to 48 in 2012). During the first six years of Poland's membership in ESA, domestic entities obtained over 330 contracts for a total amount of almost EUR 100 million.

Currently, the space sector in Poland consists of several dozen of the most active small and medium-sized enterprises (including branches of European space companies), several large enterprises operating in the ICT, defense and aviation industries, research institutes and renowned technical universities.

5 Based on: https://www.esa.int/Space_in_Member_States/Poland/Polska_w_kosmosie, (accessed 11 February 2021).

6 Based on: https://www.gov.pl/web/rozwoj-praca-technologia/kolejna-misja-kosmiczna-z-udzialem-polskiej-firmy, (accessed 11 February 2021).

In 2012, the Space Industry Employers' Union (ZPSK) was established, currently associating over 60 entities. An important group of stakeholders of the Polish space sector is also the public administration, which creates demand for solutions derived from the use of satellite data. They are used to improve the work of the administration (for instance crisis management, spatial development, and environmental monitoring). On the other hand, public administration is made up of institutions responsible for the national space policy. The leading role in this respect is played by the Ministry of Entrepreneurship and Technology (MpiT), whose representative is the chairman of the Polish delegation to ESA.

With the dynamic development of the domestic space sector, new challenges appear for Polish enterprises and research units. The Polish Space Strategy (PSK), adopted by the resolution of the Council of Ministers of 26 January 2017, mentions as goals facing the Polish space sector, among others: increasing its competitiveness and increasing its share in the turnover of the European space sector, development of satellite applications, contributing to the construction of the digital economy, expanding capabilities in the area of state security and defense with the use of space technologies and satellite techniques, and building human resources for the Polish space sector.

3.1.1 Rosetta[7]

Rosetta is an ESA cornerstone mission to chase, go into orbit around, and land on a comet. It is studying the Jupiter-family comet 67P/Churyumov-Gerasimenko with a combination of remote sensing and *in situ* measurements. The spacecraft arrived at the comet on 6 August 2014 following a 10-year journey through the Solar System. Between August and November 2014, the spacecraft orbited the comet and gathered data to characterise the environment and the comet nucleus.

On 12 November 2014, Rosetta's lander Philae was deployed to the surface. Philae carries a suite of instruments for imaging and sampling the comet nucleus. The Rosetta orbiter will track the comet through perihelion (August 2015), examining its behaviour before, during and after closet approach. The mission ended in a controlled landing on the comet's surface on 30 September 2016.

The Research Centre of the Polish Academy of Science (CBK PAN) developed the MUPUS (Multi Purpose Sensor for surface and subsurface science)

---

7 *Sięgając do Gwiazd – Polski sektor kosmiczny 4 lata w ESA,* Broszura Polskiej Agencji Rozwoju Przedsiębiorczości, (Warsaw, 2016).

instrument for the mission. The instrument is a mechanically advanced manipulator, equipped with a penetrator, the task of which is to punch into the surface of Comet 67P / Churyumov-Gerasimenko. The penetrator contains several detectors that, after the planned landing in 2014, will allow studying the physical properties and composition of the comet's nucleus.

Scientist from Space Research Centre and Institute of Geophysics of the Warsaw University participate in several Rosetta experiments: OSIRIS, VIRTIS, CONSERT and MUPUS. The main Polish instrumental contribution to the Rosetta mission is the experiment MUPUS. It is led by Professor Tilman Spohn from the Institute for Planetary Research (DLR, Berlin) and comprises teams from Germany, Poland, Austria and the United Kingdom as well as scientists from other countries. The objective of the experiment is to use a suite of instrument to investigate physical (thermal, mechanical) parameters of the cometary nucleus. Another important contribution of the Polish team to MUPUS was development of thermal sensors.

3.1.2 Cassini-Huygens

The Sensor THP (Thermal Properties) – a sensor for measuring temperature and thermal conductivity was developed and manufactured in Poland. The sensor was mounted onboard the Huygens lander, which in January 2005 landed on the surface of Titan – Saturn's moon. Measurements made by the sensor revealed the surface properties of this celestial body.

3.1.3 Proba 3

As part of the GSTP technology development programme, several Polish entities participate in the Proba 3 mission, which will be the world's first mission to verify precise formation flights' technology. Simultaneously, the Programme carries out an important scientific task of observing the solar corona (outer layer of the solar atmosphere), including in solar storms, that is, where strong explosions causing magnetic discharges which, depending on their severity, may threaten Earth's energy or telecommunications systems.

3.1.4 JUICE

The Jupiter Icy moons Explorer mission (JUICE) will study the gas giant Jupiter and its largest moons using 11 scientific instruments. Two of them are Polish experiments: submillimeter waves developed with the Space Research Centre of the Polish Academy of Sciences (CBK PAN) and plasma and radio waves developed by CBK PAN and Astronika. The spacecraft is scheduled to launch in 2022 and arrive in Jupiter in 2030. Several other entities from Poland (for instance, Mobica and Space Forest) are also involved in the production of elements of the probe itself.

3.1.5 Mars Express

Polish engineers have developed a Power Supply Unit and a Pointing System for the Planetary Fourier Spectrometer (PFS). The spectrometer's task is to analyze the spectrum of radiation reflected and emitted by the surface and atmosphere of Mars.

3.1.6 The Herschel Space Observatory

The telescope launched in 2009 serves, among others, to explain the formation of galaxies and star formation and to study gas and dust clouds and comet matter. The Polish contribution to the construction of this telescope is significant. At the CBK PAN, the Local Oscillator's key elements for the heterodyne far-infrared (HIFI) spectrometer was developed – here the HLCU (HIFI Local Oscillator Control Unit) block was designed and built, which is a complete power supply, control, and control system for the Local Oscillator.

3.1.7 A Polish Trace on Mars

One of the most spectacular planetary missions in recent years is the mission of the Mars Science Laboratory. The Curiosity planetary robot, which has been exploring the surface of Mars since 2012, is equipped with a number of scientific instruments. One of them is a tunable laser spectrometer, which includes non-cooled MCT infrared detectors designed and manufactured by VIGO System. The task of the spectrometer is to collect information about the environment on the surface of Mars.

3.2 *Polish Devices in Space*

3.2.1 Polish Satellites

Lem and Heweliusz are a pair of Polish artificial satellites that are part of the international constellation BRITE (BRIght-star Target Explorer). The BRITE project aims to astronomically observe the brightest stars in the Milky Way. Upon their launch, "Lem" and "Heweliusz" became the first Polish scientific satellites.

The Lem was launched into orbit on November 21, 2013, from the Russian Yasny military base, aboard the Dnieper rocket (a modified ballistic missile). The launch of Hevelius on board the Long March-4B rocket took place on August 19, 2013 from the Chinese Taiyuan spaceport. In both cases, contact with the satellites was established during their first flight over Poland. Lem and Heweliusz are functioning until today.

The first two Polish scientific satellites were created as part of the Polish-Canadian-Austrian BRIght Target Explorer (BRITE) Programme. Both satellites, *Lem* and *Heweliusz*, are nano class, weighing less than 10kg. Their task is to study the largest and brightest stars in our galaxy to understand their internal structure better. The satellites' construction is the responsibility of Polish engineers and scientists from the Space Research Centre of the Polish Academy of Sciences and the Nicholas Copernicus Astronomical Centre of the PAN.

The BRITE constellation consists of six satellites: apart from two Polish (BRITE-Lem and BRITE-Heweliusz, two Austrian (UniBRITE and BRITE-Austria)) and two Canadian (BRITE-Toronto and BRITE-Montreal) satellites, five of them are observing, as BRITE -Montreal never reached its planned orbit.

3.2.2 Optical Instruments

For the "Pi of the Sky" gamma-ray observation project, polish company Creotech Instruments has developed a series of CCD (Charge Coupled Device) cameras that enable fast data processing and analysis also in real time. Cameras were installed at the Las Campanas Observatory in Chile, on the southern edge of the Atacama Desert, at an altitude of 2.4 thousand meters. Cameras provide scientists with data on the formation of black holes. Additionally, the network of "Pi of the Sky" telescopes will be used to detect and monitor space debris, Space Situational Awareness. The network of robotic telescopes allows observation of a large area of the sky and can also detect and monitor space debris. Thanks to the "Pi of the Sky" project, the world's first film about the birth of a black hole was made.

3.2.3 Time Measurement Systems

Piktime Systems designs and builds precise time receivers that allows one to compare the satellites' signals and then determine the difference in their clocks' indications. Piktime Systems' solutions are used by the time laboratory of the central ground control station of the European satellite navigation system Galileo in Italy (Galileo Control Centre, Precise Time Facility).

3.3 *Applications of Satellite Techniques on Earth*

3.3.1 Satellite Imagery in the Public Sector

Polish companies offer a wide range of services based on the analysis of satellite imagery. The delivered products include studies of urban agglomerations' development for spatial planning, analyzes environmental changes for nature protection, and various maps supporting forest management. The data used in Poland come from, among others, from the European Earth observation program Copernicus, the Galileo system and EGNOS. Effective use of satellite data in the work of public administration helps to plan, take appropriate actions and react effectively. Thanks to this, it is possible to significantly reduce losses caused by natural disasters, climate change, drought or floods. It is also a great way to skilfully plan land development, infrastructure development and protect the health of residents, and also represents a powerful tool for effective crisis management.

Building the MikroGlob Satellite Earth Observation System is also one of the priorities of Polish National Space Program project. The aim of the system will be to ensure the autonomous ability to provide high-resolution satellite imagery for users related to the state security and defense sector and to meet the needs of public administration in this regard.

The MikroGlob constellation is to consist of micro-class satellites that will be equipped with optical sensors imaging the Earth in the red, green, blue and near infrared bands, produced with the participation of Polish scientific and industrial entities.

In addition, the microsatellite constellation will be complemented by the Terrestrial Segment, which will include two redundant locations consisting of the Mission Management Center, the Load Management Center (sensors) and the Satellite Communication System.

Creotech Instruments, Scanway and the Space Research Center of the Polish Academy of Sciences are working on the project of the first Polish observation microsatellite, called EagleEye. The microsatellite will be placed in a very low orbit and will provide high-resolution images of the Earth – at a level of 1 meter. A technical dialogue with potential rocket suppliers has already started, as well as the launch service, which is to provide the satellite with an optimal operational orbit. The launch of the satellite into low Earth orbit is planned for 2023.

3.3.2 Road Navigation

The Polish satellite navigation system Automapa has gained tremendous popularity thanks to the integration of various satellite techniques, limiting themselves to Galileo/EGNOS and GPS. The system uses maps that are regularly updated by detecting new structures in satellite images. The maps themselves contain a complete road grid, 3-D visualizations of buildings, and their exact addresses. Based on user traffic analysis, there is a mechanism that allows one to detect and avoid traffic jams or unexpected traffic jams. The most up-to-date maps and information about the road situation are available on the Target.pl map portal.

3.3.3 Vehicle Monitoring

Poland, due to its location, belongs to the group of so-called transit countries. To reduce costs, better manage the fleet of vehicles, and improve safety, more and more Polish transport companies decide to equip their vehicles' with satellite monitoring. This is possible, among others, thanks to the AutoControl 2.0 platform developed in Poland, the scope of which covers all of Europe.

3.3.4 Precision Agriculture

Agricultural land constitutes approximately 60% of the total area of Poland. This fact means that the market of satellite services for agriculture has enormous growth potential. The use of new technologies helps increase the overall level of effectiveness of this sector of the economy. Polish companies offer precision farming services, providing solutions to assess local growing conditions and tools for their optimization.

3.3.5 Crisis Management

Poland's location and climatic conditions result in the regular occurrence of flooding and fire hazards. The observed climate changes give rise to concerns that material losses caused in this way will increase. As a result, Poland's crisis management institutions are starting to use satellite imagery to assess threats, plan activities, and assess damage. An example of this was the flood recovery action in 2010. The Crisis Information Centre was established in Poland, which offers operational support to rescue services and crisis management institutions using satellite techniques.

3.3.6 The Young in Space

In Poland, non-governmental and student organisations are very active groups in the space sector.

They contribute to informing the public about the benefits of investing in the space industry and places where young people gain their first experience in this industry.

Polish students participated in most of the Agency's educational programmes long before Poland joined ESA. These included mainly projects related to the construction of satellites such as the Young Engineers Satellite 2 (YES2), SSETI Express, European Student Earth Orbiter (SEO), and the European Student Moon Orbiter (ESMO).

Moreover, Polish students' scientific and technological experiments were tested during parabolic flight campaigns and flights of stratospheric balloons.

In 2012, the first Polish student satellite, PW-Sat, was launched into orbit to test the passive de-orbiting system. The satellite built in conformity with the

CubeSat standard was built at the Warsaw University of Technology in cooperation with the Space Research Centre of the Polish Academy of Sciences. An equally important event was the two-time victory of Polish robots, built by students from the Białystok University of Technology, in the prestigious University Rover Challenge in the United States, organized by Mars Society, an international (but non-governmental) organisation.

The most active Polish organisations dealing with educational projects include Mars Society Polska, Student Astronautics Club, the Polish Rocket Society, ARISS Polska, and the Copernicus Project.

4 Financial Settlements between Poland and ESA – Geographic Return

By joining ESA in 2012, Poland undertook, among other things, to contribute annually to compulsory programmes that finance space research, develop key space technologies and education programmes, and cover the standard costs of ESA. Poland also has the option of paying contributions to optional programmes. The amount of the contribution for compulsory programmes is calculated by ESA in relation to the value of the Member State's net national income over a three-year period. The contribution rate for optional programmes depends on the Member State.[8]

8 In the absence of a legal definition for this chapter's purposes, it was assumed that the space sector is all entities involved in the systematic application of engineering and scientific fields to explore and use outer space, according to Wachowicz, E., *Polish space sector. Subject structure – development opportunities – fundraising* Collective work, POLSA, 2017. According to the cited definition of entities in the space sector, there are two conditions that an entity should meet in order to be included in the space sector, ie:
- documented participation in the European supply chain – through registration in the database of entities maintained by, for example, the ESA for industrial entities and organisations;
- conducting research and/or implementation of industrial works related to space technologies and satellite techniques – for scientific entities.

The third prospective criterion – for industrial entities – may estimate the turnover related to space activities (determining the share of revenues from space activities in the total amount of revenues). An example of a turning point could be the level of 25% (According to: Development of the space sector – report of the Polish Supreme Audit Office, KGP.430.017.2019 Reg. No. 44/2020/P/19/021/KGP, Warsaw, (20 May 2020)) Registration in the ESA entities' database is necessary for gaining access to tenders organized by this organisation and applying for participation in implemented projects. On 28 February 2020, a total of 14,961 entities were registered in the catalog of the ESA (https://esastar-emr.sso.esa.int/PublicEntityDir/PublicEntityDir) website (accessed 2 February

In the years 2016–2019, Poland paid a total of EUR 165,400,000 to ESA, that is, about PLN 620,000,000, as contributions to mandatory and optional programmes. Out of this amount, EUR 93,100,000 was allocated to compulsory programmes.[9]

In individual years, the amount of the compulsory contribution was:

2016 – EUR 21,600,000; 2017 – EUR 21,800,00; 2018 – EUR 23,000,000 and in 2019 – EUR 26,700,000. For 11 optional programmes, Poland allocated a total of EUR 72,300,000, including in: 2016 – EUR 15,600,000 (72% of the obligatory contribution), 2017 – EUR 17,500,000 (80%); 2018 – EUR 18,300,000 (80%), and in 2019 – EUR 20,900,000 (78.2%). The amount of the obligatory contribution in 2016 did not differ significantly until 2015, when EUR 21,700,000 was paid. However, the participation in optional programmes was significantly higher (in 2015 – EUR 8,500,000).

ESA's industrial policy is based on the so-called geographic return.[10] In 2019, Poland's contribution accounted for 0.8% of the entire ESA budget, while the geographic return in 2016 – 2018 ranged from 0.86 to 1.04. This was significantly more than other countries ending the transition periods, for instance, for Austria the ratio was 0.83; for the Czech Republic 0.79; for Denmark 0.85; and for Finland 0.87.

Pursuant to the agreement on Poland's accession to ESA, a special PLIIS mechanism was established for five years, that is, until the end of 2017. It assumed that 45% of the Polish contribution to compulsory programmes was to be allocated to adapting the Polish industry, the scientific community, and other entities to ESA requirements. In practice, this meant organizing competitions dedicated exclusively to Polish entities. ESA experts assessed projects

---

2021), including 473 from Poland. Out of 12 entrepreneurs surveyed by the Supreme Audit Office, seven declared that they obtain from 50% to 100% of their revenues from activities related to space exploration or the use of satellite data, three reported a range from 20% to 50%, and one from 0.2% up to 2.1%.

9 Development of the space sector – report of the Polish Supreme Audit Office, KGP.430.017.2019 Reg No 44/2020 / P / 19/021 / KGP, Warsaw, 20 May 2020.

10 The general rule governs all ESA contracts' geographical distribution that for each country, the share of its industry in ESA contracts should be as close as possible to that country's share in the Agency's budget. The measurement of the return is the coefficient calculated for each country – the relation between the amount of actually received contracts and the expected value (which is the percentage share in the Agency's financing multiplied by the total sum of contracts awarded to all the ESA members), taking into account the technological value of the awarded contracts. According to their technological value, assessing programmes and projects is to ensure that ESA will implement as many projects as possible with the highest technological parameters. The ideal breakdown of contracts concluded by the Agency should result in all countries achieving a coefficient of 1.

under PLIIS without the participation of representatives of the Polish side. Then, the assessed projects were recommended by the Inter-ministerial Team for Space Policy in Poland. The final decision about the implementation was made by the Joint Task Force Poland – ESA (the ESA – Poland Task Force). After the interim review was carried out in 2015, ESA submitted a request to extend the transition period until the end of 2019. On 12 January 2017, Poland's agreement with ESA was amended by extending the PLIIS mechanism until the end of 2019.

Considering the ESA settlement mechanism (deductions from the obligatory premium), in 2015–2019, ESA allocated EUR 46,700,000 under the PLIIS mechanism, that is, 42% of the sum of obligatory premiums shown on ESA invoices. This amount was reduced by ESA's internal costs, which effectively put at the disposal of Polish entities contract options with a total value of EUR 37,400,000. The contract amount of contracts concluded between ESA and Polish entities from 1 January 2015, to 30 September 2019, amounted to EUR 28,900,000, which means a "return" of 77.3%.

Apart from PLIIS, Polish entities concluded 42 contracts worth EUR 15,700,000 under ESA mandatory programmes.

By 2016, 81 contracts with a total contractual value of EUR 21,900,000 were concluded under 11 optional programmes. In 2017–2019, 64 contracts were concluded under six optional programmes with a total value of EUR 20,700,000.

5 Task Implementation in the Field of Space Policy in Poland

The Minister of Entrepreneurship and Technology, by Order No. 15 of 10 May 2019, established the Space Policy Team as an auxiliary body of the minister responsible for the economy. The goal of the Team is to provide support in the implementation of tasks in the field of space policy in Poland. The tasks of the Team include:

- giving opinions and recommending projects to the minister competent for the economy that are to be financed from the Polish contribution in individual ESA programmes for Polish entities;
- cooperation with the ESA-PL Task Force in developing activities specified in the contract with ESA;
- proposing solutions aimed at supporting the Polish space sector in acquiring industrial and scientific projects to ensure the optimal use of the Polish contribution to ESA;
- analysis and evaluation of the implementation of the assumptions of Polish space policy and the national space sector programme; recommending the

amounts of financial contributions to optional ESA programmes to the minister of the economy; and
- recommending appropriate provisions to the minister for the next financial year concerning the amount of the optional contribution to be paid to ESA.

6 European Union Projects of Which Poland Is a Part

6.1 *The Galileo System*

On 15 December 2016, the European Commission officially launched the first services of the Galileo system, that is:
- the baseline service widely available – free of charge for all users;
- public regulated access (PRS) – for public administrations and the secret services; and
- search and rescue (SAR) – a European contribution to the COSPAS-SARSAT International Satellite Alerting and Locating System, based on the system of radio signal transmitters.[11]

Galileo is the equivalent of the American GPS (Global Positioning System) and the Russian GLONASS (Global Orbiting Navigation Satellite System). Work on the project was started in 1999 on France's initiative, and its direct precursor is the Satellite Regional Support System – EGNOS.

The Galileo system consists of three segments – space, terrestrial, and the user segment. The first of them consists of 30 satellites located in three orbits around the Earth. Such a large number of satellites has a positive impact on the system's quality of operation and accuracy. For comparison: the American GPS consists of 24 satellites.

The terrestrial segment consists of infrastructure that enables satellite control, monitoring their operation, signal and data processing, and management of the entire terrestrial part. The third part of Galileo – the user segment – is used to operate the created system. This segment includes a whole range of receivers intended for various user groups, depending on the needs and application.

11 The COSPAS-SARSAT system: General operating principle in an emergency, and activated distress signal transmitter emitting a distress signal on a frequency of 406MHz. The danger signal is received by the satellites of the Cospas – Sarsat system and sent to the system's ground components – LUT. Then, the received distress signal is sent to the System Mission Control Centre – MCC and to the Search and Rescue Coordination Centres – RCC, which initiate a search and rescue operation to help people in distress.

Galileo's use is almost limitless and will cover a wide variety of fields – the economy, military sector, administration, and research. Satellite navigation supports transport (air, sea, road, rail, and pedestrian), the insurance and tourism sector, electricity and data transmission management, agriculture, and defense supervision. Transmitters that determine and transmit their position allow for the quick location of missing planes, ships, vehicles, people, and crisis management (earthquakes, forest fires, and floods).

For a private user, Galileo provides assistance in navigating unknown terrain and providing information about it, facilitates chronically-ill people's supervision, and improves rescue operations.

The Institute of Telecommunications verified the availability of Galileo signals on Poland's territory as part of a measurement campaign commissioned by the Ministry of Digital Affairs (Ministerstwo Cyfryzacji) in 2016. The system's services were not continuously available in the first period due to an insufficient number of satellites in orbit. In December 2019, all owners of receivers adapted to Galileo can use its services, for example, in satellite navigation (mobile phones), in precision agriculture, fleet management, eCall[12] in cars, critical infrastructure management, surveying, et cetera. The full use of Galileo services is possible since 2020.

6.1.1 EGNOS

The following services are available within the EGNOS system:

- from 1 October 2009 – free of charge (Open Service) – providing information necessary for positioning and timing, intended mainly for satellite navigation in the area covered by the EGNOS system;
- from 2 March 2011 – the Safety of Life service – its purpose is to support civil aviation in the field of approaching to landing in poor visibility; in the future, the service may be used in other areas (for instance, maritime, rail, and road transport); and
- from 26 July 2012 – access to EGNOS data (EDAS) – the service is aimed at users who require increased performance for commercial and professional purposes; it provides access to real-time EGNOS data and historical data collected and generated by the EGNOS terrestrial infrastructure.

12 Per Regulation (EU) 2015/758 of the European Parliament and of the Council of 29 April 2015 on type-approval requirements for the implementation of the eCall onboard system based on the 112 emergency number, from 31 March 2018, every brand new car in the EU it must have a satellite receiver to track the signals of the European Galileo navigation system.

On 14 airports in Poland, namely at Bydgoszcz, Gdańsk, Cracow, Katowice, Lublin, Łódź, Warsaw, Modlin, Poznań, Rzeszów, Szczecin, Olsztyn, Wrocław and Zielona Góra, the so-called LPV 200 approach procedure, is the most accurate of the EGNOS services. According to GSA data, in 2019, all of Poland remains within reach of EGNOS services. To improve the coverage and service parameters for the eastern part of the European Union, it is planned to establish a RIMS station in Ukraine in the second quarter of 2020. According to the European Commission, the priority is to cover all EU Member States' territories by the end of 2025 with EGNOS services.[13]

The European Community allocated EUR 3,400,000,000 to implement the Galileo and EGNOS projects in 2007–2013. Actions related to these programmes from 1 January 2014, to 31 December 2020, are expected to cost a maximum of EUR 7,100,000,000.[14]

Poland's contribution to the financing of the Galileo and EGNOS programmes in 2016–2019 amounted to a total of EUR 112,700,000, and in individual years to EUR 18,800,000, EUR 29,100,000, EUR 32,600,000, and EUR 32,200,000, respectively. This represented, respectively: 3.22%, 3.16%, 3.28%, and 3.38% of the total payments transferred by the European Union for the implementation of these. An amount of EUR 35,000,000 is planned for 2020 – the rate is 3.56%.

ESA implements the tasks commissioned by the European Commission in the area of Galileo and EGNOS. The Agency conducts proceedings concerning procurement for the construction of systems. Most of the contracts were concluded by the most significant European entities (before Poland joined the European Union or before the ESA accession). Based on a permanent contract with the Galileo system operator, CBK PAN provides GNSS observation data from the so-called BOR-1 reference station. The contract value for 2016–2019 is PLN 4,200,000 gross per year.

6.2 *The ESA Programmes*

Participation in ESA programmes became possible from the moment of Poland's accession to this Agency. In 2014–2020, 11 Polish entities (entrepreneurs, scientific, and research units) concluded contracts with ESA to implement 26

13 Development of the space sector – report of the Polish Supreme Audit Office, KGP.430.017.2019 Reg No 44/2020/P/19/021/KGP, Warsaw, 20 May 2020.

14 Council Regulation (EU, Euratom) No 1311/2013 of 2 December 2013, laying down the multiannual financial framework for 2014–2020 (Journal of Laws UE L 347 of 20 December 2013 884 as amended).

projects in the field of telecommunications and navigation. Their value totaled EUR 5,500,000.

Poland's geographic return in ESA programmes in 2016–2018 ran from 0.9 to 1.04. Among the eight areas for the use of space and satellite technologies classified by ESA,[15] in 2018 Poland achieved the highest rate of return in Earth observation (1.27) and in satellite navigation (1.13).[16]

6.2.1 The NAVISP Programme

In 2016, Poland joined the NAVISP Programme-Navigation Innovation and Support Programme, a programme supporting the development of Galileo's European global satellite navigation system.

The purpose of NAVISP[17] is to implement innovative activities. The Programme consists of three components:

- Element 1 – aimed at generating innovative concepts, techniques, technologies, and systems;
- Element 2 – which aims to maintain, improve the capacity and competitiveness of the Member States' industries in the field of technologies and services in the global satellite navigation market; and
- Element 3 – focused on supporting national navigation activities.

In 2016, Poland joined Element 2 with a total amount of EUR 2,100,000. Under the Programme, four Polish entities implemented three projects concerning the development of receivers for the Galileo system and IT systems. The amount of co-financing totaled EUR 1,550,000. The amount of EUR 1,500,000 is planned for the period 2017–2021. The geographic return coefficient for Poland should be 2.24.

15 Earth observation, research, manned flight and exploration, space transportation and return-to-earth technologies, satellite telecommunications, satellite navigation, fundamental technologies and techniques, and situational awareness systems.

16 In the years 2012–2019 (first half), Polish entities constructed six artificial satellites that were launched into space. They were:
- PW-Sat released on 13 February 2012,
- BRITE-PL-1 "LEM" – on 21 November 2013,
- BRITE-PL-2 "HEWELIUSZ" – on 19 August 19 2014,
- "PW-Sat2" – on 3 December 2018,
- "KRAKsat" and "Światowid" – on 3 July 2019.

17 Navigation Innovation and Support Programme (NAVISP) is a programme supporting the development of the European global satellite navigation system Galileo. The Programme aims to stimulate the satellite navigation industry.

6.2.2 The ARTES Programme

One of the key programmes of ESA in the field of satellite telecommunications is the ARTES programme.[18] Advanced Research in Telecommunications Systems enables European and Canadian industries to research innovative concepts through research and development to create state-of-the-art satellite products and services. Poland has been participating in it since 2016. The Programme includes both relatively undemanding projects, aimed at companies taking their first steps in the satellite sector, and complex activities (for example, building complete satellite systems, including testing them in orbital conditions) and suchlike.

Poland participated in the following elements of the ARTES programme:

- FP (future preparations) – strategic and market analyses and support for satellite communication standards. This element is compulsory for countries joining the Programme. The subscription amount depends on a given country's GDP value (The Polish premium is EUR 250,000). Polish entities have not won any contracts so far.[19]

---

18 Under the Advanced Research in Telecommunications Systems programme, European and Canadian industries research innovative concepts through research and development to create state-of-the-art satellite products and services. The ARTES programme transforms R&D investment into successful commercial products and services by offering varying degrees of support to projects with different operational and commercial maturity levels.

ARTES has three branches:

- Support and development of new or next-generation Satcom products and technologies up to their first flight opportunity is part of Core Competitiveness,
- The ESA's Partnership Projects with satellite operators and manufacturers support co-funding to share the risk of investing in new technologies. This accelerates their introduction to the market, keeping Europe ahead in satcoms,
- Business Applications develops everyday applications and services that use satcom technology to improve existing solutions or fill the gaps left by terrestrial ones.

19 ARTES Future Preparation (FP) is dedicated to strategic analysis, market analysis, technology and system feasibility studies, and to the support of satellite communication standards. The range of activities covered by ARTES FP include:

- Monitoring economic conditions and overall market trends to assess potential in the European and Canadian Satcom markets;
- Understanding future market needs while considering all actors participating in the Satcom industry;
- Understanding competition and synergy with terrestrial systems;
- Building telecom product strategy through Research & Development activities;
- Validating performance/feasibility of new concepts with an end-to-end system perspective;
- Supporting standardization and regulatory activities.

- NEOSAT (Next Generation Platform – The next-generation platform)[20] – focused on creating a production line, thanks to which two leading European companies in the space sector, Airbus DS and Thales Alenia Space, will be able to build satellites weighing from three to six tons. In the years 2013–2020, the Polish contribution totaled EUR 2,120,000. Two entities concluded the agreements and the geographic return rate for Poland was 1.
- IAP (Integrated Application Promotions – Promotion of integrated applications)[21] – promotion of integrated applications that use data from existing resources (for instance, from Earth observation, satellite navigation, satellite communications, space flight) and integrate them with terrestrial services. They most often relate to satellite techniques, including in agriculture, tourism, education, infrastructure development and suchlike. The total Polish contribution amounted to EUR 5,800,000. In the so-called Phase II (2013–2016), 19 Polish entities participated in 22 projects; the grant's total value is EUR 2,260,000. The geographic return rate was 1.33. In 2017–2019, 21 entities operating in Poland participated in 31 projects; the total amount of co-financing was EUR 4,400,000 and the geographic return ratio was 0.96.

---

20 Neosat is the next generation platform initiative, leading to two successful Partnership Projects managed by the ESA in cooperation with the French Space Agency, CNES. They are Spacebus Neo with Thales Alenia Space and Eurostar Neo with Airbus, which are dedicated to developing, qualifying, and validating in-orbit, next-generation satellite platforms for the core-satellite communications market. Neosat has significantly reduced satellites' costs by introducing innovation at all levels and optimizing the new satellites for fully electric propulsion. Since product line developments started at the end of 2015, more than 10 Neosat satellites have been sold by the European industry to six satellite operators, generating an exceptional investment return. For every €1 invested, more than €20 is expected to be returned to the Programme's participating States and their industries, according to an independent study by Euroconsult in partnership with Technopolis and Oxford Economics. The Neosat Partnership Projects have federated industry around large-scale programmes, achieving competitive leaps forward and economic impacts. Under the leadership of the prime contractors Thales Alenia Space and Airbus, companies from across the ESA Member States have developed the new satellite product lines and are supplying the recurring building blocks. System engineering, satellite assembly, integration, and test activities have taken place in France and the United Kingdom, which are the two main contributors from the 17 nations that participate in Neosat.

21 The ARTES IAP programme is dedicated to the development, implementation, and pilot operations of Integrated Applications. These applications utilize data from existing space assets, such as Satellite Communication, Earth Observation, Satellite Navigation, and Human Spaceflight technologies, combined with terrestrial services.

ARTES IAP projects cover Feasibility Studies and Demonstration Projects. Any organisation can propose to develop a new commercially promising space-based application or service. It may be, e.g., a federation of users, a commercial company, a public body, or a non-governmental organisation.

6.2.3 European Earth Monitoring Programme (GMES) – Copernicus

In 2010, the European Union launched the European Earth monitoring programme (GMES), providing access to accurate environmental and security data and information. In 2014, the GMES programme's name was changed to Copernicus, and the rules for its implementation at the European level were established.

The individual EU Member States could create national structures to receive and process data from the Programme. The creation of such structures in Poland is the second specific objective of the Polish Space Strategy (Polska Strategia Kosmiczna-PSK). Development of satellite applications – contribution to the construction of the digital economy. The intervention directions include ensuring constant, fast, and reliable access to satellite data and popularizing the use of satellite data in public administration at various levels.

The draft plan for implementing the Copernicus Programme in Poland was drawn up in 2011 by the Institute of Geodesy and Cartography and the Space Research Centre of the Polish Academy of Sciences.

In the years 2014–2020, a total of EUR 4,300,000,000 will be allocated to implementing the Copernicus EC Programme. Poland does not bear separate costs of participation in the Programme, apart from the ESA contributions, which co-finance the Programme. The so-called 'Staff costs' incurred by the ministry connected with the implementation of the Programme, including, among other things, salaries, costs of employee delegations, expert visits, and information and training projects in 2016–2019, amounted to approximately PLN 1,100,000.

6.2.4 EUMETSAT

The European Organisation for the Exploitation of Meteorological Satellites (EUMETSAT) was established in 1986 to ensure the continued operation of the meteorological satellite system built by ESA.[22] The Organization's main task is to implement its own satellite programme to provide Member States with, among others, weather and earth monitoring, climate forecasting and tracking. Pursuant to the Act of 9 January 2009, on the ratification of the Convention on the Establishment of the European Organisation for the Exploitation of Meteorological Satellites (EUMETSAT), drawn up in Geneva on 24 May 1983,[23] the Republic of Poland acceded to this Convention. However, at the time of

22 Convention for the Establishment of a European Organization for the Exploitation of Meteorological Satellites (EUMETSAT), Geneva, done 24 May 1983, entered into force 19 June 1986; 1434 UNTS 3.

23 Journal of Laws of 2009, No 38, item 297.

its signing, the Protocol on the privileges and immunities of the European Organisation for the Exploitation of Meteorological Satellites, drawn up in Darmstadt,[24] was not taken into account. This fact resulted in the deprivation of the possibility of financing EUMETSAT international conferences organized in Poland and Polish specialists' participation in courses and internships abroad. Moreover, Polish entrepreneurs were excluded from any tenders for EUMETSAT. Poland joined the Protocol only in 2014.

Poland participated in five obligatory EUMETSAT programmes:[25]

- The Meteosat Transition Programme (MTP), covering the construction, launching, and operational exploitation of the geostationary satellites Meteosat – 4 (1989–1995), Meteosat – 5 (1991–2007), Meteosat – 6 (1993–2012), and Meteosat – 7 (1997–2017). The last of the satellites were transferred to the so-called cemetery orbit in April 2017. During the period under the control of Institute of Meteorology and Water Management (Instytut Meteorologii i Gospodarki Wodnej)[26] it used the data of the last satellite that was placed over the Indian Ocean and included Poland.
- Meteosat Second Generation (MSG), a programme covering the construction of the launch and operational exploitation of the second-generation geostationary satellites: Meteosat – 8 (launch date – 2003), Meteosat – 9 (2005), Meteosat – 10 (2012) and Meteosat – 11 (2015). Until the end of the audit in December 2019, the Institute used all the satellites in this series.
- The EUMETSAT Polar System (EPS) is a programme covering the construction, launch, and operational exploitation of the Metop – A (launched in 2006), Metop – B (launched in 2012), and Metop – C (launched in 2018) polar satellites. Until the end of the audit in December 2019, the Institute used all the satellites in this series.
- MTG is a programme covering the construction of third-generation geostationary satellites. It will include five satellites. Their operation is planned for the years 2021–2036. The scheduled launch of the first MTG-I1 satellite is to take place in October 2021 and the MTG-S1 in 2023.

24 Amending Protocol to the Convention for the establishment of a European organisation for the exploitation of meteorological satellites ("EUMETSAT"), Darmstadt, done 5 June 1991, entered into force 19 November 2000; 2223 UNTS 230.

25 Development of the space sector – report of the Polish Supreme Audit Office, KGP.430.017.2019 Reg No 44/2020/P/19/021/KGP, Warsaw, 20 May 2020.

26 Institute of Meteorology and Water Management – National Research Institute – an institution that performs meteorological and hydrological services on the territory of Poland.

- EUMETSAT Polar System-Second Generation (EPS-SG) is a programme covering the construction of second-generation polar satellites. It will include six satellites (three pairs). The first pair of satellites are planned to be placed in orbit in November 2022 and November 2023.

6.2.5 The European Southern Observatory (ESO)

Formally, this entity is called the European Organisation for Astronomical Research in the Southern Hemisphere. It is an intergovernmental organisation associating 16 Member States, including Poland and the host countries Chile and Australia, as strategic partners. The main mission of ESO, established by the 1962 Convention,[27] is to provide astronomical and astrophysical observatories with the most modern research equipment, enabling them to conduct their research under the best conditions.

6.2.6 GovSatCom – Governmental Satellite Communications

The Programme is implemented with the participation of 16 countries, European Defense Agency-EDA and ESA. The goal of this Programme is to create reliable, secure government satellite communications for institutions responsible for security, crisis management, critical infrastructure, and border protection. The Programme is expected to be fully implemented in 2025. The programme's estimated costs in the operational phase, financed from the EU budget, will range from EUR 100,000,000 to EUR 150,000,000 per year.

7 Polish Space Agency Activity

The Polish Space Agency (POLSA) was established under the Act of 26 September 2014, on the Polish Space Agency. From 20 July 2019, that is, from the date of entry into force of the amendment to the Act on POLSA,[28] the

---

27 Convention for the establishment of a European Organization for Astronomical Research in the Southern Hemisphere (hereafter ESO Convention), Paris, done 5 October 1962, entered into force 17 January 1964; 502 UNTS 225.

28 According to Article 3 clause 2 of the POLSA Act, the Agency's tasks included, among other things, representing the Polish economic and scientific interest in the field of exploration and use of space, 27 internationally, in particular as part of participation in the programmes of the European Union, the European Space Agency, the European Organisation for the Exploitation of Meteorological Satellites (EUMETSAT) and the European Defense Agency (EDA) (Article 3 (2) (3)); providing advice on the use of outer space (Article 3 (2) (8)) and providing information and promotion activities in the field of using outer space (Article 3 (2) (13)). The tasks are in line with the specific objective No 1 of PSK Increasing the competitiveness of the Polish space sector and increasing its share

Agency is subordinate to the minister competent for the economy (previously the Prime Minister). The tasks of the Agency include:

1) initiating, preparing, and implementing assumptions, main directions of research and development programmes in the field of research and use of outer space;
2) representing the Polish economic and scientific interest in the field of research and use of space in the international arena;
3) advising on the use of outer space;
4) keeping a register of outer space objects according to the rules specified in the Convention of 14 January 1975,[29] on the registration of outer space objects launched into outer space;[30]
5) conducting educational, information, and promotional activities in the field of space use; and
6) identifying, in cooperation with the minister competent for higher education, the needs of training specialists in space use and supporting the training of experts in space technology.

As of today, the Polish Space Strategy is the only normative act that has been adopted into the Polish legal system. And this even despite the fact that international agreements to which Poland is a party impose an obligation on

---

in the European space sector's turnover, the direction of intervention increasing participation in EU space programmes – Horizon 2020, Copernicus, Galileo, SST, GovSatCom.

29 Convention on Registration of Objects Launched into Outer Space, New York, done 14 January 1975, entered into force 15 September 1976; 1023 UNTS 15; TIAS 8480; 28 UST 695; UKTS 1978 No. 70; Cmnd. 6256; ATS 1986 No. 5; 14 ILM 43 (1975).

30 Poland is a party to the Treaty on the Principles of State Activities in the Exploration and Use of Outer Space, Including the Moon and Other Celestial Bodies, drawn up on January 27, 1967 (Journal of Laws of 1968, item 82), the Convention on the Registration of Launched Objects into outer space of January 14, 1975 (Journal of Laws of 1979, item 22) and the Convention on International Liability for Damage Caused by Space Objects of March 29, 1972 (Journal of Laws of 1973, No. item 154). These treaties require national law to regulate, inter alia, such issues as:
– rules of consent to activities in outer space by national entities and the designation of an authority responsible for the supervision of such activities,
– rules for keeping a national register of space objects,
– state liability and compensation issues.

In order to ensure the fulfillment of the obligation arising for Poland under Article 2 of the United Nations Convention, it is necessary to develop a draft law on the National Register of Space Objects, which is to contain primarily provisions on keeping a register of space objects launched into space by Polish entities, with the simultaneous notification of this information to the Secretary General of the United Nations. The register will be kept by the Polish Space Agency, which will also supervise the space activities of Polish entities. Work on that is still in progress.

our state to regulate such issues as rules for consent to activities in space by national entities and the designation of an authority responsible for the supervision of such activities; rules for keeping a national register of space objects; and state liability and compensation issues.

To date, in Poland none of them has been regulated to the obvious detriment of the development of the space sector. The lack of such legal acts leads to such situations as the failure to register with the United Nations (UN) two Polish satellites from SatRevolution launched in 2019. Failure to register such objects is a breach of the provisions contained in the Outer Space Treaty and the Convention on the Registration of Objects Launched into Outer Space, to which Poland is a party. Failure to respect the provisions of international law obviously affects the importance of our country in the international arena.

Particularly acute is the lack of clear rules on corporate liability and related insurance issues. This leads to a situation where insurance companies, due to the lack of a clear legal framework, do not want or even cannot cooperate with the space sector because they do not know where its liability starts and ends. Of course, there were attempts to regulate these issues. Work on the draft act on the register of space objects has been going on since 2013, with poor results.

Work is currently underway on a draft law on space activities, which is to regulate such issues as:

- rules and conditions for the performance of space activities;
- the principles and administrative organization of ongoing supervision over space activities;
- liability for damage caused by a space object, insofar as the matter is not governed by international agreements;
- the procedure at the national forum in the case of a space damage involving a space object for which the Republic of Poland is a state of the art; and
- rules for the operation of the national register of space objects.

At present, the use of outer space, including celestial bodies and orbits, is governed by conventional and customary international space law standards, which is part of public international law. Poland played an important role in the development of these standards by acting constructively at the forum of the United Nations (mainly the Committee on the Peaceful Uses of Outer Space – COPUOS) and the doctrine of international law. Poland is a founding member. Poland is a Member State of the International Mobile Satellite Communications Organisation (IMSO),[31] a party to the Agreement on the

31 Convention on the International Mobile Satellite Organization, London, done 3 September 1976, entered into force 16 July 1979, as amended 1998, amended version entered into force 31 July 2001; ATS 2001 No. 11.

establishment of the international space communications organisation system "INTERSPUTNIK"[32] and a party to the most important international conventions on the use of outer space:

- The Treaty on the Principles of the Activities of States in the Study and Use of Outer Space, Including the Moon and Other Celestial Bodies of 1967;[33]
- The Agreement on the rescue of cosmonauts, the return of cosmonauts, and the return of objects launched into space from 1968;[34]
- The Convention on International Liability for Damage Caused by Space Objects of 1972;[35]
- The Convention on Registration of Objects Launched into Outer Space, 1975;[36]
- The Convention Establishing the International Maritime Satellite Communications Organisation (INMARSAT) and the International Maritime Satellite Communications Organisation (INMARSAT) 1976 Convention[37] as well as the Protocol on the Privileges and Immunities of the International Maritime Satellite Communications Organisation (INMARSAT) of 1981;[38]
- Agreements on the International Satellite Telecommunications Organisation INTELSAT;[39] and
- The Convention Establishing the European Satellite Communications Organisation EUTELSAT.[40]

7.1 *Benefits of Participating in the Galileo and EGNOS Programmes*

The main advantage of the European GNSS systems is that they are under civilian control, unlike other global systems under military oversight. In the Galileo system, according to the assumptions, the quality of services after the final system launch is to be better than in other systems. Individual users, companies, and administrations use the services offered by GNSS. A survey conducted in

32 Agreement on the Establishment of the "INTERSPUTNIK" International System and Organization of Space Communications, Moscow, done 15 November 1971, entered into force 12 July 1972; 862 UNTS 3; TIAS 859 (1973) No. 12343; Space Law – Basic Legal Documents, C.VIII.1.

33 Journal of Laws 68.14.82.

34 Journal of Laws 69.15.110.

35 Journal of Laws 73.27.154.

36 Journal of Laws 73.27.154.

37 Journal of Laws 80.7.19.

38 Journal of Laws 80.10.27.

39 Journal of Laws 94.110.530.

40 Journal of Laws 95.24.130.

2015 by the EURISY organisation in cooperation with the then Ministry of the Economy showed that 78% of the surveyed offices in Poland (both central and 32 local ones) use the service based on satellite navigation.

The state of implementation of Galileo and EGNOS applications is as follows:[41]

- Mobile telephony – leading GNSS providers, representing over 95% of the GNSS chipset market, produce components ready to support Galileo; 31 global manufacturers of smartphones/tablets have implemented solutions enabling the system's use. There are over 1 billion Galileo-enabled phones on the market (184 different models); by the end of 2019, about 40% of all receivers offered on the market will be operated by Galileo.
- Road transport – 24 car manufacturers market models equipped with EGNOS and Galileo, in line with the EU Regulation on the implementation of the e-Call system;[42] Galileo is tested worldwide in more than 25 autonomous vehicle prototypes (75% of all prototypes); collection systems over 72% of toll roads in the European Union are based on the use of GNSS.
- Aviation – 328 EGNOS-based approach procedures have been implemented at 228 global airports since October 2019. Over 156 receiver models used in drones available on the market (35 manufacturers) can use the Galileo and EGNOS system.
- Railway – the GSA is working to include EGNOS in the European Rail Traffic Management System (ERTMS).
- Sea transport – around 20% of receivers installed on ships use the Galileo signal (15% in 2018), and 90% of receivers use the EGNOS open service; 19 global manufacturers offer receivers that include Galileo.

41 Development of the space sector – report of the Polish Supreme Audit Office, KGP.430.017.2019 Reg No 44/2020/P/19/021 / KGP, Warsaw, 20 May 2020.

42 According to Regulation (EU) 2015/758 of the European Parliament and of the Council of 29 April 2015, on type-approval requirements for the implementation of the eCall onboard system based on the 112 emergency number and amending Directive 2007/46 / EC (Journal of Laws UE L 123 of 19/05/2015 77, as amended), from 31 March 2018, every brand new car in the EU will have to have a satellite receiver that tracks the signals of the European navigation system Galileo. The technical requirements for the use of the Galileo signal in eCall systems have been specified in EC Delegated Regulation 2017/79 of 12 September 2016, laying down detailed technical requirements and test procedures for the EC type-approval of motor vehicles with regard to their eCall onboard systems based on 112 onboard separate technical units and components based on 112 eCall and supplementing and amending Regulation (EU) 2015/758 of the European Parliament and of the Council with regard to exemptions and applicable standards (Journal of Laws L12 of 17 January 2017 44).

- Surveying – Satellite and navigation support system providers include Galileo services. In 2019, 37 networks were adapted to receive Galileo signals (including the Polish ASG-Eupos network). More than 57% of mapping receivers are available for Galileo, and around 97% of such mapping receivers are compatible with EGNOS.
- Agriculture – approximately 90% of new tractors in Europe equipped with a GNSS receiver can use EGNOS, while approximately 56% of navigation receivers have Galileo functionalities implemented.

According to the data presented by the European Commission and the GSA, solutions based on GNSS will constitute an increasing share in the EU economy. It is estimated that satellite navigation services contribute to almost 11% of the EU economy.[43] Besides, as indicated by the European Commission, Galileo's implementation will generate additional revenues of € 90 billion for the EU economy over 20 years.[44] This applies to direct revenues to the space sector, receiver, and application manufacturers and indirect revenues to society in the form of more efficient transport, communication, security management et cetera.

8 Commercial Involvement in Poland's Space Market

The exploration and use of outer space is an undertaking that requires States to have enormous material, infrastructural, technological, and organisational resources. Only the largest countries with the highest technological development can make such an effort. The US space agency NASA's annual budget in 2018 was over $ 20.7 billion, which is almost three times more than the total annual national defense spending in Poland. The awareness of the above-mentioned limitations prompted some of the so-called Old Europe leaders to create the European Space Research Organisation (ESRO)[45] and the European Organisation for the Development of Launch of Launchers (ELDO),[46] which in

43 Report from the Commission to the European Parliament and the Council on the implementation of the Galileo and EGNOS programmes and the European GNSS Agency's performance.

44 https://ec.europa.eu/growth/sectors/space/galileo_en (accessed 2 February 2021).

45 Convention for the Establishment of a European Space Research Organization, Paris, done 14 June 1962, entered into force 20 March 1964, expired 30 October 1980; 158 UNTS 35: UKTS 1964 No. 56; Cmnd. 2489.

46 Convention for the Establishment of a European Organization for the Development and Construction of Space Vehicle Launchers, London, done 29 March 1962, entered into force 29 February 1964, expired 30 October 1980; 507 UNTS 177; UKTS 1964 No. 30; Cmnd. 2391; ATS 1964 No. 6.

1975 were combined, thus giving rise to the aforementioned European Space Agency. Uniting ten countries (currently 22 countries), the European Space Agency, based in Paris, has set itself to implement a joint European programme for the study and use of space. In the following years, the organisation achieved a number of significant successes in the form of building its own launchers, its own communication, and satellite navigation systems. The current ESA strategy (2015 – 2025) is based, among others, on the Space 4.0i vision. The foundations of this vision are the integration of the space sector with the economy and society, the competitiveness of the European sector on a global scale, European autonomy in the space industry, and the private sector's involvement. The strategy assumes a high degree of innovation by taking up technological challenges, including those with a high degree of risk. Furthermore, the strategy considers it important that the public has a significant awareness of the Agency's activities by disclosing information.

All Member States of the European Space Agency contribute (in proportion to their gross domestic product) to mandatory programmes[47] costs and the organisation's common costs. The compulsory programmes include three programmes:

- Science Programme – space research, solar system physics, astronomy, and basic physics;
- General Studies Programme – a think tank of the European Space Agency, defining the organisation's strategy for the coming years; and
- Technology Research Programme – development of space technologies, development of equipment for space research.

Data from the European Space Agency on the Polish space sector show that by joining the Agency in 2012, Polish entrepreneurs (despite the small number of enterprises dealing strictly with space activities) had a large potential of knowledge, experience, and organisational culture. In order to prepare the operators, the scientific community, and other entities for the requirements of the Agency, it was decided that the Programme for Supporting Polish Industry in the ESA (PLIIS) would be launched. According to the Programme, 45% of Poland's contribution to the organisation's budget could be allocated to competitions addressed exclusively to the Polish space sector or to co-finance Polish participation in selected ESA projects and missions.

The competition was held in five categories: flight hardware activities, research and development activities, preparatory activities, space applications,

47 ESA Convention and Council Rules of Procedure (ESA SP-1317, December 2010, 7th edition) Publisher: ESA Communications, ESTEC, Postbus 299, 2200 AG Noordwijk The Netherlands.

products, and services. The Programme for Supporting Polish Industry in ESA was in force until 2019. It was supposed to guarantee Polish industry participation in national and international contracts in the areas of the highest technologies with huge growth potential. The remainder of the contribution for compulsory programmes (55%) was distributed per the general ESA procurement rules.

In addition to the mandatory programmes, Member States are free to join optional programmes that are funded exclusively by participating countries. Currently, Poland participates in 10 optional programmes:

- Earth Observation Envelope Programme 5 – making satellite data available through better Earth observation and the development of new products and applications in disciplines such as agriculture, urbanization, forestry, and others.
- General Support Technology Programme – building know-how in industry development to develop a technology that reduces the risk of future missions.
- Space Situational Awareness – space weather monitoring (tracking the sun's activity) detecting asteroids and comets that may be a threat to the earth, tracking active and inactive satellites and space debris.
- Integrated Applications Promotion (Artes) – creating software that integrates historical space data related to satellite communication, earth observation, satellite navigation, and historical non-space data.
- Prodex – enabling industrial entities from the Member States to participate in research experiments conducted by the European Space Agency. Future Launchers Preparatory NEO – work on new systems for launching into space.
- European Exploration Envelope Programme – a programme for exploring space and celestial objects under which research missions are carried out, that is, Mars Express, Ulysses et cetera.
- Next Generation Platform (NEOSAT) – the creation of a new satellite platform used by the industrial sector.
- The Navigation Innovation and Support Programme – acceleration of industrial competencies and innovations in the satellite navigation sector, finding ways to integrate satellite navigation with non-space technologies (IoT).
- Artes Future Preparation – defining key elements in the area of market opportunities, regulatory barriers, standards, future needs with regard to the development of telecommunications satellites.

As was mentioned, with regard to the budget of the European Space Agency, mention should be made of the existence of the policy of sustainable geographical return, according to which the number of contracts awarded to enterprises from certain countries is based on a coefficient related to the percentage share in financing ESA programmes and projects. This means that most of the premium paid by Poland returns to Poland in the form of contracts for industry and research and development units. The programmes implemented under the European Space Agency consist of several projects made available in the form of regular competitions. They are announced via the EMITS portal. The selection of subcontractors for medium-sized projects is carried out on average every three years, the selection of subcontractors for large projects – on average once every five years.

8.1 *The Main Participants of the Polish Space Sector and Their Participation in ESA Projects*

The number of operating enterprises in the space sector is estimated at 230 entities (POLSA, 2018).[48] The space industry is the main area of activity for 40 companies in Poland.[49] Due to how they are established, these enterprises can be divided into the following groups:

- Entities based on the knowledge and experience of people involved in university and institute projects are enterprises created as a result of the need to commercialize competencies and solutions developed during research activities. The emergence of this group of entities was most often associated with ESA's possibilities of financing projects. There are at least three scenarios. First, of separating the market topics from the research structure by creating a spin-off company – the entities from which this type of activity was separated were the *Przemysłowy Instytut Automatyki Przemysłowej* (PIAP Space), the Space Research Centre of the Polish Academy of Sciences (Space, Astronika), the AGH University of Science and Technology (SATIM Satellite Monitoring), and the Wrocław University of Technology (Scane Way). Second, the creation of a joint venture company by a university or an institute with a private enterprise, an example of which may be the Astri company. It was established as a result of cooperation between the Space Research Centre of the Polish Academy of Sciences and Airbus Defense and Space, specializing in electronics and optomechatronics. And third, the creation of a new entity by people previously participating in student projects, an example of which is KP Labs – a company dealing in the production of advanced IT solutions

48 The space market in Poland, cooperation between science and business in ESA projects, Warsaw University of Technology – Innovation Management and Technology Transfer Center of the Warsaw University of Technology, (Warsaw, 2019).

49 Development of the space sector – report of the Polish Supreme Audit Office, KGP.430.017.2019 Reg No 44/2020/P/19/021/KGP, (Warsaw, 20 May 2020).

in the field of computer vision and machine learning, established by a group of engineers associated with the Silesian University of Technology. Entities that separate the existing companies taking up activities in the space sector were created due to the expansion of the company's existing activities to the space sector and then the establishment of a new company focused on the space industry. An example of this type of entity can be a company established in 2015, dealing with power supply systems and drives (production of hydrogen peroxide) – Jakusz SpaceTech Sp. z o.o. It was established from the core company named Jakusz Sp. z o.o., which has in its field of activity protection against the effects of an explosion, and disposal of ammunition.

– Entities that are Polish branches of international groups to which they belong, among others: PZL OKĘCIE, GMV Innovation Solutions, Mobica Limited Sp. z o.o., SpaceForest Ltd, Thales Alenia Space Polska, and SENER.
– Entities which are expanding their activities to the space sector and entities whose existing products and services are used in the space industry.
– Entities with many years of experience in the space sector.

Due to the main types of activity, many Polish entities operating in the space sector specialize in the use of satellite data and the creation of databases. In many cases, the main area of activity for these entities is simultaneously the development of ground and onboard space software, which are used in the creation of situational awareness systems and in the preparation of communication protocols for conducted missions.[50]

9 The EU Budget Perspective for 2021–2027

From the budget perspective for 2021–2027, the European Union plans to launch a new space programme. It will consolidate several parallel projects that will include tasks related to the development of satellite navigation and earth observation systems and new security components. The axis of the programme will be the improvement and simplification of cooperation

50 As part of the optional programmes, competitions are open to all companies from the countries participating in the Programme. Since 2016, Poland has participated in the implementation of 10 optional programmes: 1.) Earth Observation Envelope Programme 5th Period EOEP 5; 2.) ARTES Future Preparation; 3.) ARTES Next Generation Platform NEOSAT; 4.) ARTES Integrated Application Promotions IAP; 5.) Navigation Innovation and Support Programme NAVISP; 6.) Further Launchers Preparatory Programme FLLP; 7.) European Exploration Envelope Programme E3P; 8.) Space Situational Awareness Programme SSA; 9.) General Support Technology Programme GSTP; 10.) Prodex.

between the three entities. At the EU level, the managing authority will remain the European Commission. At the same time, the EU Agency for the Space Programme (currently the GSA) will take over navigation tasks, marketization of space technologies, and security accreditation. At the European level, the key technical and operational partner of the European Union will be ESA (which participates as a separate international organisation in the implementation of many EU space projects). Although the new programme does not envisage a significant qualitative change, it confirms the growing importance of space issues, which impact the economy, environmental protection, and citizens' quality of life and security. Its budget is expected to amount to EUR 13–15 billion (compared to EUR 11.1 billion in the previous budget perspective). The growing importance of space in European countries' policies is also confirmed by ESA's highest budget so far, which will amount to EUR 14.4 billion for 2020–2022 (apart from contributions from Member States, about 20% of the budget is the EU contribution).

9.1 *Joint Projects*

The most considerable undertaking in the upcoming EU budget perspective will be expanding the global satellite navigation system Galileo, which is to provide European countries with complete independence in space-based products and services, such as navigation, synchronization of financial transactions, and search and rescue operations. Currently, Galileo is operating on a limited scale but is scheduled to be fully operational by the end of 2020. Although it is a fully civilian system, it will allow Europe to build a significant technological advantage by providing three times more accurate positioning than military systems – as compared with the US GPS and the Russian GLONASS.

An essential element of the new Programme will also remain Copernicus – an extensive satellite observation system (combined with terrestrial, air, and sea). It provides comprehensive information on the state of the natural environment, climate change, and emergencies and will be expanded to include further elements (including improvement of border surveillance). Copernicus is currently made up of a European satellite constellation, but the system also connects to other public and commercial satellites. To increase its independence, the European Union plans to put in orbit another 20 satellites by 2030.

The Governmental Satellite Communications Initiative (GOVSATCOM) will also be launched (currently in preparation). It will be used by the Member States and EU agencies' services responsible for security matters (including the European Defense Agency, the European Border and Coast Guard Agency, the European Maritime Safety Agency). The advantage of the system is its reliability compared to commercial solutions and lower cost and easier use than in the case of military architecture. The Space Observation and Tracking (SST) project, which collects information on the position of space objects and the space environment's characteristics (satellites, debris, weather), will also be maintained. However, the European Union will allocate little resources to both of these systems under development for the time being.

9.2 *The Importance of Cooperation*

Conducting a coherent space policy at the EU and ESA level allows States to develop their capabilities better while increasing Europe's independence from space technology leaders such as the United States, Russia, China, Japan, and India. Even the biggest players on the European market – the so-called European five (Germany, France, Italy, Spain, and Great Britain), do not decide to independently implement space programmes due to the necessary financial and technical capabilities. Collaboration is essential when running large projects. This is confirmed by the financial and technological difficulties faced by the United Kingdom in building its own satellite navigation system due to the decision to withdraw from work on Galileo after leaving the European Union.

Intensive development of the so-called New Space, or the private sector, is an additional space exploration element. The participation of enterprises (including small and medium-sized enterprises and start-ups) reduces costs while increasing the level of innovation and competitiveness of the solutions provided. To maintain Europe's potential, the new EU space programme assumes support for this branch of the economy, including through access to risk financing and innovation partnerships, including thanks to the Invest EU Fund and Horizon Europe.

At the same time, the European Union is discussing future international standards, for example, by proposing a Code of Conduct for Outer Space Activities.[51] However, the lack of significant progress in the global debate on this subject results from States' divergent positions regarding the scope and method of regulating activities in space (mainly its military use). Nevertheless, the largest space projects are implemented in cooperation with organisations outside of Europe, including NASA (Moon exploration) and Roscosmos (the Mars research expedition).

51 Negotiating a Code of Conduct for Outer Space Activities, https://www.armscontrol.org/blog/2015-06-04/negotiating-code-conduct-outer-space-activities, (accessed 5 August 2021).

10 Conclusion

The growing dependence on space-based technologies will make the coming years of great importance for the development of the EU's space potential. The new EU programme can support countries in tackling the current pandemic crisis, for example, by creating patterns of disease spread through satellite communication technologies and by developing industry through the creation of start-ups and making enterprises more innovative. However, it will be of key importance to maintain European countries' common position towards international competition. Maintaining communication channels (for instance, within ESA after the United Kingdom left the European Union) will be of great importance, as well as the coordination of ESA and EU activities, including avoiding the overlap of competencies after the creation of a new EU Space Programme Agency on the basis of the current GSA.

It will also be necessary to ensure independent European access to space, mainly in the field of satellite launches by reusable rockets and its own ground infrastructure. Another element improving the safe operation of the system will be alerted under the SST project (currently generated on the basis of data from the American system), in the development of which has so far been involved in seven countries: France, Germany, Italy, Spain, Poland, Portugal, and Romania.

For Poland, it will be of key importance to further increase research centres and enterprises' involvement in space programmes.[52] First of all, it would help increase the financial outlays for optional ESA projects (the low premium for 2020–2022 coincides with the end of the preferential period for Poland from 2020). The good use of funds by Polish entities so far provides opportunities for further development of the domestic sector, allowing, for example, to increase the potential of Polish enterprises from creators of single technologies to suppliers of subsystems (according to estimates, they would be able to complete contracts in the amount of up to EUR 102 million, which is twice the current Polish contributions). However, maintaining this trend will depend on the increased interest of the State sector in the use of space technologies. For the development of Polish potential, it will also be important to finalize

52 In the space sector, there are four levels of company development:
- Mission integrators (leading European concerns: Airbus DS, Thales Alenia Space, and OHB),
- System integrators,
- Subsystem integrators,
- Suppliers of technologies and components (current Polish level).

the procedure for opening the first ESA incubator, which will support start-up enterprises operating in the field of space technologies. In Europe, there are already 17 countries that have established individual incubators or their networks at the national or regional levels. It is also worth analyzing the possibility of including Poland in the development of new areas (for example, in the field of space security and the construction of next generations of satellites) and support for the development of applications and services for the flagship Copernicus and Galileo programmes.

The Polish space sector's development should go in the direction of research, technology supply, and production of satellite components for the production of subsystems, and in the long term, even satellite systems. It is a feasible task, assuming significantly increased public support for the production of products (subsystems) that would be implemented in a flight version.

The basic features of the national space law being developed in Poland includes in particular:

- subjecting this law to the rigors of the principle of primacy of an international norm over a domestic one;
- the unilateral character of the creation of this law by state bodies and its control by designated bodies (for instance, hierarchical constitutional review of the law by the Constitutional Tribunal);
- the universality of this law, which means the possibility of determining the behavior of all entities operating in the territory of the Republic of Poland – hence the addressees of the national space law standards may be all state authorities, citizens, foreigners, stateless persons, legal persons (both public and private), and in the end the state itself;
- shaping the subject of the regulation of this law, which relates to space activities performed on the territory of the Republic of Poland, on board ships registered in the Republic of Poland and aircraft registered in the Republic of Poland;
- covering with the scope of the matter of this law both the norms of public law and the norms of private law;
- difficulty in codifying this law due to the interdisciplinary nature of its matter, including transport, spatial development, crisis management, telecommunications, medicine, agriculture, forestry, environmental protection, geology, meteorology;
- the existence of an institutionalized system for the enforcement of this right; and
- the instrumental nature of this law in the implementation of the national space policy.

By becoming a member of the European Union, and then of the European Space Agency, Poland assumed joint responsibility for the implementation of the European space policy. Poland can boast of prestigious scientific projects, and Polish companies and research centers are able to provide advanced techniques and technologies and implement multi-million contracts. Research on satellite techniques is carried out by scientists all over the country, including at the Warsaw University of Technology and Wrocław University of Technology, at the Military University of Technology and at the Space Research Center of the Polish Academy of Sciences. The Department of International Aviation and Space Law operates at the Faculty of Law and Administration of the University of Warsaw.

It is worth recalling that since the beginning of the space age, Poland has actively participated in the efforts of the United Nations to arrive at legal solutions regulating various issues related to the legal status of outer space and celestial bodies and the activities of states in space.

Therefore, there is an urgent need to regulate the issues related to the necessity to fulfill the obligations of the Republic of Poland, resulting from the international agreements binding on it in the field of space law, in connection with the increased activity of Polish entities in the use of space. For several years, legislative work has been underway to prepare a government draft law on space activities and the National Register of Space Objects, which is to implement the provisions of the Treaty on the Principles of State Activities in the Study and Use of Outer Space, including the Moon and Other Bodies, as well as the Convention on International Liability for Damage Caused by Space Objects and the Convention on the Registration of Objects Launched into Outer Space. The proposed act is to contain, first of all, provisions on granting a license to conduct space activities and supervision over these activities and keeping a register of space objects launched into space by Polish entities, with the simultaneous notification of this information to the Secretary General of the United Nations. The register is to be kept by the Polish Space Agency.

CHAPTER 6

The Polish Legal System – an Overview

Dominika Ewa Harasimiuk

1 Introduction and Historic Background

The Polish legal system is based on a continental legal system, rooted in the civil law tradition. The shape of Poland's modern legal system dates back to the Enlightenment period, when on 3 May 1791, the first constitution in continental Europe was enacted for the Polish-Lithuanian Commonwealth.[1] It established a constitutional monarchy, one of the foundations of which was political equality between townspeople and noblemen, while peasants were placed under government protection. Due to the Republic's political weakness and pressing external forces, the Commonwealth was soon divided by Russia, Prussia, and the Austro-Hungarian Empire. Due to the Partitions in 1772, 1793 and 1795, Poland ceased to exist on the political maps of Europe until 1918, when it regained its independence and sovereignty. The period of the Partitions was a period of application of three different legal systems on the territory of the former Commonwealth. The reconstruction of independent statehood post-1918 was aligned with an effort to establish a coherent legal system for reborn Poland. Many of the newly enacted statutes, mostly in the field of administrative, civil, and commercial law had their inspiration in Austrian or German codes.[2]

The outbreak of the Second World War ruptured the 20 year-long period of efforts to establish a modern legal system and governance in Poland. In 1945 with the end of the Second World War, Poland, its economy, and legal system fell under Soviet domination. Together with a socialist political system, the centrally-planned economic system was under the governance of the Polish United Workers' Party and the Constitution of the Polish People's Republic (1952).

1 Mirosław Granat, Katarzyna Granat, *The Constitution of Poland. A Contextual Analysis* (Bloomsbury Hart Publishing 2019) 9–10.

2 Stanisław Biernat, Monika Kawczyńska, 'The Role of the Polish Constitution (Pre-2016): Development of a Liberal Democracy in the European and International Context' in Anneli Albi, Samo Bardutzky (eds), *National Cosntitutions in European and Global Governance: Democracy, Rights, the Rule of Law* (Springer Open 2019) 746–747.

 | DOI:10.1163/9789004542860_008

In 1989 with the peaceful transformation initiated by the first semi-democratic elections in Poland held on June 4th, the Polish people decided to enter onto the path of democratic changes and necessary economic reforms leading towards a market economy. It was another breakthrough moment, which at the same time was a challenge to replace and amend many existing post-communist regulations with the ones corresponding to the new capitalist and democratic system. At the same time, Poland regulated its relations with the European Economic Community, by concluding the Association Treaty in 1991.[3] It was a clear signal that the long-term goal was a full membership as part of the European Union. Before joining the European Union, Poland became member of the Council of Europe (1991), the OECD (1996), and NATO (1999). The pre-accession period, during which official negotiations with the European Union took place (1998–2002), allowed for the process of approximation of Polish law with the *acquis communautaire*. It meant that already as a candidate country, Poland had to align its national laws, rules, and procedures with the European Community to give effect to the whole body of this legal system. The negotiation processes results were concluded in the accession treaty, signed on 16 April 2003, which entered into force on 1 May 2004, marking the moment from which Poland is a Member State of the European Union.[4]

2 An Outline of the Polish Constitutional System

The Polish legal and political system's foundations are governed by the Constitution of 2 April 1997.[5] The Constitution contains a preamble and is divided into 13 chapters. Chapter 1 entitled 'The Republic,' clarifies the constitutional foundations of the State's organisation. The State's supreme power is vested in the Nation, which exercises it through democratic processes of either a direct, participative character or through its Nation's representatives (Article 4 of the Constitution). The Republic of Poland is a unitary democratic State founded on the principle of the rule of law and implementing the principles of social justice (Articles 2–3 of the Constitution). The rule of law principle

3 Europe Agreement establishing an association between the European Communities and their Member States, on the one part, and the Republic of Poland, on the other part signed in Brussels on 16 December 1991 (1993) OJ L348/184 (Journal of Laws 1994, No 11, item 38).

4 OJ (2003) L236/17.

5 Journal of Laws 1997 No 78, item 483, as amended. See also: Granat, Granat (n 1) 22. Maria Kruk, 'Przyczynek do rozważań o inspiracjach Konstytucji RP z 1997 r.'(2002) 12 Państwo i Prawo 3–16.

in the Polish constitutional system has been subject of interpretation by the Constitutional Court, which had used it as a source of other general principles of law, like legal certainty, protection of acquired rights, protection of legitimate expectations, proportionality, non-retroactivity, and sufficient *vacatio legis*.[6] Article 2 of the Constitution is considered as a *lex generalis*, which implies that the courts applying the Constitution shall rely on more specific provisions intended to protect rights and freedoms.[7] One of the aspects of the rule of law as a principle setting democratic standards is reflected in the provision of Article 7 of the Constitution, which states that the organs of public authority function on the basis of and within the limits of the law (the principle of legality).

The abovementioned Chapter 1 also confirms the independence and territorial integrity of the State (Article 5 of the Constitution), the principle of separation of powers, and balance between the legislative, executive and judicial powers (Article 10 of the Constitution) together with the principle of political pluralism (Article 11 of the Constitution).[8]

An essential part of the Constitution is devoted to the establishment of the system of fundamental rights protection. Chapter 2, 'The Freedoms, Rights and Obligations of Persons and Citizens,' contains a rather comprehensive catalog of fundamental rights and freedoms, whose enforcement is strengthened by the fact that the provisions of the Constitution shall apply directly unless the Constitution provides otherwise (Article 8.2 of the Constitution). The catalog listed in Chapter 2 includes general principles, among which there are: respect for human dignity and personal freedom, equality before the law, gender equality, and rules concerning the acquisition and protection of Polish citizenship (Articles 30–37 of the Constitution). Further on, the Constitution provides guarantees for personal freedoms and rights (Articles 38–56 of the Constitution), political rights and freedoms (Articles 57–63 of the Constitution), and economic, social, and cultural rights (Articles 64–76 of the Constitution). Chapter 2 also stipulates guarantees and means for the defense of freedoms and rights (Articles 77–81 of the Constitution), which include: the right to compensation for any harm done by any action of an organ of public authority contrary to the law, the right to appeal against judgments and decisions made at the first instance, the right to appeal to the Constitutional Tribunal for its judgment on the conformity to the Constitution of a statute or another normative act upon which basis a court or organ of public

6 Biernat, Kawczyńska (n 2) 759.

7 Ibid 762.

8 Ibid 748.

administration has made a final decision on freedoms or rights specified in the Constitution, and the right to apply to the Commissioner for Citizens' Rights for assistance in protection of freedoms or rights infringed by organs of public authority.[9] The Commissioner for Citizen's Rights is the independent constitutional organ responsible for safeguarding the freedoms and rights of persons and citizens.

The territorial system of Poland is based on the decentralization of public power. The reconstruction of local government was one of the most important elements of the political transformation process, which commenced after 1989.[10] Currently, according to the Constitution, citizens who live in territorial units form self-governing communities. The preamble of the Constitution confirms the principle of subsidiarity, which is intended to 'strengthen the powers of citizens and their communities.' In broad terms, it can be understood as a principle used by the public administration in the area of dividing powers between central and local government organisations.[11]

In 1998, administrative reform was introduced, according to which the country is divided into 16 voivodships (in Polish: *województwa*), which are divided into smaller units of poviats and further to basic units of local government, which are communes (in Polish: *gminy*). Chapter 7 of the Constitution covers detailed constitutional provisions governing the organisation and functioning of local government. According to it, there is a presumption of competences in favor of municipalities, which are established as the primary local authority. Units of local government possess legal identity, and the courts protect their self-governing character. Local authorities are ensured with adequate public funding to perform their duties. Finally, local governments are subject to supervision by the Prime Minister, the voivodes (governors) and the regional audit chambers, only in terms of the legality of their actions.[12] Local governments perform public tasks, that are not reserved to other public organs, and citizens being members of units of local government elect their constitutive

---

9 See more on the system of fundamental rights protection in Poland, Piotr Tuleja, 'Komentarz do Article 30 i nast.' in Piotr Tuleja (ed), *Konstytucja Rzeczypospolitej Polskiej. Komentarz*, (Wolters Kluwer Polska 2019) Article 30. Marek Chmaj (ed), *Wolności i prawa człowieka w Konstytucji Rzeczypospolitej Polskiej* (Wolters Kluwer Polska 2016).

10 Michał Kulesza, Dawid Sześciło, 'Local Government in Poland' in Angel Manuel Moreno Molina (ed), *Local government in the Member States of the European Union: a comparative legal perspective,* (Madrid, INAP 2012) 485–486.

11 For more on the practical implementation of this principle, see: Robert Gawłowski. Saulius Nefas, Krzysztof Makowski, 'Subsidiarity Principle- Its Realization in Self-Government in Lithuania and Poland' (2020) 10 Administrative Sciences 2–3.

12 Kulesza, Sześciło (n 10) 490–491.

and executive organs. Citizens may also decide by means of a local referendum about matters concerning the functioning of their respective communities.

3 System of Sources of Law

The system of sources of law in Poland is governed by the Constitution, which in its Chapter 3 regulates the closed catalogue of the sources of law, incorporating in it international and European Union law. The major classification distinguishes two categories – universally binding law and internally binding law. Such a dualist approach indicates that each legal act must belong to either of the two categories.[13]

Universally binding acts are addressed to all legal subjects and are intended to regulate their rights and obligations. According to Article 87 of the Constitution, the sources of universally binding law are: the Constitution, statutes (in Polish: *ustawy*), ratified international agreements, and regulations. In addition to this catalog, the Constitution includes local law into the universally binding sources. However, such local laws, which are the result of the operation of local self-government organs, are universally binding only in the territory of the organ that issued such an enactment. The catalog indicated in Article 87 of the Constitution is enumerative. Also, in terms of the legislative competence, only those subjects which are explicitly listed in the Constitution can adopt universally binding law.[14]

Under Polish law, for the statutes, regulations, and local laws to enter into force, they need to be published. Also ratified international agreements and other international agreements are published in the same manner as statues. Promulgation journals in Poland are the Official Journal of Laws of the Republic of Poland (in Polish: *Dziennik Ustaw Rzeczpospolitej*) and local law journals, which are published by the voivodships.

Acts other than universally binding as set in Article 87 of the Constitution constitute internal law. The Constitution does not contain an enumerative list of these acts and merely provides their examples. In principle, internal acts bind only the organs that have adopted them and those which are subordinated to the issuing organs and organisational units. The Constitution, while indicating examples of such acts, points at resolutions (in Polish: *uchwała*) adopted by the *Sejm* or the Council of Ministers or orders (in Polish: *zarządzenie*) issued

13 Granat, Granat (n 1) 40; Piotr Radziewicz 'Komentarz do art. 87' in Tuleja (n 9) Article 87.
14 Ibid.

by the President of the Republic of Poland, the President of the Council of Ministers and ministers. These acts may be published in the Journal of Laws of the Republic of Poland, yet in most cases are published in the Official Journal of the Republic of Poland (in Polish: *Monitor Polski. Dziennik Urzędowy RP*) and in the local official journals.

As for Poland's universally binding legal acts, the Constitution provides its enumerative list and organizes them into an official hierarchy, where the Constitution itself occupies the highest position. As mentioned above, the National Assembly adopted the current Constitution on April 2, 1997, which was approved by a national referendum (May 25, 1997) and entered into force on September 17, 1997. Its adoption marked the important moment of departing from the post-communist system of government towards a democratic, sovereign State founded on the rule of law, with a separation of powers and fundamental rights protection. The explicit, symbolic provision breaking with totalitarian ideologies, can be found in Article 13 of the Constitution, which prohibits political parties and other organisations whose programmes are based upon totalitarian methods and the modes of activity of nazism, fascism, and communism. The same provision covers the prohibition of those organisations that sanction racial or national hatred, the application of violence for the purpose of obtaining power, or for the purpose of influencing State policy. This provision refers to the concept of the so-called "militant democracy", which presumes that the State shall have effective legal instruments allowing for the elimination from the public sphere of those organisations, whose goal is to destroy fundamental democratic values.[15] Article 13 of the Constitution as such does not constitute the basis for the delegalization of political parties or organisations. In the Polish legal system, decisions regarding the application of Article 13 belong to the Constitutional Tribunal (in the case of political parties) and common courts (in the case of other organisations).

The Polish Constitution has a legal character and can be enforceable in the courts, which constitutes a particularly important procedural guarantee for the rights and freedoms contained in Chapter 2, briefly discussed above.[16]

As mentioned above, the Polish Constitution's overall structure is based on the Preamble and 13 chapters containing 243 articles. Apart from setting the major foundations for the Republic (Chapter 1), providing a framework for the freedoms, rights, and obligations of persons and citizens (Chapter 2), and organizing the system of sources of law (Chapter 3), the Constitution regulates

15 Piotr Tuleja 'Komentarz do art. 13' in Tuleja (n 9) Article 13.
16 Biernat, Kawczyńska (n 2) 748.

the system of governance – Chapter 4, devoted to the legislative (the Sejm and the Senate), Chapter 5 and 6, which regulate the executive (the President of the Republic and the Council of Ministers and government administration, respectively), Chapter 7, which relates to local government and the judicial powers, which are regulated by Chapter 8 (Courts and Tribunals). The Constitution also provides rules for the bodies of State control and the defence of rights (Chapter 9), public finances (Chapter 10), and extraordinary measures (Chapter XI). Finally, Chapter XII provides procedures for amending of the Constitution, and Chapter XII contains final and transitional provisions.

In the context of the amendment process regulated by the Chapter XII, the Polish Constitution is considered 'rigid', since the procedures leading to amendments are detailed and require broad political consent (for example, the amendment bill must be submitted by at least one-fifth of the statutory members of the Sejm, the Senate or the President; such a bill to be adopted by the Sejm requires a majority of at least 2/3 of the votes in the presence of at least one-half of the statutory number of members of the Sejm and by the Senate by an absolute majority of votes in the presence of at least one-half of the statutory number of members of the Senate).[17]

In terms of the hierarchy of Polish legal acts, the statute (in Polish: *ustawa*) is the basic universally binding law that in the hierarchy occupies a particular position. The statute has a subordinate position versus the Constitution and international agreements ratified with prior consent granted by the statute. Also, according to Article 91.3 of the Constitution, statutes shall be subordinated to the laws established by international organisations to which Poland had transferred the competence of organs of State authority in relation to certain matters.[18] The mentioned provision is applied in reference to the European Union's secondary law and allows for its direct application in the Polish legal system, and regulates its precedence in case of a conflict of laws with statutes. Statutes have a superior position versus regulations and local laws.

In terms of the legal character of a statute, it should be stressed that it has normative power, extensive material scope, and as such, it is a basic legal act that allows for the exercise of State policies. Through statutes, individuals' rights and obligations are regulated as well as the functioning of basic State organs.[19] In the field of the Polish space policy, the functioning of the Polish

---

17 Ibid, 751. For more on the amendment procedure, see Maria Kruk, 'Kilka uwag o trwałości i zmianach Konstytucji RP z 1997 r. na tle 10-lecia praktyki konstytucyjnej' in Cezary Mik (ed), *Maria Kruk, Konstytucja. Prawo i praktyka. Wybór studiów. Księga jubileuszowa* (Wydawnictwo Sejmowe 2019) 137–152.

18 See Article 90 and 91.3 of the Constitution.

19 Radziewicz (n 13).

Space Agency is regulated by the Act of 26 September 2014 on the Polish Space Agency,[20] which will be discussed in paragraph 6 of this chapter.

It should be noted that statutes are the basic instruments of giving effect to constitutional norms, which many times, despite their direct applicability, may necessitate more detailed procedural and institutional regulation.[21]

The statutes are adopted by the Sejm, in the legislative procedure regulated by Articles 118– 123 of the Constitution, which may consist of up to three readings. In principle, such a procedure is initiated by the Deputies' proposals, the Senate, the President of the Republic or the Council of Ministers. The right of a legislative initiative also belongs to a group of at least 100,000 citizens.

The Polish Constitution incorporates international agreements which are concluded and ratified by Poland into the Polish legal system. As such, the national system of sources of law is multilayered and consists of laws adopted at the international, EU, and national levels. The Polish legal system distinguishes two basic types of international agreements – the ones requiring ratification and the ones requiring mere acceptance. As to the first type of international agreements, one may subdivide them into those agreements requiring prior consent granted by a statute and ones which do not necessitate such consent. In any case, the ratification remains within the competence of the President of the Republic of Poland. According to Article 89.1 of the Constitution, the prior consent granted by the statute is required for the ratification of the agreements which concern:

1) peace, alliances, political or military treaties;
2) freedoms, rights or obligations of citizens, as specified in the Constitution;
3) the Republic of Poland's membership in an international organisation;
4) considerable financial responsibilities imposed on the State; [and]
5) matters regulated by statute or those in respect of which the Constitution requires the form of a statute.

Among ratified international agreements requiring consent expressed in the statute, there is one particular kind, which allows for the Republic of Poland to transfer to an international organisation the competence of organs of State

20 *Ustawa z 26.10.2014 o Polskiej Agencji Kosmicznej* (Act of 26.10.2014 on Polish Space Agency), Journal of Laws 2014, item 1533.

21 Radziewicz (n 13).

authority in relation to certain matters.[22] The Constitution in its Article 90.1 contains such a clause, labelled 'integration clause' or 'European clause' in legal literature, which had served as the legal basis for accession to the European Union, but also applies to agreements that change the scope of transferred powers, the essential elements of those powers, as well as the conditions for exercising transferred powers.[23] Thus, it is also used in case of ratification of amending treaties of the European Union. The Constitution in Article 90.2–4 regulates the procedure of ratification of agreements transferring powers to the international organisation. The statute granting such consent may be adopted by a two-thirds majority vote of both chambers of Parliament, or by a nationwide referendum.

Once an agreement is ratified and published, it becomes a part of the domestic legal system and may be applied directly. As was indicated above, in terms of hierarchy of norms, where a ratified international agreement contradicts the statute, agreements have precedence over statutes.

Regulations and local laws occupy lower levels in the hierarchy of Polish norms. Regulations are implementing acts towards statutes; thus they must be subordinated and compliant with the statutes based on which they are adopted. Also, regulations shall be compatible with all universally binding norms taking precedence over statutes. The general rule concerning regulations relates to the fact that specific authorization in the statute is needed for them to be adopted. The goal for such authorization is a proper implementation of the statute. The authorization shall specify the organ appropriate to issue the regulation, the material scope to be regulated, and guidelines concerning the provisions of such an act.[24]

The lack of proper authorization entails the formal invalidity of the regulation. The Act of 26 September 2014 on the Polish Space Agency provided such an authorization for the adoption of the Statute on the Polish Space Agency, which was introduced by the regulation of the Prime Minister adopted on the 17 June 2015.[25]

22 See Article 90.1 of the Constitution. See also Andrzej Szmyt, 'Uregulowania konstytucji krajowej w perspektywie integracji europejskiej oraz kierunki niezbędnych uzupełnień'(2014) 1 Studia Iuridica Toruniensia 361–376.

23 Mirosław Granat, 'Uwagi o pojmowaniu art. 90 Konstytucji RP przez Trybunał Konstytucyjny' (2014) 22 Studia Iuridica Lublinensia 527.

24 Article 92 of the Constitution.

25 *Rozporządzenie Prezesa Rady Ministrów z dnia 17 czerwca 2015 r. w sprawie nadania statutu Polskiej Agencji Kosmicznej* (Regulation of the Prime Minister on the statute of the Polish Space Agency), Journal of Laws 2015, item 861.

The personal scope of authorization covers organs expressly stated in the Constitution. The authorized organs to issue the regulations are the President of Republic of Poland (Article 142.1 of the Constitution), the Council of Ministers (Article 146.4, point 2 of the Constitution), the Prime Minister (Article 148, point 3 of the Constitution), the National Broadcasting Council (Article 213. 2 of the Constitution), the Chairman of the Committee who is a member of the Council of Ministers (Article 149.2 and 3 of the Constitution), and the minister that manages the relevant area of public administration (Article 149.2 of the Constitution). The Constitution in Article 92.2 introduces the prohibition of sub-delegation.

4 The Political System of Government

The constitutional political system of government in Poland is founded on the parliamentary-cabinet democratic model, which is characterized by the strong position of the Parliament and its relations with the government as the second governing element, together with the dominant position of both – Parliament and the government – versus the Head of State (President).[26] Such a system's primary feature is the government's accountability to the Parliament, which shall support the government and have confidence in its actions. It implies that the parliamentary political majority shall form the government.

The fundamental principle regulating the system of government is the principle of separation of powers, which in its traditional meaning shall assure balance between legislative, executive, and judicial powers. The separation of powers, the balance of powers, and cooperation between powers can be seen as an expression of the broad general principle explaining the functional division of constitutional powers and their mutual relations.[27] The legislative power entails law-making functions in the Polish legal system, and the function of political control. The executive function is connected to the implementation (realisation) of public tasks as set out in the Constitution; legislative acts adopted by Parliament, and international agreements binding upon Poland. The judicial functions relate to the administration of justice, but also to interpreting and judging the law and the determination of constitutional liability.[28]

26 Maria Kruk, 'Wprowadzenie do problematyki parlamentarnego systemu rządów' in Mik (n 17) 354–355.

27 See, Ryszard M. Małajny, 'Podział władzy w Konstytucji RP z 1997 roku. Analiza formalna' (2017) 6 Przegląd Sejmowy 97–99.

28 Paweł Sarnecki, 'Komentarz do art. 10' in Leszek Garlicki, Marek Zubik (eds), *Konstytucja Rzeczypospolitej Polskiej. Komentarz. Tom I* (2nd edn, Wydawnictwo Sejmowe 2016) Article 10.

It should be stressed that, based on the established doctrinal and constitutional case-law approach, relations between the legislative and executive power are different from relations between the two and the judiciary. While between legislative and executive powers one can notice the intersection and overlapping of competences, their relation with the judiciary is built upon the proper separation and division of competences. The justice system's very nature results from the fact that it should be carried out exclusively by courts and tribunals, and other authorities should not interfere with its activities.[29]

Different State organs perform these three branches of power. The legislative power belongs to the Parliament, which in Poland has a bi-cameral structure and consists of the Sejm (Lower Chamber) and the Senate (Upper Chamber). The Sejm and Senate are thus proper legislators – only the Parliament has the power to adopt statutes by which citizens' and legal persons' legal positions may be determined. The Parliament also exercises political control over the activities of the Council of Ministers, within the scope provided by the Constitution and relevant statutes. Members of the Council of Ministers shall be collectively and individually responsible to the Sejm for the activities of the Council of Ministers and matters falling within their competence assigned to them by the Prime Minister, respectively. From the viewpoint of the Sejm, such a political control can take the form of the right to pass a vote of no confidence in the Council of Ministers or towards an individual minister.[30] Also, the Deputies have the right of interpellation. The Parliament may examine activities of the Council of Ministers and interrogate its members on the issues falling within the scope of their competence.[31]

The Sejm is composed of 460 Deputies, elected in universal, equal, direct, and proportional elections, conducted by way of secret ballot.[32] The Senate is composed of 100 Senators, who are similarly elected with the difference that for the Senate election, a majority method of election instead of a proportional one is applied. The term of office for both chambers of the Polish Parliament is four years. Yet, the Senate's constitutional term of office is directly connected to the term of the Sejm since any shortening of the term of office of the Sejm means automatic shortening of the term of office of the Senate.[33]

---

29 Zbigniew Kmieciak, 'Rozłączność kompetencji organów władzy w świetle orzecznictwa sądowego w przedmiocie ochrony praworządności'(2020) 10 Państwo i Prawo 113. See also: Judgment of the Constitutional Tribunal, 21.11.1994, K 6/94, OTK 1994, No 2, item 39.

30 See Articles 156–159 of the Constitution.

31 See Articles 115 of the Constitution.

32 For more on the electoral principles, Marek Safjan, Leszek Bosek eds, *Konstytucja RP. Tom II. Komentarz do art. 87–243* (Wydawnictwo CH Beck 2016) para 17–40.

33 See Article 98.3 of the Constitution.

The executive branch of power is vested in two State authority centers – the President of the Republic of Poland and the Council of Ministers (the Government). Such a dualist approach indicates that both organs are autonomous and self-contained in reference to their structure and competence.[34] The President – the Head of State – is the highest representative of the Republic of Poland and the guarantor of the continuity of State authority. The Nation elects the President of the Republic in universal, equal and direct elections conducted by secret ballot.[35] The term of office is 5 years and can be renewed once. The President's general role is to ensure the observance of the Constitution to assure the protection of the sovereignty and security of the State together with the inviolability and integrity of its territory. More detailed competences of the President defined in the Constitution relate to his role as the Republic's supreme representative. As such, the President represents the State in foreign affairs. Within these matters, the President ratifies and renounces international agreements, appoints and recalls Poland's diplomatic representatives to other States and international organisations, receives letters of credence, and letters of recall diplomatic representatives of other States and international organisations accredited to him.[36] It should be noticed that the President must cooperate with the Prime Minister and the Minister of Foreign Affairs in the field of foreign policy, and his role is not fully autonomous. The President also performs the function of the Supreme Commander of the Armed Forces. In times of peace, this power is exercised through the Minister of National Defence.[37]

The President may actively participate in Poland's law-making process by exercising the right of legislative initiative and the right to refuse to sign an adopted statute. All bills adopted by the Parliament must be signed by the President, who also orders their promulgation in the Journal of Laws of the Republic of Poland. If the President is willing to refuse to sign the bill, he may either refer it to the Constitutional Tribunal for adjudication of its conformity with the Constitution or may refer the bill to the Sejm for its reconsideration.[38]

34 Maria Kruk, 'Kilka uwag o koncepcji władzy wykonawczej w Konstytucji RP z 1997 r.' in Mik (n 17) 487. See more on the division of competence between the President of the Republic and the Council of Ministers, Bartłomiej Opaliński, *Rozdzielenie kompetencji władzy wykonawczej między Prezydenta RP oraz Rade Ministrów na tle Konstytucji Rzeczypospolitej Polskiej z 1997 roku* (Wolters Kluwer 2012).

35 See Article 127 of the Constitution.

36 See Article 133 of the Constitution.

37 See Article 134 of the Constitution.

38 See Article 122 of the Constitution.

The presidential veto, in principle, is considered an element of assuring the balance between legislative and executive power.[39]

The power to refer the bill to the Constitutional Tribunal is one of the expressions of the duty of the President to observe the Constitution. If the Constitutional Tribunal declares a given bill incompatible with the Constitution, the President cannot sign it. The reference to the Sejm for reconsideration may result in the rejection of the presidential veto, by three-fifths majority vote in the presence of at least half of the statutory number of Deputies.

The second branch of executive power in Poland rests in the hands of the government, which is officially called the Council of Ministers and is chaired by the President of the Council of Ministers (the Prime Minister). The President of the Republic first nominates the Prime Minister, who is responsible for forming the Council of Ministers, which once established, is appointed by the President of the Republic of Poland. The whole process of the government's appointment is concluded by the formal vote of confidence by the Sejm.[40]

The Council of Ministers consists of ministers who govern particular branches of government administration (ministries) and perform tasks assigned to them by the Prime Minster.

The Council of Ministers' overall competence consists of conducting the internal and foreign policy of the Republic of Poland and is based on the general presumption managing all State affairs that are not reserved to other State organs.[41] Article 146.4 of the Constitution contains a non-exhaustive list of more detailed functions belonging to the Council of Ministers. They include ensuring the implementation of statutes, adoption of regulations, coordination and supervision of State administration organs' work, protection of the interests of the State Treasury, adoption of the draft of the State Budget and its implementation, ensuring the internal and external security of the State, exercising the general control concerning international relations (with other States and international organisations), the conclusion of international agreements requiring ratification and acceptance and renouncing of other international agreements, and exercising the general control in the area of national defence.

In terms of political relations between the Council of Ministers on one side and the Parliament and the President of the Republic on the other, it should be stressed that the Polish constitutional system is not founded on dualist control mechanisms. The members of the Council of Ministers, both collectively and individually, are only responsible to the Sejm. The President of the Republic

39 Maria Kruk, 'Zakres władzy prezydenta' in Mik (n 17) 534.
40 See Article 154–155 of the Constitution.
41 See Article 146 of the Constitution.

does not have robust tools, which can be used to oppose the government's policies.[42]

The number and competencies of ministers and their ministries vary depending on the decision of the Prime Minister. The statute on the branches of government administration[43] provides the possibility to shape the competencies of ministers and to limit or expand the list of ministers.

According to Article 9 of the statute on the branches of government administration, the development and implementation of the space policy in Poland, also in the international context, particularly in cooperation with the European Union and the European Space Agency, belongs to the minister responsible for economy. Currently, the space policy is run by the Ministry of Economic Development and Technology.

5 The Judicial System

Judicial power in the Polish constitutional system occupies a special place governed by Article 173 of the Constitution, which stipulates that 'the courts and tribunals constitute a separate power and shall be independent of other branches of power.' Such a separation of judiciary power ensures that courts and judges act independently and impartially while performing their judicial functions. The separation is also understood from the organisational perspective as a feature guaranteeing the institutional autonomy of courts and the Tribunal, whose role is to administer justice.[44] Neither legislative nor executive power may move into the sphere of an independent adjudication.[45] There are, however, some functional links between the judiciary and executive, which in the Polish legal system take the form of the Minister of Justice's administrative supervision over common courts[46] or the mechanism of the appointment of judges by the President of the Republic. Nevertheless, such links may not create pressure or influence over courts and judges' independent and impartial functioning.

---

42 Kruk, 'Kilka uwag …' (n 34) 488–489.

43 *Ustawa z 4.09.1997 r. o działach administracji rządowej* (Statute on the branches of government administration), consolidated text Journal of Laws 2020 item 1220, 2327.

44 Maria Kruk, Marcin Olszówka, Mariusz Godlewski, Mikołaj Jarosz, Marzena Laskowska, Jacek Zaleśny, *Ochrona praw i wolności. System instytucjonalny w Rzeczypospolitej Polskiej*, (Difin 2019) 51.

45 See, the judgment of the Constitutional Tribunal, 19 July 2005, K 28/04.

46 See, *ustawa z 27.07.2001 Prawo o ustroju sądów powszechnych* (Statute on the law governing the organisation of common courts), consolidated text Journal of Laws 2020 item 2072.

Poland's judicial system is based upon the constitutional principle assuring that everyone shall enjoy the right to have a matter adjudicated by the court.[47] This principle is stated in Article 45 of the Constitution and is the source of more detailed rights which are a right to a fair trial and a right to have a case adjudicated without undue delay. A right to a fair trial implies that the court does not act arbitrarily, hence is competent, impartial, and independent. The concept of a fair trial guarantees the right to be heard, assures that the final judicial decisions are duly justified with their grounds clearly explained and that the procedure is predictable from the participants' viewpoint.[48]

A general constitutional principle confirms that under procedural law in Poland both administrative bodies' and courts' decisions made at the first instance are subject to appeal.[49] The provision of Article 176 brings a more detailed rule according to which court proceedings shall have at least two stages. The implementation of this rule necessitates the establishment of a level-based structure of the court system, where there are courts of lower and higher instances. As such, the provision discussed determines the organisation of the justice system in Poland.[50] In general, the administration of justice in Poland is implemented by the Supreme Court, common courts, administrative courts, and military courts. The detailed rules concerning the jurisdiction of given courts are regulated in procedural statutes: the criminal procedural code,[51] the civil procedural code,[52] and law on the procedure before administrative courts.[53]

In consequence, in relation to the justice system in civil and criminal matters, there is a three-tiered court system (the common courts system), consisting of the district courts (*sądy rejonowe*), regional courts (*sądy okręgowe*), and courts of appeal (*sądy apelacyjne*). The common courts deserve a special position in the judicial system since Article 177 of the Constitution stipulates that they have a general competence to implement the administration of justice in all matters, except those which are reserved by statutes to other courts.

47 Arkadiusz Bieliński, 'The Right to Have a Matter Adjudicated by a Court and Alternative Dispute Resolution – Selected Issues'(2017) 22 Białostockie Studia Prawnicze (2017) 236–237.

48 See, the judgment of the Constitutional Tribunal, 16 January 2006, SK 30/05.

49 See, Article 78 of the Constitution.

50 Kruk, Olszówka et al. (n 44) 68.

51 Consolidated text, Journal of Laws 2020 item 30.

52 Consolidated text, Journal of Laws 2020 item 1575.

53 Consolidated text, Journal of Laws 2019 item 2325.

The military courts are the military regional courts and military garrison courts. They perform judicial control within the Polish Army in criminal cases and other cases that were subscribed to them by relevant statutes.

The administrative court system belongs to 16 regional administrative courts adjudicating in first instance and the Supreme Administrative Court, which controls the regional administrative courts' decisions. Administrative courts adjudicate on jurisdictional and competence disputes between local government organs, self-government appeal colleges, and between those bodies and government administration organs. The administrative courts' control also concerns the conformity check of resolutions passed by organs of local government and normative acts of territorial organs of government administration with statutes.

The Supreme Court is the highest judicial organ in Poland, which exercises supervision over common and military courts in reference to their judgments. In terms of the Supreme Court's competence, one shall distinguish its role as the highest court administering justice. As such, the Supreme Court assures conformity with the law and uniformity of case law of common and military courts by deciding upon measures of cassation appeal and adopting law-interpreting resolutions. Also, since 2017, based on the statute on the Supreme Court, a new measure – an extraordinary complaint – was introduced, which is intended to rectify judgments of the common courts which objectively infringe the legal order.[54]

The Supreme Court is also responsible for the final handling of electoral protests and for determining the validity of national parliamentary and presidential elections, elections to the European Parliament, as well as the validity of any national referendum and any constitutional referendum. It is also competent to decide upon disciplinary proceedings concerning legal professions (advocates, legal counsels, notaries, judges). Finally, the Supreme Court issues legal opinions on the statutes and other normative acts and proposals, based on which, after their adoption, courts shall function and adjudicate.

In the Polish legal system, apart from the courts mentioned above, the system of legal protection includes two tribunals – the Constitutional Tribunal and the Tribunal of State. The Constitutional Tribunal is a judiciary organ, being a separate body from the general court system. Its role is to safeguard the Constitution as the supreme law in the Polish legal system. As such, the Constitutional Tribunal adjudicates on the conformity of statutes and international agreements with the Constitution, on the conformity of statues

54 Consolidated text, Journal of Laws 2021 item 154, Article 89.

with ratified international agreements whose ratification necessitated prior consent granted by statute, on the conformity of legal acts adopted by central state organs with the Constitution, ratified international agreements and statues, on the conformity with the Constitution of the activities of political parties, on complaints concerning constitutional infringements and on competence disputes between central constitutional state organs. Judgments of the Constitutional Tribunal have universally binding character and are final. However, their proper effect is produced upon publication in a proper official journal in which original normative acts had been promulgated.[55]

The Constitutional Tribunal is composed of 15 judges chosen individually by the Sejm. Elected judges before taking the office shall take an oath before the President of the Republic. The term of office is 9 years and is not renewable. Judges of the Constitutional Tribunal during their term shall be fully independent and subject solely to the Constitution.

The second Tribunal regulated by the Constitution is the Tribunal of State. It is an organ of constitutional accountability and control, which is performed over the highest state officials. The provision of Article 198 of the Constitution contains an enumerative list of persons who are constitutionally accountable to the Tribunal of State. It includes the President of the Republic, the Prime Minister and members of the Council of Ministers, the President of the National Bank of Poland, the President of the Supreme Chamber of Control,[56] members of the National Council of Radio Broadcasting and Television,[57] persons to whom the Prime Minister has granted powers of management over a ministry, and the Commander-in-Chief of the Armed Forces. Also, under limitations set out in Article 107 of the Constitution,[58] Deputies and Senators may be constitutionally accountable before the discussed Tribunal.

55 See Articles 188–190 of the Constitution.

56 The Supreme Chamber of Control is a constitutional body, which is a chief organ of state audit. Subject to its audit activities are organs of government administration, the National Bank of Poland, State legal persons and other State organisational units, local government organs, communal legal persons and other communal organisational units. See, Articles 202–203 of the Constitution.

57 The National Council of Radio Broadcasting and Television is a constitutional organ responsible for safeguarding the freedom of speech, the right to information together with the public interest regarding radio broadcasting and television. See, Article 213 of the Constitution.

58 Article 107 of the Constitution states that 'Deputies shall not be permitted, to the extent specified by statute, to perform any business activity involving any benefit derived from the property of the State Treasury or local government or to acquire such property.' The breach of this prohibition may give rise to the constitutional accountability before the

The President of the Supreme Court is at the same time the President of the Tribunal of State. The remaining members are: 2 deputy-presidents and 16 members elected by the Sejm from candidates who are not members of the Parliament. Candidates need to have Polish citizenship, full public rights, should have no criminal record and should not be employed in the public administration sector. Deputy-presidents and at least half of the remaining members shall have qualifications to perform judicial functions.[59]

Since 2015, Poland is struggling with a constitutional crisis which impacts the functioning of its justice system. The crisis is mostly connected to the reforms that have been undertaken between 2016 and 2017 by the governing Law and Justice Party and affected the Constitutional Tribunal, the Supreme Court, the National Council of the Judiciary[60] and the whole system of the common courts. The initial phase of the constitutional crisis is linked to the irregularities with the appointment of judges to the Constitutional Tribunal. The government formed after elections in fall 2015 started taking control of the Constitutional Tribunal by replacing duly appointed judges with its own nominees and appointing its own president. The whole process, which politicized and undermined the independence of the Constitutional Tribunal, had its legal foundations in statutes adopted in the years 2015 and 2016,[61] amending the Act on the Constitutional Tribunal and finally replacing it by two statutes: on the Status of Judges of the Constitutional Tribunal[62] and on the organisation and rules of procedure before the Constitutional Tribunal.[63]

The reforms continued, and in 2017, the package of three amending laws were proposed, concerning the Act on the Supreme Court, the Act on the National Council of the Judiciary and the Act on the Organisation of the Common Courts. These amendments were supposed to increase the executive's

Tribunal of State, which may adjudicate on the forfeiture of the mandate. This provision is also applied to Senators.

59 Kruk, Olszówka et al. (n 44) 286–287.

60 National Council of Judiciary is the constitutional organ responsible for assuring independence of judges, by examining and evaluating candidates for appointment as judges to the Supreme Court, common courts, administrative courts and military courts. See, Articles 186–187 of the Constitution.

61 See more on the origins and the course of the constitutional crisis impacting the Constitutional Tribunal, Marek Zubik, 'A.D. 2015/2016. Anni Horribili of the Constitutional Tribunal in Poland' (2018) 2 Przegląd Konstytucyjny 46–55. More detailed analysis of the problem can also be found in opinions delivered by the Venice Commission of the Council of Europe, <https://www.venice.coe.int/webforms/documents/default.aspx?country=23&year=all> (accessed 05.02.2021).

62 Consolidated text, Journal of Laws 2018, item 1422.

63 Consolidated text, Journal of Laws 2019, item 2393.

control over judicial power, undermining its independence understood in both an internal sense, referring to the independence and impartiality of judges, and external independence, understood as a systemic resistance of the court system from the influence of executive and legislative powers.

Finally, the most controversial amendments were introduced at the end of 2017, with the adoption of the new Act on the Supreme Court[64] and the law amending the Act on the National Council of the Judiciary.[65] Three most significant changes impacted the functioning of the Supreme Court. Firstly, the extraordinary complaint system was introduced allowing to undermine common courts' rulings, which objectively infringes on the legal order. Such complaints may be lodged within five years after issuance of such a questionable ruling, and during the first three year period of application of the new law, the system of extraordinary complaints extends to decisions that became final after October 17, 1997. Secondly, the disciplinary proceedings concerning judges and representatives of other legal professions were changed and the new Disciplinary Chamber in the Supreme Court was established as a relevant court in these matters, with much autonomy and judges receiving earnings 40% higher than judges from other chambers of the Supreme Court. In July 2022 the Disciplinary Chamber was replaced by the Professional Liability Chamber. Finally, the most significant changes referred to the very composition of the Supreme Court. The new law lowered the retirement age of the judges of the Court to 65 years old (before it was 70). There was an option of an extension of the service, yet it was dependent on the President of the Republic's consent. Such a change was aimed at the forced renewal of the composition of the Supreme Court.

As for the National Council of the Judiciary, the main change relates to the composition of this body and the method of selecting the majority of its members, who are judges. According to Article 187.1 of the Constitution, the Council (NCJ) consists of 25 members, 15 of whom are judges of Polish courts. The remaining members are: four deputies, two senators, the First President of the Supreme Court, the President of the Supreme Administrative Court, the Minister of Justice, and a representative of the President of the Republic of Poland. Before the reform, 15 judicial members were elected by the judges from among their representatives. Under the new rules, the judges are elected by

64 *Ustawa o SN z 8.12.2017* (Statute of the Supreme Court), consolidated text, Journal of Laws 2018, item 5.

65 *Ustawa z 8.12.2017 o zmianie ustawy o KRS oraz niektórych innych ustaw* (Statute amending the statute on the National Council of Judiciary and other statutes), Journal of Laws 2018, item 3.

the Sejm, which raises concerns related to the separation of judiciary power from legislative one. Candidates for judicial members of the NCJ are indicated to the Sejm by groups of at least 2,000 Polish adult citizens or a group of 25 professionally active judges. The election of new judicial members of the NCJ showed significant irregularities, which were primarily related to the lack of transparency of the whole process. Lists containing names of those who had supported individual candidates had not been disclosed. The described lack of transparency undermines such an important constitutional organs's legitimacy, whose role is to assure the independence of judges, the court system, and the judicial authority in general.[66]

All the reforms mentioned above raised serious concerns relating to Poland's possible breach of the fundamental values based on which the European Union is founded and, in particular, the rule of law principle.[67] This chapter's general scope does not allow to take up a thorough analysis of this complex problem. Thus, only a general outline of significant actions taken towards Poland will be indicated. The European Union has tried several measures, which were intended to annul the undertaken reforms.[68] In particular, the European Commission first used political mechanisms of a soft character by launching the framework mechanism intended to strengthen the rule of law in 2016.[69] When this did not bring a satisfactory result, the Commission opened proceedings under Article 7 of the Treaty on European Union.[70] However, this mechanism also proved ineffective and did not reach the decision-making stage due to complex procedural requirements. Having realized the weakness

66 Anna Rakowska-Trela, 'Krajowa Rada Sądownictwa po wejściu w życie nowelizacji z 8.12.2017 r. – Organ nadal konstytucyjny, czy pozakonstytucyjny?' in Łukasz Bojarski, Krzysztof Grajewski, Jan Kremer, Gabriela Ott, Waldemar Żurek (eds) *Konstytucja. Praworządność. Władza sądownicza. Aktualne problemy trzeciej władzy w Polsce* (Wolters Kluwer Polska 2019) 122.

67 See, Article 2 of the Treaty on the European Union, which states: 'The Union is founded on the values of respect for human dignity, freedom, democracy, equality, the rule of law and respect for human rights, including the rights of persons belonging to minorities. These values are common to the Member States in a society in which pluralism, non-discrimination, tolerance, justice, solidarity and equality between women and men prevail.'

68 Maciej Bernatt, Michał Ziółkowski, 'Statutory Anti-Constitutionalism' (October 31, 2018) 28 Washington International Law Journal (2019) 2–3 < https://ssrn.com/abstract=3384304> (access 02.02.2021).

69 Commission, 'A new EU Framework to strengthen the Rule of Law' (Communication) COM (2014) 0158 final.

70 Commission, 'Proposal for the Council Decision on the Determination of a Clear Risk of a Serious Breach by the Republic of Poland of the Rule of Law' COM (2017) 835 final.

of political control, the Commission decided to use regular judicial measures, by which the Commission performs the role of the 'guardian of the Treaties.' Hence, the Commission brought actions for infringement against Poland to the Court of Justice of the European Union (CJEU) under Article 258 of the Treaty on the Functioning of the European Union. The charges which were raised concerned violation of equal treatment of judges of common courts[71] and the violation of the independence of the Supreme Court.[72] The general issue of both proceedings focused on the problem of lowering the retirement age of judges, which may impact the independence of justice in Poland and as such may undermine the treaty obligation stated in Article 19 of the Treaty on European Union, concerning the adoption of national remedies sufficient to ensure effective legal protection in the fields covered by EU law. In both cases, Poland lost before the CJEU.

The Court of Justice of the European Union also had several opportunities to pronounce itself about the interpretation of the treaty provisions in the context of Polish reforms of the judiciary through the preliminary reference procedure (Article 267 of the Treaty on the Functioning of the European Union), which is a tool for a bottom-up, judicial dialog between the national courts and tribunals and the Court of Justice. As a result of one of such procedures, on 19 November 2019, the CJEU ruled that the Supreme Court may examine whether the Supreme Court's Disciplinary Chamber is independent to hear cases related to the retirement of the Supreme Court judges.[73] The CJEU raised concerns about the capacity of the new Disciplinary Chamber's capacity as an independent and impartial court, primarily due to the process of appointment of their members and involvement in this process of the new National Council of the Judiciary whose legitimacy, due to transparency issues, is questionable. The CJEU ruled that if the Supreme Court considers that the Chamber 'does not satisfy the requirements of judicial independence under EU law,' it should refrain from applying provisions of Polish law related to the Chamber's functioning. In addition, the CJEU ruled that the National Council of the Judiciary may propose candidates for judges if it can be considered independent of the legislative and executive authorities.

The controversies over Polish judiciary reforms are ongoing, and the CJEU will have several opportunities in the future to pronounce itself about their legality and compliance with the fundamental values of European integration.

71 See, Case C-192/18 *Commission v Republic of Poland*, ECLI:EU:C:2019:924.
72 See, Case C-619/18 *Commission v Republic of Poland*, ECLI:EU:C:2019:531.
73 See, joined Cases C-585/18, C-624/18 and C-625/18 A.K. v Krajowa Rada Sądownictwa and CP and DO v Sąd Najwyższy, ECLI: EU:C:2019:982.

6 Public Administration Organs Responsible for Space Policy

As mentioned above, space policy falls under the scope of the Council of Ministers and, in particular, belongs to the responsibilities of the Ministry of Economic Development and Technology and in the field of research and education related to space belongs to the Ministry of Education and Science. However, there is a public administration organ that performs more specialized tasks regarding space policy – the Polish Space Agency (POLSA), which was established in 2014.[74] Its main task it to support the Polish space industry by assuring cooperation between the world of business and science. POLSA also works as a body supporting entrepreneurs in obtaining funds from the European Space Agency (ESA). The Polish Space Agency promotes the development of satellite technology that is used in communication, navigation, environmental monitoring, and weather forecasting. At the same time, POLSA pursues a general goal by assuring the security of the country and contributing to the increase of Polish defense capabilities through the use of satellite systems.

POLSA implements the Polish National Space Programme, whose main objective is to establish a system of appropriate tools and mechanisms for advisory and financial support for Poland's space industry.

The discussed Agency's strategic goal is to ensure that by 2030 the Polish space sector in selected areas is fully competitive globally. Also, there is a need to ensure the independence of Poland in the access and use of satellite data.

The Polish Space Agency's activities cover international cooperation, support to the Polish space sector, managing data solutions for administrative authorities, research and development, education, and defence.

In the area of international cooperation, POLSA is working closely with the European Space Agency and the European Union, by providing support to Polish applicants for the space programmes. POLSA intends to integrate the national industrial sector in projects implemented by the European Organisation for the Exploitation of Meteorological Satellites (EUMETSAT).

Providing support to the Polish space sector is done through the advisory services rendered by POLSA. An important aspect of POLSA's activities relates to the incentives for operators of high-tech or IT to invest and get involved in the space industry.

---

74 See, n 20. Bogdan Wiszniewski, 'Building Polish space sector – from small island of excellence to a national innovation ecosystems' (2019) 52-8 IFAC PapersOnLine 211–220 <https://www.sciencedirect.com/science/article/pii/S2405896319304045> (accessed 2 February 2021).

In the area of satellite data management, POLSA is promoting solutions to support Polish central and local governments. The intention is to realize a noticeable increase of the efficiency of the public administration, which will have better access and use of services based on satellite data technology (for example, earth observation, navigation and telecommunications).

Finally, POLSA is active in the area of R&D and education, by supporting scientific institutions and companies in fundraising for scientific and industrial research. The Agency is also involved in educational activities aiming at the popularization of knowledge of space research.

Polish space policy is strongly related to research and development. The Space Research Centre of the Polish Academy of Sciences (SRC PAS – CBK PAN) is the only research institute in Poland which is fully responsible for the research in the fields of terrestrial space, the solar system and the Earth, with the use of satellite techniques and space technology. The SRC PAS was established in 1977 and ever since has participated in several research projects and scientific space missions. Main activities of the SRC PAS include research based on the results of satellite experiments on space physics; participation in international space missions and research programmes; and development of space technologies, including the construction of space and satellite instruments. An important area of activity also concerns the use of satellite techniques in telecommunication navigation and earth observation. The Space Research Centre is an important participant of Polish academic life, with doctoral programme and extensive cooperation with various universities. The PAS SRC also supports Polish space industry through its expertise, education and technology transfer.[75]

It should also be mentioned that space policy is becoming one of the priorities of the industrial development. The Polish Industrial Development Agency provides special support programmes and cooperates closely with the Polish Space Industry Association, which was established in 2012 and associates 70 Polish companies and R&D institutions operating in the space sector. The Polish Space Industry Association runs a continuous dialogue with public administration organs, which is directed at the growth of Polish space sector. In particular, it intends to influence legislative processes by providing analyses and recommendations, which can be useful in policy and law-making strategies.

75 See, <https://www.cbk.waw.pl/index.php?option=com_content&view=section&id=10&Itemid=13 > (accessed 13 July 2021).

7 The Polish Legal System in the Context of EU Law

Poland is an EU Member State since 1 May 2004. The accession was preceded by the period of association, under the European agreement establishing the association between the European Economic Community and their Member States on the one part and the Republic of Poland on the other.[76] Already during the association period, Poland was obliged to harmonize national laws with the European Community (now, European Union) law.[77] The accession to the European Union has impacted the Polish legal system to a great degree since EU law started to be the additional source of rights and obligations. As indicated above in paragraph 3 of this chapter, the Constitution in its Article 90.1 contains an 'integration clause,' which provides a particular ratification procedure for the international agreements under which the Republic of Poland transfers to an international organisation or international institution the competence of State bodies in relation to certain matters. This procedure has been used twice – in relation to the ratification of the Accession Treaty, which was signed in Athens on 16 April 2003,[78] and in relation to the Lisbon Treaty signed on 13 December 2007.[79] The consent for the ratification of the Accession Treaty was granted by a national referendum, while in the case of the Lisbon Treaty, the consent was given by the Sejm and the Senate.[80]

As a consequence of Poland's accession to the European Union, the system of sources of EU law was integrated into the Polish legal system. Thus, in Poland, the treaties concerning the European Union and on the functioning of the European Union are directly applicable and directly effective. The same applies to the directly applicable sources of EU secondary law, namely EU regulations and decisions. In case of directives, they necessitate the implementation to the national legal system. In Poland, EU directives are being implemented through statutes.

Overall, Poland complies with the general rules concerning the division of competences between the European Union and its Member States. The provision of Article 90 of the Constitution is considered to be an expression of the principle of conferral,[81] based on which the European Union as an

---

76 Europe Agreement establishing an association between the European Communities and their Member States, on the one part, and the Republic of Poland, on the other part signed in Brussels on 16 December 1991, (n 3).

77 See, Article 69 of the Europe Agreement.

78 See, n 4.

79 OJ (2007) C 306/1.

80 Biernat, Kawczyńska (n 2) 750.

81 See, Articles 3.6, 4.1, 5.1 of the Treaty on the EU.

international organisation acquires its policy and law-making powers necessary to achieve treaty goals.

Also, at the level of the national legislative processes, Poland assures the respect of EU law. At the stage of deciding to prepare a legislative proposal, there is an obligation to take into account the analysis of the present legal state, including European Union law. Every statute's justification should contain, among others, a declaration of its conformity with EU law or a declaration that the bill's subject matter is not covered by EU law.[82]

In terms of the respect of the principle of supremacy of EU law extending over the national Constitution, it should be noted that this issue, both at the theoretical and at the practical level, was the subject of the Constitutional Tribunal's judgement regarding the Accession Treaty.[83] At the time, the Constitutional Tribunal noticed that the fact of the co-existence of two legal orders – national and EU – may result in the possibility of collision between the norms of national Constitutions and EU law. The collision happens once there is an irreconcilable inconsistency between the two, and such a collision may not be removed by traditional interpretation methods. The Constitutional Tribunal took the position of denying the possibility of resolving that collision by assuming the supremacy of EU law. Such a position of the Constitutional Tribunal, even if at first glance it may be considered as opposing the CJEU's understanding of supremacy,[84] is explained from the viewpoint of the constitutional role of the Constitutional Tribunal as an organ safeguarding the Polish Constitution. Furthermore, in the discussed judgment, the Constitutional Tribunal explained that in the case of such a collision it is up to the Nation as a sovereign, or a State authority organ authorized by the Constitution to represent the Nation, to decide if the Constitution needs to be amended, or EU provisions need to be modified, or as an ultimate solution Poland shall withdraw from the European Union. Taken into consideration of the above-mentioned interpretation by the Constitutional Tribunal, so far, there was just one amendment of the Polish Constitution related to the membership in the European Union.[85] It concerned the collision between constitutional provision of Article

82 Dominika E. Harasimiuk, 'Analysis of compliance of bills with the European Union law in parliamentary work in 2015–2016' (2020) 3 Ius Novum 122.

83 See, the judgment of the Constitutional Tribunal, 11 May 2005, K 18/04.

84 More on general principle of supremacy of EU law and the national response, see, Trevor Hartley, *The Foundations of European Union Law* (Oxford University Press 2014). 243–245, 259–280.

85 *Ustawa 8.09.2006 o zmianie Konstytucji Rzeczypospolitej Polskiej* (Statute amending the Constitution of the Republic of Poland) Journal of Laws 2006, No 200, item 1471.

55.1 prohibiting Polish citizens' extradition with the Council Framework Decision 2002/584 on the European Arrest Warrant.[86]

86 Council Framework Decision of 13 June 2002 on the European arrest warrant and the surrender procedures between Member States (2002/584/JHA), (2002) OJ L 190/1.

CHAPTER 7

Draft of the Polish Space Act

Ewa Jasiuk

1 Introduction

The space sector is currently developing very dynamically and is one of the most innovative and technologically advanced areas, and its economic importance is growing worldwide.[1] Today, space is one of the fastest-growing industries. The telecommunications sector alone generates revenues of over EUR 100 billion annually – thanks to advances in satellite technology, including global ones.[2] Knowledge related to the use of space is very often, and will certainly also be in the future, used to a greater extent by other sectors. This fact gives it special value and importance. Expert support and technological knowledge from the space sector can be useful to various enterprises, institutions, and bodies, including the public administration. It has been little more than half a century since the launch of the first satellite, but in this time space has acquired a different meaning. In the meantime, several legal regulations of an international nature were created.[3] Also, in their domestic law, States have made efforts to create legal regulations in the field of space law, which very often complied with international law obligations. The experience of other countries in the world justifies the need to prepare appropriate legal regulations also in Poland. Lucien Rapp is quite right when he writes that "(...) Of the 22 members of the European Space Agency (ESA), only seven members have adopted an internal legal framework governing space operations. Except for

1 One of the most important trends in recent years is the creation of ever smaller satellites – some of them weigh only 1 kg. On this subject, see: Satellites – a miniature revolution, https://evertiq.pl/news/25799 (accessed December 29, 2020). See also: PWC Report (2019). *Main Trends and Challenges in the Space Sector*. Available online at: https://www.pwc.fr/fr/assets/files/pdf/2019/06/fr-pwc-main-trends-and-challenges-in-~the-space-sector.pdf.

2 New Space, https://www.airbus.com/public-affairs/brussels/our-topics/space/new-space.html (accessed on: December 29, 2020).

3 See: V. Halunko, *Cosmic law: present and future*, https://www.researchgate.net/publication/335595976_Space_Law_the_Present_and_the_Future (accessed on: December 29, 2020).

 | DOI:10.1163/9789004542860_009

TABLE 4 The content of the space laws of the member states of ESA

	France	Austria	Netherlands	Belgium	UK
Authorization and licensing	YES	YES	YES	YES	YES
Continuous supervision of non-governmental activity	YES	YES	YES	YES	YES
Insurance	YES	YES	YES	YES	YES
Limitation of liability	YES	YES	YES	YES	NO
Registration process	YES	YES	YES	YES	YES
Transfer of ownership in space	YES	YES	YES	YES	NO
Space debris removal	YES	YES	NO	NO	YES
State strategic interest	YES	YES	YES	YES	YES

SOURCE: L. RAPP, SPACE LAWMAKING, HTTPS://WWW.THESPACEREVIEW.COM/ARTICLE/3523/1 (ACCESSED ON: JULY 29, 2021)

Norway, the other states have laws regulating all the mechanisms related to space operations."[4]

The tables below offer a comparative survey within and outside ESA countries:

Polish enterprises also need support from legal regulations. Today, this support is very often the key to success for enterprises in the space sector. That is why it is so important for Poland to prepare comprehensive legal regulations in

4 L. Rapp, Space lawmaking, https://www.thespacereview.com/article/3523/1 (accessed on: July 29, 2021).

TABLE 5 The material scope of space laws

	France	USA	China	Russia	Australia
Space objects launch/return	YES	YES	YES	YES	YES
Space objects control	YES	YES	NO	YES	NO
Ground segment operations	NO	YES	NO	YES	YES
Space technology	NO	NO	NO	YES	NO

SOURCE: L. RAPP, SPACE LAWMAKING, HTTPS://WWW.THESPACEREVIEW.COM/ARTICLE/3523/1 (ACCESSED ON: JULY 29, 2021)

TABLE 6 The personal scope of space laws

	France	USA	China	Russia	Australia	UK
Territorial application	YES	YES	YES	YES	YES	NO
Extra-territorial application	YES	YES	YES	YES	NO	NO
Personal application	YES	YES	YES	YES	YES	YES

SOURCE: L. RAPP, SPACE LAWMAKING, HTTPS://WWW.THESPACEREVIEW.COM/ARTICLE/3523/1 (ACCESSED ON JULY 29, 2021)

TABLE 7 The content of space laws of states outside ESA

	USA	Russia	China	Australia
Authorization and licensing	YES	YES	YES	YES
Continuous supervision of non-governmental activity	YES	YES	YES	YES
Insurance	YES	YES	YES	YES
Limitation of liability	YES	YES	N/A	YES
Registration procerss	YES	YES	YES	YES
Transfer of ownership in space	YES	NO	YES	YES
Space debris removal	YES	NO	YES	NO
State strategic interest	YES	YES	YES	NO

SOURCE: L. RAPP, SPACE LAWMAKING, HTTPS://WWW.THESPACEREVIEW.COM/ARTICLE/3523/1 (ACCESSED ON: JULY 29, 2021)

this area. However, it is worth taking into account the legal solutions adopted by other countries.

For example, in the United States, there are laws that are designed to facilitate commercial space activities, such as the Commercial Space Launch Act of 1984. However, it should be remembered that the regulations in force in the United States give quite broad powers to the US government, which can interfere with commercial space activities quite significantly, thanks to the 10th amendment to the US Constitution, which states: "This Constitution, and the Laws of the United States which shall be made in Pursuance thereof; and all Treaties made, or which shall be made, under the Authority of the United States, shall be the supreme Law of the Land; [emphasis added] and the Judges in every State shall be bound thereby, any Thing in the Constitution or Laws of any State to the Contrary notwithstanding."[5] M. J. Listner rightly claims: "Fundamentally, this means when the United States ratifies an international treaty like the Outer Space Treaty and its progeny, the provisions of those treaties have the same legal effect as a federal statute passed by Congress and signed into law by the President. Therefore, not only is the federal government legally committed to abide by the terms of a treaty like the Outer Space Treaty, so are the private citizens under the United States' domestic jurisdiction. Moreover, the Outer Space Treaty's standing as the supreme law of the land delegates to the federal government of the United States the power over commercial space activities that some advocates claim is reserved to private individuals by the 10th Amendment."

Currently, there is a strong need to create regulations that will allow avoiding unnecessary problems in the future and at the same time affect the dynamics of the development of the space industry in Poland. In connection with human activity in space, new problems have arisen and are still arising, requiring appropriate legal regulations.[6] At the same time, it should be remembered that the law is a living matter, undergoing changes and transformations, especially when it regulates an industry in which technical progress is very speedy. Therefore, it is important to issue appropriate national regulations of a timeless and universal nature, meeting Poland's international obligations and social needs. However, this is an arduous task that requires an appropriate approach. Proper legal regulations in the space sector are a necessity that should not be underestimated, especially as the development of rocket flight technology offers more and more opportunities. The creation of international space law is in the common interest of all mankind, and the effectiveness of this law will not be ensured without appropriate national regulations. It is states that regulate space activities through the enactment of national laws and regulations, and there is a need for appropriate international regulations.[7] V. Halunko rightly claims: "After a long period of relative stability (stagnation) of space law humanity has moved to a new stage of its development, which is characterized by the use of outer space at the expense of finances and funds of private companies. Therefore, the world community and space law face new challenges. Objectively, space law is beginning to develop actively. The leading

5 See, M. J. Listner, International space law and commercial space activities: the rules do apply https://www.thespacereview.com/article/2305/1 (accessed on: December 29, 2020).

6 S. Swaminatham, *The Applicability of Space Law Principles to Basic Space Science: An Update*, http://adsabs.harvard.edu/pdf/2005UNPSA.16.117S (accessed on: December 29, 2020).

7 L. Rapp, Space lawmaking https://www.thespacereview.com/article/3523/1 (accessed on: July 29, 2021).

directions of space law development should be: standardization of legal space terms, approval of private space law, promotion of private capital involvement in space programs, development of the theory of the right to use space bodies, regulation of the rights and legitimate interests of space tourists, development of sanctions agreed by the world community for violation of space law, subjects and procedures for their application."[8]

It should be noted that international law should keep pace with technological progress. It happens, however, that law-making is a bit ahead of technological progress, as an example: the system regulating the activities of States on the moon and other celestial bodies adopted by the United Nations in 1979.[9] However, it must be remembered that some legal issues related to space have not been regulated in international law to this day. An example should be the definition of the beginning of space, or the issue of space mining,[10] the issue of the use of nuclear energy in space. For example, the definition of the beginning of outer space has been the subject of many debates at the United Nations, but so far no agreement has been reached in this regard, and it is difficult to deny the seriousness of this problem and the need to regulate it. However, there are still different approaches and many theories.[11]

It should be noted that the growing involvement of private and commercial companies in space exploration, acting both jointly and individually, is universal in space known as "NewSpace" – as opposed to "OldSpace". NewSpace companies develop innovative technologies, conduct research and manage

8 V. Halunko, Space Law: the Present and the Future, file:///C:/Users/Admin/Downloads/Space_Law_the_Present_and_the_Future.pdf (accessed on: July 29, 2021), p. 17.

9 G. Zhukov, Y. Kolosov, International Space Law, Moscow, 2014 https://mgimo.ru/upload/2016/05/KOLOSOV_space_law_eng.pdf (accessed on: July 28, 2021).

10 Marco Ferrazzani, head of the legal services department at ESA, is in favour of adopting international rules for a new legal framework that will encourage respect and fair distribution of extracted resources. "When space mining becomes technologically feasible, economically beneficial and physically realistic, conditions to pursue dialogue and reconcile international rules could be established." on the other hand Tanja Masson-Zwaan, deputy director of the International Institute of Air and Space Law at Leiden University, elaborates: "There is a need for an international regime, whether through adoption of a binding treaty or soft-law mechanisms, because it will ensure compliance with the principles of international space law, increase legitimacy of space-mining activities, provide legal certainty to stakeholders, and develop an approach to benefit sharing. An adaptive governance approach of addressing issues step-by-step and involving all actors in the discussion would be most effective."https://eandt.theiet.org/content/articles/2018/01/outer-space-laws-and-legislation-regulating-the-province-of-all-mankind (accessed on: July 28, 2021).

11 See Zob. T. Masson-Zwaan, Space Law in the 21 St century, http://www.commonlii.org/in/journals/NLUDLRS/2012/35.pdf (accessed on: July 28, 2021).

projects. Examples include Planetary Resources and Deep Space Industries, which, as Catherine Doldirina writes, "(...) want to mine asteroids and even other planets to sell the resources they have mined." "SpaceX plans to use rockets to transport people from one continent to another on 30-minute suborbital flights, while several companies are currently developing technologies for commercial space transportation and tourism."[12] In turn, Lesley Jane Smith claims that "Recent developments and the changing paradigm of space exploration – from being dominated by government programs to being driven by the interests of private companies – are a challenge for regulators." and further adds: "Space traffic management is an issue that has been on the agenda for quite some time, specifically due to the ever-increasing amount of all kinds of space junk (or, as the professionals call it, "space debris")." Suborbital flights will make such a system more complex, since air and space traffic management will have to be coordinated. Lesley Jane Smith, Professor of Law at Leuphana University and solicitor at Weber-Steinhaus & Smith in Bremen, says that this coordination will go much further: "New hybrid technologies will enable access into and return from outer space to become commonplace. This will require a supra-system of regulations that effectively replace the long-standing 'sector-driven' rules that apply to air, to space, and to the other communication regimes. Space traffic management cannot be reduced to an isolated category of operations. The global scale of space exploration poses a major challenge for regulators. Today, no single state can operate a space traffic management system. This means that all countries, international organizations and private companies have to coordinate and cooperate."[13] It is very important that countries cooperate with each other and jointly create an international space law that meets the needs of the entire international community, not just certain countries or groups of countries. We cannot forget about the ongoing work of the UN COPUOS working group, which creates guidelines that will help establish a space traffic management system that will eliminate space debris.[14]

---

12 C. Doldirina, Outer space is subject to international law. This means that all countries and parties must work together to develop effective space legislation for future needs. https://eandt.theiet.org/content/articles/2018/01/outer-space-laws-and-legislation-regulating-the-province-of-all-mankind/ (accessed on: July 28, 2021).

13 L. J. Smith, Access into and return from outer space [will] become commonplace.' https://eandt.theiet.org/content/articles/2018/01/outer-space-laws-and-legislation-regulating-the-province-of-all-mankind (accessed on: July 28, 2021).

14 See, https://www.nationalgeographic.com/science/article/space-junk (accessed on: July 28, 2021) and https://letstalkscience.ca/educational-resources/stem-in-context/space-junk (accessed on: July 28, 2021).

Masson-Zwaan at Leiden University, aptly referring to the discussed issues, stated that: "Development of international space law depends on the dialogue among all stakeholders, with the UN COPUOS continuing to play an important role as a forum where all states can talk in a neutral environment and eventually agree on necessary additions to the existing legal framework for space activities."[15]

It is therefore important that States, party to international conventions, issue appropriate national laws ensuring the effectiveness of the conventions.

Outer space offers great opportunities in terms of its use. As Wojciech Góralczyk and Stefan Sawicki wrote, 'The possibility of the practical use of extra-atmospheric space arose first in the military field (observation from space objects and the possibility of placing weapons of mass destruction in orbits) and in the field of satellite communications, which can be used both for military purposes, and civilian (radiotelegraphy, transmission of television programmes).'[16] Many changes have occurred since the time these words were written, and important political and ethical questions as well as problems related to space exploration have arisen.[17] Outer space continues to raise the interest of countries around the world in its use.[18] For example, in 2018, the United States presented a new idea for the use of space. President Donald Trump's government has put forward a proposal to create a space force, the sixth type of US military – alongside the existing army, navy, air force, marines and coast guard. Vice President Mike Pence said: '(...) space environment was once peaceful and uncontested, now it is crowded and adversarial, with more and more threats arising from there. The time has come to prepare for the fact that extraterrestrial space will become a battlefield.' The United Nations Office for Outer Space Affairs (UNOOSA), reported that '(...) in early 2019, nearly 5,000 satellites were orbiting the Earth. Since 1957, when the Soviet Union first launched the Sputnik satellite into Earth's orbit, approximately 8,378 satellites have been sent up into outer space.'[19] However, Guglielmo S. Aglietti

15 https://eandt.theiet.org/content/articles/2018/01/outer-space-laws-and-legislation-regulating-the-province-of-all-mankind (accessed on: July 28, 2021).

16 W. Górlaczyk, S. Sawicki, *Public International Law in Outline*, Warsaw 2007, p. 244.

17 M. K. Simpson, *Planetary defence, global cooperation and world peace,* Handbook of Cosmic Hazards and Planetary Defence, eds J. Pelton and F. Allahdadi (Cham Springer, 2015), 1055–1067.

18 USA creates space forces, https://www.polityka.pl/tygodnikpolityka/swia-t/1759900,1,usa-tworzy-sily-kosmiczne.read (accessed 12 December 2020) *Polityka* 33.2018 (3173) of 13 August 2018; *Ludzie i wydarzenia. Świat*, 10 Original text title: *Amerykańska armia kosmiczna.*

19 A 'war in space' would be a disaster. Returning to rule-based collaboration is the only way to keep peace in space. See: https://theconversation.com/war-in-space-would-be-a-catastrophe-a-return-to-rules-based-cooperation-is-the-only-way-to-keep-space-peaceful-150947 (accessed on: December 29, 2020).

also writes: 'Under the name of 'New Space,'[20] there is an ongoing 'revolution' in the space sector with new players/commercial entrepreneurs/businesses[21] entering a domain traditionally occupied by institutional players ('Old Space', that is space agencies working with large companies) to exploit the new opportunities opening in front of them. These could include new services, offered through applications of space data (from precision navigation/agriculture, surveillance, to earth environment monitoring, et cetera), to more futuristic opportunities, such as space tourism or asteroid mining. Successful entrepreneurs from other sectors, from Richard Branson in the United Kingdom to Elon Musk in the United States, have entered the 'space' arena, taking risks and challenging the conservatism of the established 'Old Space' business model.'[22] The share of nations in space has also changed over the years with Asian countries, led by China, Japan and India, joining the United States, Russia and European countries.[23]

With the growing number of satellites in space, satellite technology is developing rapidly, with more and more innovations.[24] The competition between the space industry and scientific research is also noticeable in the world.[25] Poland will most likely focus on conducting scientific research and using

---

20 In other words, 'New Space' or the phenomenon of Space 4.0. concerns the commercialization of the space sector. Private entities are starting to play a leading role in space, and not the State as before. These include, in particular, companies such as SpaceX and the so-called 'GAFA' (Google, Apple, Facebook and Amazon). Recently, companies from Poland have had their increasing share in it. In January 2019, six projects related to the construction of micro- and nanosatellites were implemented in our country, according to data from the Polish Space Agency. See more at: https: //www.wnp.pl/tech/polska-branza-kosmiczna-zyskuje-na-rozkieta-new-space,337386.html (accessed on: December 29, 2020).

21 M. Hall, *Cosmic philosophies: who, how, what?* Space Daily. Available online at: https://www.spacedaily.com/reports/NewSpace_Philosophies_Who_How_What_999.html.

22 Guglielmo S. Aglietti, *Current challenges and opportunities for space technologies* https://www.frontiersin.org/articles/10.3389/frspt.2020.00001/full (accessed on: December 29, 2020).

23 B. C., Brittingham, *Does the World Really Need New Space Law?* https://www.peacepalacelibrary.nl/ebooks/files/35550927X.pdf (accessed on: December 29, 2020).

24 Satellites – a miniature revolution that is found overhead, https://cordis.europa.eu/article/id/415436-satellites-mini-revolution-unfolds-above-us/pl (accessed on: 29/12/2020), as well as: S. Hobe, The Impact of New Developments on International Space Law (New Actors, Commercialization, Privatization Increase in the Number of 'Space-faring Nations'). Uniform Law Review 2010, No 15 869–881.

25 It is estimated that the total revenues of the entire global services market will exceed over EUR 5 billion in 2021, which will represent a significant increase from EUR 2 billion

existing technologies, and to a lesser extent, will be engaged in independent space exploration. Poland is a country that also has significant achievements in this area, for instance, advanced satellite components are manufactured in Gdynia. It cannot be overlooked that Polish companies in the space sector are successfully operating, for example, Polish companies together with NASA participated in groundbreaking Mars research. The Polish company Astronika manufactured the equipment to land on the Red Planet and then drill its surface to a depth of 5 m. The company, as a coordinator of the production process, hired several Polish research centers to subcontract.[26] It should be remembered that the merits of Polish citizens also go back to 1924 and the observations of the Red Planet made at that time by Stanisław Andruszewski together with students from the University of Adam Mickiewicz in Poznań.[27] In turn, the first Polish commercial satellite, *Światowid,* which flew into space from the cosmodrome (spaceport) in Virginia, was created by the Wrocław company SatRevolution, which started its business by creating popular mobile games.[28] The task of the satellite was, among others, real-time monitoring of the earth's surface, researching air quality and road traffic congestion in cities.

Światowid was released into space from the Japanese Kibō International Space Station module on July 3, 2019 at 11:50 UTC. At that time, in Poland, in order to conduct space activities, read to send objects into space, the permission of the president of the Polish Space Agency was not required, as it is currently indicated in the draft Act on Space Activity and on the National Registry of Space Objects.

---

in 2016. See more, at: https://cordis.europa.eu/article/id/415436-satellites-mini-revolution-unfolds-above-us/en (accessed on: December 29, 2020).

26 See: https://tech.wp.pl/przelomowa-misja-na-marsa-nasa-zbada-planete-razem-z-polakami-6319981121607809a (accessed on: December 11, 2020), https://naukawpolsce.pap.pl /aktualnosci/news%2C29342%2Cw-sobote-start-mission-nasa-z-udzialem-polakow.html (accessed 11 December 2020), and https://news.astronet.pl/index.php /2019/10/23/virgin-orbit-oglosilo-misje-na-marsa-polscy-scientists-accept-in-it's-share (accessed on: December 11, 2020), https://www.parp.gov.pl/component/content / article / 57773: infrared-specialists-ie-Poles-on-Mars (accessed on: December 11, 2020).

27 Poland recalls the Polish Mars research, https://www.urania.edu.pl/wiadomosci/polsa-przypomina-o-polskich-badaniem-marsa-4876.html (accessed on: December 11, 2020).

28 https://cyfrowa.rp.pl/technologie/33521-pierwszy-polski-satelita-komercyjny-leci-w-kosmos, https://businessinsider.com.pl/technologie/nowe-technologie/pierwszy-polski-satelita- commercial-swiatowid / lqwyhsj, and https://naukawpolsce.pap.pl/aktualnosci/news%2C28824%2Cpierwszy-polski-satelita-komercyjny-ma-zostac-umieszczony-na-orbicie-w-2018, and also: https: / /www.pb.pl/pierwszy-polski-satelita-komercyjny-ma-zostac-umieszczony-na-orbicie-w-2018-r-908530 (accessed on: December 11, 2020).

At that time, the State was internationally responsible for the activities of companies registered in Poland that operated in space, including objects sent there. The 1972 Convention adopts the principle of absolute liability of the State launching a space object for damage caused to the surface of the earth or to the aircraft. As Grzegorz Brona writes, 'Poland can pride itself on forty years of activity in the field of space research and exploration. During this period, Polish scientists and engineers designed and built over seventy instruments that were used, among others, in such space missions as: Cassini-Huygens, Mars Express, Rosetta, Venus Express, Herschel or Phobos-Grunt.'[29]

The successes of Polish entrepreneurs, as can be seen in the Supreme Audit Office[30] report, result, among others, from the Minister of Development's involvement in shaping economically advantageous relations with the European Space Agency (ESA), especially in the area of winning contracts for Polish entrepreneurs.

The successes of Polish entrepreneurs in space justify the need to properly regulate, above all, such issues as establishing the rules for giving consent to activities in space by domestic entities; designate an authority responsible for the supervision of such activities; and establish the rules for keeping the national registry of space objects, rules on State liability and compensation issues.

The above-mentioned regulatory needs are also an obligation resulting from Poland's international obligations. At the same time, in Poland, along with the emerging challenges, there is an opportunity to develop new regulations that will stimulate further technological progress and affect Polish entrepreneurs' further success. In addition, it should be remembered that the national regulations are in line with international law and thus do not limit the activities of enterprises. Still, on the contrary, they should be a factor motivating entrepreneurs to act more intensively. Consideration should also be given on how to enforce the agreed rules and regulations at the international level.[31] Space law should be created so that it does not introduce unnecessary bureaucracy and does not restrict the freedom to generate new ideas and implement new

29 *Polski sektor kosmiczny. Katalog wybranych podmiotów*, Polska Agencja Kosmiczna 2018, 3.

30 Rozwój sektora kosmicznego, informacje o wynikach kontroli KGP.430.017.2019, *Nr ewid* 44/2020 / P / 19/021 / KGP, https://www.nik.gov.pl/plik/id,22462,vp,25136.pdf (accessed on: December 11, 2020).

31 See: B. C. Brittingham, *Does the World Really Need New Space Law?* https://www.peacepalacelibrary.nl/ebooks/files/35550927X.pdf (accessed on: December 11, 2020).

applications. The law should serve the freedom to develop and use new technologies while respecting human rights.[32]

Poland is a party to the following international conventions relating to space:[33]

1. Treaty on Principles Governing the Activities of States in the Exploration and Use of Outer Space, including the Moon and Other Celestial Bodies (hereinafter: the 'Outer Space Treaty'), drawn up in London, Moscow and Washington on 27 January 1967.[34]
2. Convention on Registration of Objects Launched into Outer Space (hereinafter: the 'Registration Convention') open for signature in New York on 14 January 1975.[35]
3. Convention on International Liability for Damage Caused by Space Objects (hereinafter: the 'Liability Convention'), drawn up in London, Moscow and Washington on 29 March 1972.[36]
4. The Agreement on the Rescue of Astronauts, the Return of Astronauts and the Return of Objects Launched into Outer Space, drawn up in London, Moscow and Washington on 22 April 1968.[37]

The conventions as mentioned above impose a number of legal and international obligations on Poland, so in connection with those obligations, the draft Act on Space Activity and on the National Registry of Space Objects was prepared.

Therefore, in Poland, there is a need to issue appropriate legal provisions resulting, among others, from the needs of entrepreneurs and the necessity to fulfill obligations resulting from the above-mentioned international agreements. Legal provisions dictated by the indicated necessities should define, first of all:

- rules for consent to activities in space by national entities,
- designation of an authority responsible for the supervision of this type of activity,
- rules for keeping a national registry of space objects,

32 See: Morozova, E. and Vasyanin, Y., (2019). *International space law and satellite telecommunications.* Oxford Research Encyclopedia of Planetary Science. Available online at: https://oxfordre.com/planetaryscience/view/10.1093/acrefore/9780190647926.001.0001/acrefore-9780190647926-e-75.

33 https://www.rp.pl/Kosmos/170809948-Nowe-przepisy-o-polskich-firmach-w-kosmosie.html (accessed on: December 11, 2020).

34 Journal of Laws 1968, No 14, item 82.

35 Journal of Laws 1979, No 5, item 22.

36 Journal of Laws 1973, No 27, item 154.

37 Journal of Laws 1969, No. 15, item 110.

- State liability and compensation issues,
- keeping a registry of space objects launched into outer space by Polish entities, with simultaneous notification of this information to the Secretary General of the United Nations, and
- issues related to the obligation to insure the activities of space entities under a third-party liability agreement.

It should also be mentioned that thanks to membership in, for example, such international organisations as the European Space Agency (ESA), the European Organisation for the Exploitation of Meteorological Satellites (EUMETSAT), as well as the European Union, more and more attention is paid to legal regulations relating to outer space.

It can be mentioned, for example, that on January 12, 2017, Deputy Prime Minister Mateusz Morawiecki and Jan Wörner, Director General of the European Space Agency (ESA), signed an agreement under which the application of transitional measures were extended to Poland as a member of ESA until December 31, 2019. It was related to the further possibility for entrepreneurs and scientific units to use the Polish Industry Incentive Scheme (PLIIS), launched especially for Poland. Undoubtedly, the content of the agreement should be considered a negotiating success for Poland, given that for the first time in history, the European Space Agency agreed to extend the transition period for a member State. However, it should be remembered that the purpose of PLIIS, closed at the end of 2019, was to increase the competences of local companies in the space sector and to make it easier for them to compete in ESA open tenders and further commercial contracts. Which, in turn, as was already mentioned, justifies the need to properly regulate, first of all, such issues as establishing the rules for granting consent to activities in space by national entities; designate an authority responsible for the supervision of such activities; and establish the rules for maintaining a national registry of space objects, rules on State liability and compensation issues.

2 Work on the Creation of the Polish Space Act in Poland

In Poland, work on the development of the Polish Space Act began in 2013. In turn, the draft assumptions for the draft Space Act were submitted to the government work list in the second half of 2014.[38] The draft assumptions for the

38 The issue of creating The Act on Space Activity and on the National Registry of Space Objects (hereinafter 'Draft Space Act') was consulted during the preparation of the update of the 'Programme of activities for the development of space technologies and the use of

draft Act on the National Registry of Space Objects was adopted by the Council of Ministers in June 2016. In 2017, a modified draft combining the assumptions of both acts was sent for inter-ministerial consultations and public consultations.[39] However, work on the project proceeded with some problems and delays.

This was confirmed by the post-audit statement of the Supreme Audit Office, amended by Resolution No. 26/2020 of the College of the Supreme Audit Office of April 16, 2020, P / 19/021 development of the space sector covering the audit period from January 1, 2016 to June 30, 2019. Taking into account these activities and the evidence presented before and after that period, which had an impact on the assessment of the controlled activities, the Supreme Audit Office negatively assessed the failure or ineffectiveness of some activities of the minister competent

The above document states that: 'The Minister did not create a system for coordinating the implementation of the PSS, nor did he conduct ongoing monitoring of the degree of implementation of the strategic objective, specific objectives, and implementation indicators assigned to individual objectives.' As is stated further in the document: 'The consequence of the lack of a sufficient number of employees in the relevant organisational unit of the ministry was excessive length of work on the draft Act on Space Activity and on the National Registry of Space Objects. The lack of this Act – in the opinion of the Supreme Audit Office – significantly weakens the conditions for the development of the Polish space sector and contributes to Poland's failure to

satellite systems in Poland,' ie, the 'National Space Sector Development Plan.' Working meetings lasted throughout the first semester of 2013, and inter-ministerial arrangements and public consultations were held in July 2013. Then, during the consultation conferences, the issue of the need to pass the Polish Space Act was additionally discussed. The above document mentions as one of the tasks, the 'Development of the draft Space Act and related delegated acts.' Moreover, on 30 August 2013, the Inter-ministerial Team for Space Policy in Poland adopted Resolution No 10 on the establishment of a Working Team for Space Act. The aim of the team's work was to develop a draft of the assumptions for the space Act as part of cooperation between the public administration and the scientific and industrial community. On 3 July 2014, the draft assumptions for the Space Act were submitted to the Government Work List (ZD105). The draft assumptions for the draft Act on the National Registry of Space Objects (the name of the draft was changed as suggested by the Government Legislation Centre (RCL) at the stage of inter-ministerial consultations and was adopted by the Council of Ministers on 7 June, 2016.

39 The draft Act on space activity after consultations, https://www.rp.pl/Opinie/310169975-Projekt-ustawy-o-dzialalnosci-kosmiczna-po-konsultacji.html (accessed on: December 11, 2020), and https://www.space24.pl/projekt-ustawy-o-zmianie-ustawy-o-polskiej-agencji-kosmicznej-po-konsultacjach-miedzyresortowych-i-publicznych (accessed on: June 24, 2021).

meet its international obligations under the United Nations Convention on the Registration of Objects Launched into Outer Space. Failure to fulfill obligations under international law, among others, negatively affects the image of Poland as a country that aspires to actively participate in European space policy.'

The relevant provisions of the 'space act' are particularly important considering Poland's obligations under international agreements, but also the expectations of entrepreneurs who successfully operate in this sector. Therefore, work on the project should be carried out with dynamism and efficiency appropriate for this type of project. Preparation of an appropriate project will certainly contribute to the increase in the Polish space sector's competitiveness and will increase the country's share in the turnover of the European space sector.

It should be remembered, however, that in 2017 the Legislative Council operating at the Prime Minister's office assessed '(...) as generally positive,'[40] the draft Act on Space Activity and on the National Registry of Space Objects (hereinafter 'Draft Space Act'), prepared by the Ministry of Development, submitting the following recommendations:[41]

1. Recommendation No 1 – The justification for the draft Act should be expanded.
2. Recommendation No 2 – The scope of the act should be narrower.

The Legislative Council emphasizes that the scope of the draft act is too wide. It should apply only to activities carried out from the territory of Poland or on board a ship or aircraft registered in Poland, that is to space objects whose registration state is Poland. It should be noted that, in turn, the act currently applies, *inter alia*, to space activities carried out by Polish citizens regardless of their place of residence, which raises doubts in the Legislative Council.

3. Recommendation No 3 – Laws are needed to regulate the liability for space damage caused on Polish territory to Polish citizens by space objects registered in Poland.

In its opinion, the Legislative Council indicates that the draft act should regulate the liability for space damage caused on Polish territory to Polish citizens by space objects registered in Poland.

40 The opinion of the Legislative Council was prepared by Prof. Dr. Hab. Anna Łabno (specialist in the field of constitutional law, University of Silesia), Prof Dr Hab Anna Wyrozumska (specialist in the field of public international law and EU law, University of Łódź), Dr. Hab. Tomasz Bąkowski, prof. UG (specialist in the field of administrative law, spatial planning and development and construction law) and the vice-chairman of the Legislative Council, Dr Hab Maciej Kaliński, prof. of UW (specialist in the field of civil law, in particular compensation law, re-privatization, bills of exchange and the check law).

41 https://www.space24.pl/projekt-ustawy-o-dzialalnosci-kosmicznej-i-krok-pod-lupa-rady-legislacyjnej (accessed on: December 11, 2020).

Today, the act includes only the definition of damage as loss of life, injury or other threat to the health of foreign natural persons or loss or damage to property or property of countries other than the Republic of Poland or foreign natural or legal persons or property of international intergovernmental organizations.

4. Recommendation No 4 – The ambiguities in the space licensing requirements should be removed.

In the opinion of the Legislative Council, some requirements for obtaining a license to conduct space activities are not sufficiently specified. As an example, one can mention the requirement of knowledge and experience in the implementation of projects in the field of space activities, stipulated in the draft act. It should be noted that it is difficult to define what this is supposed to mean in practice and what is the boundary between having knowledge and experience, and not having them. The Legislative Council also has reservations about the requirement to develop a detailed description of the planned activity. It seems to the Legislative Council a highly complicated task to draw a clear line between the detailed and imprecise description of planned space activities. Additionally, it points out that the draft act does not contain sufficient guidelines to issue a regulation containing provisions specifying the types of documents confirming the fulfillment of the above conditions. This gives the Prime Minister, as the executive body, too wide a range of independence, which in consequence violates the principles of protecting the interests of the entity that intends to conduct space activities.

5. Recommendation No 5 – More detailed guidance is needed on the amount of fees.
6. Recommendation No 6 – Lifetime insurance cover for space activity.
7. Recommendation No 7 – The sanctioning of space activities conducted in violation of the conditions set out in the permit may lead to a build-up of administrative proceedings and supporting further work on the bill.

3 Analysis of the Project – the Act on Space Activity and on the National Registry of Space Objects

After a detailed analysis of the provisions of the Act on Space Activity and on the National Registry of Space Objects, some doubts have arisen. The first relates to the status and identification of the launching State. According to Article 3 of the Draft Space Act '(…) whenever the Act refers to the launching State – this shall be understood as a State within the meaning of Article 1 (a) of the Convention on the Registration of Objects Launched into Outer

Space, open for signature in New York on 14 January 1975.'[42] According to that Convention, the term 'launching State' means:

'1. A State which launches or procures the launching of a space object; [and]

2. A State from whose territory or facility a space object is launched.'

Likewise, the Convention on International Liability for Damage Caused by Space Objects, drawn up in London, Moscow and Washington on March 29, 1972,[43] defines the expression 'launching State' as:

'1. A State which launches or procures the launching of a space object; [or]

2. A State from whose territory or facility a space object is launched.'

The given definitions are compatible. The conclusion is that the status of a launching State is acquired by law itself the moment a space object is launched into space.

According to Article II of the Convention on International Liability for Damage Caused by Space Objects ('Liability Convention'), the launching State shall be liable to pay compensation for damage caused by its space object on earth's surface or to an aircraft in flight.[44] However, under Article III of the Liability Convention, if the damage was caused elsewhere than on the surface of the earth, the issuing State shall be liable for the damage caused, if it resulted from its fault or the fault of persons for whom it is responsible. Article V of the Liability Convention provides that when two or more countries jointly launch a space object, they are jointly and severally liable for any damage caused. Also, these countries may agree on the sharing of financial obligations among themselves, in which they are jointly and severally liable. Such agreements, however, are without prejudice to the right of a State sustaining damage to seek full compensation under the Convention from any or all of the issuing States jointly and severally liable.

In the Draft Space Act, and more precisely in Article 4(2), point 13, of the Draft Space Act, a permit to conduct space activities may be issued under the following conditions: conclusion of an agreement defining which State is the launching State, in the case when more than one State can be considered the launching State. This Article contradicts the provisions of the Registration Convention and the Liability Convention.[45] The status of a launching State is

42 Journal of Laws 1979, item 22.

43 Journal of Laws 73.27.154.

44 Absolute liability.

45 Note that it is not up to any pair of countries to determine who is the launching State, as that already is determined by the Liability Convention; is the idea here to conclude an agreement on which of the launching States would ultimately take the burden of paying compensation or whether it would be somehow shared (ref. Article V(2), Liability Convention; cf. also the Baikonur arrangements between Russia and Kazakhstan).

obtained under international law the moment a space object is (attempted to be) launched into space. Therefore, when a Polish satellite is launched from another State's territory, very often two, or maybe even more, launching States are involved, jointly and severally liable in the event of damage caused by a jointly launched space object. On the other hand, any agreements between States do not have any impact on the status of the issuing State, apart from the distribution among the issuing States of the financial liabilities arising from the damage suffered, and, as also indicated above, this does not affect the question of liability to the aggrieved party. The presented doubt is significant, particularly with regard to the obligation to bear liability for damage caused by a space object.

Another doubt arises in connection with the content of Article 25 of the Draft Space Act. It states that: 'The owner of the space facility before the operator applies for a permit, is obliged to conclude a liability insurance contract for damage.'[46] The State Treasury will be indicated as the insured person in the insurance contract.[47] According to Article 28, the owner may be released from the obligation to conclude an insurance contract, if the space object will be used for the purposes of essential national security, science, research or education.[48]

---

46 This insurance is not subject to the provisions of the Act of 22 May 2003 on compulsory insurance, the Insurance Guarantee Fund and the Polish Motor Insurers' Bureau, Journal of Laws 2016, item 2060, and it covers liability for damage caused in connection with space activities during the duration of the insurance coverage and for the year after the termination of this protection. The insurance company may not contractually limit the payment of compensation.

47 The Prime Minister shall determine, by way of a regulation, the amount of the minimum sum insured for one event, the effects of which are covered by the insurance contract, taking into account the type of space facility and the scale of potential threats associated with its use.

48 A space object used for science, research or education purposes may be a space object which meets all of the following criteria:

1) is scientific and the research equipment used to conduct scientific research or development works, is within the meaning of the Act of 30 April 2010 on the principles of financing science (Journal of Laws 2016, item 2045 and item 2260 and of 2017, item 859);
2) the launch of the space object is an important stage in the implementation of the research programme, which includes scientific research or development work, and the aim of which is to obtain results and data for the development of science and innovation;
3) the research programme carried out with the use of the launched space object is of significant importance for the development of science or the increase in the level of innovation in Poland;

The owner of the facility who is one of the following entities (within the meaning of the applicable regulations) may apply for an exemption from the obligation to conclude an insurance contract:

1. a research unit,
2. a university,
3. scientific network,
4. scientific consortium,
5. scientific and industrial center,
6. scientific center of the Polish Academy of Sciences, or
7. university's research center.

According to Article 29(1) of the Draft Space Act on exemption or refusal of exemption from the obligation to conclude an insurance contract referred to in Article 25(1) is resolved by the minister competent for science by way of an administrative decision, at the request of the owner.

Thus, the Minister responsible for science will decide on the exemption or refusal of the exemption from the obligation to conclude an insurance contract for the purposes of science, research or education, but also for the purposes of the basic interest of State security (Article 28 item 1). However, would it not be necessary to regulate the issue, whereby the Minister responsible for science should be applying to the Minister of National Defence, the Minister responsible for foreign affairs and the head of the Internal Security Agency for a position in the field of the fundamental interest of state security, or taking into account the scope of competence to investigate the premises of the basic interest of state security? This could be provided for by the Minister of National Defence, instead of the minister responsible for science.[49] Thus, perhaps it would be more expedient that decisions regarding the exemption or refusal of the exemption from the obligation to conclude an insurance contract in the event that the space object is to be used for the purposes of science, research or education should be issued by the minister for science, and in the

---

4) the owner of the facility agrees to use the obtained results of scientific research or development work for the purpose of conducting activities promoting science and educational activities;

5) the owner of the facility has submitted a declaration stating that the space facility will be used mainly for scientific research or development work, and that the possible economic use of the facility will be of an auxiliary nature, ie, activities of limited scope, directly related to the operation of a given facility and necessary for its operation or inherent in its main non-economic purpose.

49 In the previous provisions of the draft Act, and even in Article 7, Sec. 2 of the draft, in the course of the proceedings, the President of the Polish Space Agency requests the Minister of National Defence, the minister responsible for foreign affairs and the head of

case of intended use of the object for the basic purposes of State security, the Minister of National Defence.

Further doubts regarding the provisions of the Draft Space Act arise in relation to the competences of the Prime Minister with regard to the Polish Space Agency. They result from the changes introduced to the Act on the Polish Space Agency. According to Article 2 of the Act on the Polish Space Agency, 'The Agency is subordinate to the minister competent for economy,' whereas previously it was the Prime Minister. It would be worth introducing a uniform solution, as leaving the current wording will result in an unnecessary division of competences. Issues related to the conduct of space activities and registration of space objects will be governed by the regulations of the Prime Minister, and issues related to the functioning of the Polish Space Agency by the regulations of the minister responsible for the economy. The division of competences used does not serve the efficiency of action, but can only introduce chaos.

4 Fulfillment of Poland's International Obligations in the Field of Space Law, and the Draft Space Act

The applicable provisions of international law must be specified by implementing them into the domestic law of States, party to international conventions. It is in the well-understood interest of all States that appropriate provisions of domestic law be issued that would satisfy their obligations under international law. Thanks to this approach, it will be possible to avoid many problems related to the use of space, on the one hand, and on the other hand, it will stimulate legal activities in space. Recently, a significant increase in human activity in the use of space can be noticed. Such a state of affairs creates the necessity to be appreciated by the representatives of the doctrine of this branch of law and to engage in the process of its creation.

The need to issue relevant legal provisions is, as mentioned earlier, related to the need for the Republic of Poland to fulfill its obligations under international agreements in the field of space law, but also, as we read in the justification to the Draft Space Act, this need arose '(...) in connection with an increase in the activity of Polish entities in the use of space.'[50]

---

the Internal Security Agency to take a position on the impact of space activities on the security and interest of the State, as well as the performance of international obligations by the Republic of Poland.

50 Despite the lack of appropriate legislation, in 2018 the space sector in Poland consisted of several dozen of mostly active small and medium-sized enterprises (including branches

The proposed Act will implement the provisions of the Outer Space Treaty, the Liability Convention and the Registration Convention.

The above-mentioned treaties, as mentioned earlier, provide for the necessity to regulate in national law, in particular:
- rules of expressing consent to activities in space by domestic entities;
- designation of an authority responsible for the supervision of such activities;
- rules for keeping the national register of space objects; and
- State liability and compensation issues.

The Act on Space Activity and on the National Registry of Space Objects will apply to entities based in the territory of the Republic of Poland, both public and private. The Draft Space Act makes it clear that the supervision over space activities is exercised by the President of the Polish Space Agency and he, in accordance with Article 37, has the right to control space activities.

In addition, it should be remembered that the Draft Space Act must comply with the basic principles of space law, which were included in the Outer Space Treaty, that is the principle of freedom for research and use of space for the sake and in the interest of all countries, the principle of non-appropriation of outer space, and the principle of the peaceful use of outer space.

The Draft Space Act is the first national legal act in the field of space policy.

Pursuant to Article 1 of the Draft Act[51] on Space Activity and on the National Registry of Space Objects, the Act regulates:
1) rules for the performance of space activities; and
2) rules for keeping the National Registry of Space Objects.

The Draft Space Act applies to space activities conducted:
1) on the territory of the Republic of Poland;
2) on board space facility platforms, including Polish sea-going ships or aircraft registered in the Republic of Poland; or
3) by Polish citizens regardless of their place of residence; or
4) conducted by legal persons or organizational units without legal personality with their seat in the territory of the Republic of Poland.

Space activities in Poland, as provided for in Article 2 of the project, may be performed on the terms specified in the Act of July 2, 2004, on the freedom of economic activity.[52]

---

of European space companies), several large enterprises operating in the ICT, defence and aviation industries, research institutes and renowned technical universities. In 2012, the Space Industry Employers' Union (ZPSK) was established, uniting over 60 entities in 2018 – see more, at: *Polski sektor kosmiczny. Katalog Wybranych podmiotów*. Polska Agencja Kosmiczna (2018) 5 – 96.

51 The draft Act of 10 July, 2017.

52 Journal of Laws 2016, item 1829 and of 2017, item 460.

Article 3 defines 'space activities', 'space objects', 'operators', the 'launching State', and 'damages.'

In the case of two definitions, the legislator refers to the definitions contained in international conventions to which Poland is a party. It does so in the case of the definition of "launching State" by referring in this case to Article I (a) of the Convention on Registration of Objects Launched into Outer Space, opened for signature in New York on January 14, 1975, and for the definition of damage by referring to Convention on International Liability for Space Damage Caused by Space Objects, drawn up in Moscow, London and Washington on March 29, 1972. The definition of a space object in this draft is compatible with the definition contained in the Convention on International Liability for Space Damage Caused by Space Objects, drawn up in Moscow, London and Washington on March 29, 1972.

It should be noted that the definition of a space object contained in the discussed draft is compatible with the definition of the Convention on International Liability for Space Damage Caused by Space Objects, drawn up in Moscow, London and Washington on March 29, 1972, and the Convention on the Registration of Objects Launched into Outer Space (Registration Convention).

In accordance with Article VI of the Outer Space Treaty, 'States Parties to the Treaty shall bear international responsibility for national activities in outer space, including the Moon and other celestial bodies, whether such activities are carried on by governmental agencies or by non-governmental entities, and for assuring that national activities are carried out in conformity with the provisions set forth in the present Treaty. The activities of non-governmental entities in outer space, including the Moon and other celestial bodies, shall require authorization and continuing supervision by the appropriate State Party to the Treaty.' Taking into account the above provision, a State should regulate issues related to the performance of space activities. Therefore, the third chapter of the project is devoted to the authorization to conduct space activities.

According to Article 4 of the Draft Space Act space activities may be performed only after obtaining a permit issued at the request of the operator. This permit is issued, refused, amended or revoked by the President of the Polish Space Agency by way of an administrative decision after meeting strict conditions. The application for the issue, change or transfer of a permit is subject to a fee, which is the income of the Polish Space Agency.[53] The Polish Space Agency (POLSA) was established by the Act of 26 September 2014,[54] and has also been

53 The amount as well as the manner and procedure for paying the fees, taking into account the type and value of the space object, are specified by the Prime Minister by way of a regulation.

54 Journal of Laws 2014, item 1533.

equipped with tasks in the field of research and development of space technology, including satellite engineering and their application for utility, economics, defence, state security and scientific purposes. Additionally, it deals with the preparation and implementation of the National Space Plan. In accordance with the project under discussion, the President of POLSA issues a permit to conduct space activities. It does so within 6 months from the date of submitting the application, which is submitted together with complete documentation confirming the fulfilment of strictly defined conditions referred to in Article 4(2) of the Draft Space Act. In the course of the proceedings, the President of POLSA requests the Minister of National Defence, the minister responsible for foreign affairs and the head of the Internal Security Agency to take a position on the impact of space activities on the security and interest of the State, as well as the performance of international obligations by the Republic of Poland.

The permit may specify the conditions for the performance of space activities established for the protection of national security, the safety of persons or property, the environment, and to ensure the performance of international obligations by the Republic of Poland.

Complying with the obligations arising from Article II of the Registration Convention,[55] it was also necessary to regulate the issues related to the National Registry of Space Objects.

The purpose of this Convention is to provide States parties with additional measures and procedures to facilitate the identification of space objects, assuming that "(…) the system of compulsory registration of objects launched into outer space will facilitate, in particular, the identification of these objects and will contribute to the application and development of international law in the field of research and use of outer space." The project under discussion meets these obligations in the fourth chapter, entitled: 'The National Registry

55 When analyzing national space legislation in the world, the following models of regulation of these issues in the internal orders of individual countries stand out, namely:
- complete absence of national regulations and application of only international law,
- complete absence of national regulations and application of only international law,
- application of soft law,
- regulating only registration issues in a generally applicable act,
- regulation of registration issues and partly other issues in a generally applicable act,
- regulating the methods of conducting space activities.

According to the UN report, the registry of space objects exist in the following countries: South Africa, Algeria, Argentina, Australia, Austria, Belgium, Belarus, Brazil, Chile, China, France, Spain, the Netherlands, Japan, Canada, Kazakhstan, Colombia, South Korea, Germany, Nigeria, Norway, Russia, Sweden, Ukraine, the United States of America, Venezuela, United Kingdom, and Italy.

of Space Objects.' The registry contains information on space objects launched into orbit around the earth, for which the Republic of Poland is the issuing country. Pursuant to the Outer Space Treaty, the Republic of Poland retains jurisdiction and control over an object released into outer space included in the registry and over the object's crew on board when they are in outer space or on a celestial body. The obligation to keep the registry is imposed by the Draft Space Act on the President of POLSA. Article 14 of the draft specifies which information is to be entered in the Registry. Entry in the registry in accordance with the draft Act takes place at the operator's request. The registry is kept in electronic form and is public. The application for entry into the Registry is submitted in Polish and English. Pursuant to the provisions of the draft, the President of POLSA is obliged to immediately submit to the Secretary General of the United Nations, information about entering a space object into the Registry, through the minister responsible for foreign affairs. The procedure for submitting an application for entry is determined by the Prime Minister by way of a regulation.

It should be noted that the above-mentioned provisions meet the obligations arising from Article VI of the Space Treaty – the obligation to 'authorize and constantly supervise' the space activities carried out. It should be added that Article II of the Registration Convention requires the States that are parties to the Convention, to create and administer a registry of space objects launched into outer space, with simultaneous notification of such information to the Secretary-General of the United Nations. It should be emphasized that the act of registration of a space object entails the right to exercise jurisdiction by the State and to exercise certain prerogatives, and the obligation to bear international responsibility for the operation of such an object, since the aforementioned article states: 'When a space object is launched into Earth's orbit or beyond, the launching State shall register the space object by means of an entry in an appropriate registry which it shall maintain. Each launching State shall inform the Secretary-General of the United Nations of the establishment of such a registry.'

In turn, Chapter 5 of the discussed project is devoted to fees. Pursuant to its provisions, an operator applying for a permit to conduct space activities or to make an entry or change an entry in the National Registry of Space Objects is obliged to pay a fee. The amount of the fee depends on the type and value of the space object.

Chapter 6 was entitled: 'Liability for damage.'

The provision of Article 22 of the Draft Space Act states that 'the Republic of Poland is liable for the damage, on terms set out in international law.' Therefore, in the event of liability for damage, the international conventions must be applied, in particular: the Liability Convention, in which Article II states: 'A launching State shall be absolutely liable to pay compensation for damage caused by its space object on the surface of the Earth or to aircraft in flight.' Further, Article III clarifies: 'In the event of damage being caused elsewhere than on the surface of the Earth to a space object of one launching State or to persons or property on board such a space object by a space object of another launching State, the latter shall be liable only if the damage is due to its fault or the fault of persons for whom it is responsible.' In turn, according to Article 24 of the Draft Space Act, 'In the event that the Republic of Poland has to pay compensation in connection with damage caused by space activities, funds to cover it come from the special-purpose reserve of the State budget for financing the liabilities of the State Treasury.'

However, it must be remembered that pursuant to Article 23(1) of the Draft Space Act, in the event that the Republic of Poland has paid compensation for the damage, the State Treasury has recourse claim to the owner up to the amount of the insurance sum.

In matters not regulated by the Act (currently the Draft Space Act), the provisions of the Civil Code apply to the liability of the owner.

In accordance with the provisions of the above-cited Convention, the launching State bears absolute liability for damage that a launched object has caused to the surface of the earth or to an aircraft in flight, and if the damage was caused elsewhere than on the surface of the earth, the issuing State is responsible for the damage occurred, when it resulted from his fault or the fault of persons for whom it is responsible. It should be emphasized that in this case, the nature of the facility (governmental or non-governmental) does not matter.

This state of affairs affects the wording of the definition of "launching State", which is the same wording in both the Registration Convention, opened for signature in New York on January 14, 1975, and the Convention on International Liability for Damage Caused by space objects, done at Moscow, London and Washington on March 29, 1972, both conventions define the expression "State launching into space" as:

1.a State that launches or causes a space object to be launched, [and]
2. the country from whose territory or facilities the space object was launched.

The presented definition means that, regardless of the place where the damage occurred, also in a place other than on the earth's surface, the issuing State is responsible for the damage, if it was caused by its fault or the fault of persons for whom it is responsible.

In accordance with the Liability Convention, a claim for compensation for damage is made through diplomatic channels. In the event of unsatisfied claims through diplomatic negotiations, the interested parties shall, at the request of one of them, establish a Claims Commission.

Chapter 7 is entitled: 'Liability insurance for damage.' As it is stated in the explanatory memorandum to the Draft Space Act of 20 July 2017,[56] 'Due to the specific nature of insurance of objects launched into space, this insurance will be treated differently than other compulsory insurance. Due to the fact that third party liability insurance of entities launching space objects is a niche insurance line for business on a global scale, the detailed terms and conditions of the third party liability insurance will be specified in the contract by both parties to the insurance, on market terms, in such a way that it can be reinsured on global markets specializing in this type of insurance. It was assumed that the minimum sum insured would be 60 million euros for one space object, however, this amount is too high, especially in the case of start-ups. The Prime Minister, by way of an ordinance, shall determine the amount of the minimum sum insured, taking into account the type of space object and the risk of damage.'

Pursuant to Article 25 of the Draft Space Act, 'The owner of a space object, before the operator applies for a permit, is obliged to conclude a liability insurance contract for damage.' The State Treasury will be indicated as the insured person in the insurance contract. The insurance is not subject to the provisions of the Act of 22 May 2003 on compulsory insurance, the Insurance Guarantee Fund and the Polish Motor Insurers' Bureau.[57] The insurance covers liability for damage caused in connection with space activities during the period of insurance coverage and for a year after the termination of such protection. The insurance company may not contractually limit the payment of compensation. This regulation is important taking into account the financial responsibility of the State assumed in the Draft Space Act and with a view to protecting its interests. In the event of damage caused by a space object for which Poland is the issuing State, the State Treasury will be required to pay compensation to the third country. However, it will be entitled to a recourse claim for the compensation paid up to the sum insured from the owner of the facility. The remaining amount will be covered by the State Treasury as part of the special-purpose funds unless the damage was caused solely by the operator or in connection with breach of the terms of the permit granted to him. Then the

56 http://prawoikosmos.pl/wp-content/uploads/2017/07/dokument300891-1.pdf (accessed on: July 15, 2021).

57 Journal of Laws 2016, item 2060.

State Treasury will be entitled to pursue a recourse claim up to the full amount of compensation paid.

However, it should be emphasized that, in accordance with the Draft Space Act, the insurance contract will indicate the State Treasury as the insured. It is the owner of the space facility who, before the operator applies for a permit, is obliged to conclude a third party liability insurance contract.

Furthermore, the Draft Space Act provides for the right to be exempted from the liability insurance for the owner of a space object if the space object is used for the purposes of the basic interest of State security, science, research or education, and the owner of the object applying for the exemption is one of the scientific entities, such as, for example, a university, a research center of the Polish Academy of Sciences, or a scientific consortium.

However, it will be up to the decision of the minister responsible for science whether the exemption from the insurance obligation is dismissed or refused.

When damage caused by a space object exempt from liability insurance occurs, the determination of the circumstances, causes and effects of the event that caused the damage will be the responsibility of a special commission appointed each time by the President of the Polish Space Agency. The Commission's findings will be consultative and advisory, and the conclusions and recommendations issued are to prevent similar events in the future. However, the Commission does not make findings on the fault and liability of those who caused the damage. The Commission acts on the basis of the Regulations established, by order, by the President of the Polish Space Agency.

Exemption from the obligation to obtain civil liability insurance for damages in the case of objects performing activities for the public interest, science or education, as well as limiting the liability of entities launching space objects of a different nature up to the amount of the sum insured, except in the case when the damage was caused by willful misconduct or gross negligence, is an important record from the point of view of the interests of the Polish State and the whole of humanity, because the lifting of these obligations will affect the dynamics of the development of the Polish space sector.

It is noteworthy that, in accordance with the Liability Convention, Poland will be liable for damage caused to foreign entities by space objects launched by Polish entities and registered in the national registry.

Liability for damage to the ground and to aircraft during flight is absolute. In turn, liability for damages caused outside the ground will depend on the establishing of fault. Therefore, the burden of covering the damage shall be borne by the State Treasury.

Chapter 8 shows that the President of the Polish Space Agency exercises supervision over space activities.

Chapter 9 of the Draft Space Act provides for the imposition of financial penalties in the event that entities conduct space activities in a manner inconsistent with the Act and conduct space activities without a permit.

5 Conclusions

The discussed Draft Space Act is a response to the needs of the broadly understood space industry in Poland. Undoubtedly, the project is a long-awaited proposal, which should be assessed positively despite the indicated doubts. The preparation of the bill was a necessity, especially considering the activities of Polish enterprises and scientific institutions that are successful in the space industry, as well as the involvement of other countries in space activities. The accuracy of the legislative solutions in the field of issuing a license to conduct space activities by way of an administrative decision, or providing for the possibility of exemption from the obligation to conclude an insurance agreement against liability for damage caused by a space object should be emphasized.

It is particularly important that the provisions of the Draft Space Act are compatible with the changes resulting from the draft amending the Act on the Polish Space Agency,[58] especially with regard to the body supervising the Polish Space Agency, that is, the minister responsible for the economy. It should be mentioned that the previously proposed changes to the amendment to the Act on the Polish Space Agency were related to the adaptation of the supervision of the POLSA to European practice, in particular of those countries that are members of the European Space Agency (ESA). It should also be emphasized that the Draft Space Act complies with European Union law, noting that according to Article 2c, paragraph 3 of the Treaty of Lisbon, "In the fields of research, technological development and space, the Union has competence to carry out activities, in particular to define and implement programs, but the exercise of these powers must not result in Member States being prevented from exercising their competences."

58 Source – act amending POLSA https://www.gov.pl/web/rozwoj-praca-technologia/rada-ministrow-przyjela-projekt-nowelizacji-ustawy-o-polskiej-agencji-kosmicznej#:~:text=Rada%20Ministr%C3%B3w%20przyj%C4%99%C5%82a%20projekt%20nowelizacji%20ustawy%20o%20Polskiej,Agencji%20Kosmicznej%20%28PAK%29%2C%20kt%C3%B3r%C4%85%20przyj%C4%99%C5%82a%20dzi%C5%9B%20Rada%20Ministr%C3%B3w. (accessed on: July 15, 2021).

This is very important considering that the regional regulations are a very important element of legal protection in the field of space law, quite strongly affecting activities in space.

The provisions contained in the Draft Space Act are in line with the basic principles of space law as expressed in the Outer Space Treaty, that is, the principle of freedom of research and use of outer space for the benefit and interest of all countries, the principle of non-appropriateness of outer space, the principle of the peaceful use of outer space, but also implement previously made international commitments.

The described project regulates many important issues from the point of view of space activities. It will certainly have an impact on Poland's activities in space and will lead to even greater activity of Polish enterprises and Polish science.

The work on the Space Act raises concerns in Poland due to its duration. Therefore, pursuant to Article 193 paragraph 1 and 2 of the Regulations of the Sejm of the Republic of Poland,[59] an interpellation of March 16, 2021, number 24603, on the "excessive length of work on the Draft Space Act" was presented by the Members of the Sejm of the Republic of Poland: Mrs Paulina Hennig-Kloska, Mrs Hanna Gill-Piątek, Mrs Joanna Mucha, Mr Mirosław Suchoń and Mr Tomasz Zimoch. In response to the above interpellation, prepared by Mr Robert Tomanek, Undersecretary of State, it was stated that: "With regard to the Draft Space Act, it should be emphasized that that the project being developed by the Ministry of Economic Development, Labour and Technology is the second draft of the Act devoted to principles of conducting space activities.

The following factors have an influence on the pace of work on the Act:

a) the scope of necessary supplements and changes resulting from the arrangements of the previous draft Act;
b) parallel work on the National Space Program (KPK); and
c) ongoing work on the Recovery and Resilience Plan for Poland (KPO).

The scope of necessary supplements resulting from the arrangements of the previous draft Act, including in particular: clarification of the notional grid, the subject scope, the need to re-analyze the way of regulating the obligatory insurance of space activities and the rules of operator's liability for damage caused by a space object, caused the need for re-analysis, which resulted in the commencement of work on a new project."[60] In the discussed answer to the

59 Resolution of the Sejm of the Republic of Poland of 30 July 1992 on the Regulations of the Sejm of the Republic of Poland (M. P. of 2019, item 1028, as amended).

60 https://orka2.sejm.gov.pl/INT9.nsf/klucz/ATTC4WHF8/%24FILE/i24603-01.pdf (accessed on: July 16, 2021).

interpellation, one could optimistically read that "After being entered into the list of legislative and program works of the Council of Ministers, it is planned that in the second half of 2021 the draft will be directed to interministerial consultations and social consultations, and then submitted to the Standing Committee of the Council of Ministers and the Council of Ministers, which will open the way to refer the draft for deliberation by the Parliament."

CHAPTER 8

Intellectual Property Protection for Space Activities in Poland: A Study of Polish Patent Law

Katarzyna Krupa-Lipińska

1 Introduction

Since more than 20 years the issue of intellectual property (IP) is given special attention in the context of space activities. The World Intellectual Property Organization (WIPO) indicated a few reasons for such interest. One of them is the tendency of shifting of space activities from state-owned to private or commercial ones, which investors are more conscious of their tangible and intangible properties primarily due to the commercial benefits they are providing.[1] This argument is strengthened by the recent boost of private space tourism in the form of commercial flight launched in 2021 by Virgin Galactic,[2] Blue Origin and SpaceX – the last one, called "Inspiration4", circled the earth solely with an amateur crew (and with no professional astronaut) on board. What is more, Blue Origin announced in October 2021 the project of building a commercial space station called "Orbital Reef" with an internal volume similar to the International Space Station (ISS).[3] The legal certainty would definitely encourage the private sector to invest in space research and cooperation.

Another reason indicated by WIPO is the globalization of space activities in the form of international cooperation, which also calls for a reliable international legal framework to address the mosaic of legal systems that might apply to such cooperation. The disadvantage of cooperation agreements between cooperating parties is that they regulate crucial intellectual property issues only between the given parties and do not apply to third parties.[4]

1 WIPO, *Intellectual Property and Space Activities. Issue paper prepared by the International Bureau of WIPO*, 4–5, point 18–21 <https://www.wipo.int/export/sites/www/patent-law/en/developments/pdf/ip_space.pdf> accessed 1 September 2021.

2 At the end of 2021 Virgin Galactic said to have about 700 customers that bought tickets for a suborbital space ride <https://www.space.com/virgin-galactic-sells-100-space-tourist-tickets> accessed 13 November 2021.

3 <https://edition.cnn.com/2021/10/25/tech/blue-origin-space-station-jeff-bezos-scn/index.html> accessed 11 November 2021.

4 WIPO, *Intellectual Property and Space Activities* (n 1) 4–5, point 19–21.

 | DOI:10.1163/9789004542860_010

At the turn of the century increase in the interest in IP rights protection in the context of space activities resulted in establishing certain provisions in international legal documents. For example, in 1996 a United Nations Resolution Adopted by the General Assembly, the Declaration by the United Nations Committee on the Peaceful Uses of Outer Space on International Cooperation in the Exploration and Use of the Outer Space for the Benefit and the Interest of All States, Taking into Particular Account the Needs of Developing Countries, stated in its second paragraph that:

> States are free to determine all aspects of their participation in international cooperation in the exploration and use of outer space on an equitable and mutually acceptable basis. Contractual terms in such cooperative ventures should be fair and reasonable and they should be in full compliance with the legitimate rights and interests of the parties concerned as, for example, with intellectual property rights.[5]

International activities relating to laws regulating outer space and intellectual property have been also led by WIPO and included a study conducted in 1997 with the help of consultants from Europe, Japan and the United States of America on the possible need for rules and/or principles for the protection of industrial property, which end up with the conclusion that – as for that time – "there was no need for special international legislative provisions concerning the protection of inventions created or used in outer space, but that it is desirable that the International Bureau of WIPO give information on the existing protection of such inventions to interested States and organizations".[6] Interestingly though, the issues that has been raised included clarification on the principle of Article 5*ter* of the Paris Convention[7] as well as whether there is a need to clarify by Member States of WIPO that the laws applicable to inventions in the territory of a country will also apply in the spacecraft registered by (under jurisdiction of) the said country and the standardization of contractual clauses on the protection of inventions and confidential information

5 <https://www.unoosa.org/oosa/en/ourwork/spacelaw/principles/space-benefits-declaration.html.> accessed 11 November 2021.

6 WIPO, *Intellectual Property and Space Activities* (n 1) 9, point 36.

7 Article 5*ter* of the Paris Convention relates to non-infringement of the rights of a patentee by the use on board vessel of devices forming the subject of patent provided that such use devices are used there exclusively for the needs of the vessel as well as the use of devices or accessories forming the subject of the patent in the construction or operation of aircraft or land vehicles of other countries when those aircraft or land vehicles temporarily or accidentally enter the said country.

created or used in international cooperative agreements between the space faring nations.[8] The plenary of the Third United Nations Conference on the Exploitation and Peaceful Uses of Outer Space (UNISPACE III) held in Vienna from 19–30 July 1999 adopted (with amendments) the recommendation that has been made by the Workshop on Intellectual Property Rights in Space and included it in the Report of the Conference. The recommendations called – first – for more attention to the protection of intellectual property rights "in the view of the growth in the commercialization and privatization of space-related activities". Second, further exploration of the harmonization of intellectual property standards and legislation relating to intellectual property rights in outer space should be made with the goal of "enhancing international coordination and cooperation at the level both the State and the private sector". Third, "all States should provide appropriate protection of intellectual property rights involving space-related technology, while encouraging and facilitating the free flow of basic science information" and fourth, "educational activities concerning intellectual property rights in relation to outer space activities should be encouraged".[9]

2 Intellectual Property Law

The term "intellectual property" is not uniformly understood in legal doctrine. In general the differences relate to the question whether the given term applies only to copyrights and related rights or whether it includes also industrial property rights. The later understanding, that is that the term "intellectual property" is a collective (superior) term that includes both copyrights and industrial property rights, follows from the international treaties, in particular Article 2 (viii) of the Convention Establishing the World Intellectual Property Organization[10] and Article 1 (2) of the TRIPS Agreement[11] and currently is

8 WIPO, *Intellectual Property and Space Activities* (n 1) 8–9, point 35–36.

9 ibid 9, point 37.

10 Signed at Stockholm on July 14, 1967 and as amended on September 28, 1979, in force in Poland from 23.03.1975, Journal of Laws 1975 No 9, item 49. The article 2 (viii) states that: ""intellectual property" shall include the rights relating to: – literary, artistic and scientific works, – performances of performing artists, phonograms, and broadcasts, – inventions in all fields of human endeavor, – scientific discoveries, – industrial designs, – trademarks, service marks, and commercial names and designations, – protection against unfair competition, and all other rights resulting from intellectual activity in the industrial, scientific, literary or artistic fields".

11 Agreement on Trade-Related Aspects of Intellectual Property Rights – Annex 1C to the Marrakesh Agreement Establishing the World Trade Organization signed in Marrakesh

widely represented in Polish doctrine.[12] Following this approach it is legitimate to claim that the given term relates to: copyrights and related rights, database and industrial property rights, including: patents, utility models, industrial designs, trademarks, service marks, trade names, indications of source or appellations of origin, and the repression of unfair competition (Article 1(2) of the Paris Convention for the Protection of Industrial Property[13]) as well as protection of new plant varieties, topographies of integrated circuits and know-how. The given broad meaning of the term "intellectual property" is applied in the Agreement concerning Cooperation on the Civil International Space Station 1998 (IGA)[14] in its Article 21 (1) by its reference to the Convention Establishing the World Intellectual Property Organization.

As a rule, the same intangible good may be protected by different intellectual property rights, so the protection might be cumulative. For example, a design might be protected by registered or unregistered design right, copyright and repression of unfair competition law. There are, however, certain exceptions, for instance an identical technical solution cannot be a patented invention and utility model at the same time. Legal grounds of intellectual property protection are independent from each other[15] and there is no need to declare one legal basis as *lex specialis* in relation to another. It is for the entitled person to choose on which legal basis he or she seeks the protection.[16]

Intellectual property law is a branch of civil law, which means that under Polish law the Polish Civil Code has auxiliary application (for example relating

on 15.04.1994, came into effect on 01.01.1995, in force in Poland from 03.04.1996, Journal of Laws 1996 No 32, item 143. According to Article 1 (2) "For the purposes of this Agreement, the term "intellectual property" refers to all categories of intellectual property that are the subject of Sections 1 through 7 of Part II", that is: copyright and related rights; trademarks; geographical indications; industrial designs; patents; the layout-designs (topographies) of integrated circuits; protection of undisclosed information.

12 On the contrary eg Andrzej Szewc in Andrzej Szewc and Gabriela Jyż (eds), *Prawo własności przemysłowej* (2nd ed., C.H.Beck 201) 24.

13 Paris Convention for the Protection of Industrial Property of 20 March 1883 (as amended on September 28, 1979) that enter into force on 3 June 1984, in force in Poland on 22.10.1931, Journal of Laws1932 No 2, item 8. (Paris Convention).

14 Agreement Among the Government of Canada, Governments of Member States of the European Space Agency, The Government of Japan, The Government of the Russian Federation, and the Government of the United States of America Concerning Cooperation on the Civil International Space Station done in Washington on 29th January 1998.

15 Alicja Adamczak and Michał du Vall, *Ochrona własności intelektualnej* (Uniwersytecki Ośrodek Transferu Technologii 2010) 23–24.

16 Piotr Kostański and Łukasz Żelechowski, *Prawo własności przemysłowej* (2nd ed, C.H. Beck 2020) 6.

to contracts on intellectual property rights).[17] The intellectual property law include also *ius publicum* norms, that is administrative norms, which enable the implementation of the protection (for example norms relating to administrative procedure before Polish Patent Office, its organization and tasks), financial law (for example payments for protection of industrial property rights) and penal provisions for the infringements of intellectual property rights, which strengthen their protection.[18]

3 Industrial Property Law

3.1 *Introduction*

According to Article 1(2) of the Paris Convention the objects of the protection of industrial property are: patents, utility models, industrial designs, trademarks, service marks, trade names, indications of source or appellations of origin, and the repression of unfair competition.[19] Currently the given term is understood broadly and it includes also protection of new plant varieties, topographies of integrated circuits and know-how.[20] In general, the term "industrial property" is not uniform, as it relates to goods of different kinds[21] in terms of their function, legal character and the ways of obtaining protection.[22] More accurately it might be said that the intangible goods relating to industrial property belong to an open catalogue, which changes in time due to technical and social development and – apart from absolute intellectual property rights – they also include, for example, protection of trade secrets and know-how. On the other hand, the catalogue of absolute industrial property rights is closed and dependent upon a legislative decision restricted by international

17 Ryszard Skubisz in Ryszard Skubisz (ed), *System Prawa Prywatnego. Prawo własności przemysłowej*, (Tom 14A, C.H.Beck 2012), 84–85; Szewc (n. 12) 6.

18 Adamczak and du Vall (n 15) 23; Szewc (n 12) 6.

19 Article 1 (3) Paris Convention clarifies that "Industrial property shall be understood in the broadest sense and shall apply not only to industry and commerce proper, but likewise to agricultural and extractive industries and to all manufactured or natural products, for example, wines, grain, tobacco leaf, fruit, cattle, minerals, mineral waters, beer, flowers, and flour."

20 Michał du Vall in Ewa Nowińska and Urszula Promińska and Michał Du Vall (eds), *Prawo własności przemysłowej* (5th ed, LexisNexis 2011) 18.

21 Michał du Vall, *Prawo patentowe* (Oficyna a Wolters Kluwer business 2008) 20 with reference to Fryderyk Zoll, ‚*Wstęp*' in Adam Ponikło and Jan Gutowski, *Polskie prawo patentowe z komentarzem* (Geberhner i Wolff 1935) 3.

22 Du Vall (n 21) 18.

agreements.[23] In Poland those rights are regulated in the Industrial Property Law Act of 30 June 2000, with amendments[24] and concern the protection of inventions, utility models, industrial designs, trademarks, geographical indications and topographies of integrated circuits. The given rights are restricted in territory and time,[25] originate in constitutive administrative decisions issued by the Polish Patent Office, might be invalidated at any time, and their exclusivity is restricted to professional usage. The intangible goods relating to industrial property that are not absolute industrial property rights are primarily protected by general rules of the Polish Civil Code of 23 April 1964 and the Unfair Competition Suppression Act of 16 April 1993.[26,27]

Industrial property rights might be divided into two categories: the rights relating to production, which extends the state of the art (for example inventions or utility models) and those which serves to distinct products or traders (for example trademarks, geographical indications, or trade names). From the perspective of space activities, the production rights traditionally play a crucial role, as they relate to the extension of the state of the art in space technology. Due to that fact, the further analysis in this chapter will primarily concern patent law. It needs to be mentioned however, that due to the development of space tourism the issues concerning trademarks and designs possess a potential to play a more important role in the future.

3.2 *Legal Basis*

As mentioned, in Polish law the basic legal act relating to industrial property law is the Industrial Property Law Act. The protection of new plant varieties is prescribed in the Protection of Plant Varieties Act of 26 June 2003,[28] combating of unfair competition and protection of know-how is regulated in the Unfair Competition Suppression Act and personal goods as well as company name is regulated in the Civil Code. The detailed legal rules are prescribed in regulations. In addition, according to Article 87 of the Constitution of the Republic of Poland of 2 April 1997[29] (the Polish Constitution), the sources of universally binding law are also ratified international agreements. Poland is bound

23 Kostański and Żelechowski (n 16), n 9–10.

24 Statute of 30 June 2000 – *Prawo własności przemysłowej*, Journal od Laws from 2021, item 324.

25 Except geographical indications.

26 Statute of 16 April 1993 r. Combating of unfair competition, Journal of Laws 2021, item 1655.

27 Kostański and Żelechowski (n 16), 9–10.

28 Statute of 26 June 2003 concerning Protection of Plant Varieties, Journal of Laws 2021, item 213.

29 Journal of Laws No. 78, item 483.

by many ratified international agreements relating to industrial property law and in particular to patent law, for example the Paris Convention of 20 March 1883 with revisions, the TRIPS Agreement,[30] the Convention on the Grant of European Patents (European Patent Convention) of 5 October 1973 with revisions[31] and the Act revising the Convention on the Grant of European Patents of 29 November 2000,[32] the Patent Cooperation Treaty of 19 June 1970 with amendments,[33] and the Strasbourg Agreement Concerning the International Patent Classification of 24 March 1971 as amended on 28 September 1979.[34]

According to Article 91(1) of the Polish Constitution, "[a]fter promulgation thereof in the Journal of Laws of the Republic of Poland (*Dziennik Ustaw*), a ratified international agreement shall constitute part of the domestic legal order and shall be applied directly, unless its application depends on the enactment of a statute", and pursuant to Article 91(2), "[a]n international agreement ratified upon prior consent granted by statute shall have precedence over statutes if such an agreement cannot be reconciled with the provisions of such statutes". On 1 May 2004 Poland joined the European Union and in that regard according to Article 91(3) of the Polish Constitution, "[i]f an agreement, ratified by the Republic of Poland, establishing an international organization so provides, the laws established by it shall be applied directly and have precedence in the event of a conflict of laws". Therefore, European Union regulations relating to industrial property rights, like for example Regulation (EU) 2017/1001 of the European Parliament and of the Council of 14 June 2017 on the European Union trade mark[35] or Council Regulation (EC) No 6/2002 of 12 December 2001 on Community designs,[36] are directly applicable.

---

30 Agreement on Trade-Related Aspects of Intellectual Property Rights (hereafter TRIPS Agreement), Annex 1C to the WTO Agreement, Marrakesh, done 15 April 1994, entered into force 1 January 1995; 1869 UNTS 299; UKTS 1996 No. 10; Cm. 3046; ATS 1995 No. 38.

31 Convention on the Grant of European Patents (European Patent Convention) done in Munich of 5 October 1973 as revised by the Act revising Article 63 EPC of 17 December 1991 including its Protocols that forms its integrated part, Journal of Laws 2004, No 79, item 737.

32 Act of 29 November 2000 revising the Convention on the Grant of European Patents done in Munich 5 October 1973, Journal of Laws 2007, No 236, item 1736.

33 Patent Cooperation Treaty done at Washington on June 19, 1970, amended on September 28, 1979, modified on February 3, 1984 Journal of Laws 1991, No 70, item 303 with attachment.

34 Strasbourg Agreement Concerning the International Patent Classification done on Strasbourg at March 24, 1971, as amended on September 28, 1979 Journal of Laws 2003 r. No 63, item 579.

35 OJ L 154, 16.6.2017, 1–99.

36 OJ EC No L 3 of 5.1.2002, 1 with amendments OJ EC No L 386 of 29.12.2006, 14.

According to Article 4(1) of the Industrial Property Law Act, "where an international agreement or the provisions of European Union laws binding and directly applicable in all Member States provide for special procedures for granting protection for inventions, utility models, industrial designs, trademarks, geographical indications or topographies of integrated circuits, the provisions of this Law shall apply accordingly to the subject matter not governed by that agreement or these provisions, or falling within responsibilities of national authorities".

According to Article 5 of the Industrial Property Law Act foreign persons shall enjoy the rights under this Law on the basis of international agreements. It relates mainly to Articles 2 and 3 of Paris Convention which prescribes national treatment for nationals of countries of the Paris Union and nationals of countries outside the Union who are domiciled or who have real and effective industrial or commercial establishments in the territory of one of the countries of the Union. As for 2022 there are 179 Contracting Parties to the Paris Convention (Members of the Paris Union),[37] therefore the given rule has a general application. A similar provision may be found in Article 1(3) of the TRIPS Agreement, namely that Members shall accord the treatment provided for in this Agreement to the nationals of other Members. Here, "nationals" means persons, natural or legal, who are domiciled or who have a real and effective industrial or commercial establishment in that customs territory. In the rare case the applicant is not domiciled or does not have a real and effective industrial or commercial establishment in one of the countries which are Member States of the Paris Union or the TRIPS Agreement, the reciprocity rule applies (as per Article 5(2) of the Industrial Property Law Act).

3.3 *Relevance of the Place of Invention*

From the perspective of space activities industrial property goods may be divided into those that have been created on earth and relate to outer space activities and those created in outer space.[38] Intellectual property goods created in outer space might be further divided into those created in outer space "as such" or in an object launched into outer space (see paragraph 5). In that regard it should be underlined that at the stage of application and obtaining of an exclusive right in the territory of Poland the place where the invention, utility

37 WIPO information at: <https://wipolex.wipo.int/en/treaties/ShowResults?search_what=C&treaty_id=2> accessed 11 November 2021.

38 Mariusz Tomasz Kłoda, *Prawo własności intelektualnej w działalności kosmicznej* (*Intellectual property rights and space activities*), Researchgate uploaded 27 April 2021, accessed 1 November 2021.

model or industrial design had been created is irrelevant. Therefore, whether an industrial property good relating to space activity had been created on Earth or in outer space (both in outer space "as such" or in an object launched into outer space) is irrelevant for the possibility to obtain patent at the territory of Poland by applying to the Polish Patent Office by national (via Polish Patent Office – PPO), European (via European Patent Office – EPO) or international Patent Cooperation Treaty (via World Intellectual Property Organization – WIPO) procedure. It is explicitly prescribed in Article 27(1) of the TRIPS Agreement that "patents shall be available and patent rights enjoyable without discrimination as to the place of invention". What matters in applying for a patent is the nationality (domicile) of the applicant, as analyzed on the grounds of Article 5 of the Industrial Property Law Act. What is more, the Industrial Property Law Act provides in Article 40 that a person having its registered office or domicile in the Republic of Poland may file a patent application for seeking patent protection in another country via the Polish Patent Office following the procedure: 1) prescribed in an international agreement or European Union laws as prescribed in Article 4 of the Industrial Property Law Act, or 2) prescribed in the Industrial Property Law Act itself – after application concerning that invention with the Polish Patent Office. The justification for the given provision is that the Polish Patent Office should have a chance to evaluate and select inventions that potentially may concern defense or state security.[39] In case the Polish Patent Office finds that such invention concerns national defense (for instance, it is a new category of weapon or military equipment and methods of combat) or the security of the State (for instance, technical means applied by civil services authorized to carrying out actions and reconnoitering operations, as well as new categories of equipment and methods of use thereof by the said services) it may consider it to be a secret invention, which constitute a classified information and which right to patent is transferred for the State subject to compensation (Articles 56–59 of the Industrial Property Law Act). Contrary to regulation in some other national legal systems,[40] the obligation in Polish law provided in Article 40 of the Industrial Property Law Act is not dependent upon the subject of application, therefore it has a general applicability. Interestingly though, the given provision does not possess any sanction, so it is a *lex imperfecta*.[41]

---

39 Agnieszka Żebrowska-Kucharczyk and Magdalena Tagowska, ‚Komentarz do art. 40" in Arkadiusz Michalak (ed), *Prawo własności przemysłowej. Komentarz* (C.H.Beck 2016) 121.

40 Anna Maria Balsano, ',Intellectual Property Rights and Space Activities' (1994), 79 ESA Bulletin <https://www.esa.int/esapub/bulletin/bullet79/balsano.htm> accessed 10 November 2021.

41 Żebrowska-Kucharczyk and Tagowska (n 39) 121.

The given problem according to outer space activities is prescribed in Article 21(3) of the IGA, which states that "[i]n respect of an invention made in or on any Space Station flight element by a person who is not its national or resident, a Partner State shall not apply its laws concerning secrecy of inventions so as to prevent the filing of a patent application (for example, by imposing a delay or requiring prior authorization) in any other Partner State that provides for the protection of the secrecy of patent applications containing information that is classified or otherwise protected for national security purposes. This provision does not prejudice (a) the right of any Partner State in which a patent application is first filed to control the secrecy of such patent application or restrict its further filing, or (b) the right of any other Partner State in which an application is subsequently filed to restrict, pursuant to any international obligation, the dissemination of an application".

At the same time it needs to be mentioned that in Polish law there is also no rule like the one existing in Section 105 of Chapter 35 of the United States Code (Inventions in outer space) which prescribes that "any invention made (…) in outer space on a space object or component thereof under the jurisdiction or control of the United States shall be considered to be made (…) within the United States for the purposes of this title except with respect to any space object or component thereof that is specifically identified and otherwise provided for by an international agreement to which the United States is a party, or with respect to any space object or component thereof that is carried on the registry of a foreign state in accordance with the Convention on Registration of Objects Launched into Outer Space" and that "any invention made, (…) in outer space on a space object or component thereof that is carried on the registry of a foreign state in accordance with the Convention on Registration of Objects Launched into Outer Space, shall be considered to be made (…) within the United States for the purposes of this title if specifically so agreed in an international agreement between the United States and the state of registry".[42]

3.4 *Priority*

The general rule in Polish industrial property law, including patent law, is that the 'first in time' in applying for the right is also the 'first in law.' Therefore, the date according to which the requirements of obtaining protection are evaluated is of primary importance and it is called the priority. The following kinds of priority are distinguished:

42 Added Pub. L. 101–580, §1(a), Nov. 15, 1990, 104 Stat. 2863 <https://www.congress.gov/101/statute/STATUTE-104/STATUTE-104-Pg2863.pdf> accessed 1 November 2021.

1) Ordinary priority, that is with reference to the date of filing a patent application with the PPO or the EPO and;
2) Previous priorities which might take the form of:
   - Conventional priority, that is with reference to the date that an application has been duly filed in the designated country on conditions laid down in international agreements (in particular State Parties to Paris Convention or any Member of the World Trade Organization) and the application for patent or utility model is duly filed with the PPO or the EPO within 12 months from that application.[43] According to the European Patent Convention the right of priority shall have the effect that the date of priority shall count as the date of filing of the European patent application (Article 89).
   - Priority from the date of displaying industrial property good in the exhibition. According to the Industrial Property Law Act, priority to obtain industrial property right counts from the date that the invention, the utility model or the industrial design was displayed, in Poland or elsewhere in the world, at an official or officially recognized exhibition, provided that the patent, utility model or industrial design application has subsequently been filed with the Patent Office within six months of that date. Priority to obtain a right of protection of a utility model or a right in registration of a design shall also be granted where the utility model or the industrial design has been displayed at a public exhibition in Poland other than that mentioned above, if the given exhibition was mentioned by the President of the Patent Office in a communication in the "*Monitor Polski*" Official Gazette of the Republic of Poland and the filing of an application was done within 6 months from that date (Article 15[1] of the Industrial Property Law Act). This situation is differently regulated (but to the same effect) in the European Patent Convention as displaying the invention at an official, or officially recognized, international exhibition falling within the terms of the Convention on international exhibitions signed at Paris on 22 November 1928 and last revised on 30 November 1972 constitutes a non-prejudicial disclosure (not be taken into consideration) if it occurred no earlier than six months preceding the filing of the European patent application (as per Article 55 (1) (b) of the European Patent Convention).

43 In case of application for design protection and trademark protection – design or trademark should be duly filed in PPO or EUIPO within 6 months.

3.5 *The Right to a Patent*

Another important question is: once the invention, utility model or industrial design has been created, who can obtain industrial property right to it? The answer lies with the rights labelled: the right to a patent for invention, the right of protection for a utility model and the right in registration for an industrial design, which are prescribed in Article 11 of the Industrial Property Law Act. The given rights may be assigned (the contract should be in writing on pain of invalidity) or may be subject to succession. They belong to the creator or – in case they have been made jointly by a number of persons – the given rights belong to the creators jointly. If the invention, utility model or industrial design has been made by a creator in the course of employment duties or in the execution of any other contract, it belongs to the employer or the commissioner (unless otherwise agreed by the parties). In case those intangible goods have been made in connection with the execution of an agreement concluded between economic entities, then the given agreement may designate the entity to which the given rights shall belong to. If an invention, a utility model or an industrial design has been made by a creator with the assistance of an economic entity, the latter may enjoy the right to exploit them in its own field of activity (it might be stipulated in the agreement on the provision of assistance that the given right shall, however, belong in whole or in part to the economic entity).

4 Patentable Inventions

As mentioned, space technology is one of the most sophisticated and advanced areas of technological development. Since the beginning of the 21st century the state-owned activities using space technology shift to private and commercial activities, which involve expensive investments. This situation calls for the mechanisms of effective protection of intellectual property, based on a fair and competitive legal environment. Such effective protection is important for numerous reasons indicated by WIPO, namely: 1) it gives competitive benefits to right holders (notably the possibility to conclude licensing agreements or exclude competitors from using a certain technology), 2) it improves the overall image of the company (a patent portfolio may serve as proof of technical competence of the company); 3) it gives the possibility to negotiate a cross-license, especially in a situation in which a certain space technology combines various high-tech solutions to which different subjects are entitled; and 4) it gives the States the possibility to establish and maintain security interests in intellectual property.[44]

The major exclusive right that protects technological solutions is patent for invention. In Poland, patent protection may stem from a decision of the PPO or the EPO. The term "invention" is neither defined in Polish law nor in the European Patent Convention. The Polish legal doctrine defines it as "a technical solution directed to fulfill practical needs with the use of new means of influence on a matter or utilization of its proprieties, providing in a full and complete manner the rules of proceedings which guarantee achievement of intended outcome".[45] Invention needs to have a technical character, the lack of which precludes further analysis of its patentability.[46] The concept of an invention within a meaning of the European Patent Convention relates to the case law of the German Federal Court of Justice and its concept of "technical teaching", that is: "a teaching to methodically utilize controllable natural forces to achieve a causal, perceivable result".[47] In other words, "technical teaching" is "an instruction addressed to a skilled person as to how to solve a particular technical problem using particular technical means".[48]

Inventions are different by their nature, therefore typically four categories are distinguished, namely: 1) products (such as substances and mixtures or fragments of live organisms), 2) apparatuses (such as tools and machines), 3) methods and 4) applications of substances or mixtures for methods of treatment or diagnosis. With regard to methods concerning space activities, for example, in 2020 attention has been given to the patent granted on 30 June of that year (with application on 3rd January 2017) by the United States Patent and Trademark Office (USPTO) to NASA, which relates to the invention called "method for transferring a spacecraft from geosynchronous transfer orbit to lunar orbit"[49] – what is basically a method of transferring spacecraft to the moon cheaper and faster than previously available.

---

44 WIPO (n 1) 5, point 21.

45 Stanisław Sołtysiński in Janusz Szwaja and Andrzej Szajkowski (ed.), *System prawa własności intelektualnej. Prawo wynalazcze* (Vol. 3, Ossolineum 1990) 29–32.

46 Case II GSK 372/10 [16.03.2011] Supreme Administrative Court (NSA) Legalis.

47 EPO Board of Appeals decision of 9.12.2010, G 0002/07 (OJ 2012,130) Broccoli/PLANT BIOSCIENCE, 60 <https://www.epo.org/law-practice/case-law-appeals/pdf/g070002ex1.pdf> accessed 1 November 2021.

48 Derk Visser, *The Annotated European Patent Convention* (21 ed., H.Tel 2013) 55.

49 Patent no. US 10,696,423 B1. According to the abstract the invention concerns "method for placing a spacecraft into a lunar orbit, either by standard (i.e. impulsive) or ballistic (i.e. non – impulsive) capture, from an Earth orbit that is significantly inclined relative to the lunar orbit plane, with no constraint on the local time of perigee for the starting orbit".

As mentioned, neither the Polish legislator nor the European Patent Convention gave a positive definition of invention; rather, they provided for a negative, non-exhaustive list in Article 28 of the Industrial Property Law Act respectively Article 52(2) of the European Patent Convention, which indicates what (in particular) shall not as such be regarded as invention. First of all it should be underlined that exclusion relates to: 1) discoveries, scientific theories and mathematical methods. In outer space activities a certain discovery might relate to outer space and its bodies as such (stemming from outer space exploration), but it may also refer to the outcomes of the scientific and commercial research conducted in a microgravity environment, that is where physical and biological phenomena of materials and substances are not influenced by earth's gravity and may lead to certain discoveries concerning their proprieties and functioning.[50] The exclusion of being an invention also relates to: 2) purely aesthetic creations, 3) schemes, rules and methods for performing mental acts, playing games doing business, 4) computer programs – which in case of a space activities plays a crucial role; and 5) presentations of information. Article 28 of the Industrial Property Law Act also mentions creations or methods whose incapability of exploitation may be proven or exploitation of which will not bring the result expected by the applicant, under the generally accepted and recognized principles of science. The provisions concerning biotechnological inventions also contain two additional indications of what cannot constitute patentable invention, namely 1) the human body, at the various stages of its formation and development, and 2) the simple discovery of one of its elements, including the sequence or partial sequence of a gene.

The invention to be patented needs to fulfill certain patentability criteria which – apart from technical character – are: 1) novelty, 2) inventive step and 3) industrial application (as per Article 24 of the Industrial Property Law Act and Article 52(1) of the European Patent Convention).

Novelty means that the invention does not form part of the state of the art (as per Article 25(1) of the Industrial Property Law Act and Article 54 (1) of the European Patent Convention). The state of the art comprises everything that was made available to the public by means of a written or oral description, by use, displaying or disclosure in any other way, before the date according to which priority to obtain a patent is determined. Also the content of any patent applications or utility model applications which enjoy the earlier priority but were not made available to the public are considered as comprised in the state

---

50 Eg the experiments in outer space are conducted in relation to faucets and tires. See <https://money.cnn.com/2018/08/05/news/companies/goodyear-delta-faucet/index.html> accessed 11 November 2021.

of the art, provided that they were published in the manner as specified in the Industrial Property Law Act. It should be underlined that novelty is examined widely, that is, the examined state of the art is the one revealed not only in the territory where the protection is sought, but in the whole state of the art available anywhere in the world. In the context of space activities, it should probably be specified that availability to the public should be understood broadly and include all the revealed technical solutions, regardless of the place of disclosure. It would be legitimate then to claim that a technical solution disclosed in outer space might also hinder the novelty of an invention, the priority of which is later than that disclosure.

What is more, the Industrial Property Law Act and the European Patent Convention protect an applicant from abusive prior disclosure stating that there is a possibility to grant patent protection for the invention, if its disclosure took place six months before filing patent application and it was caused by an evident abuse in relation to the applicant or his legal predecessor.

The invention involves inventive step if, having regard to the state of the art, it is not obvious to a person skilled in the art. In deciding whether there has been an inventive step, the content of any patent applications or utility model applications which enjoy the earlier priority, not made available to the public, are not taken into consideration (as per Article 26 of the Industrial Property Law Act and Article 56 of the European Patent Convention). The distinction in the examination of novelty and inventive step is that while evaluating novelty the items of prior art are compared individually with the applied invention, while in case of inventive step the evaluation relates to the combination ('mosaics') of prior art and the question whether the person skilled in the art would deduce from it the technical solution that is applied for.[51] Therefore, the inventive step is established by EPO by using "the problem and solution approach". The question that might arise in the context of space activities and – in general – highly sophisticated technology involved in it, relates to the proper establishment of a model of a person skilled in the art that would make such an assessment on the basis of the combined material of the state of art that he/she is acquainted with. It is explained that "[t]he skilled person neither has the level of knowledge of the average member of the public at large (…), nor that of advanced senior scientist (…). The skilled person resembles an ordinary practitioner possessing the common general knowledge in the specific technical field at the relevant date. (…) The skilled person is not creative, has no imagination (…) and is a captive of established prejudices in his field (…)".[52]

51 Visser (n 48) 103.
52 ibid 104.

The knowledge of the person skilled in the art relates to the technical field to which invention belongs to. There then needs to be identified a standard of knowledge and skills that people working in this particular technical field commonly possess. In case of such a specific technical field as that of space activities, with not so many technical experts who possess such an exclusive technical knowledge, the construction of a model of a person skilled in the art may cause certain problems. What is more, in the fields in which the inventions are created by a group of researchers from different technical fields (as it might be in the case of space activities) the model of a person skilled in the art may need to possess the knowledge and skills of a specialist from those different technical fields.[53]

In turn, the susceptibility of industrial application means that by means of the given invention a product may be produced or a process may be used, in a technical sense, in any kind of industry, including in agriculture (Article 27 of the Industrial Property Law Act and Article 57 of the European Patent Convention). The term "industry" is understood broadly, therefore it includes also the space industry.

Polish law and the European Patent Convention also designate the types of inventions that are excluded from patenting, even if they would fulfill patentability criterions (as per Article 29 of the Industrial Property Law Act and Article 53 of the European Patent Convention). The given exceptions to patentability are in line with the global standard prescribed in Article 27 (2) and (3) of the TRIPS Agreement. According to Article 29 of the Industrial Property Law Act, patents shall not be granted for:

1) Inventions the exploitation of which would be contrary to public order or morality; the exploitation shall not be deemed to be so contrary merely because it is prohibited by law. The given provision became particularly important with the development of biotechnological inventions, therefore it has been clarified that biotechnological inventions whose exploitation would be contrary to public order or morality in particular are: a) processes for cloning human beings, b) processes for modifying the germ line genetic identity of human beings, c) uses of human embryos for industrial or commercial purposes, d) processes for modifying the genetic identity of animals which are likely to cause them suffering without any substantial medical benefit to man or animal, and also animals

53 Krystyna Szczepanowska-Kozłowska in Ewa Nowińska and Urszula Promińska and Krystyna Szczepanowska-Kozłowska (eds), *Własność przemysłowa i jej ochrona* (LexisNexis 2014) 52.

resulting from such processes (as per Article 93[3](2) of the Industrial Property Law Act).

2) Plant or animal varieties or essentially biological processes for the production of plants or animals and products obtained in such process; this provision does not apply to microbiological processes or to other technical processes nor to the products made thereof unless they are not plant or animal varieties. The process for the production of plants or animals is essentially biological if it consists entirely of natural phenomena such as crossing or selection.

3) Methods for treatment of the human or animal body by surgery or therapy or diagnostic methods applied on human or animal bodies; it does not apply to products, and in particular to substances or compositions applied in diagnostics or treatment.

5 Patent

The scope of protection granted by patent is determined by the claims contained in the patent specification. The given claims might be interpreted in the light of the patent specification and drawings (as per Article 63(2) of the Industrial Property Law Act). A patent granted for a process of manufacture also covers products directly obtained by means of that process (as per Article 64(1) of the Industrial Property Law Act).

Patent right is defined in Polish law in a positive and negative way. The positive (synthetic) designation of patent right means that patent confers the exclusive right to exploit the invention, for profit or for professional purposes, throughout the territory of the Republic of Poland (as per Article 63(1) of the Industrial Property Law Act). The negative (analytical) definition relates to the acts that are forbidden by third parties in relation to the patented invention. A patent holder then has the right to prevent any third party not having his consent from exploiting his invention for profit or for professional purposes by way of performing the acts consisting of making, using, offering, putting on the market, or storing a product that is the subject matter of the invention, exporting or importing the product for such purposes, or employing a process that is the subject matter of the invention, as well as using, offering, putting on the market, storing of products directly obtained by that process, or exporting or importing the given products for such purposes.

A patent right, as any exclusive industrial property right, is restricted to the territory of the Republic of Poland. Generally, the territorial scope of protection of industrial property rights is one of the most difficult issues regarding space activities. However, this feature of patent right is universally accepted in national patent regimes, as it stems from Article 4 *bis* of the Paris Convention and is derived from State sovereignty. The exclusive industrial property rights prescribed in the industrial property laws are created by the administrative decisions of an administrative offices of particular States, like in Poland by the Polish Patent Office, and therefore they might be binding only at the territory of that State.[54]

At the stage of application and obtaining patent in Poland the place where the invention has been created is irrelevant. What matters is the nationality (domicile) of the applicant upon the rules prescribed in Article 5 of the Industrial Property Law Act (analyzed above). Once patent is granted the right is restricted to the territory of the Republic of Poland. According to Article II of the Treaty on Principles Governing the Activities of States in the Exploration and Use of Outer Space, including the Moon and Other Celestial Bodies (Outer Space Treaty) from 26 January 1967, in force in Poland from 22 December 1967,[55] outer space (as such) is not appropriated by any State, therefore – obviously – it cannot be treated as a territory of the Republic of Poland and a patent granted at the territory of Poland does not confer protection in outer space (as such). The more complex problem relates to the patent protection at an object launched into outer space. According to the Article VIII of the Outer Space Treaty, "A State to the Treaty on whose registry an object launched into outer space is carried shell retain jurisdiction and control over such object, and over any personnel thereof, while in outer space or on a celestial body". According to Article II of the Convention on Registration of Objects Launched into Outer Space (Registration Convention), "Where a space object is launched into earth orbit or beyond, the launching State shall register the space object by means of an entry in an appropriate registry which it shall maintain. Each launching State shall inform the Secretary General of the United Nations of the establishment of such a registry" and according to Article III, "1. The Secretary-General of the United Nations shall maintain a Register in which the information furnished in accordance with article IV shall be recorded. 2. There shall be full and open access to the information in this Register".

There are two problems stemming from the above-mentioned provisions. First, that the registry should be maintained by the launching State. In Poland there is no such national registry so far, but the legislative work regarding its

54 Piotr Kostański in Kostański and Żelechowski (n 16) 168.

55 Journal of Laws 1968, No 14, item 82.

establishment is progressing. Currently the draft statute on space activities and a national register of space objects, dated 10 July 2017,[56] is in the legislative stage of public consultations.[57] Polish space objects would thereby be registered directly in the United Nations Register of Objects Launched into Outer Space upon the information addressed to the Secretary-General. Second, the utmost important problem in the given context is whether retaining "jurisdiction and control" over an object means that also rights under a given legal regime, which are restricted to the territory of launching State, are in force in the object registered by that launching State. The United States in its federal law, namely Section 105 of Chapter 35 of the United States Code, regulated this issue by stating that " (a) Any invention (…) used or sold in outer space on a space object or component thereof under the jurisdiction or control of the United States shall be considered to be (…) used or sold within the United States for the purposes of this title, except with respect to any space object or component thereof that is specifically identified and otherwise provided for by an international agreement to which the United States is a party, or with respect to any space object or component thereof that is carried on the registry of a foreign state in accordance with the Convention on Registration of Objects Launched into Outer Space" and that "(b) Any invention (…) used or sold in outer space on a space object or component thereof that is carried on the registry of a foreign state in accordance with the Convention on Registration of Objects Launched into Outer Space, shall be considered to be made, used or sold within the United States for the purposes of this title if specifically so agreed in an international agreement between the United States and the state of registry". Regrettably, Article 13(3) of the Polish draft statute on space activities and a national registry of space objects (at least in its current version of 2017) only repeats the provision of Outer Space Treaty stating that in accordance with this Treaty the Republic of Poland retains jurisdiction and control over an object launched to outer space which is registered in the registry and over the personnel on its board, while they are in outer space or on a celestial body. The answer to the question of intellectual property law applicable on a space object is a subject of legal debate. Some claim that applicability of a national law of the State of registry of a space object is doubtful[58] while others

56 <https://legislacja.rcl.gov.pl/docs//2/12300856/12449052/12449053/dokument300886.pdf> accessed 1 November 2021.

57 Information available at the Governmental Legislation Centre (*Rządowe Centrum Legislacji*) <https://legislacja.rcl.gov.pl/projekt/12300856/katalog/12449052#12449052> accessed 1 November 2021.

58 Anna Maria Balsano, *Industrial Property Rights in Outer Space in the International Governmental Agreement (IGA) on the Space Station and the European Partner,* 35th

here allow an analogy to the ships which fly a State's flag on the high seas and on aircraft which are registered by that State.[59]

The territorial protection of patents, the doctrine of no-appropriation of outer space and the necessity to disclose the invention before the patent is granted is called in a Polish doctrine the "space patent paradox" and is explained in the following way by M.E. Wachowicz and M. Bury:

> [A] patent's coverage is limited to the particular territory that issues the patent. However, outer space is no one's territory. There is no Space Patent Office or Space Patent Court. Furthermore, there is no legal system that would allow a patentee to enforce patent in extra-terrestrial space. On the first thought it seems to be a space patent paradox as an applicant would disclose invention and obtain no protection for the field of application that is most important to him. However, it must considered where is the money in space industry and what are the principles of its flow/distribution. It should be observed that space instruments and devices are manufactured on Earth and in the limited number of countries. Suppliers of those devices receive either public or private funds for their products and often compete for the orders from the agencies. It leads to the quite obvious conclusion that although space devices are applied in space the money in them can be made on Earth and in quite specific locations. Patent protection provides possibility to win some of the orders by ruling out the competitors if the patent protection covers these very locations.[60]

Within international cooperation the problem of governing law is regulated by agreements concluded between parties taking part in such cooperation. The best example is Article 21(2) of the IGA[61] concerning the International Space Station (ISS) which states that "[s]ubject to the provisions of this Article, for purposes of intellectual property law, an activity occurring in or on a Space

---

Colloquium on the Law of the Outer Space, Washington D.C., August 28 to September 5, 1992.

59 Arnold Varharenwald, ',Industrial Property on the Space Station "„Freedom'", 1993 E.I.P.R., vol. 15, No. 9 at footnote 22 referring to Beier and Stauder „*Weltraumistationen und das Recht des geistgen Eigentums*"", GRUR Int. (1985) at 9 note 22 and 8 note 18.

60 Marta E. Wachowicz and Marek Bury, ',Space technology transfer problems in the context of protecting the space heritage'(2017) 42 Space Policy 67.

61 Agreement among the government of Canada, governments of Member States of the European Space Agency, the Government of Japan, The Government of the Russian Federation, and the Government of the United States of America concerning cooperation on the civil International Space Station.

Station flight element shall be deemed to have occurred only in the territory of the Partner State of that element's registry, except that for ESA-registered elements any European Partner State may deem the activity to have occurred within its territory. For avoidance of doubt, participation by a Partner State, its Cooperating Agency, or its related entities in an activity occurring in or on any other Partner's Space Station flight element shall not in and of itself alter or affect the jurisdiction over such activity provided for in the previous sentence".

One of the important rules in patent law is the exhaustion of rights in relation to a particular product embodying the invention or manufactured by means of the invention. According to this rule the rights conferred by a patent shall not extend to acts concerning a product embodying the invention or manufactured by means of the invention, consisting in particular of its being offered for sale or further put on the market, if that product has been put on the market on the territory of the Republic of Poland by the patent holder or with his consent. The given provision (Article 70(1) of the Industrial Property Law Act) constitutes the so-called 'national exhaustion of a patent right.' The Polish legislator also regulated regional exhaustion of a patent right by stating that a patent shall neither be considered infringed by an act of importation into the territory of the Republic of Poland or other acts referred above, in respect of a product that has earlier been put on the market on the territory of the European Economic Area (EEA, comprising the Member States of the European Union, Iceland, Norway and Liechtenstein) by the patent holder or with his consent (as per Article 70(2) of the Industrial Property Law Act). It is claimed that regional exhaustion of patent (as well as for example of utility model, industrial design, and topographies of integrated circuits) mitigates the consequences of the rule of territorial protection of a patent, for in case of its lack the free movement of goods in a common market would be hindered in relation to innovative products protected by patent.[62] The Polish legislator did not, however, prescribed international exhaustion of patent, therefore if the product protected by patent has been put on a market outside EEA, the exhaustion of the right does not apply.

The Polish legislator prescribed also certain restrictions to the patent, that is the acts that do not constitute patent infringements, which are prescribed in Article 69 of the Industrial Property Law Act. They include:

1. The communication privilege, which means that the exploitation of an invention concerning means of transport or their parts or accessories, temporarily located on the territory of the Republic of Poland, or

62 Kostański in: Kostański and Żelechowski (n 16) 191.

concerning goods which are in transit through its territory is allowed. The given provision relates to Article 5 *ter* of the Paris Convention and guarantees freedom of transport. It is of particular relevance to outer space activities as the question arises whether it may be applied also to the spacecraft in a situation of a temporary presence in a foreign State, for instance if the transport of flight elements depends on launchers registered in another State.[63] The given problem has been recognized and regulated with respect to the International Space Station. In Article 21(6) of the IGA it is therefore prescribed that "[t]he temporary presence in the territory of a Partner State of any articles, including the components of a flight element, in transit between any place on Earth and any flight element of the Space Station registered by another Partner State or ESA shall not in itself form the basis for any proceedings in the first Partner State for patent infringement".

2. The exploitation of an invention for national purposes, to a necessary extent, without the exclusive right, where it is has been found indispensable to prevent or eliminate a state of emergency relating to vital interests of the State, in particular to security or public order.
3. The examining privilege, which means employment of an invention for research and experimental purposes, for the evaluation thereof, analysis or teaching.
4. The registration privilege (the so-called Bolar's exemption), that is the exploitation of an invention by making, using, storing, offering, or putting it on the market, or exporting or importing it for the purpose of performing the acts as required under the provisions of law for obtaining, also by third party, registration or authorization, being requisite for certain products to be allowed for putting them on the market due to its purpose, in particular those being pharmaceutical products at the territory of European Economic Area or another State.
5. The pharmaceutical privilege, that is the extemporaneous preparation of a medicine in a pharmacy on a physician's prescription.
6. The farmer's privilege, that is the use of a biological material for the purpose of its breeding or discovery and introduction of new plant varieties.

Patent rights might also be abused, which means that patent might be formally used within the scope of its protection, but in a way that is not in conformity with the purpose of its grant. The general, legal provision that relates to

63 Meeting of Consultants on inventions made or used in outer space, Geneva March 6 and 7, 1997, question (g).

abuse of right is prescribed in Article 5 of the Polish Civil Code and states that the right cannot be exercised in a manner contradictory to its social and economic purpose or equity. In such case the behavior of the entitled person is not deemed as an exercise of his or her right and is not protected. The Industrial Property Law Act also contains special rules on the abuse of patent, namely that the patent holder or the licensee may not abuse his rights, in particular by preventing the invention from being exploited by a third party, if such exploitation is necessary for the purpose of meeting home market demands and is particularly dictated by public interest considerations, and consumers are supplied with the product in insufficient quantity or of inadequate quality, or at excessively high prices. However, preventing third parties from exploiting the invention within a period of three years from the date of the grant of the patent shall not be considered an abuse of rights. The Patent Office has the right to request a patent holder or a licensee to submit any explanations as to the scope of the exploitation of the invention for the purpose of establishing whether or not the patent is abused (as per Article 68 (1)-(3) of the Industrial Property Law Act). Where the Patent Office finds that the patent is abused it may decide that a compulsory license may be applied for and shall announce it in "*Wiadomości Urzędu Patentowego*" (as per Article 82(3) of the Industrial Property Law Act).

The second situation of patent abuse takes place when it has been established that the patent holder enjoying the right of priority of an earlier application (the earlier patent) prevents, by refusing to conclude a license contract, the meeting of home market demands through the exploitation of the patented invention (the dependent patent), whose exploitation would encroach upon the earlier patent. In such case, the holder of the earlier patent may demand that an authorization be given to him for the exploitation of the invention that is the subject matter of the dependent patent (cross-license). In that case the Polish Patent Office may grant a compulsory license, which is conditional upon ascertainment that the exploitation of the invention that is the subject matter of the dependent patent, where both inventions concern the same subject matter, involves an important technical advance of considerable economic significance. In case of an invention concerning semi-conductor technology, a compulsory license may only be granted to counteract unreasonable anti-competitive practices.

The other possibilities for the Polish Patent Office to grant a compulsory license, that is the authorization to exploit a patented invention of another person are in a case where: 1. it is necessary to prevent or eliminate a state of national emergency, in particular in the field of defence, public order, the protection of human life and health, as well as the protection of natural environment, or 2. it has been established that the patent has been abused within the meaning of Article 68 of the Industrial Property Law Act (referred to above). A compulsory license may be granted, if the applying party is able to prove that it has earlier made, in good faith, efforts to obtain a license. This requirement may be waived in the case of a compulsory license to be granted for the purpose of preventing or eliminating a state of national emergency or where it is announced that a compulsory license may be applied for (as per Article 82(4) of the Industrial Property Law Act). The compulsory license is non-exclusive (as per Article 83 of the Industrial Property Law Act). The person exploiting the invention under a compulsory license is obliged to pay a royalty to the patent holder and the Patent Office shall determine the scope and duration of a compulsory license, the detailed terms and conditions of its exercise, as well as the amount, in proportion to the market value of the license, of the royalty and the manner and time limits of payment (as per Article 84 of the Industrial Property Law Act).

Patent protection is also restricted in time as it lasts for a maximum of 20 years counted from the date of filing patent application with the Patent Office. The payment is due on annual basis by payment of fees, that increases in time, to the Patent Office. After the expiry of patent, for instance by the lapse of time (that is after 20 years) or due to non-payment for the next year of protection, the invention enters the public domain. Apart from the given situations, the patent lapses also due to the surrender of the patent by the patent holder before the Patent Office, with the consent of the parties having rights in the patent. In case of biotechnological inventions the patent lapses also when the invention became irreversibly unfeasible for exploitation due to the lack of access to the biological material, which is needed for that purpose and which became inaccessible and unfeasible for reproduction on the basis of the description. In those cases, except termination of patent after 20 years, the Patent Office shall make decisions on the lapse of a patent. Patent lapses on a date, on which an event has occurred that is considered as giving rise to the lapse of the patent. In the case of failure to pay a renewal fee within the prescribed time limit, a patent lapses on the date on which a preceding period of protection has expired. The date of the lapse of the patent is confirmed in a decision (as per Article 90 of the Industrial Property Law Act) and the lapse of a patent is recorded in the Patent Register (as per Article 92 of the Industrial Property Law Act).

A patent might be also declared invalid in whole or in part at the request of any person who is able to prove that the statutory requirements for the grant of a patent have not been satisfied, the invention has not been shown in sufficiently clear and exhausted manner, so that the person skilled in the art could realize the invention, the patent has been granted for the invention not covered by the content of application or initial application, and finally, if the patent claims does not determine the subject of protection in a clear and concise way or are not in full supported by the description of the invention (as per Article 89 of the Industrial Property Law Act). Invalidation is recorded in the Patent Register.

6 Patent Related Contracts

Patents may be assigned or be subject to succession. The transfer contract shall be in writing on pain of invalidity. The transfer of a patent shall be binding on third parties as from the date of its entry in the Patent Register (as per Article 67 of the Industrial Property Law Act).

Patents may be also licensed. The license might be restricted, which means that in the contract restricted exploitation of the invention may be provided for. Such a license should be directly stipulated in a contract, otherwise the license should be considered to be the full license, in other words: the licensee shall have the right to exploit the invention to the same extent as the licensor. The license contract shall be in writing on pain of invalidity. The license shall terminate at the latest on the lapse of the patent, however the parties are free to provide for a longer duration of the contract in respect of the provisions other than those governing the license, and in particular those involving payable services necessary for the purpose of exploiting the invention.

The license might be either non-exclusive, which means that the grant of a license to one party does not prevent other parties from being granted a license, as well as the patent holder from concurrent exploiting of the invention, or exclusive, which means that exclusive exploitation of the invention in a specific manner is reserved. If the license should be exclusive it should be stipulated directly in a contract (as per Article 76(1–4) of the Industrial Property Law Act). The licensor shall be required to transfer to the licensee all the technical know-how which is necessary to exploit the invention that is available to him at the time of concluding the contract (unless otherwise agreed in the license contract pursuant to Article 77 of the Industrial Property Law Act). A licensee may grant a further license (sub-license) only with the patent holder's consent. The law does not permit granting further sub-licenses. At the request of the interested party the license may be recorded in the Patent Register. The holder of an exclusive license recorded in the Register may, to the same extent as the patent holder, enforce his claims in the event of infringement, unless the license contract stipulates otherwise (as per Article 76(5–6) of the Industrial Property Law Act). Unless otherwise agreed between the parties, the provisions on license contracts shall apply accordingly to contracts for exploitation of an invention applied for protection with the Patent Office and for which no patent has as yet been granted, as well as to contracts for exploitation of an invention not applied for protection but being part of a company's know-how (as per Article 79 of the Industrial Property Law Act). Where a licensed patent is transferred, the license contract shall be binding on the successor in title (as per Article 78 of the Industrial Property Law Act).

There is also a possibility to declare an open license. A patent holder may submit to the Patent Office a declaration of licenses of the right to exploit the invention (the open license), which is irrevocable and non-liable to change. The submission of such a declaration is recorded in the Patent Register. Where the declaration of an open license is submitted, renewal fees due for patent protection are reduced by one half. The same applies to a single renewal fee or a fee for the first protection period, if the fee so reduced is received together with the declaration at the latest at the prescribed term.

An open license is full and non-exclusive. Its royalty may not exceed 10 percent of the profits obtained by the licensee in each year of exploiting the invention, after deduction of the expenses incurred. An open license may be acquired by way of conclusion of a license contract or by starting exploitation of the invention without entering into (or before the conclusion of) negotiations. In the latter case the licensee shall be obliged to inform the licensor of that fact in writing within one month of the date of start to exploiting the invention. The licensee shall pay the maximal royalty within one month from the end of each calendar year in which the licensee has exploited the invention, unless a royalty in a lower amount is provided for in the licensor's declaration and unless the contract does not stipulate otherwise (as per Article 80 of the Industrial Property Law Act).

Specific regulation of patent licenses in the context of space activities has been developed in the IGA in relation to ESA-registered element of the International Space Station. In Article 21(5) of the IGA it has been provided that "[w]ith respect to an activity occurring in or on an ESA-registered element, no European Partner State shall refuse to recognize a license for the exercise of any intellectual property right if that license is enforceable under the laws of any European Partner State, and compliance with the provisions of such license shall also bar recovery for infringement in any European Partner State". The given provision may serve as a model-rule for the future international acts relating to intellectual property rights and space activities. Since Poland is not a European Partner State to the International Space Station this provision has no relevance in Polish legal system.

7 Patent Infringement

7.1 *Jurisdiction*

Patented inventions that relate to outer space might concern for example space objects or assets manufactured or used on earth. If the invention is patented in Poland and one of the acts infringing patent took place in Poland, then the patent holder may start the litigation proceeding against the infringer. Since 1 July 2020 the exclusive jurisdiction over cases of patent infringement as well as cases of intellectual property relating to computer programs, inventions, utility models, topography of integrated circuits, plant varieties and trade secrets of a technical nature, lies with the District Court in Warsaw (as per Article 479[90] of the Polish Code of Civil Procedure). In such proceedings the rules of civil procedure apply, which include a separate proceeding on intellectual property rights (Section IVg, Article 479[89]- 479[129] of the Polish Code of Civil Procedure). If the infringement took place at the Polish-registered space object, the jurisdiction of the Polish court would apply.

It needs to be mentioned, that in case the infringement relates to situations involving so-called foreign elements there is a necessity to establish applicable law, on the basis of Article 13 of the Rome II Regulation:[64] "[f]or the purposes of this Chapter, Article 8 shall apply to non-contractual obligations arising from an infringement of an intellectual property right" and according to Article 8, "[t]he law applicable to a non-contractual obligation arising from an infringement of an intellectual property right shall be the law of the country for which protection is claimed", which means the *lex loci protectionis*. According to Article 3 of the Rome II Regulation, the application of the Regulation is universal, that is "[a]ny law specified by this Regulation shall be applied whether or not it is the law of a Member State". Therefore the law that might be applied is either the law of an EU Member State or of another State, and in the latter case it is not dependent on conflict of law reciprocity.[65]

The specific provision stemming from the IGA relates to the International Space Station and its ESA-registered element. According to Article 21(4) of the IGA, "Where a person or entity owns intellectual property which is protected in more than one European Partner State, that person or entity may not recover in more than one such State for the same act of infringement of the same rights in such intellectual property which occurs in or on an ESA-registered

64 Regulation (EC) No 846/2007 of the European Parliament and of the Council of 11 July 2007 on the on the law applicable to non-contractual obligations (Rome II), OJEU 31.7.2007, L 199/40.

65 Maksymilian Pazdan, *Prawo prywatne międzynarodowe* (10th ed, LexisNexis 2007) 79.

element. Where the same act of infringement in or on an ESA-registered element gives rise to actions by different intellectual property owners by virtue of more than one European Partner State's deeming the activity to have occurred in its territory, a court may grant a temporary stay of proceeding in a later-filed action pending the outcome of an earlier-filed action. Where more than one action is brought, satisfaction of a judgment rendered for damages in any of the actions shall bar further recovery of damages in any pending or future action for infringement based upon the same act of infringement". Again, this provision may serve as a model-rule for the future international regulations relating to the infringement of intellectual property rights in a space objects of international character. As for today, due to non-participation of Poland in the International Space Station as a European Partner State, this provision has no relevance to Polish law.

7.2 *Claims for an Infringement of Patent Rights*

In case the patent has been infringed, according to Polish law a patent holder (or any person who is permitted by law to do so) may demand the infringing party to cease the infringement or to surrender the unlawfully obtained profits. In case the infringement has been caused by fault, a patent holder may also seek redress of the damage. The given redress is either a) in accordance with the general principles of law or b) by the payment of a sum of money in the amount corresponding to the license fee or of another reasonable compensation, which while being vindicated would have been due on account of consent given by the patent holder to exploit his invention. What is more, when judging on the infringement of a patent the court may, at the holder's request, decide on publishing the judgement in full or in part, or mention the judgement, in a manner and at the extent as specified by the court. If the act of infringement was committed unintentionally the person infringing patent may request the court to order that that he/she should pay the holder an adequate amount of money, if the cessation of the infringement or the judgement would be excessively severe for the infringing person and the payment of the adequate sum of money properly meets the interests of the patent holder (as per Article 287 of the Industrial Property Law Act).

The limitation period for claims for infringement of the patent is three years. The period concerned runs separately in respect of each individual infringement, from the date where the right holder has learned about the infringement of his patent and about the infringing person. However, in any case, the claim become barred by prescription five years after the date on which the infringement has occurred. The given period is suspended for the time between the filing of the patent application with the Patent Office and the grant of the patent (as per Article 289 of the Industrial Property Law Act).

8 Space Applicable Inventions – Contractual Relationships

M.E. Wachowicz and M. Bury rightly noticed, that the "space technology transfer process is different than in other fields of technology. The difference is caused by significantly higher investment costs, atypical requirements that space equipment has to meet, the need for dedicated infrastructure and highly specialized human resources – namely engineers".[66] Due to the high costs of making the inventions which can operate in space, there are certain ways of obtaining funding for Polish entities.

One of them is conclusion of a contract with European Space Agency (ESA), which assists numerous R&D tasks both to private and public bodies, like universities, research laboratories, and suchlike.[67] Article III(3–4) of the Convention for the establishment of a European Space Agency of 30 May 1975 (the ESA Convention) stipulates that "3. When placing contracts or entering into agreements, the Agency shall, with regard to the resulting inventions and technical data, secure such rights as may be appropriate for the protection of its interests, of those of the Member States participating in the relevant programme, and of those of persons and bodies under their jurisdiction. These rights shall include in particular the rights of access, of disclosure, and of use. Such inventions and technical data shall be communicated to the participating States. 4. Those inventions and technical data that are the property of the Agency shall be disclosed to the Member States and may be used for their own purposes by these Member States and by persons and bodies under their jurisdiction, free of charge". To that end ESA uses the General Clauses and Conditions for European Space Agency Contracts (GCC) currently in a version from 5 July 2019. According to conditions concerning intellectual property rights for an ESA study, research and development contract the rules are divided into those of a general regime and a special regime for partly funded contracts. In general clauses it is stated for instance that:

– "The Contractor shall own all Intellectual Property Rights and have the right to apply for and to own any Registered Intellectual Property Rights arising from work performed under the Contract. At the Contractor's request and

66 Wachowicz and Bury (n 60) 66.

67 Balsano (n 40).

expense the Agency shall carry out all reasonable tasks including executing any document required to vest such title in the Contractor" (Clause 39.1).

- "The Contractor shall as soon as possible report to the Agency any results arising from work performed under the Contract which may in the Contractor's opinion be protected as Registered Intellectual Property Rights and state whether it intends to apply for such protection. At the Contractor's specific request in order to allow for filing of patent applications the Agency shall not Disclose any information, data or results supplied for a period of 12 Months from the date it was reported to the Agency" (Clause 40.1).
- "If the Contractor does not wish to apply for Registered Intellectual Property Rights (or wishes to abandon Registered Intellectual Property Rights) arising from work performed under the Contract it shall inform the Agency. After such notification the Agency shall consult the Contractor and investigate the reasons for the failure to apply or for the abandonment of such rights. Following this consultation the Agency may inquire whether Third Parties would be interested in protecting or exploiting such rights the Contractor owns. If the Agency finds a suitable Third Party, the Agency can require the Contractor to assign to the Third Party the rights necessary to apply for such Registered Intellectual Property Rights or require the Contractor to license the Third Party such abandoned Registered Intellectual Property Rights on Favourable Conditions to be agreed between the Contractor, the Agency and the Third Party. For the avoidance of doubt the Contractor may not unreasonably object to the terms of any such assignment or licence" (Clause 39.4).
- According to the use of Intellectual Property Rights the GCC prescribes that "All Intellectual Property Rights arising from work performed under the Contract shall be available to: a) the Agency, Participating States and Persons and Bodies to use on a free, worldwide licence with the right to grant sublicences for the Agency's Own Requirements (such licence to be granted by the Contractor or the Agency as set out in the standard licence which the licensee shall enter into if required); b) Participating States and Persons and Bodies to use on Favourable Conditions for a Participating State's Own Public Requirements (such licence to be granted by the Contractor as set out in the standard licence which the licensee shall enter into if required); c) academic and research institutions to use on a free licence without the right to grant sublicenses for their own scientific research purposes (excluding commercial purposes) providing the Contractor agrees such use is not contrary to its Legitimate Commercial Interests (such licence to be granted by the Contractor as set out in the standard licence which the licensee shall enter into if required); d) any Third Party on Market Conditions to use for

purposes other than the Agency's Own Requirements or a Participating State's Own Public Requirements providing the Contractor agrees such use is not contrary to its Legitimate Commercial Interests" (Clause 41.1.).

In the special regime for a partly funded contract it is stipulated for instance that:

- "The Contractor shall own all Intellectual Property Rights and have the right to apply for and to own any Registered Intellectual Property Rights arising from work performed under the Agency Contract. At the Contractor's request and expense the Agency shall carry out all reasonable tasks including executing any document required to vest such title in the Contractor" (Clause 52.1.).
- "The Agency shall be granted the rights, including the access, to Intellectual Property Rights set out in clauses 53 to 57" (Clause 53.2).
- "The Contractor shall as soon as possible report to the Agency any results arising from work performed under the Agency Contract which may in the Contractor's opinion be protected as Registered Intellectual Property Rights and state whether it intends to apply for such protection. At the Contractor's specific request in order to allow for filing of patent applications the Agency shall not Disclose any information, data or results supplied for a period of 12 Months from the date it was reported to the Agency" (Clause 54.1.).
- "The Contractor shall inform the Agency of any application to register results, information or data arising from work performed under the Agency Contract and within 2 Months of the date of filing, provide details of the office where the application was filed, the application number, the filing date, the inventor's name and applicant's name, the reference number of the relevant Agency Contract and where possible provide a copy of the application (including description, any claims and drawings). Following the filing of the application the Contractor shall inform the Agency whether it has been used as the basis for applications in other countries. Following the grant of such applications the Contractor shall inform the Agency of any proceedings which allege that granted rights are invalid or require amendment" (Clause 54.2).
- "All Intellectual Property Rights arising from work performed under the Agency Contract shall be available to: a) the Agency to use on a free, worldwide licence for the Agency's Own Requirements (such licence to be granted by the Contractor as set out in the standard licence which the licensee shall be entered into if required); b) Participating States and Persons and Bodies to use on Financial Conditions for the Agency's Own Requirements (such licence to be granted by the Contractor as set out in the standard licence which the licensee shall enter into if required); c) any Third Party on Market Conditions to use for purposes other than the Agency's Own Requirements

providing the Contractor agrees such use is not contrary to its Legitimate Commercial Interests" (Clause 55.1.).

The other available finance sources for space activities inventions might also be granted by the National Science Centre (*Narodowe Centrum Nauki* – NCN), the National Centre for Research and Development (*Narodowe Centrum Badań i Rozwoju* – NCBR) and EU funding programs, like Horizon Europe, with the respective provisions in their regulations concerning intellectual property rights.

9 Conclusion

The recent shift from state-owned projects concerning space activities to private ones calls for more attention to the problems of intellectual property protection. The national patent systems are to a large extent unified, however there are still differences between them. Any initiative the goal of which is to unify patent law relating to outer space activities should therefore be welcomed. In a foreseeable future the problems might relate to trademark and design law as well as copyright law to a greater extent, therefore a general regulation should be preferred.

In the Polish legal system the issues addressing space law and intellectual property law are covered by separate legal acts. The application of general rules of intellectual property law to the demands of space industry and space activities in general should not pose a problem. However, the preferable regulation included in space law should relate to the law applicable at space objects in the same or similar way as Article 21(2) of the IGA or Section 105 of Chapter 35 of the United States Code. Unfortunately, the current draft of a Polish statute for space activities and a national registry of space objects (2017) only repeats in its Article 13(3) the provision of Outer Space Treaty providing that in accordance with this Treaty the Republic of Poland retains jurisdiction and control over an object launched to outer space which is registered in the registry and over the personnel on board, while they are in outer space or on a celestial body. Taking into consideration that currently there is no Polish national registry of space objects and that any Polish space objects are therefore registered directly in the United Nations Register of Objects Launched into Outer Space pursuant to the information provided to the Secretary-General, the current legal system is far from satisfying in that regard. It is therefore strongly suggested that the final provisions of the given statute clarify the law concerning intellectual property rights, and in particular the law applicable to objects launched into outer space. Apart from that issue it seems that, as for today, the most visible problems on intellectual property in relation to space activities are possibly solved by the accurate interpretation of the Industrial Property Law Act, taking into consideration the specific context of those activities, like for example in case of communication privilege or the disclosure of prior art that may hinder novelty and individual character of the invention.

CHAPTER 9

The Polish Vision on Space Activities

A Review of Current and Proposed Legislation and Space Policy Developments – Looking towards the Future

Julia Anna Hetlof and Agnieszka Kunert-Diallo

1 Introduction and Rationale for National Space Legislation

As Polish space law is still at the beginning of its legislative road, its purpose and scope will depend on current policy determinations as well as on the level of national engagement in space activities broadly understood. In general, there are three types of approaches followed by States in their regulation of space activities.

The first approach assumes compliance with international treaty obligations with no specific domestic regulatory framework in place. Currently, this approach is only noticeable in States with no or little involvement in space activities as the majority of the space-faring nations have implemented or are in the process of enacting national legislation to provide some degree of national legal, regulatory or policy framework for their space activities.[1]

Notably, the trend to establish domestic space frameworks is a relatively recent phenomenon as space activities first developed in the domain of international relations and public international law. The early phases of the Space Age were dominated by the United States and the former Soviet Union, two superpowers conducting their publicly-funded and strictly controlled activities, with no real need for developing specific national space regulations.[2] This approach has changed with the increasing number of space actors, more space-faring nations and ultimately, with the entrance of the private entities competing in the space sector, which precipitated the need to regulate their activities by the

---

1 At the time of this writing, at least 25 States have adopted national legislation or other regulations directly related to outer space activities – based on the country submissions to UNOOSA. https://www.unoosa.org/oosa/en/ourwork/spacelaw/nationalspacelaw/index.html (accessed 1 February 2021); Annette Froehlich and Vincent Seffinga, eds, *National Space Legislation: A Comparative and Evaluative Analysis* (Springer, 2018) 2.

2 See Chapter 4 of this book, for the historical development of the international space law.

 | DOI:10.1163/9789004542860_011

respective 'appropriate state.'[3] Emergence of NewSpace technologies, advancing innovative and more affordable space capabilities, have opened up exciting new business opportunities for private actors in new spacefaring States. At the same time, the new players in the space sector expect guidance from their national authorities, which are suddenly faced with regulating this new developing market.

One of the main roles of national space law is to ensure the rules that govern outer space activities at the national level are in accordance with the international space law regime.[4] In other words, in order to properly discharge their obligations stemming from international commitments, States have a strong interest in developing proper legal tools to monitor and control such activities as to their national effects.[5] Accordingly, the second approach taken by States relies on national space legislation as an instrument to implement their international legal obligations, *in particular with respect to authorization and supervision of non-governmental (that is, private) space activities under their jurisdiction*.[6]

Notwithstanding the level of national involvement in space activities, the scope and extent of each State's national legislation could (and in fact should) vary due to many different factors, such individual international commitments, each country's goals, needs and practical considerations.[7] Taking all of the divergent needs and requirements into consideration, the 2013 Resolution on National Legislation recommends a number of provisions that States should include in their national space legislation so that 'outer space is used for peaceful purposes and [...] the obligations under international law and those specifically contained in the United Nations treaties on outer space are implemented.'[8] Specifically, the recommendations entail the regulation of

3 Also see Chapter 4, for more on State responsibility under international space law regime and discussion why space activities of private entities require State authorization and supervision by the 'appropriate state.'

4 Ram Jakhu and Joseph N. Pelton, eds, *Global Space Governance: An International Study* (Springer, 2017) 88.

5 Frans von der Dunk, 'Fundamental Provisions for National Space Laws' Space, Cyber and Telecom Law Program Faculty Pubs 11 (2006) 93; Frans von der Dunk, 'Current and Future Development of National Space Law and Policy' United Nations/Brazil Workshop on Space Law: Disseminating And Developing International And National Space Law: The Latin America And Caribbean Perspective (United Nations, New York, 2005).

6 Ibid; Froehlich and Seffinga (n4) 6.

7 UNGA Recommendations on National Legislation Relevant to the Peaceful Exploration and Use of Outer Space (2013) UN Doc A/RES/68/74 (hereinafter 'Resolution on National Legislation').

8 Ibid.

(i) authorization of space activities, which should include the conditions for granting, altering or revoking such authorization and the transfer of ownership of space objects;
(ii) continuous supervision of space activities conducted by private entities;
(iii) the scope of the legislation, to determine to which type of activities the legislation applies or where, geographically it is applicable – that is, the legal definition of 'space activities' or 'outer space';[9]
(iv) protection of environment, including space debris;
(v) registration of space objects in a national registry;
(vi) mechanisms for the State to seek recourse against private entities in case of damage for which international liability of the State has been engaged;
(vii) appropriate coverage for damage caused by space objects or private entities via mandatory insurance requirements; and
(viii) enforcement mechanisms to ensure compliance with the domestic requirements.[10]

While State regulation of space activities, especially those conducted by private entities, is mandated by the international space legal regime, it should strike a proper balance so as not stifle the developing industry with overregulation. As the majority of States are focused on the fulfilment of international obligations, their legislation tends to be limited to the scope of State responsibility and liability for the acts stemming therefrom.

The last, third pattern observed in the most advanced domestic legislations, best exemplified by the United States, includes areas not covered by international agreements and thus presenting its own policy and regulatory approach, for example by outlining more comprehensive rules for liability arrangements and broader licensing regime(s). The United States has probably the most robust and detailed national space law and regulatory regime addressing commercial space activities of any nation.[11] One of the distinctive characteristics of such mature framework is that it effectively combines extensive policies, statutes and regulations applicable to the space industry while fostering its growth and development.[12]

Poland's vision of space legislation seems to be heading towards the second approach of regulation touching areas such as licencing and liability rules

9 See Chapter 3 of this book, for discussion on unresolved legal issues of air and space boundary and applicability of space law.
10 Froehlich and Seffinga (4) 6–7; Resolution of National Legislation (n10).
11 Milton 'Skip' Smith, 'The Space Law Review: USA' the LawReview (Dec 17, 2020) https://thelawreviews.co.uk/title/the-space-law-review/usa.
12 Ibid.

that, based on international space law, are clearly subject to national competences. The policy basis for such approach has been already presented in the 2017 Polish Space Strategy and the Polish National Space Program; the latter however is still under development and the progress of national space policy mostly depends on assumptions and projects adopted based on this executive document.

2 Existing Legislation and Its Applicability to National Space Activities: Administrative and Policy Coordination

As of the date of this writing, the only existing Polish legislation strictly relating to space activities is the Act establishing the Polish Space Agency (POLSA), as the primary administrative authority for space activities in Poland.[13] However, there are other governmental bodies and tools, which are part of the legislative branch and that have been utilized to develop and coordinate Polish space sector activities, such as the Inter-ministerial Board for Space Policy (in existence between November 2012 and January 2019) and the Space Policy Team, from June 2020 to the present day. The role of these bodies was presented in the historical context of Polish space policy and strategy development in Chapter 2 of this book.

2.1 *The Polish Space Agency (POLSA) and Its Statutory Tasks*

The Polish Space Agency was established with the Act of 26 September 2014 on the Polish Space Agency.[14] Until POLSA was created, there was no single body responsible for space activities, but rather different competences were scattered among various institutions and public authorities. The creation of a central institution, responsible for the oversight and development of the Polish space sector, was deemed necessary for effective use of space exploration capabilities and better opportunities for Polish companies and research institutions within the European Space Agency (ESA) framework.

POLSA is a governmental executive agency acting under the authority of the Act of 27 August 2009 on public finances, headquartered in Gdansk, and it reports directly to the minister responsible for the economy.[15] Detailed statutory tasks of POLSA, enumerated in an exemplary catalogue of Article 3, are focused on the agency's supporting role in the areas of: space industry,

13 POLSA Act, ibid (n1).
14 Ibid.
15 Act of 27 August 2009 on Public Finances, Journal of Laws of 2017, item 2077.

research, use of outer space, development of space technology including satellite engineering and using research and its results for operational, economic, defence, state security and scientific purposes. Although the catalogue of tasks is not exhaustive, some of them are worth noting. POLSA represents Poland internationally in matters within its competences, as specified in the authorization granted by applicable authorities. The agency coordinates the participation of Polish representatives in the programs of the European Union, ESA, the European Organisation for the Exploitation of Meteorological Satellites (EUMETSAT) and the European Defence Agency (EDA) in the field of space research, space technology and satellite technology. The agency is also entrusted with maintaining a register of objects launched into outer space, although the Polish Act on Space Activity and the National Register for Space Objects is still under preparation.[16] The priority tasks of POLSA also include increasing the defensive and security capabilities through the use of space and satellite systems.

POLSA has two principal organs: the President and the Council, which are acting based on the statute issued by way of regulation. The latest amendments to the statute were implemented in November 2021 and came into force on 21 December 2021.[17] There are some basic requirements that must be fulfilled by a candidate for POLSA's organs, which are commonly required for civil service, such as Polish citizenship, enjoying full civil rights, no prior criminal record, holding qualification or experience to carry out task entrusted to POLSA, and enjoying an impeccable reputation. The President has executive and management powers, is appointed for a five-year term in office and can be assisted by no more than two vice-presidents. The agency is functioning through local branches and the President appoints directors of the organizational units. His/her tasks are focused mainly on the agency's ongoing activities, including preparation of the agency's drafts for annual and five-year activity plans, annual reports on the agency's activities as well as financial statements, and managing the assets of the agency. He/she also prepares drafts of legal acts and issues opinions on legislative proposals covered by the agency's activities.

The Council of POLSA is a supervisory and advisory organ of the President and is headed by a chairperson elected among members of the Council. He/she is supported by no more than two vice presidents. The President and vice presidents are elected by the Minister responsible for the economy. The latter is also entitled to elect one of his/her representatives to the Council and

16 Draft Space Act, ibid (n3).

17 Ministry of Economic Development and Technology, Regulation on the Adoption of the Polish Space Agency Statute, Official Journal of the Republic of Poland of 2021, item 2248.

appoints four members from representatives of the scientific sector and four members from the industrial sector. Members appointed from the scientific sector are recommended by the President in consultation with the Space and Satellite Research Committee, while members appointed from the industrial sector are elected by the President among entrepreneurs operating in the field of satellite technologies participating in the implementation of ESA's projects. The rest of the members are appointed upon request by the following officials: the head of the chancellery of the Prime Minister, the Minister of National Defence, the Minister responsible for higher education and science, the Minister responsible for foreign affairs, the Minister responsible for internal affairs, the Minister competent for public administration, the Minister of Digital Affairs, the Minister of Agriculture and Rural Development, the Minister of Environment and the Minister responsible for transport. The Council is therefore represented by the majority of ministries involved, to a greater or lesser extent, in the development of the Polish space sector. Just like the President's term of office, each member of the Council is appointed for a five-year period and may be re-elected only for one more term.

As a supervisory body, the Council prepares and presents proposals regarding priorities and main directions of the agency's development, including a draft strategy for research and development programs in the field of space. The Council also provides periodic assessments of the approved annual action plans' implementation and analyses the effectiveness of the agency's activities. It also supervises the financial management of the Agency and determines the amount of remuneration of the President and vice-presidents.

Increased commercialisation of space activities and the progressive shift of risk and responsibility to the space industry requires coordination at the national level. By placing a lesser burden on the institutional side and focusing on formulation of user needs rather than technical requirements, POLSA may create capabilities for further technical and business innovations. In the broader economic sense, through effective use of its statutory prerogatives and involvement of major governmental actors, POLSA may significantly contribute to adopt a friendly legal environment enabling further development of the space sector in Poland.

3 Still at the Beginning of the Road: The Polish Space Strategy and the National Space Program

As already presented in Chapter 2 of this book, Polish space policy and strategy has been developing steadily since Poland's geopolitical changes after 1989 and, in particular, after Poland's accession to the European Union in 2004 and to the European Space Agency in 2012.

3.1 *The Polish Space Strategy*

The Polish Space Strategy was adopted by the Resolution of the Council of Ministers on 26 January 2017 with the expressed objectives to create a stable and efficient cooperation between science and industry, and to stimulate the space sector's development and economic growth by fostering innovative technologies and international cooperation.[18] The space strategy has laid out 3 strategic objectives and 5 specific goals, to be implemented by year 2030, which are described in detail in Chapter 2. Notably, one of the listed objectives is to increase the competitiveness of the Polish space sector on the European market and to raise its share to at least 3% of the latter's turnover in proportion to the Polish economic potential. The other goals entail increasing utilization of the satellite-derived data by the public administration while developing sufficient infrastructure to achieve that goal, and to effectively sustain both commercial and public needs while enhancing state defence and security.[19] The already mentioned specific goals are the measures through which the development of the Polish space sector development is expected to be achieved.

The strategy includes the SWOT analysis of the Polish space sector in both the upstream and downstream sectors to identify its strengths and weaknesses in the respective areas with indications as to the future potential for development. The 'upstream sector' conventionally refers to services related to making and sending space objects (satellites, probes, spacecraft and rovers) into space, while the segment that uses these objects to deliver products and services on earth (mostly commercial both also environmental and scientific exploitation) is called 'downstream.'[20] The upstream segment overwhelmingly comprises cost-intensive space manufacturing, to include the design, manufacture of spacecraft, payloads, systems, subsystems and components, and the infrastructure required to launch and operate them from earth. On the other hand, the downstream sector involves the provision of satellite broadcasting, communication and navigation services, earth observation and remote sensing applications, support products and services, and financial services (including space insurance).

18 Ibid (n2).

19 Ibid.

20 UK Department for Business, Energy & Industrial Strategy, 'Upstream Space: A Galaxy of Capability, A Science and Innovation Audit Summary Report' (2018) 4.

The Polish Space Strategy recognizes that the upstream sector is more difficult in terms of market access, mainly due to the lack of experienced entities in Poland, and therefore requires international cooperation to acquire 'flight heritage' and to ensure better perspectives for entities involved in activities part of the upstream segment. Thus, the strategy also recognizes the potential for the Polish space industry's access into the sector with the NewSpace developments in small and micro satellites. The downstream sector appears to be more accessible for the private entities due to lower barriers to market entry, and is more in line with the organic growth of the Polish space industry, also described as the 'bottom-up approach' in Chapter 2. The distinct phenomenon of the Polish space industry, predicated on solid scientific foundations, is its ability to combine innovative technologies with entrepreneurial spirit, indicating its potential for continued growth, especially in the niche of developing NewSpace markets.[21] At the same time, the strategy recognizes the need for substantial investments and long-term financing, mostly in the upstream, as well as in the major downstream projects, which is currently lacking.

From the public policy standpoint, the adopted space strategy, by promoting sustainable economic growth through innovative technological solutions and competitive enterprises, is compatible with a comprehensive strategy of economic development for Poland, commonly known as the Responsible Development Strategy ('SOR'), which focuses on science, innovations and technological development.[22] Moreover, popularizing the use of satellite data by the public administration will hopefully increase its effectiveness and better use of public resources, such as with intelligent transport systems, monitoring of the environment, crisis management, and hence will advance one of the national detailed goals of SOR – effective State and economic institutions for growth and social and economic inclusion. Since the space strategy indicates the public administration as the third main player in the Polish space sector (next to science and industry) and, currently, its primary user, it can also generate growth of the commercial entities in the downstream sector.

Finally, the Polish Space Strategy underlies the importance of the participation in EU and ESA projects, as well bilateral and multilateral cooperation within various international organizations and between States more advanced in the development of the space sector. However, it seeks to go beyond and to promote the national sector by building appropriate regulatory instruments, to

21 See Chapter 3 of this book, for discussion on traditional and NewSpace applications.

22 Council of Ministers Resolution No 8 of 14 February 2017, Official Journal of the Republic of Poland (Monitor Polski) of 2017, item 260.

include consulting, financial and educational tools through the development and implementation of the National Space Program.

3.2 *The Polish National Space Program*

Adoption of the National Space Program (hereinafter referred to as 'KPK' as its Polish abbreviation) constitutes one of the statutory tasks entrusted to POLSA based on Article 3 of the Act establishing the Polish Space Agency.[23] KPK should follow the goals established by the Polish Space Strategy and should be focused on particular projects that are planned to be implemented within a short period of time.

The first draft of KPK, the National Space Program for 2019–2021, envisioned 54 projects supporting the development of the Polish space sector within 3 years, grouped into 8 main areas: large projects, support of the downstream sector, innovations, international environment, internships and trainings, education, promotion, and the complementary projects.[24] The large projects were mostly designed to reach 3% of the value of the European space market's turnover by 2030.

Although developed by POLSA in December of 2018, the first draft KPK was not implemented due to lack of support by the applicable Ministry of Development, allegedly because of its failure to meet the adopted space strategy's requirements and was finally rejected at the end of 2020.[25] The current draft of KPK, the Polish Space Program for 2021–2026, was completed in mid-2021, but, as of the date of this writing, has not been yet adopted.[26]

The overriding objective of the KPK 2021–2026 is to increase the potential of the Polish space industry and research institutions to support the needs of the State and the economy, and to effectively compete on the international markets. The specific objectives mirror those of the Polish Space Strategy, as listed in the preceding section. KPK 2021–2026 indicates the following four Priorities for Actions, which are designed to achieve the strategic objectives:

---

23 POLSA Act, ibid (n1).

24 POLSA, Krajowy Program Kosmiczny na lata 2019–2021 (Tr. National Space Program for 2019–2021) https://dlapilota.pl/wiadomosci/polska/krajowy-program-kosmiczny-2019-2021-54-projekty-wspierajace-rozwoj-polskiej-branzy.

25 Jaroslaw Gowin, Minister of Development, Labor and Technology, 'Response to Parliamentary Question No. 11218 in the matter of functioning of the Polish Space Agency, realization of the Polish space strategy and cooperation with private entities' 20 October 2020, Case No. DIN-V.054.3.2020.

26 Ministry of the Development and Technology, Krajowy Program Kosmiczny na lata 2021–2026 (Tr. National Space Program for 2021–2026), ver. 0.8, 23 July 2021, https://www.gov.pl/attachment/935b6f52-92ed-41f4-9dc6-fb502c609a84.

Priority I: Developing the ability to build and launch space objects.
Priority II: Creation of the MikroGlob Satellite Earth Observation System.
Priority III: Building the National Satellite Information System (NSIS).
Priority IV: Development of the National Space Security System.[27]
KPK emphasizes the complimentary nature of the four priorities in that they constitute an integral whole. The ability to build and launch space objects (Priority I – with dedicated funding of 983 million PLN) supports the formation of the MikroGlob constellation – a national EO system (Priority II, with dedicated funding of over 1.32 billion PLN). Data from this constellation will feed the NSIS (Priority III – 281 million PLN) which, in turn, will define the needs for images from Priority II, while the National Space Security System (Priority IV – 272 million PLN) will protect the MikroGlob satellites (Priority II) and other satellites supplying data to the system provided for in Priority III. Additionally, in the future, it is expected that the sensors of the Priority IV system will be placed on satellites, for which the competences developed by Priority I will be essential, especially through development of key technologies, including telecommunications, launch, navigation and Earth observation (also in relation to downstream satellite applications), exploration, as well as ready infrastructure and trained personnel.[28]

The funding for KPK, worth over 2.5 billion PLN, is projected to come from three primary sources:

1) State budget funds, including funds from the State budget of individual ministers involved in the implementation of the Program;
2) European Union funds, for instance the EU space program and Horizon Europe; and
3) Measures of the National Plan for Reconstruction and Increasing of Immunity.[29]

Although spending was projected to start as early as 2021, the document is still in the draft phase, just like its versions from previous years.[30]

Under either proposal, participation in optional ESA projects is crucial for the development of the Polish space industry. Indeed, the Polish Space Strategy recognized that, as demand of individual industry sectors and public administration is gradually growing, the contribution in optional programmes should

27 Ibid.
28 Ibid 19.
29 Ibid 53.
30 Pawel Szygulski, 'Nowy plan dla polskiej branży kosmicznej. Budżet ma być pokaźny' (Tr. 'New Plan for Polish Space Industry. Budget is Going to be Substantial') wnp.pl (15 October 2021) https://www.wnp.pl/tech/nowy-plan-dla-polskiej-branzy-kosmicznej-budzet-ma-byc-pokazny,498136.html.

increase to the level of 150–200% of the compulsory contribution. Therefore, the contribution increase was used as a major tool to increase the competitiveness of the Polish space sector, resulting in greater access to developed technologies for security and defence and to provide applications meeting expectations of the Polish users (consumers).

While some of the tasks identified by KPK rely on international cooperation and achievements possible thanks to Poland's participation in the European Space Agency, there are still other tasks which should be implemented independently based on the international commitments arising from space treaties. Such obligations should be considered and implemented via the national space legislation.

4 Development of Polish National Space Legislation

4.1 *Proposed Axioms of Polish National Space Law*

In light of increasing space-related activities, in Poland, within the European Union and internationally, Poland has recognized the need to develop and implement national space legislation in order to foster the growth of its space sector while complying with its international obligations stemming from the space law treaties to which it is signatory. The first major draft, the Act on Space Activity and the National Register of Space Objects[31] was prepared in 2017 and its provisions are described in detail in Chapter 7 of this book. The draft went through the legislative consultations, which indicated certain areas for improvement and re-consideration, to include limiting the scope of regulated activities, more detailed license and obligatory insurance requirements, and adding a liability regime for damages caused by space objects in the territory of Poland and to the Polish citizens and entities.[32] As a result, the project went back to the drawing board, and the new draft Space Act is expected to include:

1) rules and conditions for the performance of space activities;
2) rules for and administrative organization of continuous supervision over space activities;
3) liability for damage caused by the space object, to the extent this issue is not regulated by the provisions of the international agreements;

---

31 Draft Space Act (n3).

32 Recommendations by the Legislative Council for the Prime Minister, 22 September 2017, https://www.space24.pl/projekt-ustawy-o-dzialalnosci-kosmicznej-i-krok-pod-lupa-rady-legislacyjnej.

4) a national (liability) framework in the event of space damage caused by the space object for which the Republic of Poland is the launching State; and
5) regulations relating the national register of space objects.[33]

Based on the above, Poland will mostly regulate only those aspects which are desirable from the State interest perspective and required for the functioning of commercial activities, specifically:

– granting permissions (via licensing) to conduct activities in outer space and the designation of an authority responsible for authorization and supervision of space activities – stemming from a fundamental duty under Article VI of Outer Space Treaty[34] (as discussed in Chapter 4);
– establishment of the Polish space object registry – to comply with Article II of the Registration Convention and, in addition, to ensure jurisdiction and control over such space objects and the operators thereof can be meaningfully exercised in accordance with Article VIII of Outer Space Treaty;[35]
– domestic rules of liability pertaining to commercial activities, with possible State participation in such liability and setting mandatory insurance requirements – relating, inter alia, to Article VII of Outer Space Treaty and Liability Convention's imposition of international liability on the launching (issuing) State (also discussed in Chapter 4); and
– possibly, extending the domestic liability regime to cover damages by the space object in the territory of Poland and to Polish nationals and entities, when Poland is the issuing (launching) State – as a further extension of the more victim-friendly international liability regime.

Moreover, according to the statement by the Ministry of Development responsible for the project, the new legislation will also attempt to include, to the extent possible, the UN recommendations presented in the 2019 Guidelines for Long-term Sustainability of Outer Space Activities.[36] This goal, if in fact

33 Robert Tomanek, Undersecretary of State, in Response to Statement by Mr. Slawomir Rybicki, Senator of the Republic of Poland, concerning the draft act on space activity and the National Register of Space Objects, 16 December 2020, No. DIN-V.0710.18.2020.

34 Treaty on Principles Governing the Activities of States in the Exploration and Use of Outer Space, Including the Moon and Other Celestial Bodies (Outer Space Treaty), 27 January 1967, 610 UNTS 205, Journal of Laws of 1968, no. 14, item 82, Article VI.

35 Convention on Registration of Objects Launched into Outer Space, 12 November 1974, 1023 UNTS 15 (Registration Convention), Journal of Laws of 1979 no. 5 item 22, Article II; Outer Space Treaty (n29) Article VIII.

36 Guidelines for Long-Term Sustainability of Outer Space Activities, Report of the Committee on the Peaceful Uses of Outer Space, COPUOS 62nd session, A/74/20, 20 August 2019.

reflected in the new legislative draft, would be a welcome sign in the right direction, showing more meaningful development of the national space law framework by embracing important soft law trends, thus placing Poland in the small but growing number of States with more detailed domestic space legislation.[37]

The ongoing work on the development of Polish space law has been met with enthusiastic response and involvement by Polish academia and a growing body of space law experts. One of such initiatives resulted in the first scientific-legal conference 'Space Activity – law and administration,' organized at the Polish Senate by the Senate Committee in cooperation with the Manfred Lachs Polish Space Law Center, in Warsaw on 28 May 2018. Following the conference, a study on the Legal Aspects of Space Activity was published, which considered many of the legal issues in the development of national, regional (EU) and international space law regimes.[38] One of the noted difficulties in codifying space law arises from its interdisciplinary dimension, which includes the intersection of transport, spatial development, crisis management, telecommunications, medicine, agriculture, environmental protection, meteorology and many other aspects.[39] Mrenca submits the following axioms, or characteristics, of the national space law that is currently under development in Poland:

- the primacy of international law over domestic law;
- the consistent understanding of the developing law, as adopted by the State organs and controlled by respective courts from the perspective of constitutional principles, still ensuring primacy of international (EU) law (despite some political opinions otherwise);
- the universal application of this law with respect to all persons and entities under the State's jurisdiction, making the rules applicable to all State authorities, citizens, foreigners, stateless persons, legal persons (both public and private) and finally the State itself;
- the scope of regulated space activities, which should include space activities within the territory of Poland, as well as those conducted on board ships and aircraft registered in Poland;
- the scope of the national space law should include norms of public law and private law;

---

37 Tomanek (n37) 4.

38 Katarzyna Myszona-Kostrzewa, Elzbieta Mrenca, Piotr B. Zientarski, eds., *Prawne Aspekty Dzialalnosci Kosmicznej* (Tr. *The Legal Aspects of Space Activity*) (Kancelaria Senatu, 2019).

39 Elzbieta Mrenca, 'Aksjomaty krajowego prawa kosmicznego – polska perspektywa' (Tr. 'The Axioms of the National Space Law – Polish perspective') in K. Myszona-Kostrzewa et alia, *Prawne Aspekty* (n42) 39.

- the existence of an institutionalized enforcement system; and
- the instrumental nature of this law within the scope of national space policy implementation.[40]

The extent of the final revisions following the recommendations from the legislative review is yet uncertain. However, some remarks and reflections stemming from the international law perspective might be useful for the drafters and legislators of the Polish space law and hence, will be presented in the following sections.

5 National Space Activities and Jurisdiction

Jurisdiction is considered a basic attribute of a State, whereby it exercises fundamental powers as a subject of international law.[41] Generally, jurisdiction refers to powers exercised by a State over persons, property or events, and it might include powers to legislate or to apply its laws in order to regulate persons and activities (prescription jurisdiction), the powers of a State's courts to hear and adjudicate cases (judicial or adjudicative jurisdiction), or the State's right to enforce (or punish non-compliance with) its laws (enforcement jurisdiction).[42] Under customary international law, the State's prescriptive or legislative jurisdiction may be based on (1) territoriality, (2) nationality, (3) effects, (4) national security, (5) passive personality, and (6) universality.[43] Under customary law, a State may have jurisdiction to regulate a space object if:

1. the object was launched from its territory (territorial jurisdiction);
2. the object was under the control of its nationals (nationality jurisdiction);
3. the operation of the object had significant effects on the State (for instance, media broadcasting) (effects jurisdiction); or
4. the object posed a security threat to a State (national security jurisdiction).[44]

State obligations under the space treaties, as discussed in detail in Chapter 4, involve the concepts of State responsibility, liability and the

40 Ibid.

41 Manfred Lachs, *The Law of Outer Space: An Experience in Contemporary Law-Making* (1979) 69.

42 Peter Malanczuk, Akehurst's Modern Introductin to International Law, 7th Ed (Routledge, 1997) 132; Mark Sundahl, 'Legal status of Spacecraft' in Ram S. Jakhu and Paul S. Dempsey, eds, *Routledge Handbook of Space Law* (Routledge, 2017) 42.

43 Sundahl, ibid.

44 Ibid 44.

registration requirements, which have been recognized by the proposed Draft Space Act.[45] However, while the Polish Draft Space Act recognizes the obligation stemming from Article VI of Outer Space Treaty to 'authorize and continuously supervise' the space activities of private entities, its drafters should also look at this obligation in conjunction with the first part of the same article, making States 'internationally responsible for national activities in outer space.'[46] The concept of 'national activities in outer space' has not been defined in Article VI, except for the assignment of State responsibility for space activities conducted not only by its own (governmental or public) agencies but also for its non-governmental (that is, private) entities. This distinction is important from the perspective of a State's ability to effectively limit or extend its jurisdictional reach and ultimately, affect the extent of its international liability under international space law.

According to Von der Dunk, there are three positions, or schools of thought, as to what 'national activities' refer to in the context of Article VI of the Outer Space Treaty. The first simply equates 'national activities' to 'activities of nationals,' while the second approach views the concept of 'national activities' as necessarily impacted by the principle of jurisdiction and control by the State of registration, and hence, the State's obligations and liabilities connected therewith.

Article VIII of the Outer Space Treaty provides that a State of registration

'shall *retain jurisdiction and control* over such object, and over any personnel thereof, while in outer space or on a celestial body. *Ownership* of objects launched into outer space [...] is not affected by their presence in outer space ...' [emphasis added].

The Polish Draft Space Act incorporates only the first part of Article VIII, as '[t]he Republic of Poland retains jurisdiction and control over an object launched into outer space registered in the Registry and its personnel while in outer space or on a celestial body.'[47]

International space law recognizes jurisdiction, control and ownership over space objects located beyond a State's territory and empowers the State of registration to legislate with respect to its space objects and its personnel.[48] The interplay between the right and obligation of the 'State of registration' implied in the continuing jurisdiction and control under Article VIII of Outer Space Treaty, the requirement of the 'appropriate State' to 'authorize and

45 Draft Space Act (n3).
46 Outer Space Treaty (n38) Article VI.
47 Draft Space Act (n3) Article 13(3).
48 Jakhu and Pelton (n7) 122.

continuously supervise' the private actors engaged in space activities under Article VI of Outer Space Treaty, and finally, the apparent inability of the 'launching State' to transfer its potential liability obligation in case of damage caused by the space object under Article VII of Outer Space Treaty and the Liability Convention, is also detailed elsewhere in this book.[49] These relationships are important to understand the second argument, which equates the State's national activities in outer space with all the cases where the State may be found liable for damage either as a 'launching State' (under Article VII of the Outer Space Treaty) or a 'State of registration' (under Article VIII of the Outer Space Treaty).[50]

The third school of thought takes a more logical approach, essentially equating national activities for which a State can be held responsible with those over which it is entitled to exercise some form of generally accepted jurisdiction – specifically, either based on territorial principle (launching activities, satellite communications, remote sensing and navigation activities conducted from the territory of the State concerned) or nationality principle (activities conducted by its nationals and activities involving space objects registered by that State).[51]

The Polish Draft Space Act defines the scope of its jurisdiction as applicable to the 'space activity' conducted within the territory of the Republic of Poland or on board of the platforms launching the space objects, including ships and aircraft registered in Poland (territorial and quasi-territorial jurisdiction), but also to Polish citizens and legal persons (national or personal jurisdiction).[52] However, during the legislative review process, one of the comments indicated that the scope of the applicability of the act should be narrowed down to territorial jurisdiction only, excluding the personal jurisdiction basis. Accordingly, it might be expected that the issue of jurisdiction will be reviewed again in the revised draft. It is respectfully submitted that limiting jurisdiction, or the State's ability to exercise power and control over its space objects and/or nationals involved in space activities is not desirable even within a limited scope of involvement in space activies. On the contrary, it would be beneficial for the Polish Space Act to have a wider scope, to include both the territorial

49 See Chapters 4 and 7.

50 Frans G. von der Dunk, 'International Space Law' in Frans G. von der Dunk, with Fabio Tronchetti, eds, *Handbook of Space Law* (Edward Elgar, 2015) 54, also see H.A. Wassenbergh, Public Law Aspects of Private Space Activities and Space Transportation in the Future, in *Proceedings of the Thirty-Eight Colloquium on the Law of Outer Space* (1996) 246.

51 Von der Dunk, ibid, Bin Cheng, *Studies in International Space Law* (1997) 658–63.

52 Draft Act (n3) Article 1.1.

and nationality (personal) jurisdiction over space activities conducted by the Polish nationals and companies. This is related to the discussion of 'national activities' and the State's international responsibility under Article VI of the Outer Space Treaty for the actions of its private entities.

In the context of State liability as a launching (issuing) State, it is as much liable for any damages if the launch is conducted or procured by a private entity as it would for its own actions.[53] This is a derogation from State responsibility rules under general international law, where States are only directly and fully responsible for their *own* activities, whereas under space law regime they are equally responsible for non-governmental (that is, private or commercial) activities.[54]

The 'launching State' is defined by the space treaties as a State that launches or procures the launching of a space object, or from whose territory or facility a space object is launched.[55] The Draft Space Act embraces the same definition in Article 3(4).[56] Adding the 'joint and several liability' principle of Article V of Liability Convention, the State remains liable as a launching State in multinational joint launching projects, with different launching States and/or private entities involved.[57]

Article 4(13) of the Draft Space Act further provides that, as a condition for obtaining a license, in a case of a joint launch, an agreement should be reached as to which State is considered a 'launching State.'[58] This provision appears to be an attempt to limit the State liability obligation as a launching State based on a contractual provision, which is in contravention to the international space liability regime. Given the reality of space operations, where the launching State might not have full control over the respective space activity during the entire process (launch and life in orbit), especially in case of a joint launch, the Liability Convention encourages launching States to 'conclude

53 Outer Space Treaty (n38) Article VII, and Liability Convention, Article II (absolute liability) or Article III (fault-based liability), Convention on International Liability for Damage Caused by Space Objects, 29 March 1972, 961 UNTS 187 (Liability Convention), Journal of Laws of 1973, no. 27 item 154.

54 Frans von der Dunk, 'Legal aspects of private manned spaceflight' in *Handbook of Space Law* (n55) 680.

55 Registration Convention (n39) Article 1a, Liability Convention (n58) I(c).

56 Draft Space Act (n3) Article 3(4).

57 Liability Convention (n58) Article V.

58 Draft Space Act (n3) Article 4 reads: A license to conduct space activities, hereinafter referred to as "the license", may be issued under the following conditions: (13) conclusion of an agreement determining which country is the issuing country in where more than one State can be considered an issuing State.

agreements regarding the apportioning among themselves of the financial obligation' by leaving any risk-sharing duty to the launching States.[59] However, the Liability Convention makes it clear that any such arrangements are binding only between the launching States (as to the apportionment of their joint legal obligation), leaving the 'victim State' free to seek damages from any and all launching States, which continue to be jointly and severally liable.[60] Article 4(13) of the Draft Space Act might be interpreted as an attempt to require such risk-sharing agreement, as a pre-condition for license in case of a joint launch, however, its wording should be clarified that any such agreement does not change the status of the launching State(s)' obligation under international law. It is important to note that abandonment of a space object, or a lack of control over it (for example, by contract or sale to operator from another State or due to lack of jurisdiction) cannot relieve a State from its status (and consequently, its obligation) as a 'launching State' under international space law.[61]

Based on the above, the attempt by the Polish Draft Space Act to limit the State's status (and ultimately, liability) as a launching State via contract would be ineffective within the international space law regime. However, the liability regime set up by the space treaties specifically addresses 'international responsibility' and 'international liability,' which is liability between one or more States on one hand and one or more States on the other.[62] Given this State-to-State relationship, reflective of each State's sovereignty under international law, the compensation process under the Liability Convention, involving diplomatic channels and political relationships, might be time-consuming.[63]

---

59 Liability Convention (n58) Article V.2, reinforced by UNGA Resolution 59/115, *Application of the Concept of the 'Launching State'*, UN Doc A/RES/59/115 (2005), See Armel Kerrest and Caroline Thro 'Liability for damage caused by space activities' in *Routledge Handbook of Space Law* (n55) 61.

60 Liability Convention (n58) Article V.2 states, in pertinent part: 'Such agreements shall be without prejudice to the right of a State sustaining damage to seek the entire compensation due under this Convention from any or all of the launching States which are jointly and severally liable.' Of note, in case of a damage caused by a collision of two space objects to the third State, the sharing of liability between the two launching States shall be done proportionate to the committed faults or equally, if the fault cannot be determined. Ibid, Article IV (2),Kerrest and Thro (n65) 61.

61 Noting the different liability standards based on the location of the damages – absolute liability for damage on the surface of the Earth or to aircraft in flight, Liability Convention, Article II, and fault-based liability for damage caused in space ('elsewhere than on the surface of the Earth'), Liability Convention (n58), Article III. See Jakhu and Pelton (n7) 123, Francis Lyall and Paul B. Larsen, *Space Law: A Treatise* (Ashgate, 2009) 84.

62 Von der Dunk, International Space Law (n55) 89.

63 Kerrest and Thro (n65) 68.

In addition, the liability regime set up by the Liability Convention does not apply to 'nationals of the launching State' and to foreign nationals that were participating in or invited to the launch.[64] The availability and extent of damages to such nationals are within the sole discretion of the national laws. The liability framework set up by the Liability Convention is victim-friendly, as it does not require proof of any fault or negligence in case of damage occurring on the ground (as per the absolute liability of Article II of the Liability Convention). Accordingly, a decision whether to extend the victim-oriented liability protection under the Liability Convention to its own nationals or not remains each State's prerogative. The currently reviewed Draft Space Act does not contemplate any such grounds for domestic compensation under the space law treaties. However, as previously mentioned, it is expected that the revised draft might include such provisions.[65]

Finally, since it is mostly the launching State that bears international responsibility and liability under the international space regime, it is in the interest of States to ensure that the activity planned and conducted by their non-governmental entities can be properly supervised. For the same reason, it would also serve the State's interest to secure, through the provisions of its national space law, the broadest extra-territorial jurisdiction allowed under the international and their domestic law. This can be achieved by setting out rules in the national legislation which impose registration, licensing, insurance, and other requirements on the private entities concerned. Accordingly, the Draft Space Act's scope of the application in Article 1(1) should not be curtailed to a territorial basis of jurisdiction only.

The current proposal, which includes both the territorial and nationality principles as the basis of the Polish Space Act's jurisdiction is more in line with Poland's international treaty obligations, especially in the light of the increasing private participation in space activities. As Poland's ability to participate in more advanced space activities grows, its ability to exercise its powers to control the relevant activities, including those conducted by its nationals (citizens or legal entities), should not be pre-empted by its own legislation. While beyond the scope of this study, the nationality-based or personal jurisdiction would also be crucial in policing and penalizing the criminal behaviour in

64 Liability Convention (n58) Article VII, also Article III provides that 'damage [...] to a space object of one launching state or to persons or property on board such a space object by a space object of another launching state ...' (emphasis added), See Von der Dunk, International Space Law (n55) 89.

65 Tomanek, ibid (n37).

outer space, for example by criminal liability for infringement of rules pertaining to such activities.

6 The Limit of State Sovereignty and the Unresolved Boundary Question

States are free to regulate their national space activities, as long as the fundamental tenets of international space law are not violated. Accordingly, while States cannot relieve themselves of their international liability under the space treaties, they can minimize the extent of that liability by exercising their duty to 'authorize and continuously supervise' effectively. It might be achieved by creating appropriate regulatory regimes governing space activity in the domestic framework with complex registration, licensing and liability regulations, involving mandatory insurance, certification, navigation, as well as compliance with safety and security standards, and other proscribed international norms and guidelines. If this list of recommended regulatory provisions sounds familiar, it is not by accident.

The development of national space law necessitates, to some extent, comparative analysis not only to draw similarities or to borrow solutions from other, already developed branches of law. Comparison of space law to aviation or maritime law has served this purpose. Chapter 3 of this book provides a useful comparison of the major differences between international air law and space law. The law of outer space is often compared to other domains of international law as well, which govern common spaces such as the law of the sea[66] and the law governing Antarctica[67] – the high seas, deep seabed and the landmass of Antarctica, like outer space, are all excluded from claims of sovereignty.[68]

The concept of exploitation and use of outer space as the province of all mankind, as well as principles of freedom of exploration and use of outer space, to be conducted for the benefit and in the interest of all countries, are the central tenets set up by the Outer Space Treaty, along with the non-appropriation principle.[69] These fundamental principles of the international space regime

66 United Nations Convention on the Law of the Sea (UNCLOS), 10 December 1982, 1833 UNTS 3 (entered into force 16 November 1994) Article 89.

67 Antarctic Treaty, 1 December 1959, 12 UST 794, 402 UNTS 71, 19 ILM 860 (1980), UKTS 97 (1961),Cmnd 1535, ATS 12 (1961) (entered into force 23 June 1961) Article IV.

68 Stephen Hobe and Kuan-Wei Chan, 'Legal status of outer space' in *Routledge Handbook* (n55) 27–33.

69 Outer Space Treaty (n38), Article I and II, respectively. These concepts are further developed in the Common Heritage of Mankind (CHM) principle enshrined in the Agreement

are in stark contrast to the complete and exclusive sovereignty of each State over its airspace, firmly established under the international air law regime.[70] Under Article 1 of the Chicago Convention, the principle of exclusive sovereignty of every State (not only of each signatory of the Convention) has been recognized.[71] The concept of sovereignty should be considered as the exclusive jurisdiction of the State concerned to adopt laws and regulations pertaining to the status and uses of its national airspace.[72] That exclusive sovereignty of each State arguably ends at the border between the national airspace and outer space. The location of that border, or even the need for its definition, continues to be debated in the international arena. Different physical, operational and legal considerations relating to the definition of outer space, as applicable to the scope and application of space law, are presented in Chapter 3. State practice continues to develop in this area, with some States embracing the spatialist approach in their national space legislation by setting the firm boundary (usually around 100 km) while others adopting the functional approach, by focusing on either the function of the regulated activities (space activities) or the character of the regulated subject (spacecraft or space object).[73]

The Polish Draft Space Act appears to adopt the functional approach by defining 'space activity' as 'the launch, exploitation of the space object and its re-entry to Earth,' without defining the outer space.[74] It also defines 'space object' as 'any object intended to be launched, or launched into outer space, its component parts, as well as its launch vehicle and its component parts.' By adopting the functional approach, the drafters of the Space Act might have avoided settling a theoretical dispute on the boundary between airspace and outer space, with the implied vertical limit to State sovereignty, as discussed in Chapter 3. However, they missed an opportunity to contribute to such

Governing the Activities of States on the Moon and Other Celestial Bodies, 5 December 1979, 1363 UNTS 3 (Moon Agreement) Article 11.

70 See Chapter 3 (5) of this book.

71 Convention on International Civil Aviation ('Chicago Convention') (1994) 15 U.N.T.S. 295. (Chicago Convention) Article 1, Convention Relating to the Regulation of Aerial Navigation Signed at Paris, October 13, 1919, 1 J. Air L. & Com. 94 (1930) (Paris Convention) Article 1. 2.

72 Michael Milde, *International law and ICAO* (Eleven International Publishing, 2008) 35.

73 Frans von der Dunk, 'The Delimitation of Outer Space Revisited: The Role of National Space laws in the Delimitation Issue'(1998) Space, Cyber, and Telecommunications Law Program Faculty Publications 51, 255, https://digitalcommons.unl.edu/spacelaw/51; Also See Chapter 3, for a full discussion on the lower boundary of outer space, including differences between the spatial and functional approaches and popular misapprehensions about the so called 'von Karman line' as the boundary between the airspace and outspace.

74 Draft Space Act (n3) Article 2 (1).

unresolved legal issues as free access to outer space or the right of innocent passage by foreign spacecraft through the national airspace, which are important from the international space law perspective. Moreover, adopting a pure functional approach does nothing to solve the legal uncertainty related to different registration and liability standards under the regimes of or air law and space law, which are likely to become even more relevant in the developing suborbital operations. Accordingly, it would be advisable for the drafters of the Polish Space Act to take into consideration a variety of different approaches, including hybrid proposals, as described in more detailed in Chapter 3.

7 Existing Domestic Legislation and Its Applicability to National Space Activities

As already noted, Poland has not yet adopted the Draft Space Act, or any other specific legislation governing commercial space activities except the Act on the establishment of POLSA.[75] Reference is therefore needed to the general rules contained in Polish civil law. As the main areas of interest involve the issues of State liability, the Polish Civil Code,[76] in particular provisions referring to the State Treasury's liability, are relevant in the context of space activities in Poland. In this respect, Article 435 of the Polish Civil Code, regarding persons running an enterprise, would be applicable in case of potential recognition of liability.[77] This article clearly states that a person who manages on his own account, an enterprise or an establishment set in motion by natural forces (steam, gas, electricity, liquid fuels, and suchlike) is liable for any personal or property damage caused by the operation of the enterprise or the establishment unless the damage is due to force majeure or solely to a fault on the part of the aggrieved party or a third party for whom he is not responsible.

The Draft Space Act does not determine how the principles of liability apply to space activities, narrowing only insurance requirements in case of some scientific entities. Enterprises conducting space activities would fall under Article 435 of the Polish Civil Code depending on the findings regarding the occurrence of the damage. Possible liability may also be determined based on Article 449 of the Polish Civil Code pertaining to manufacturer's risk.[78] This principle applies to liability for damage caused by a dangerous product implemented to

75 POLSA Act (n1).

76 Polish Civil Code, Polish Journal of Law of 23 April 1964, No.16, item 93.

77 Ibid Article 435.

78 Ibid 449.

the Polish law based on Council Directive 85/374/EEC of 25 July 1985 concerning liability for defective products.[79] Within this context, the defectiveness of the product should be determined by reference not to its fitness for use but to the lack of safety which the public at large is entitled to expect; such safety is assessed by excluding any misuse of the product not reasonable under the circumstances.[80] The definition of a manufacturer given by the directive and implemented under the Polish Civil Code assures a broad definition of entities liable by recognition of every manufacturer of a finished product, the producer of any raw material or the manufacturer of a component part and any person who, by putting his name, trade mark or other distinguishing feature on the product presents himself as its producer. As the Draft Space Act provides for a combination of space insurance and complementary State compensation for a State to bear international liability, the principles of liability defined under Articles 435 and 449 of the Polish Civil Code would have to be applied without any specific rules referring strictly to space activities.

However, as the Draft Space Act assumes, in case of situations involving more than one launching State, relevant agreements for apportionment of liability between the applicable States would need to be concluded. Although the extent of such agreements is not clear from the existing content of the proposal, it is quite obvious that its implementation would require arrangements with the other State to determine principles of liability.

The same approach regarding an adequate applicability should also be taken into account in case of potential criminal liability governed by the Polish Criminal Code. Based on Article 5, Polish penal law is applicable to the perpetrator who committed a prohibited act within the territory of the Republic of Poland, or on board of a Polish vessel or aircraft, unless an international law agreement stipulates otherwise. Polish penal law does not specifically refer to 'space objects,' as defined by the Draft Space Act,[81] however at least some of the space objects might qualify as an 'aircraft' within the meaning of aviation law and thus may fall within the scope of Polish penal law.[82] To assure full compliance with the intention of Article 5 of the Polish Criminal Code and to

79 Council Directive 85/374/EEC of 25 July 1985 on the approximation of the laws, regulations and administrative provisions of the Member States concerning liability for defective products, O.J. L 210, 7.8.1985.

80 Ibid 29.

81 Draft Space Act (n3) Article 2(2).

82 According to internationally accepted definition by International Civil Aviation Organization (ICAO), an 'aircraft' is '[a]ny machine that can derive support in the atmosphere from the reactions of the air other than the reactions of the air against the earth's surface' Chicago Convention (n77) Annex 1,2 and 6 definitions. For discussion on the

avoid any doubts within the scope of criminal liability, especially in the case of offences committed on board space objects, the clause would need to be changed.

As the Polish Space Strategy focuses on opportunities delivered to consumers by the new technology through communication, navigation, satellite imagery, and so on, legal aspects of personal data protection should be also considered, especially within the context of downstream sector activities. These aspects would be covered by the General Data Protection Regulation (GDPR), although there are enlisted areas excluded from the scope of this regulation when it comes to the processing of personal data by Member States when carrying out activities covering national security or by EU institutions, offices and agencies.[83]

More problematic issues may occur in case of dual-use space activities, particularly when some activities and practices within the area of national security and defense are assigned to commercial entities and thus the determination of the boundary between protection of personal data and State interests may be difficult to determine.

While the planned space legislation will provide important legal guidance pertaining to the basic operation and control of space activities, there are still other issues that need to be taken into consideration and that would be governed by various areas of law. For example, space activities as defined by the Draft Space Act would also fall under the Economic Freedom Act.[84] This means that, in addition to complying with the requirements set by the Draft Space Act, the space activity would need to be registered and properly maintained in accordance with the Code of Administrative Procedure of 14 June 1960.[85] In addition, many aspects relevant for commercial space activities are part of national telecommunications legislation, namely the Telecommunication Act of 16 July 2004.[86] This act covers orbital resources defined as positions in geostationary orbits or satellite orbits which are or may be used for the placement of artificial earth satellites for the provision of telecommunications. Hence, the capacity of the geostationary orbit is treated

---

different between 'space object' and 'aircraft' with respect to the applicability of the space law versus air law regimes, see Chapter 3.

83 Regulation (EU) 2016/679 of the European Parliament and of the Council of 27 April 2016 on the protection of natural persons with regard to the processing of personal data and on the free movement of such data, and repealing Directive 95/46/EC, OJ L 119, 4.5.2016.

84 Economic Freedom Act, Journal of Law 2016, item 1829.

85 Code of Administrative Procedure of 14 June 1960, Journal of Law 1960, No 30, item 168.

86 Telecommunication Act of 16 July 2004, Journal of Law 16 July 2004, No 171, item 1800.

as a finite natural resource, orbital positions are allocated by the International Telecommunication Union (ITU) through national administrative bodies.[87] Polish authorities have not yet made reservations for orbital resources due to the fact that satellite facilities are still not operated by Polish entities, but two nominal positions in geostationary orbit are provided for Poland. Based on decisions adopted by International Telecommunication Union (ITU), Poland obtained the following positions:

- Position for a telecommunication satellite – 15.2^{0}E. The allotment comprises: a nominal orbital position, frequency bands and bandwidths, a service area for national coverage, generalised parameters and a predetermined arc (PDA), and
- Position for a broadcasting satellite -50^{0}E, however this position is shared among other countries: Afghanistan, Sri Lanka, Iraq, Kirghizstan, Moldova, Nepal, Turkmenistan and Romania. The assignment comprises: channel numbers and assigned broadcasting frequencies, orbital position description, boresight geographical coordinates, satellite station antenna characteristics, its gain and equivalent isotopically radiated power.[88]

In November 2003, a team for the elaboration of a concept for Polish orbital resources management was established by the President of the Office of Telecommunication and Post Regulation headed by Jozef Modelski. According to the assessment conducted by the team and released in a form of report, it was pointed out that the position 15.2^{0}E is difficult to use as the nominal position 15,2 E is surrounded by big constellations of Hot Bird satellites owned by Eutelsat and ASTRA satellites covering the territory of Poland and operating in the same frequency band as the one provided for the Polish satellite. As was further explained, nation-wide coverage demands from the operator to use footprint in the shape of an ellipse with defined dimensions and oriented towards as precise coverage of the national area as possible. The second position was assessed as correct in terms of technical parameters. It was, however, noticed that the latter position is far away from the positions occupied by the

87 See also Fabio Tronchetti, *The Exploitation of Natural Resources of the Moon and Other Celestial Bodies, A proposal for a Legal Regime* (Brill 2009) 131–191; Gorove, Stephen, 'The Geostationary Orbit: Issues of Law and Policy' The American Journal of International Law 73, no. 3 (1979) 444–61; Christy Collis 'The Geostationary Orbit: A Critical Legal Geography of Space's Most Valuable Real Estate' The Sociological Review 57(1_suppl) (2009) 47–65.

88 World Radiocommunication Conference, WARC-1985, WARC-1988, WRC-2000, WRC-2003. Detailed data describing these two positions can be found in Appendix No 30, 30A and 30B of Radio Regulations of the International Telecommunication Union (Radio Regulations) (Geneva, 2020) available at https://www.itu.int/pub/R-REG-RR/en.

constellation of ASTRA and Eutelsat satellites and thus, special orientation of receiving antennas would be required. It was finally concluded that the position 50^0 E seems to be more commercially attractive than the position 15.2^0 E. Interestingly, a proposal for the leading position of Poland has been considered in this report to achieve an agreement with the rest of countries sharing position in order to sale or lease this position to a big satellite operator.[89] However, no further developments have been undertaken in this respect.

The Polish telecommunications legal framework requires tendering, and this may be complicated in combination with ITU's formal and technical procedures.

The space industry tends to utilize and advance development of the most advanced technologies and, therefore, it frequently implicates the intellectual property rights assured by the national law. The Polish system of intellectual property protection consist of two regulations: the Act of 4 February 1994 on Copyright and Related Rights[90] and the Act of 30 June 2000 – Industrial Property Law.[91] It is not clear whether those regulations would be applicable to space objects registered in Poland and, without specific national rules, problems may occur especially in case of infringements committed in space.

Since another important goal of the Polish Space Strategy concerns strengthening of national defence, space activities might implicate the Act of 29 November 2000 on Foreign Trade in Goods, Technologies and Services of Strategic Significance for State Security and for Maintaining International Peace and Security.[92] Export controls, as an integral part of State security policy, apply to international trade and implement control mechanisms and instruments relating to typical trade and customs procedures. They impose non-tariff restrictions, implying the necessity of obtaining a license for various forms of trade, including non-material transfers, when no formal customs clearance is conducted, or in case of domestic broker participation in a transaction between companies from other countries and the product in question does not enter the territory of Poland. Moreover, the difficulty in determining the usage of some products may fall under the regime of dual-use products

89 Report from a team for the elaboration of a concept for Polish orbital resources management, http://pdc.ceu.hu/archive/00002903/01/Report_from_a_Team_for_the_elaboration_of_a_concept_fo.pdf.

90 Act of 4 February 1994 on Copyright and Related Rights, Journal of Law 1994, No 24, item 83.

91 Act of 30 June 2000 – Industrial Property Law, Journal of Laws of 2001, No 49, item 508.

92 Act of 29 November 2000 on Foreign Trade in Goods, Technologies and Services of Strategic Significance for State Security and for Maintaining International Peace and Security, Journal of Laws of 2000, No 119, item 1250.

governed by the Council Regulation (EC) 428/2009[93] and a prior authorization for transfer of enlisted items, including satellites will be required.

The applicable national legislation discussed above by no means exhaust all the considerations and issues that require additional clarification under domestic legal framework.

8 Conclusions and Looking towards the Future

Outer space is no longer dominated by States as the main players, but rather has transformed into an increasingly multi-national, even global market. In Poland, the growing importance of the space sector has been recognized and institutionalized with the establishment of the Polish Space Agency (POLSA) in 2014, and most recently, with the implementation of the Polish Space Strategy in 2017 and ongoing work to develop and implement National Space Program and the Act on the Space Activities and the National Register of Space Objects ('Space Act'). In addition to the priority projects related to the development of national satellite systems, NewSpace technologies, including the creation of Polish suborbital rockets with greater private sector industry participation, constitute an important element of the Polish Space Strategy.

The creation of national regulations in the area of outer space activities is of twofold importance.

First, it is crucial for the domestic legal framework as it may impact (positively or negatively) the development of the space sector and its domestic economic growth in general. As recognized by Mrenca, the developing industry sector should reasonably expect Polish space law to be the propeller or facilitator for its expansion and not an anchor for it.[94] Accordingly, the registration, licensing and liability regimes to be implemented and enforced through the domestic space legal framework should strike the right balance between many important, albeit not always compatible interests, such as the State's and general public interests in ensuring the safe, secure and predictable conduct of space activities with proper compensation for damages resulting therefrom, on the one hand, and scientific and commercial interests in free and affordable access to use and explore the outer space and the opportunities presented therein, on the other.

93 Council Regulation (EC) 428/2009, Official Journal L 134, 29.5.2009.
94 Mrenca (n43) 48.

Second, domestic space legislation, as evidence of State practice, is important from the international space law perspective, not only as illustrative of the possible solutions (for comparative law purposes), but also because it can contribute to forming rules of customary international law. Customary international law arises from the practice of States coupled with the acceptance of the practice of law (*opinio juris sive necessitatis*), which, once established, is binding on all nations.[95] The point at which consistent State practice becomes customary international law binding on all States is open to interpretation. The evidence of custom may be found in international agreements, declarations of international organization, judicial decisions of international tribunals, and other acts of States.[96] Arguably, national space laws might evolve in the upcoming years into State practice and become *opinio juris*. Accordingly, States, such as Poland, currently in the process of developing their national space legislations should take the opportunity to weigh in on still unresolved and definitional issues, such as the delimitation of airspace and outer space, the precise meaning of 'non-appropriation', 'cooperation' or the status of outer space as an international global commons, which continue to trouble jurists to this day.[97]

Accordingly, Poland, by creating a clear and predictable national legal regime for space activities would not only enhance the debate at the international level, but also, equally, if not more importantly, promote its own commercial space sector. Finally, outer space continues to be an important domain for national military capabilities, as confirmed by setting up separate branches within the national armed forces of some States and the recognition of the outer space as important strategic domain by allies at the North Atlantic Treaty Organization (NATO).[98] Promoting de-weaponization of outer space and peaceful development of this final frontier of human activity should be the goal of any space-faring State, including the new entrants.

95 Von der Dunk, Delimitation (n79) 255.

96 Ibid 12.

97 Hobe and Chen (n74) 41.

98 At June 2019 Defence Ministers' meeting, Allies adopted NATO's Space Policy, and at the December 2019 Leaders' Meeting in London, Allies declared space a fifth operational domain, alongside air, land, sea and cyberspace. In their declaration, NATO Leaders stated: 'We have declared space an operational domain for NATO, recognising its importance in keeping us safe and tackling security challenges, while upholding international law.' NATO, NATO approach to Space (2 December 2021) https://www.nato.int/cps/en/natohq/topics_175419.htm#:~:text=and%20early%20warning.-,NATO's%20approach%20to%20space%20will%20remain%20fully%20in%20line%20with,its%20operations%2C%20missions%20and%20activities (accessed 23.01.2022).

Issues for consideration – proposals de lege ferenda for the Polish draft space act

1. The scope of regulation (jurisdiction) should not be limited to the territorial principle, but rather be wider, to include nationality (personal) jurisdiction over space activities conducted by the Polish nationals and companies.
2. Registration requirements should be more detailed, to include identification of the component parts of the space objects or clearer identifiers of the larger parts in order to facilitate identification and tracking of space debris and enhance Space Situational Awareness efforts.
3. Requirements and conditions for licensing should be more elaborate with respect to possible transfer of ownership, liability, the levels of mandatory insurance as well as environmental protection (proscribing mitigation of space debris) and sanctions for their violations.
4. Liability provisions under the Liability Convention, including the proposed indemnification clauses, should be incorporated into the domestic liability framework to include compensation for damages that occurred in the territory of Poland and to the Polish nationals and entities.
5. UN-recommended Guidelines for the Long-term Sustainability of Outer Space Activities should be followed to the largest possible extent.
6. More incentives for both 'downstream' and 'upstream' sector development should be examined and provided – tax incentives, funding, public-private partnerships (P3) initiatives.
7. Poland should continue and increase its involvement in bilateral and multilateral efforts (such as with ESA and NASA) and under UN auspices with COPUOS working groups and to promote effective soft law measures for space security by implementing such guidelines/ recommendations into its national legal regime.

As a final note, we should be mindful of the wise words of the great Polish legal mind Manfred Lachs reminding us that 'there can be no doubt that the freedom of action of States in outer space or on celestial bodies is neither unlimited, absolute or unqualified, but is determined by the rights and interest of other States. It can therefore be exercised only to the extent to which as indicated it does not conflict with those rights and interests. There should therefore be no antinomy between the freedom of some and the interest of all.'[99]

99 Lachs (n45) 117.

Concluding Remarks

Frans von der Dunk

It is clear, that from a general perspective the increasing participation of the private sector in activities in outer space presents one of the most fundamental paradigm changes and challenges also for space law.[1] Whilst the *corpus iuris spatialis internationalis* as most famously comprised of the 1967 Outer Space Treaty[2] and a few follow-on treaties of the late 1960s until mid-1970s[3] provided the overarching legal framework for all activities in outer space and was generally acknowledged to apply to all States,[4] it largely failed to address any specifics of private sector participation.

Once such private sector participation started to take shape, however (first in the realm of satellite communications and launch services, then gradually in other areas as well), it turned out that a handful of articles within the *corpus iuris spatialis internationalis* were of key importance here – and provided a major rationale for the establishment of national space legislation, next to

1 See already on this *e.g.* F.G. von der Dunk, As Space Law Comes to Nebraska, Space Comes Down to Earth, 87 *Nebraska Law Review* (2008), 498–515.

2 Treaty on Principles Governing the Activities of States in the Exploration and Use of Outer Space, including the Moon and Other Celestial Bodies (hereafter Outer Space Treaty), London/Moscow/Washington, done 27 January 1967, entered into force 10 October 1967; 610 UNTS 205; TIAS 6347; 18 UST 2410; UKTS 1968 No. 10; Cmnd. 3198; ATS 1967 No. 24; 6 ILM 386 (1967).

3 This notably concerns the Rescue Agreement (Agreement on the Rescue of Astronauts, the Return of Astronauts and the Return of Objects Launched into Outer Space, London/Moscow/Washington, done 22 April 1968, entered into force 3 December 1968; 672 UNTS 119; TIAS 6599; 19 UST 7570; UKTS 1969 No. 56; Cmnd. 3786; ATS 1986 No. 8; 7 ILM 151 (1968)); the Liability Convention (Convention on International Liability for Damage Caused by Space Objects, London/Moscow/Washington, done 29 March 1972, entered into force 1 September 1972; 961 UNTS 187; TIAS 7762; 24 UST 2389; UKTS 1974 No. 16; Cmnd. 5068; ATS 1975 No. 5; 10 ILM 965 (1971)); and the Registration Convention (Convention on Registration of Objects Launched into Outer Space, New York, done 14 January 1975, entered into force 15 September 1976; 1023 UNTS 15; TIAS 8480; 28 UST 695; UKTS 1978 No. 70; Cmnd. 6256; ATS 1986 No. 5; 14 ILM 43 (1975)).

4 For the comprehensive measure of ratification by at least the spacefaring countries, see A/AC.105/C.2/2021/CRP.10, of 31 May 2021. Furthermore, certainly the Outer Space Treaty has generally been recognized to reflect customary international law even binding upon those States not (yet) parties to it; *cf.* also F.G. von der Dunk, International space law, in F.G. von der Dunk & F. Tronchetti (Eds.), *Handbook of Space Law* (2015), 59–60.

 | DOI:10.1163/9789004542860_012

the interest in underpinning national space policies and strategies with a solid legal foundation.

First, Article VI of the Outer Space Treaty, the only clause at least referring to the private sector by using the term "non-governmental entities", required the space activities of such entities to be subjected to "authorization and continuing supervision" by "the appropriate State". While not strictly speaking requiring that such authorization and continuing supervision should take the form of national space legislation and a full-fledged national regime for authorizing and supervising private space activities, from many perspectives the establishment of such national space legislation indeed presented the most comprehensive, transparent and effective tool for the purpose.[5]

Second, Article VII of the Outer Space Treaty, as then elaborated by the 1972 Liability Convention, turned out to hold States liable also for damage caused by private space activities, as long as they qualified, one way or another, as a "launching State"[6] of the space object involved in such activities. This turned out to present a huge incentive for States to actually implement national space legislation, as it would provide the most comprehensive, transparent and effective means of ensuring that private sector space operators would on the one hand be severely scrutinized before going into space to start with, and on the other hand, once authorized to go into space, would be required to reimburse the State for any international liability claim the latter might face.

National space legislation in a wider sense of the term would encompass *all* national law to address space activities and their major downstream implications and applications, thus including for instance national laws establishing national space agencies or providing the funding for national space programmes. Yet, the authorization and supervision of private sector space activities clearly represented the most important contribution of any national laws and regulations to the legal regime regarding space activities and upholding the public interests in an environment as safe, secure, environmentally benign and generally beneficial to humanity as possible.

5 Note that for instance France for many years chose to supervise Arianespace, the private commercial launch service provider of French nationality – but with profound broader involvement of other Member States of the European Space Agency – and SpotImage, the private remote sensing company of French nationality, not by way of a national space law, but by major government shareholding in the companies concerned.

6 The launching State was defined as "(i) A State which launches or procures the launching of a space object; (ii) A State from whose territory or facility a space object is launched"; Article I(c), Liability Convention.

While the theory of national space law and its role in implementing such core clauses of in particular the Outer Space Treaty is therefore relatively straightforward, practice has always been much more fragmented, complicated and almost haphazard. Some countries with private sector space activities for a long time did not, or even today do not, possess such a general national space law, while other countries had such a national space law in place before the domestic private sector became seriously interested in going into outer space.[7]

Over time, a clear and fundamental acceleration in the adoption of national space laws and their details can be noticed. Strictly speaking, the first national law addressing any possible private sector interest in going into outer space was the 1969 Norwegian Act on Launching.[8] It comprised three Sections and totalled half a page, but did include the fundamental requirement for a private company to obtain approval from the Norwegian authorities to launch something into outer space.

In the two next decades, merely three other States effectively followed suit: the United States (by way of the FCC effectively in 1970 declaring its 1934 Communications Act[9] to apply to private satellite communication operators as well, later followed by specific acts on launching and satellite remote sensing), Sweden (Norway's neighbour) in 1982 and the United Kingdom in 1986. Of the latter two, only the UK Outer Space Act[10] comprised more than a few pages.

In the single decade of the 1990s, four more countries followed (or five, if you include Hong Kong as a separate one): South Africa in 1993; the two main countries resulting from the falling apart of the Soviet Union, Russia (in 1993) and Ukraine (in 1996); as well as Australia in 1998, the latter country producing the at that point largest national space law by far as comprised in a single document.

Then things really took off: in the 2000s, as much as eight countries for the first time adopted a national space law (while others updated or extended existing ones, and gradually more additional regulation started to be developed as well). Among the 'newcomers' was the first developing country properly

---

7 See for a comprehensive overview up to 2015 and analysis *e.g.* I. Marboe, National space law, in F.G. von der Dunk & F. Tronchetti (Eds.), *Handbook of Space Law* (2015), 127–204.

8 *Lov om oppskyting av gjenstander fra norsk territorium m.m. ut i verdensrommet*, No. 38, 13 June 1969; *National Space Legislation of the World*, Vol. I (2001), at 286; United Nations/ Nigeria Workshop on Space Law, National Legislation and Policy – Selected Texts (2005), at 159.

9 Communications Act, 19 June 1934; 47 U.S.C. 151 (1988); 48 Stat. 1064; now codified as 47 U.S.C. Chapter 5.

10 Outer Space Act, 18 July 1986, 1986 Chapter 38; *National Space Legislation of the World*, Vol. I (2001), at 293; *Space Law – Basic Legal Documents*, E.I; 36 *Zeitschrift für Luft- und Weltraumrecht* (1987), 12.

speaking (Brazil in 2001), the officially still-communist China (in 2002) and a number of smaller countries like Belgium and the Netherlands, which at best could expect national private sector activities to be developed in certain niche markets.

Almost inevitably, the 2010s so far top the bill: no less than thirteen countries adopted their first piece of comprehensive national space legislation. Among them countries as 'small' as Luxembourg and New Zealand, as well as the first Arab country, the United Arab Emirates. Again, also, existing laws were extended and further augmented by more detailed regulations and authorization regimes. By now, all national space laws and regulations would likely not fit on any standard bookshelf anymore – and that is, of course, without the actual authorizations handed out under them.

And now Poland is – maybe, hopefully – on the verge of joining the club. As the current book explores in greater detail, there are many good reasons why Poland, compared to some of the States that already *have* such a national law in place not the least of nations with the private sector potential to go into outer space, would now be interested in developing at least such a framework law. Most succinctly put: it means full-fledged implementation of several key obligations under the *corpus iuris spatialis internationalis*, it means offering a much higher level of legal certainty to *bona fide* commercial operators, and it (consequently) means offering the best approach to allow Poland both to benefit from whatever the private sector might bring to outer space and space activities and to control and minimize the potentially negative effects of such private sector involvement.

Given Poland's relatively young involvement in the overlap of space activities and private sector interest, in particular the element of promotion of a legal environment which actually incentivizes the private sector to go into outer space merits further attention, given the general, often seemingly almost ineradicable conception with the private sector that government regulation and licensing is a thing to be avoided as much as possible.

One of the most telling examples comes from the Netherlands. In 2007, the country had established its framework national space law, applying its licensing obligation *ratione materiae* to "the launch, the flight operation or the guidance of space objects in outer space".[11] Shortly thereafter, a (then) small Dutch company ISIS entered the international market for secondary payload

---

11 See Secs. 1(b), 2, *Wet houdende regels omtrent ruimtevaartactiviteiten en de instelling van een register van ruimtevoorwerpen* (*Wet ruimtevaartactiviteiten*) (hereafter Dutch Space Law), 24 January 2007; 80 *Staatsblad* (2007); *Nationales Weltraumrecht / National Space Law* (2008), at 201.

('piggy-back') launches. Given that this largely concerned small satellites which, after separation from the launch vehicle, were not really 'operated' or 'guided' anymore, the Dutch government indicated that no license would be due under the Dutch Space Law.[12]

One might perhaps expect that ISIS was pleased to learn it would not have to go through any bureaucratic procedures to get a license, incurring temporal as well as financial costs and probably being confronted with other obstacles, before it could go ahead with arranging launches for its clients. However, ISIS was smarter than that, and actually *requested* to somehow be licensed within the scope of the Dutch Space Law, as it realized the risks of *not* being licensed would ultimately be much larger than the costs of going through the licensing process.

First, ISIS realized that while the Dutch government might perhaps not consider itself a launching State under the Liability Convention by virtue of the Dutch company ISIS procuring a launch of a small and unguided satellite on behalf of a client, in case such a satellite would – even if rather unlikely, given the usually small size, short lifetime and low operating orbit – cause damage to third countries or their operators or citizens, such other countries might by contrast consider the Netherlands to be internationally liable. In the absence of a license including a clear provision on derogation by the Dutch State of such liabilities to ISIS, it would be an open question to what extent such derogation could and would be imposed *ex post facto* as based on general liability and tort considerations.

Second, granting of licenses by the Dutch government also constituted a token of trustworthiness and reputability towards potential international clients: if ISIS would be actually authorized by the Netherlands to undertake such activities, it could hardly be viewed as a shady and/or inexperienced operator which would bring in all sorts of unforeseen risks for its contractual partners. A license, in other words, would also serve as an official stamp of approval.

Third, following from the above, granting of licenses also meant that the Dutch government would at least be generally committed to making ISIS' business a success. In particular in a volatile, highly technological but at the same time highly sensitive realm as that of commercial space operations, the Netherlands could now be expected to intervene on behalf of their licensed operator in case the latter would somehow run into trouble, in terms for instance of becoming diplomatically engaged with other countries involved

12 See on this story in greater detail *e.g.* N. Palkovitz, Small Satellites, Innovative Activities, Traditional Laws, and the Industry Perspectives, in I. Marboe (Ed.), *Small Satellites* (2016), esp. 51–63.

or even using available inter-State dispute settlement mechanisms such as the International Court of Justice or the Claims Commission possibly established under the Liability Convention.[13]

Consequently, following extended discussions with ISIS and other stakeholders, the Dutch government ultimately (in 2015) officially declared that the Dutch Space Law would *also* apply to unguided satellites.[14]

The above story is not just one of the more outlying examples of how national space law and authorization regimes can actually promote and support private sector participation in space activities. It is also reflective of the fact that all those national space laws established over the last decades around the globe harbour both a certain number of more or less common features *and* a considerable number of national idiosyncratic elements. Which also means Poland would now be in the right spot to allow it to analyse more thoroughly, to learn and benefit from the over two dozen countries so far already 'in the game', while still being ahead of the overwhelming majority of countries that have *no* transparent comprehensive legal framework for incentivizing private sector participation *and* preserving and protection the interests of the general public at large in that context.

This kind of 'middle position' of Poland in the larger scheme of things, finally, also is reflected in this book, as reflecting the actual state of affairs of academic thinking and academic expertise on the topic in the country. While most of the direct-space(-law)-related themes have been properly addressed, the close reader may also have recognized that there are major elements of importance in the broader scheme of things, which have not (yet) been addressed in any detail.

A first major example thereof concerns telecommunications and telecommunications law, the latter of which addresses *inter alia* the use of radio frequencies, in principle regardless of where they would be used. At the international level, already since the 1959 World Administrative Radio Conference, the member States of the International Telecommunication Union (ITU), the UN-affiliated intergovernmental organization responsible for trying to smooth out potential conflicts regarding the international use of radio frequencies of which also Poland is a member State, officially acknowledged that this whole

13 See Arts. XIV–XX, Liability Convention.

14 See on this story in greater detail *e.g.* T.L. Masson-Zwaan, Registration of Small Satellites and the Case of the Netherlands, in I. Marboe (Ed.), *Small Satellites* (2016), 187–92.

system also applied to the use of such frequencies directed at, within or from outer space.[15]

It would thus be important also in the context of Poland and its path towards a national space law as discussed in greater detail elsewhere in this book to address how domestic Polish telecommunications law would, should and/or could apply to relevant space activities as well. Countries like the United States and the United Kingdom also have, as such, separate laws dealing with telecommunications *largo sensu*, but have taken care to ensure proper coordination and compatibilities with the space laws more directly focused on (all) space activities.

A second major example would concern the alignments of Poland in a security and military context as far as they may impact the development of the space industry. While Poland is participating in the Missile Technology Control Regime (MTCR)[16] and the Wassenaar Arrangement,[17] as well as – as an EU Member State – part of the EU-wide regime on dual-use sensitive technology controls,[18] its sovereignty in matters of defence and security means that the guidelines of the MTCR and Wassenaar Arrangement still need to be adopted by way of domestic Polish legislation, whereas the EU Regulation still allows the Member States to apply such national export controls unless differently provided for by the Regulation. Much has been written on the obstacles that such export controls would provide to commercial and civil space activities,[19] and it would be very useful in the near future to undertake a profound analysis of national Polish technology export controls from exactly that angle.

A third major example would be the membership of Poland of INTERSPUTNIK, the organization which since the early 1970s has developed into a major international player in satellite communications. Though still an intergovernmental organization as such, in recent years it has developed into a partially

15 See further on this story in great detail F.G. von der Dunk, Legal aspects of satellite communications, in F.G. von der Dunk & F. Tronchetti (Eds.), *Handbook of Space Law* (2015), 458–93.

16 Agreement on Guidelines for the Transfer of Equipment and Technology Related to Missiles (MTCR Agreement), done 16 April 1987; 26 ILM 599 (1987).

17 Wassenaar Arrangement on Export Controls for Conventional Arms and Dual-Use Goods and Technologies, Wassenaar, done 19 December 1995, effective 12 July 1996; http://www.wassenaar.org/.

18 As most recently per Regulation (EC) No 2021/821.

19 See *e.g.* F. Tronchetti, Legal aspects of the military uses of outer space, in F.G. von der Dunk & F. Tronchetti (Eds.), *Handbook of Space Law* (2015), 359–77; H.P. van Fenema, Legal aspects of launch services and space transportation, in F.G. von der Dunk & F. Tronchetti (Eds.), *Handbook of Space Law* (2015), 418–36.

commercial operation allowing distinct opportunities also for Polish telecom service providers to benefit from the availability of its multi-satellite constellation.[20] It would be interesting to see how such usage could benefit Polish commercial operators to become more closely involved in space operations themselves, and allow Polish (and other, in particular given the Internal Market for satellite communications which started to be developed in the European Union from the 1994 Satellite Directive[21] onwards) consumers to benefit therefrom in terms of access to major modern communication networks sometimes spanning the globe.

From that perspective, the present book should clearly be viewed as an initial first collection of a number of 'building blocks' for a national space law to be used for the actual activity of 'building' the national space law, while already being aware that a number of building blocks are still missing. While that may well be inevitable, as a consequence of the general level of general familiarity and expertise with the subject, given that Poland is maybe on the road to becoming, but as of yet certainly is not a true space-faring nation, such gaps will hopefully be quickly addressed in the near future. It would certainly constitute a major step forward in the direction of an appropriate, comprehensive and effective national legal regime in Poland incentivizing in the right amount private sector participation while making sure the overarching public interests in the 'global commons' of outer space – on safety, security and the environment for instance – are well protected, ultimately for the benefit of all humankind.

20 This was mainly the result of the Protocol on the Amendments to the Agreement on the Establishment of the "INTERSPUTNIK" International System and Organization of Space Communications, done November 1996, entered into force 4 November 2002; *Space Law – Basic Legal Documents*, C.VIII.2.1; 29 JSL (2003) 147.

21 Commission Directive amending Directive 88/301/EEC and Directive 90/388/EEC in particular with regard to satellite communications (Satellite Directive), 94/46/EC, of 13 October 1994; OJ L 268/15 (1994).

References

Aglietti,Guglielmo S, *'Current challenges and opportunities for space technologies'*, https://www.frontiersin.org/articles/10.3389/frspt.2020.00001/full.

Albi A and Bardutzky S (eds), *'National Constitutions in European and Global Governance: Democracy, Rights, the Rule of Law'*, (Springer Open 2019).

Bernatt M and Ziółkowski M, *'Statutory Anti-Constitutionalism'* (October 31, 2018) 28 Washington International Law Journal (2019) 485–525 < https://ssrn.com/abstract=3384304> (access 02.02.2021).

Bieliński A, *'The Right to Have a Matter Adjudicated by a Court and Alternative Dispute Resolution – Selected Issues'* (2017) 22 Białostockie Studia Prawnicze (2017) 235–242.

Biernat S and Kawczyńska M, *'The Role of the Polish Constitution (Pre-2016): Development of a Liberal Democracy in the European and International Context'* in Anneli Albi, Samo Bardutzky (eds), National Constitutions in European and Global Governance: Democracy, Rights, the Rule of Law (Springer Open 2019) 745–793.

Bierzanek R and Symonides J, *'Prawo Międzynarodowe Publiczne'* (Tr. International Public Law), (Wolters Kluwer Warsaw 2004).

Blount PJ, *'Jurisdiction In Outer Space: Challenges Of Private Individuals In Space'* 33 (J of SL 299 2007).

Bojarski Ł, Grajewski K, Kremer J, Ott G, Żurek W (eds) *'Konstytucja. Praworządność. Władza sądownicza. Aktualne problemy trzeciej władzy w Polsce'* (Wolters Kluwer Polska 2019).

Brittingham Bryon C, *'Does the World Really Need New Space Law?'* https://www.peacepalacelibrary.nl/ebooks/files/35550927X.pdf.

Butchard P, *'Principles of International Law'* House of Commons Library, Briefing Paper 9010 (21 September 2020) 3, https://researchbriefings.files.parliament.uk/documents/CBP-9010/CBP-9010.pdf.

Cheng B, *'Revisited: International Responsibility, National Activities, and the Appropriate State'* 27 (J of SL 1998).

Cheng B, *'Studies in International Space Law'* (1997).

Chmaj M (ed), *'Wolności i prawa człowieka w Konstytucji Rzeczypospolitej Polskiej'* (Wolters Kluwer Polska 2016).

Collis Ch, *'The Geostationary Orbit: A Critical Legal Geography of Space's Most Valuable Real Estate'* The Sociological Review 57(1_suppl) (2009).

Doyle S, *'A Concise History of Space Law'* Sundahl, M. J. and Gopalakrishnan, V. eds, New Perspectives On Space Law: The Proceedings of The 53rd Iisl Colloquium On The Law Of Outer Space: Young Scholar Session 1 (Int"l. Inst. Space Law 2011).

Freeland S, *'The Role of "Soft Law" in Public International Law'*, Irmgard Marboe, ed., Soft Law in Outer Space: The Function of Non-binding Norms in International Space Law (2012).

Froehlich A and Seffinga V, eds, *'National Space Legislation: A Comparative and Evaluative Analysis'* (Springer, 2018).

Gabrynowicz J, *'The Outer Space Treaty and Enhancing Space Security'*, United Nations Institute for Disarmament Research, Building the Architecture for Sustainable Space Security, (Conference Report 30–31 March 2006) UNIDIR/2006/17.

Galicki Z, *'Status prawny kosmosu'* (Tr. The Legal Status of the Cosmos) Wasilkowski A ed, Działalność kosmiczna w świetle prawa międzynarodowego, (Tr. Space activities in the light of international law) (Wrocław – Warsaw – Cracow 1991).

Galicki Z, Kamiński T, Myszona-Kostrzewa K, ed *'Manfred Lachs – an outstanding world lawyer'*, Warsaw, 2011.

Gangale T, *'The Non Karman Line: An Urban Legend of the Space Age'* 41 J of SP 2017, vol 2.

Garlicki L and Zubik M (eds), *'Konstytucja Rzeczypospolitej Polskiej. Komentarz. Tom I'* (2nd edn, Wydawnictwo Sejmowe 2016).

Gawłowski R, Nefas S and Makowski K, *'Subsidiarity Principle- Its Realization in Self-Government in Lithuania and Poland'* (2020) 10 Administrative Sciences 2–15.

Gibson J, Powell J, *'Current Space Law and Policy'* in AU-18 Space Primer (Air Command and Staff College and Space Research Electives Seminars AUP, 2009) 46 www.jstor .com/stable/resrep13939.10.

Gorove S, *'The Geostationary Orbit: Issues of Law and Policy'* The American Journal of International Law 73, no. 3 (1979).

Gowin J, Minister of Development, Labor and Technology, *'Response to Parliamentary Question No. 11218 in the matter of functioning of the Polish Space Agency, realization of the Polish space strategy and cooperation with private entities'*, 20 October 2020, Case No. DIN-V.054.3.2020.

Góralczyk W and Sawicki S, *'Prawo międzynarodowe publiczne w zarysie'*, (Warsaw, 2007).

Górbiel A, *'International Space Law'*, (Warsaw, 1985).

Górbiel A, *'Międzynarodowe prawo kosmiczne'* (Tr. International Space Law) (Warsaw 1985).

Granat M and Granat K, *'The Constitution of Poland. A Contextual Analysis'* (Bloomsbury Hart Publishing 2019).

Granat M, *'Uwagi o pojmowaniu art. 90 Konstytucji RP przez Trybunał Konstytucyjny'* (2014) 22 Studia Iuridica Lublinensia, 523–531.

Hall M, *'New Space Philosophies: Who, How, What'*, Space Daily. Available online, at: https://www.spacedaily.com/reports/NewSpace_Philosophies_Who_How_What_999.html.

Halunko V, *'Space law: the present and the future'*, https://www.researchgate.net/publication/335595976_Space_Law_the_Present_and_the_Future.

Harasimiuk D E, *'Analysis of compliance of bills with the European Union law in parliamentary work in 2015–2016'* (2020) 3 Ius Novum 120–137.

Hartley T, *'The Foundations of European Union Law'* (Oxford University Press 2014).

Hetlof J, *'Space Security: Space Debris Removal Under the International Legal Regime'*, Hrycaj A, et alia, eds, 'Prawo a Nowoczesność: Wyzwania-problemy-nadzieje' (Tr. Law and Modernity: Challenges-issues-expectations) (Warsaw 2019).

Hobe S and Chan K-W, *'Legal status of outer space'* Jakhu R and Dempsey P.S, eds, Routledge Handbook of Space Law, (Routledge, 2017).

Hobe S, *'The Impact of New Developments on International Space Law'* (*New Actors, Commercialization, Privatisation, Increase in the Number of 'Space-faring Nations* (Uniform Law Review 2010), No 15.

Hobe S, Chen K-W, *'Legal Status of outer space'* Jakhu R, and Dempsey PS, eds Routledge Handbook of Space Law (Routledge 2017).

Hobe S, et alia, eds, *'Cologne Commentary on Space Law'*, Vol. 2, (Köln 2013).

Jakhu RS, Freeman S, *'The Sources of International Space Law'*, (Beijing 2013).

Jakhu RS, *'The legal status of the Geostationary Orbit'* VII, Annals of Air and Space Law, 1982.

Jakhu RS, Steer C, Chen KW, *'Conflicts in Space and the Rule of Law'* https://papers.ssrn.com/sol3/papers.cfm?abstract_id=2722245.

Jakhu RS, Ahmad T, *'The Outer Space Treaty and States.* Obligation to Remove Space Debris: A US perspective' The Space Review (2017).

Jakhu RS, and Pelton JN, eds, *'Global Space Governance: An International Study'* (Springer, 2017).

Jankowitsch P, *'The background and history of space law'* Von der Dunk F with Tronchetti F, eds Handbook of Space Law, (Edward Elgar, Pub, 2015).

Kerrest A and Thro C *'Liability for damage caused by space activities'* Jakhu R and Dempsey P.S, eds, Routledge Handbook of Space Law, (Routledge, 2017).

Khan I, *'Article 38 of the Statute of the International Court of Justice: A Complete Reference Point for the Sources of International Law?'* The New Jurist (5 April 2019).

Kmieciak Z, *'Rozłączność kompetencji organów władzy w świetle orzecznictwa sądowego w przedmiocie ochrony praworządności'*, 113, Państwo i Prawo [The State and the Law] 2020, No 10.

Koeck HF, *'Alfred Verdross – A Visionary of Contemporary Doctrine and Practice of International Law'* Lecture delivered at the Faculty of Law and Administration of the Nicolaus Copernicus University of Toruń on 13 December 2010, Studia Iuridica Toruniensia VIII.

Konert A and Kunert-Diallo A, *'Responsibility of the space operator towards space tourists'*, Państwo i Prawo [The State and the Law], No 6/2019.

Kruk M, *'Kilka uwag o koncepcji władzy wykonawczej w Konstytucji* RP *z 1997 r.'* Mik Cezary (ed), Maria Kruk, Konstytucja. Prawo i praktyka. Wybór studiów. Księga jubileuszowa (Wydawnictwo Sejmowe 2019) 484–494.

Kruk M, *'Kilka uwag o trwałości i zmianach Konstytucji* RP *z 1997 r. na tle 10-lecia praktyki konstytucyjnej'* in Cezary Mik (ed), Maria Kruk, Konstytucja. Prawo i praktyka. Wybór studiów. Księga jubileuszowa (Wydawnictwo Sejmowe 2019) 137–152.

Kruk M, *'Przyczynek do rozważań o inspiracjach Konstytucji* RP *z 1997 r.'* (2002) 12 Państwo i Prawo 3–16.

Kruk M, *'Wprowadzenie do problematyki parlamentarnego systemu rządów'* in Cezary Mik (ed), Maria Kruk, Konstytucja. Prawo i praktyka. Wybór studiów. Księga jubileuszowa (Wydawnictwo Sejmowe 2019) 353–382.

Kruk M, Olszówka M, Godlewski M, Jarosz M, Laskowska M, Zaleśny J, *'Ochrona praw i wolności. System instytucjonalny w Rzeczypospolitej polskiej'* (Difin 2019).

Kulesza M and Sześciło D, *'Local Government in Poland'* in Angel Manuel Moreno Molina (ed), Local government in the Member States of the European Union: a comparative legal prespective, (Madrid, INAP 2012) 485–504.

Kułaga Ł, *'Odpowiedzialność międzynarodowa za szkody wyrządzone przez obiekty kosmiczne'* (tr. Liability for damages caused by space objects) Galicki Z et alia, eds, Manfred Lachs – wybitny pranik swiata (tr. Manfred Lachs – an outstanding world lawyer) (Warsaw, 2011).

Kułaga Ł, *'Przestrzeń kosmiczna – jako wspólne dziedzictwo ludzkości. Kontrowersje wokół Porozumienia regulującego działalność państw na Księżycu i innych ciałach niebieskich'* (Tr. Outer space – as a common heritage of humanity. Controversies around the Agreement regulating the activities of States on the Moon and other celestial bodies), Galicki Z et alia, eds, 'Wykorzystanie Przestrzeni Kosmicznej Świat-Europa-Polska' (Tr. The Use Of Outer Space-World-Europe-Poland) (Warsaw, 2010).

Kułaga Ł, *'The Implementation of International Agreements in the Polish Legal System. The Selected Aspects of Practice in Recent Two Decades'*, 9 Polish Rev of Int'l and Eur Law 1 (2020).

Kułaga Ł, *'Współczesne tendencje regulacyjne międzynarodowego prawa kosmicznego'* (tr.'Contemporary regulatory tendencies of international space law') Kwartalnik Prawa Publicznych, No 4 (2007).

Lachs M, *'The Law of Outer Space: An Experience in Contemporary Law-Making'* (1979).

Lankosz K, *'Eksploracja i eksploatacja Kosmosu. Czy helium 3 zmieni status prawny przestrzeni kosmicznej?'* (tr. Exploration and exploitation of space. Will Helium 3 change the legal status of outer space) Mikos-Skuza E et alia, eds, Prawo międzynarodowe – teraźniejszość, perspektywy, dylematy. Księga Jubileuszowa Profesora Zdzisława Galickiego (Tr. International Law – present, perspective, dilemmas. The anniversary edition of Prof. Zdzislaw Galicki) (Warszawa 2013) 374–375.

Lyall F, and Larsen P, 'Space Law: A Treatise', (Ashgate, 2009).

Łukaszuk L, *'Cooperation and competition in outer space. Law'*, Politics, Economy, (Toruń, 2012).

Łukaszuk L, *'International space law – origins and stages of development. Selected issues'*, International aviation and space law and technologies, ed E. Dynia, D. Kuźniar-Kwiatek, (Rzeszów, 2016).

Malanczuk M, *'Akehurst's Modern Introductin to International Law'*, 7th Ed (Routledge, 1997).

Małajny R M, *'Podział władzy w Konstytucji RP z 1997 roku. Analiza formalna'* (2017) 6 Przegląd Sejmowy 97–123.

Malinowska K, Space Insurance. International Legal Aspects, Kluwer 2017.

Mik C (ed), M Kruk, *'Konstytucja. Prawo i praktyka. Wybór studiów. Księga jubileuszowa'* (Wydawnictwo Sejmowe 2019).

Milde M, *'International law and ICAO'* (Eleven International Publishing, 2008).

Misztal A, Kułaga Ł, *'The importance of space law in Polish foreign policy'*, Kosmos in law and politics, law and politics in space, ed: K. Myszona-Kostrzewa, (Warsaw, 2017).

Misztal A, Kułaga Ł, *'Znaczenie prawa kosmicznego w polskiej polityce zagranicznej'* (Tr. The importance of space law in Polish foreign policy) Myszona-Kostrzewa K, eds, Kosmos w prawie i polityce, Prawo i polityka w Kosmosie (Tr. Cosmos in law and politics, law and politics)

Moreno Molina A M (ed), *'Local government in the Member States of the European Union: a comparative legal prespective'*, (Madrid, INAP 2012).

Morozova E and Vasyanin Y, *'International space law and satellite telecommunications.'* Oxford Research Encyclopedia of Planetary Science. (2019). Available online at: https://oxfordre.com/planetaryscience/view/10.1093/acrefore/9780190647926.001.0001/acrefore-9780190647926-e-75.

Mrenca E, *'Aksjomaty krajowego prawa kosmicznego – polska perspektywa'* (Tr, The Axioms of the National Space Law – Polish perspective) in Myszona-Kostrzewa K et alia, eds, Prawne Aspekty Dzialalnosci Kosmicznej (Tr. The Legal Aspects of Space Activity) (Kancelaria Senatu, 2019).

Myszona-Kostrzewa K, *'Directions of the development of international space law'*, Directions of development of contemporary international law, ed: K. Karski, (Warsaw 2015).

Myszona-Kostrzewa K, Mrenca E, Zientarski P, eds., *'Prawne Aspekty Dzialalnosci Kosmicznej'* (Tr. The Legal Aspects of Space Activity) (Kancelaria Senatu, 2019).

Nowacki M, *'Działalność dyplomatyczna profesora Manfreda Lachsa'* (Tr. Diplomatic activity of Professor Manfred Lachs) Galicki Z et alia, eds, Manfred Lachs – wybitny pranik swiata (tr. Manfred Lachs – an outstanding world lawyer) (Warsaw, 2011).

Olesz J, *'Stay tuned, PW-Sat3 is coming!'* (5 October 2021) https://pw-sat.pl/en/whats-next-pw-sat3/.

Opaliński B, *'Rozdzielenie kompetencji władzy wykonawczej między Prezydenta RP oraz Rade Ministrów na tle Konstytucji Rzeczypospolitej Polskiej z 1997 roku'* (Wolters Kluwer 2012).

POLSA, Krajowy Program Kosmiczny na lata 2019–2021 (Tr. National Space Program for 2019–2021).

Prezas I, *'A bilateral treaty developing legal effects erga omnes? Reflections on the Prespa Agreement between Greece and North Macedonia settling the name dispute'* 65 QIL Zoom-in (2020).

Radziewicz P, *'Komentarz do art. 87'* in Piotr Tuleja (ed), *'Konstytucja Rzeczypospolitej Polskiej. Komentarz'*, (Wolters Kluwer Polska 2019) Article 87.

Rakowska-Trela A, *'Krajowa Rada Sądownictwa po wejściu w życie nowelizacji z 8.12.2017 r. – Organ nadal konstytucyjny, czy pozakonstytucyjny?'* in Łukasz Bojarski, Krzysztof Grajewski, Jan Kremer, Gabriela Ott, Waldemar Żurek (eds) Konstytucja. Praworządność. Władza sądownicza. Aktualne problemy trzeciej władzy w Polsce (Wolters Kluwer Polska 2019) 107–122.

Safjan M and Bosek L (eds), 'Konstytucja RP. Tom II. Komentarz do art. 87–243' (Wydawnictwo CH Beck 2016).

Sarnecki P., *'Komentarz do art. 10'* in Leszek Garlicki, Marek Zubik (eds), *Konstytucja Rzeczypospolitej Polskiej. Komentarz. Tom I (2nd edn)*, (Wydawnictwo Sejmowe 2016) Article 10.

Sięgając do Gwiazd-Polski sektor kosmiczny 4 lata w ESA, Broszura Polskiej Agencji Rozwoju Przedsiębiorczości, [Reaching for the Stars – the Polish Space Sector, 4 years in the ESA, Brochure by: PARP], (Warsaw, 2016).

Simpson M K, *'Planetary Defence, Global Cooperation and World Peace'*, in: Joseph Pelton and Firooz Allahdadi eds, Handbook of Cosmic Hazards and Planetary Defence, (Cham Springer, 2015).

Słomczyńska I, *'European space policy'*, (Lublin, 2017).

Smith MS, *'The Space Law Review: USA'* the LawReview (Dec 17, 2020) https://thelawreviews.co.uk/title/the-space-law-review/usa.

Steel C, *'Sources and law-making processes relating to space* activities' Jakhu R, and Dempsey PS, eds, Routledge Handbook of Space Law (Routledge, 2017).

Sundahl M, *'Legal status of Spacecraft'* Jakhu R and Dempsey P.S, eds, Routledge Handbook of Space Law, (Routledge, 2017).

Swaminatham S, *'The Applicability of Space Law Principles to Basic Space Science: An Update'*, http://adsabs.harvard.edu/pdf/2005UNPSA.16.117S.

Szafarz R, *'Manfred Lachs – światowej sławy uczony, sędzia i patron'* (Tr. Manfred Lachs – world-famous scientist, judge and patron) Galicki Z et alia, eds, Manfred Lachs – wybitny pranik swiata (Tr. Manfred Lachs – an outstanding world lawyer) (Warsaw, 2011).

Szmyt A, *'Uregulowania konstytucji krajowej w perspektywie integracji europejskiej oraz kierunki niezbędnych uzupełnień'* (2014) 1 Studia Iuridica Toruniensia 361–376.

Sztucki J, *'Problemy Prawne Kosmosu'* (Tr. Legal problems of the Cosmos) (Polski Instytut Spraw Miedzynarodowych, 1965).

Szygulski P, *'Nowy plan dla polskiej branży kosmicznej. Budżet ma być pokaźny'* (Tr. New Plan for Polish Space Industry. Budget is Going to be Substantial) wnp.pl (15 October 2021) https://www.wnp.pl/tech/nowy-plan-dla-polskiej-branzy-kosmiczn ej-budzet-ma-byc-pokazny,498136.html.

Tomanek R, Undersecretary of State, in Response to Statement by Mr. Slawomir Rybicki, Senator of the Republic of Poland, concerning the draft act on space activity and the National Register of Space Objects, 16 December 2020, No. DIN-V.0710.18.2020.

Trnavci G, *'The Meaning and Scope of the Law of Nations in the Context of the Alien Tort Claims Act and International Law'*, Penn Law: Legal Scholarshipo Repository (2014).

Tronchetti F, *'The Exploitation of Natural Resources of the Moon and Other Celestial Bodies, A proposal for a Legal Regime'* (Brill 2009).

Tuleja P (ed), *'Konstytucja Rzeczypospolitej Polskiej. Komentarz',* (Wolters Kluwer Polska 2019).

Tuleja P, *'Komentarz do art. 30 i nast.'* in Piotr Tuleja (ed), *'Konstytucja Rzeczypospolitej Polskiej. Komentarz',* (Wolters Kluwer Polska 2019) Article 30.

Von Bogdandy A, *'Pluralism, direct effect, and the ultimate say: On the relationship between international and domestic constitutional law',* Int'l J of Con Law 3 no 3 and 4 (Oxford University Press, 2008).

Von der Dunk FG, *'International Organizations in Space Law',* Von der Dunk F, with Tronchetti F, eds, Handbook of Space Law, (Edward Elgar, 2015).

Von der Dunk FG, *'Advanced Introduction to Space Law'* (Edward Elgar, 2020).

Von der Dunk FG, *'Current and Future Development of National Space Law and Policy'* United Nations/Brazil Workshop on Space Law: Disseminating And Developing International And National Space Law: The Latin America And Caribbean Perspective (United Nations, New York, 2005).

Von der Dunk FG, *'International Space Law'*, Von der Dunk F, with Tronchetti F, eds, Handbook of Space Law (Edward Elgar, 2015).

Von der Dunk FG, *'Legal aspects of private manned spaceflight'* F. von der Dunk, with F. Tronchetti, eds, Handbook of Space Law (Edward Elgar, 2015).

Von der Dunk FG, *'Private Enterprise and Public Interest in the European 'Spacescape''* (Leiden U, Leiden 1998).

Von der Dunk FG, *'Too-Close Encounters of the Third Party Kind: Will the Liability Convention Stand the Test of the Cosmos 2251-Iridium 33 Collission?'* (2010) Space, Cyber and Telecom. L Program Faculty Publications 28, https://digitalcommons.unl .edu/spacelaw/28.

Von der Dunk FG, *'Transfer of Ownership in Orbit: From Fiction to Problem'* in Mahulena Hofmann and Andreas Loukakis, eds, Ownership of Satellites: 4th Luxembourg Workshop on Space and Satellite Communication Law (2017) 36.

Wachowicz E, *'Polish space sector. Subject structure – development opportunities – fund-raising.'* Collective work, POLSA, (2017).

Wassenbergh H.A, *'Public Law Aspects of Private Space Activities and Space Transportation in the Future'* in Proceedings of the Thirty-Eight Colloquium on the Law of Outer Space (1996).

Wassenbergh H, *'An International Institutional Framework for Private Space Activities'* (1997) XXIII Annals of A&SL 529.

Wilmanowicz M, *'European Space Agency. Scientific Journals of Civilization Approach'*, 2018, No. XIV (1), 152–163.

Wiszniewski B, *'Building Polish space sector – from small island of excellence to a national innovation ecosystems'* (2019) 52–8 IFAC PapersOnLine 211–220 <https://www.sciencedirect.com/science/article/pii/S2405896319304045> (access 02.02.2021).

Wiśniowski W, Wolański P, *'Rola Instytutu Lotnictwa w badaniach kosmicznych',* Prace Instytutu Lotnictwa, No 1 (234), 2014, 10–11.

Wyzner E, *'Manfred Lachs – Profesor, Szef, Mentor i Przyjaciel'* (Tr. Manfred Lachs – Professor, Boss, Mentor and Friend), Galicki Z, et alia, eds, Manfred Lachs – wybitny pranik swiata (tr. Manfred Lachs – an outstanding world lawyer) (Warsaw, 2011).

Zubik M, *'A.D. 2015/2016. Anni Horribili of the Constitutional Tribunal in Poland'* (2018) 2 Przegląd Konstytucyjny 46–55.

Żylicz M, *'O początkach międzynarodowego prawa kosmicznego'* (Tr. On the beginnings of international space law) Galicki Z et alia, eds, Wykorzystanie Przestrzeni Kosmicznej Świat-Europa-Polska (Tr. The Use Of Outer Space-World-Europe-Poland) (Warsaw, 2010).

Legal Acts and Documents

Act of 26 September 2014 on the Polish Space Agency, Journal of Laws of 2014 item 1533, as amended by Act of 13 June 2019, Amending the Act on The Polish Space Agency and The Act on Government Administration Departments, Journal of Laws of 2019, item 1248.

Act of 26 September 2014, on the Polish Space Agency, (Journal of Laws of 2018, item 601, as amended).

Act of 27 August 2009 on Public Finances, Journal of Laws 2017, item 2077.

Act of 29 November 2000 on Foreign Trade in Goods, Technologies and Services of Strategic Significance for State Security and for Maintaining International Peace and Security, Journal of Laws of 2000, No 119, item 1250.

Act of 30 June 2000 on Industrial Property Law, Journal of Laws of 2001, No 49, item 508.

Act of 4 February 1994 on Copyright and Related Rights, Journal of Laws of 1994, No 24, item 83.

Act on Space Activity and the National Register of Space Objects, project dated 10 July 2017 (Draft Space Act) https://legislacja.rcl.gov.pl/docs//2/12300856/12449052/12449053/dokument300886.pdf (accessed 23.01.2022).

Action Programme for the Development of Space Technologies and the Use of Satellite Systems in Poland, Ministry of Economy, 26 June 2012.

Agreement between the Government of the Republic of Poland and the European Space Agency Concerning the Accession of Poland to the Convention for the Establishment of a European Space Agency and Related Terms and Conditions, done at Warsaw on 31 July 2012, ratified on 24 October 2012, entered into force on 19 November 2012, published January 16, 2013, Journal of Laws of 2013, item 61.

Agreement between the Republic of Poland and the European Organisation for the Exploitation of Meteorological Satellites (EUMETSAT) on cooperation, done and signed in Warsaw on 15 December 1999, Journal of Laws 2002 No 2020, item 1706.

Agreement Governing the Activities of States on the Moon and Other Celestial Bodies, 5 December 1979, 1363 UNTS 3 (Moon Agreement).

Agreement on the amendment of the Agreement between the Government of the Republic of Poland and the European Space Agency on the accession of Poland to the Convention on the Establishment of the European Space Agency and related conditions, signed in Warsaw on 12 January 2017, Journal of Laws of 2017, item 261.

Agreement on the Principles of State Activities in the Study and Use of Outer Space, Including the Moon and Other Celestial Bodies of January 27, 1967 (Journal of Laws No 14, item 82, Annex No 2, 15 May 1968).

Agreement on the Rescue of Astronauts, the Return of Astronauts and the Return of Objects Launched Into Outer Space (Rescue Agreement), 22 April 1968, 672 UNTS 119 Journal of Laws of 1969, No 15, item 110.

Agreement regulating the activities of States on the moon and other celestial bodies, signed on 18 December 1979.

Agreement Relating to the International Telecommunications Satellite Organization (INTELSAT Agreement), Washington, done on 20 August 1971, entered into force on 12 February 1973, 1220 UNTS 21 (1971), Journal of Laws of 1994, No 110, item 530.

Agreement Relating to the International Telecommunications Satellite Organization (ITSO) (ITSO Agreement), Washington, done on 20 August 1971, entered into force 12 February 1973, as amended 13 November 2000, amended version entered into force 30 November 2004, 23 UST 3813 and 4091, TIAS 7532.

Antarctic Treaty, 1 December 1959, 12 UST 794, 402 UNTS 71, 19 ILM 860 (1980), UKTS 97 (1961), Cmnd 1535, ATS 12 (1961) (entered into force 23 June 1961).

Audit of the Supreme Audit Office on Development of Space Sector, No. 44/2020/P/19/021/KGP, 77.

Biuletyn Informacyjny Klubu Teledetekcji Środowiska Polskiego Towarzystwa Geograficznego, Nr 106 (lato'96) Warszawa, 1996.07.15., ISSN 1425-7688, https://ptgeo.org.pl/wp-content/uploads/2017/09/OK-106.pdf.

Code of Administrative Procedure of 14 June 1960, Journal of Laws of 1960, No 30, item 168.

Compendium, Space Debris Mitigation Standards Adopted by States and International Organisations, (5 September 2018), http://www.unoosa.org/documents/pdf/space law/sd/Space_Debris_Compendium_COPUOS_5_sep_2018.pdf.

Constitution and Convention of the International Telecommunication Union (ITU), 22 December 1992, 1825 UNTS 143, UN Reg. No I-31251.

Constitution of the Republic of Poland of 2 April 1997, Dz.U. 1997 nr 78 poz. 483.

Convention for the Establishment of a European Organization for the Exploitation of Meteorological Satellites (EUMETSAT), done in Geneva on 24 May 1983, entered into force 19 June 1986. Germany, Bundersgesetzenblatt, Jahrgang 1987, Part 11 (1987), 256, Journal of Laws of 2009, No 38, item 297 (entered into force 27 March 2009).

Convention for the Establishment of a European Space Agency, opened for signature on 30 May 1975 and entered into force on 30 October 1980 (CSE/CS) (73)19, rev.7.

Convention for the establishment of the European Space Agency, done in Paris on 30 May 1975, Journal of Laws of 2013, item 61.

Convention on International Civil Aviation ('Chicago Convention') (1994) 15 U.N.T.S. 295 (Chicago Convention).

Convention on International Liability for Damage Caused by Space Objects (Liability Convention), 29 March 1972, 961 UNTS 187 Journal of Laws of 1973, No 27, item 154.

Convention on International Liability for Damage Caused by Space Objects of March 29, 1972 (Journal of Laws No 27, item 154, appendix, 30 June 1973).

Convention on International Liability for Damage Caused by Space Objects, 29 March 1972, 961 UNTS 187 (Liability Convention), Journal of Laws of 1973, no. 27 item 154.

Convention on Registration of Objects Launched into Outer Space (Registration Convention), 12 November 1974, 1023 UNTS 15 Journal of Laws of 1979 No 5, item 22.

Convention on the International Maritime Satellite Communications Organization (INMARSAT Convention) on 3 September 1976, entered into force 16 July 1979, 1143 UNTS 105.

Convention on the International Mobile Satellite Organization (IMSO Convention), London, September 3, 1976, entered into force July 16, 1979, as amended 1998, amended version entered into force 31 July 2001; ATS 2001 No 11, Journal of Laws of 2003, No 140, item 1347.

Convention on the Registration of Objects Launched into Outer Space of 14 January 1975 (Journal of Laws No 5, item 22, annex, of 30 March 1979).

Convention Relating to the Regulation of Aerial Navigation Signed at Paris, October 13, 1919, 1 J. Air L. & Com. 94 (1930) (Paris Convention).

COPUOS, 'Space Law' www.unoosa.gov/oosa/en/ourwork/spacelaw/index.html.

Corfu Channel (the UK v Albania) [1949] ICJ Reports 4.

Council Directive 85/374/EEC of 25 July 1985 on the approximation of the laws, regulations and administrative provisions of the Member States concerning liability for defective products, O.J. L 210, 7.8.1985.

Council of Ministers Resolution No 6 of 26 January 2017 on the Adoption of the Polish Space Strategy (hereinafter Polish Space Strategy), Official Journal of the Republic of Poland of 2017 (Monitor Polski) item 203.

Council of Ministers Resolution No 8 of 14 February 2017, Official Journal of the Republic of Poland (Monitor Polski of 2017), item 260.

Council Regulation (EC) 428/2009, Official Journal L 134, 29.5.2009.

Development of the space sector – report of the Polish Supreme Audit Office, KGP.430.017.2019 Reg No 44/2020 / P / 19/021 / KGP, Warsaw, 20 May 2020.

Draft Act of 10 July 2017. Act of ... ... 2017 on Space Activity and on the National Registry of Space Objects.

Economic Freedom Act, Journal of Laws of 2016, item 1829.

EO Portal Directory, 'COSPAS-SARSAT', https://directory.eoportal.org/web/eoportal/satellite-missions/c-missions/cospas-sarsat#foot14%29.

EUMETSAT Resolutions and Declarations 1986–2019. https://www-cdn.eumetsat.int/files/2020-07/pdf_leg_res_full.pdf.

European Cooperating State Agreement between the European Space Agency and the Government of the Republic of Poland, done in Warsaw on 27 April 2007, ratified by Poland on 28 March 2008, entered into force on 26 April 2008. Poland, Journal of Laws of 2008 No 154, item 959.

European Cooperating State Agreement between the European Space Agency and the Government of the Republic of Poland, Journal of Laws No154, 26 August 2008.

Evaluation of implementation of Polish Space Strategy and its KPIs, https://www.pspa.pl/index.php/pl/projekty/polska-strategia-kosmiczna-psk/ocena-realizacji-wskaznikow-polskiej-strategii-kosmicznej.

France v Turkey, PCIJ, A/10.

Fundamental Provisions for National Space Laws' Space, Cyber and Telecom Law Program Faculty Pubs 11 (2006).

Government Statement of 5 June 1994, on the Republic of Poland's accession to the Convention Establishing the European Satellite Communications Organisation EUTELSAT, opened for signature in Paris on 15 July 1982, (Journal of Laws of 1995), No 24, item 131.

Guidelines for Long-Term Sustainability of Outer Space Activities, Report of the Committee on the Peaceful Uses of Outer Space, COPUOS 62nd session, A/74/20, 20 August 2019.

http://www.isunet.edu.

https://bip.kprm.gov.pl/kpr/form/r29,Plan-dzialan-na-rzecz-rozwoju-technologii-kosmicznychi-wykorzystania-systemow-s.html (accessed 3 February 2021).

https://dlapilota.pl/wiadomosci/polska/krajowy-program-kosmiczny-2019-2021-54-projekty-wspierajace-rozwoj-polskiej-branzy.

https://newjurist.com/article-38-of-the-statute-of-the-international-court-of-justice.html#:~:text=Article%2038(1)of%20the,principles%20recognized%20by%20civilized%20nations.

https://www.esa.int/Space_in_Member_States/Poland/Polska_w_kosmosie (accessed 2 February 2021).

https://www.gov.pl/web/rozwoj-praca-technologia/kolejna-misja-kosmiczna-z-udzialem-polskiej-firmy (accessed 11 February 2021).

https://www.senat.gov.pl/prace/komisje-senackie/konferencja,2,10705,konferencja-dzialalnosc-kosmiczna-prawo-i-administracja.html (accessed 2 February 2021).

International COSPAS-SARSAT Program Agreement (COSPAS-SARSAT Agreement), Paris, done 1 July 1988, entered into force on 30 August 1988, Monitor Polski of 2006, No 13, item 172.

International Law Commission (ILC), Draft Articles on Responsibility of States for Internationally Wrongful Acts (Draft Articles), Supplement No 10 (A/56/10), Chapter IV.E.1 (2001), Article 42(a).

Joint ESA/Poland Mid Term Review Report, June 2015, Warsaw.

Judgement of 29.12.1999, ISA/Po 3057/98, ONSA 2001, no 1, item 34.

Judgment of the Constitutional Tribunal of 11.5.2005, K18/04.

Judgment of the Constitutional Tribunal of 27.4.2005, P1/05.

Justification for the draft Act of 10 July 2017 of the Act of … … … … 2017 on Space Activity and on the National Registry of Space Objects.

Liechtenstein v Guatemala, ICJ Reports 1955.

Ministry of Economic Development and Technology, Regulation on the Adoption of the Polish Space Agency Statute, Official Journal of the Republic of Poland of 2021, item 2248.

Ministry of the Development and Technology, Krajowy Program Kosmiczny na lata 2021–2026 (Tr. National Space Program for 2021–2026), ver. 0.8, 23 July 2021. https://www.gov.pl/attachment/935b6f52-92ed-41f4-9dc6-fb502c609a84.

National Space Programme 2021–2026, draft version 0.8, 23 July 2021, https://www.gov.pl/web/rozwoj-technologia/prekonsultacje-krajowego-programu-kosmicznego-na-lata-2021--2026-kpk.

NATO, NATO approach to Space (2 December 2021) https://www.nato.int/cps/en/natohq/topics_175419.htm#:~:text=and%20early%20warning.-,NATO's%20approach%20to%20space%20will%20remain%20fully%20in%20line%20with,its%20operations%2C%20missions%20and%20activities (accessed 23.01.2022).

Nicaragua v USA, ICJ Reports 1986.

Operating Agreement on the International Maritime Satellite Organization (INMARSAT Operating Agreement) on 3 September 1976, entered into force 16 July 1979, 1143 UNTS 2013, Journal of Laws of 1980, No 7, items 19, 20.

Operating Agreement Relating to the International Telecommunications Satellite Organization (INTELSAT Operating Agreement), Washington, D.C., done on 20 August 1971, entered into force 12 February 1997, 1220 UNTS 149 (1971).

Opinion of 19 December 2014, on the draft assumptions of the Draft Act – Space Law (Minister of Economy), Legislative Council at the Prime Minister, RL030332 / 14, point I.3.

Plan for the European Cooperating States (PECS): Objectives, Rules, and Procedures, Journal of Law No 154, 26 August 2008.

Polish Civil Code, Journal of Laws of 23 April 1964, No.16, item 93.

Polish Space Instruments, Period 1970–2016, Warsaw, 2016.

Polish space sector 2020. Analysis of current situation, trends and technologies from national and international perspective, Polish Space Agency, May 2021, Warsaw.

Polish Space Strategy, 2017, Resolution No 6 of the Council of Ministers of 26 January 2017, on the adoption of the Polish Space Strategy (MP item 203).

Prosecutor v Tadic, IT-94-1-T, 10/8/1995.

Prosecutor v Tadic, IT-94-1A, 15/7/1999.

PWC Report (2019): Main Trends and Challenges in the Space Sector. Available online at: https://www.pwc.fr/fr/assets/files/pdf/2019/06/fr-pwc-main-trends-and-challenges-in-~the-space-sector.pdf.

Radio Regulations of the International Telecommunication Union (Radio Regulations) (Geneva, 2020) available at https://www.itu.int/pub/R-REG-RR/en.

Recommendations by the Legislative Council for the Prime Minister, 22 September 2017, https://www.space24.pl/projekt-ustawy-o-dzialalnosci-kosmicznej-i-krok-pod-lupa-rady-legislacyjnej.

Regulation (EU) 2016/679 of the European Parliament and of the Council of 27 April 2016 on the protection of natural persons with regard to the processing of personal data and on the free movement of such data, and repealing Directive 95/46/EC, OJ L 119, 4.5.2016.

Regulation No 102 of the Prime Minister of 16 November 2012, on the Inter-ministerial Board for Space Policy in Poland (MP item 852, as amended).

Regulation No 15 of the Minister of Entrepreneurship and Technology of 10 May 2019, on the appointment of the Space Policy Team, Journal of Laws of the Minister of Entrepreneurship and Technology 2019, item 15.

Regulation No 200 of the Prime Minister of 28 November 2018, on abolishing certain subsidiary bodies of the Council of Ministers and the President of the Council of Ministers (MP, item 1191).

Report of the Committee on the Peaceful Uses of Outer Space, COPUOS 62nd session, A/74/20, (20 August 2019).

Resolution No 6 of the Council of Ministers of 26 January 2017, on the adoption of the Polish Space Strategy (MP item 203).

Telecommunication Act of 16 July 2004, Journal of Law16 July 2004, No 171, item 1800.

The Act of December 12, 2013, on the ratification of the Protocol on Privileges and immunities of the European Organisation for the Exploitation of Meteorological Satellites (EUMETSAT), drawn up in Darmstadt on 1 December 1986, Journal of Laws of 2014, item 190.

The Agreement on the Establishment of the Intersputnik International System and Organization of Space Communications (as amended by the Protocol on Amendments of 30 November 1996) established the Intersputnik International Organization of Space Communications (INTERSPUTNIK) 861 UNTS 3, in effect in Poland as of 12 July 1972, Journal of Laws of 1974, No 40, item 234.

The Barcelona Traction Case, Belgium v Spain, ICJ Reports 1970.

The Convention Establishing the European Telecommunications Satellite Organization (EUTELSAT), Paris, done 15 July 1982, entered into force 1 September 1985, as amended 20 May 1999, amended version entered into force 28 November 2002; Cm. 4572; Space Law – Basic Legal Documents, C.II.1.

The Delimitation of Outer Space Revisited: The Role of National Space laws in the Delimitation Issue (1998) Space, Cyber, and Telecommunications Law Program Faculty Publications 51, 255, https://digitalcommons.unl.edu/spacelaw/51.

The ESA Industry Portal (2019). http://About Us/Business with ESA, (accessed 2 February 2021).

The Legality of the Threat or Use of Nuclear Weapons, Advisory Opinion (1996) ICJ Rep 226.

The strategy of actions related to space in Poland in the conditions of membership in the European Union, Committee on Space Research, Polish Academy of Sciences, November 2003, http://www.kbkis.pan.pl/images/stories/Strategia_Full_Version.pdf.

Towards an Enlarged Partnership – ESA's Relations with the Czech Republic, Hungary, Poland and Romania, Baudin C, Legal Affairs Department, ESA, Paris, Bergquist K, International Relations Department, ESA, Paris, ESA Bulletin 107 – August 2001.

Treaty Banning Nuclear Weapon Tests in the Atmosphere, in Outer Space and Under Water (Limited Test Ban Treaty), 5 August 1963, 14 UST 1313, 480 UNTS 43 entered into force 10 October 1963, Journal of Laws of 1963, No 52, item 288.

Treaty on Principles Governing the Activities of States in the Exploration and Use of Outer Space, including the Moon and other Celestial Bodies drawn up in Moscow, London and Washington on 27 January 1967, (Journal of Laws of 1968, No 14, item 82).

Treaty prohibiting the testing of nuclear weapons in the atmosphere, outer space and underwater signed on 5 April 1963.

UK Department for Business, Energy & Industrial Strategy, *'Upstream Space: A Galaxy of Capability, A Science and Innovation Audit Summary Report'* (2018).

UNGA Recommendations on National Legislation Relevant to the Peaceful Exploration and Use of Outer Space (2013) UN Doc A/RES/68/74 (hereinafter 'Resolution on National Legislation').

UNGA Res 1802, International Co-operation in the Peaceful Uses of Outer Space, 14 December 1962, UN Doc RES 1802(XVII).

UNGA Res 1962, Declaration of Legal Principles Governing the Activities of States in the Exploration and Use of Outer Space, 13 December 1963 UN Doc. RES 1963(XVIII).

UNGA Res 37/92, Principles Governing the Use by States of Artificial Earth Satellites for International Direct Television Broadcasting, 10 December 1982, UN Doc RES 37/92.

UNGA Res 41/65, Principles relating to remote sensing of the Earth from outer space, 3 December 1986, UN Doc RES 41/65.

UNGA Res 47/68, Principles Relevant to the Use of Nuclear Power Sources in Outer Space, 14 December 1992, UN Doc RES 47/68.

UNGA Res 76/76, International Co-operation in the Peaceful Uses of Outer Space, 9 December 2021, UN Doc A/RES/76/76.

UNGA Res. 1348, Question of the Peaceful Uses of Outer Space, 13 December 1958, UN Doc. RES 1348(XIII).

UNGA Res. 1472, International Cooperation in the Peaceful Uses of Outer Space, 12 December 1959 UN Doc. RES 1472(XIV).

UNGA Res. 1721, International Co-operation in the Peaceful Uses of Outer Space, 20 December 1961, UN Doc. RES 1721(XVI).

UNGA Res. 51/122, Declaration on International Cooperation in the Exploration and Use of Outer Space for the Benefit and in the Interest of All States, Taking into Particular Account the Needs of Developing Countries, 13 December 1996, UN Doc A/RES/51/122.

UNGA Res. 59/115, Application of the concept of the 'launching State', 10 December 2004; UN Doc. A/RES/59/115.

UNGA Res. 62/101, Recommendations on enhancing the practice of States and international intergovernmental organizations in registering space objects, 17 December 2007, UN Doc. A/RES/62/101.

UNGA Res. 62/217, International cooperation in the peaceful uses of outer space, (22 December 2007).

UNGA Res. 68/74, Recommendations on national legislation relevant to the peaceful exploration and use of outer space, 16 December 2013, UN Doc. A/RES/68/74.

UNGA Resolution 59/115, Application of the Concept of the 'Launching State', UNGAOR, 59th Sess, UN Doc A/RES/59/115 (2005).

United Nations Convention on the Law of the Sea (UNCLOS), 10 December 1982, 1833 UNTS 3 (entered into force 16 November 1994).

United Nations, Charter of the United Nations, 24 October 1945, 1 UNTS XVI (UN Charter).

United Nations, Statute of the International Court of Justice, 18 April 1946, available at: https://www.refworld.org/docid/3deb4b9c0.html [accessed 12 January 2022].

Urania, Postępy Astronomii, No 1/2011, 34–35.

Vienna Convention on the Law of Treaties (VCLT), 23 May 1969, 1155 UNTS 331.

Index

Printed in the United States
by Baker & Taylor Publisher Services